TODAY'S WORD

A Daily Devotional

God's Word is a light to my path.

By Ken and Dottie Phillips

Today's Word
A Daily Devotional
by Ken and Dottie Phillips

Printed in the United States of America

ISBN 9781625093523

www.xulonpress.com

October 18, 2014

Thomas Edmund Stopa!

Thank you for your partnership
with World Bible Society and
The Hunger Solution.

Please enjoy this book of Devotions
with our compliments

Ken Dotle
Phil 1:6

PREFACE

Since 2008 we have been writing a FREE daily devotional that we have sent to thousands of people that have subscribed for them. Now we have put together 366 edited versions of past devotionals and placed them in this TODAY'S WORD devotional book.

It is our prayer as you receive this TODAY'S WORD daily devotional book that you will commit to reading it daily and that God will have something special just for you that day.

As we have researched and written each devotional our lives have been blessed by God. We are continually blessed by the more than 100 email responses we receive each day.

We want to give a special word of thanks to one of our daughters (Sheri Domke) and two of our daughter-in-laws (Debby Phillips and Jody Phillips) for their help in formatting and editing each day's devotional. We are grateful to you for volunteering your valuable time to help us with this project.

May we encourage you to consider?

First, receive our free daily devotionals by email. Go to our web site www.thehungersolution.org and subscribe. Each day you will receive a new and different devotional.

Second, if you are interested to know more about us you may read our book, NO PROBLEMS ONLY SITUATIONS! This book will take you through our life journey, married for 56 years, raising six children and now having 20 grandchildren while we ministered full time in several ministries and consulted more than 40 Christian Children's missions. You will go with us to many of the 100 countries we have been in and share with us the valleys and mountains we went through raising our family. You can order this book by going to our web site.

It is our prayer that these daily devotionals will be a blessing to you and draw you closer to our Lord.

Ken and Dottie Phillips

PROLOGUE

I was blessed to be raised by Ken and Dottie Phillips. As one of their six children, I was responsible for more than a few of their grey hairs. But their unwavering love and support help to mold and shape me into the person that I am today.

One of my strongest memories is of our family dinners. Every night - summer, winter, weekends – without fail, we had a family dinner at home. My mom would make a delicious meal that we would sit down to and, after a prayer of thanks to God for the food, we would enjoy together. Following our meal, we always had a devotional time led by my father. We began by reciting bible verses that our parents had us learn. There were between 75 and 100 verses that we memorized and each night, my dad would ask each of us to recite one or two that he randomly selected for each of us. The younger kids started out with very easy verses, such as "In the beginning, God created the Heavens and the Earth," and the older ones recited longer and more difficult passages. But because we were constantly hearing the verses, it became very easy to learn the verses our older siblings recited. Because of this tradition, I have a large catalog of verses that I can find encouragement and strength in every day of my life. I can still recite every verse that we learned as children.

Following our bible verse recitations, my dad would read the bible to us. When we were younger, he read from a children's bible that had bible stories that we could easily understand. As we grew older, he would read chapters and passages from the bible. After a time of discussion of the passage, we would share prayer requests and then each of us in turn would say a prayer, starting with my youngest brother and ending with one of my parents. This time of prayer, sharing and devotion helped to create a family unit whose focus was on a relationship with Christ. My siblings and I are all very close to this day and each of us has a strong, personal relationship with Christ. We all have children of our own and are raising them to know and love Christ in their own lives. I attribute our relationships with Christ in large part to the time we spent at the dinner table with our parents.

Developing and keeping a family devotion time like my parents had with us, requires dedication and commitment. I remember many evenings thinking to myself that I would rather be out with my friends, doing my homework or watching television. But our family devotion time was not an option. I am sure that there were many nights that my parents were exhausted from a long day at work and taking care of six kids, but they never let that get in the way of their commitment to our family devotions.

In many of the daily devotions in this book, my parents refer to the importance of our nightly dinners and family devotions. In this day and age, it is difficult at best to find the time and energy for a daily devotional. But it is important to make time for God. Find time in the morning, evening or whenever practical to spend on your devotions, be it alone or with your loved ones. By reading and applying the devotions in the following pages, God will bless you and you will find peace and contentment in Him.

SHERI DOMKE

DAUGHTER

TODAY'S WORD FOR JANUARY 1

PROMISE

And this is the promise that He has promised us, eternal life. I John 2:25

God has given us over 7000 promises in His Word. When Joshua was old and knew his life was about over, he gave a farewell speech to the Children of Israel. He said in Joshua 23:14, "You know with all your heart and soul that not one of all the promises the Lord your God gave you has failed. Every –promise has been fulfilled and not one has failed."

God made two very significant promises, one to Noah and one to Abraham. Even today we can see rainbows and the country of Israel confirming that when God makes a promise it is never broken.

In Genesis 9:12-15 God said to Noah, "this is the sign of the covenant which I make between Me and you, and every living creature that is with you, and for perpetual generations; I set My rainbow in the cloud and it shall be the sign of the covenant between Me and the earth, that the waters shall never again become a flood to destroy all flesh."

In Genesis 12:2-3 God told Abraham, "I will make you a great nation; I will bless you and make your name great; I will bless those that bless you; I will curse those that curse you; and in you all the families of the earth shall be blessed."

God kept His promise to Noah and now a rainbow after a storm reminds us that He would never destroy the earth with a flood. He kept His promise to Abraham by making him a great nation [Israel] and making his name great.

The greatest promise ever made was the promise made by God to send His only Son to this earth to pay for the sins of everyone who has or will live on this earth so that they might have eternal life. This promise of eternal life is for everyone who is willing to ask God for forgiveness for their sins and then accepts Jesus into their heart entering into a personal relationship with Him.

Today, parents make promises to children and then do not follow through. Spouses make promises, families make promises, and bosses make promises. For the most part these promises are disregarded as if they were never made. There is a key to unlock these promises in our life and that is character.

Do you realize the positive impact that is made on a child's mind when promises are made and kept? When not kept there is a negative impact that can have long term repercussions. When you keep a promise you will be considered reliable and looked to as a person of integrity with character.

God set the example in keeping His promises with Noah and Abraham and as Christians, God expects nothing less from us. From this day on we need to commit to make promises that we are sure we can honor. Relationships are put in jeopardy when promises are not kept. It is time to honor your promises.

TODAY'S WORD FOR JANUARY 2

OBEY

If you obey my commandments you will remain in my love, just as I have obeyed My Father's commandments and remain in His love. John 15:9

Obedience is the result of love and loyalty and they cannot be separated. Obedience to God is a demonstration of our love for Him, doing what Christ has commanded us to do, and living as He wants us to live. Jesus set the example for us by being obedient to His father and obeying His commands. Obedience brings reward and disobedience has consequences.

We read in Numbers 20:7-12 that Moses struck the rock to get water rather than just speaking to the rock as God commanded him to do. Moses did not obey God and therefore forfeited his privilege of entering the Promised Land with the Children of Israel. How painful it must have been for Moses, after leading the Israelites out of Egypt and all through the wilderness for forty years, not to be able to enter the Promised Land with them.

When we obey God, He uses ordinary people to do extra ordinary things. The disciples obeyed when Jesus said: "Follow me and I will make you fishers of men" (Mark 1:17). The disciples were just ordinary men but because they were willing to obey God He used them in mighty ways. He used them to spread the gospel message and to begin His church. They were given the power to perform miracles and God, through them, healed many people. God can do wonders if you are obedient and willing to follow Him. Trusting and obeying the Lord brings fulfillment and joy to life. We must learn to obey.

Have you noticed that children never need to be taught to disobey? Disobedience is a result of our sinful nature and because of the sin we were born with, we all must be taught to obey. God uses His Word to instruct us in being obedient to Him. He allows us to suffer consequences when we disobey.

We learned as we were raising our children that to teach obedience it was necessary to set clearly the standards and acceptable boundaries and make them aware of the consequences for disobeying them. Then when these standards were not honored and when we had given fair reminders, we would give the appropriate punishment such as taking away a privilege that was important to the child, for not obeying.

The punishment has to be seen by the child as a significant loss so that they will truly regret being disobedient. We also learned that it did not help to yell or threaten; this only built up resentment and never had good results. When administering punishment to the child for not obeying, it is very important that the punishment be appropriate for the nature of the disobedience and for the age of the child. Punishment must be consistent and fair. God has set His standards for us in His Word. In I John 2:5-6 we read, "If anyone obeys His Word, God's love is truly made complete.

TODAY'S WORD FOR JANUARY 3

PRIORITIES

But seek first the kingdom of God and His righteousness and all these things shall be added unto you. Matthew 6:35

A priority is something that is considered to be more important than anything else. Most people today do not set any kind of priorities in their lives. In our generation people literally live from one minute to another with absolutely no direction or any kind of priority of purpose. People are so focused on themselves that they do not have any concern for others. They live totally for self.

To be a success in business you must have a business plan. This plan will outline the priorities that are necessary to establish and grow the business. The same is necessary if you want a happy family. You must have a plan and a listing of daily priorities. Then outline how you will spend your time and schedule your activities.

We encourage you today to set goals and priorities in your life. God leaves no doubt as to what our first priority is to be. He states it very clear in Matthew 22:37-38: "You shall love the Lord your God with all your heart, with all your soul, and with all your mind. This is the FIRST and GREATEST commandment."

Thus, your first priority must be your relationship with God. Every day you need to set aside time to read and study the Bible and to pray. You need study tools to help you grow spiritually. You need to be concerned enough to make it a priority.

Your second priority is to your family. Parents have the responsibility of providing not only for their children's physical needs but also for their spiritual needs. This includes involving them in reading the Bible, praying and going to a church. This requires a commitment of your time, and unless you make it a priority, it will not happen. Countless things will come up and become excuses for not having time. Your family must be second to God in your list of priorities.

Parents need to live by example because our children watch, listen and follow in our footsteps. Children need positive role models in their lives beginning with their parents. Parents have a responsibility to help their children do their school work and guide them in their school activities. Those times of sitting with our children at the kitchen table, helping them with school work were wonderful times of bonding.

Priorities are dreams with a deadline and remember you cannot dream a dream too big for God. You need to set your priorities each day. Every morning write down your priorities for the day. Try it and you will be amazed at how much you will accomplish. When you are setting your priorities ask yourself the question: "What must be the focus of my attention today?" Then ask, "Does it control me?" If it is not Christ centered, then change it. The key thought here is "control." The priorities you set will control your life.

The reason many people do not go very far in life is because they side step opportunity and shake hands with procrastination. Every day is a new opportunity to serve the Lord. Do you make that your priority or do you procrastinate?

TODAY'S WORD FOR JANUARY 4

FAITHFULNESS

Do you not know that those who run in a race all run, but one receives the prize? Run in such a way that you may obtain it. I Corinthians 9:24

Life is full of reversals. We as Christians are not excluded from reversals in our lives that bring disappointments causing us to want to give up. This is not what God wants from us. He wants faithfulness and a spirit of never quitting to prevail in our lives.

To have faithfulness in our lives means to be constant, firm and enduring in our love for our Lord. We are to be loyal and steadfast in devotion and allegiance. A person that shows faithfulness to God can be assured that God will work all things out for good for them (Romans 8:28).

Paul challenges us in the race that is the Christian life, to keep running (above verse). He gave these words to the believers in the church at Corinth.

The Greeks enjoyed two great athletic events, the Olympic games and the Isthmian games, and because the Isthmian events were always held in Corinth, believers there were quite familiar with this analogy that Paul used of running to win. We are to run faithfully the race God has given us and we should be driven by the knowledge that we run to honor our King and to receive from Him an eternal crown at the end of our race.

David in Psalms 89:1 said that He will sing of the loving kindness of the Lord forever; and will make known the faithfulness of God with his mouth. The word loving kindness means loyal love or unfailing love. This is what God gives us as believers and He expects the same from us in return.

In the genealogy of Adam to Noah, Genesis 5, one man is singled out as a man who walked with God. In Genesis 5:4 it says that "Enoch walked with God." Walking with God requires faithfulness and commitment. It was written about Enoch that God rewarded him for his obedience. Enoch did not have to experience death. God just took him to be with Him because he walked daily with God and had an unswerving obedience to God in the midst of a corrupt culture.

We urge you to be challenged by the faithfulness of Enoch, as we are, and to renew your commitment to walk faithfully with God in all that you do each and every day. Just think what it would be like if people that saw you would make just one comment: "He or she walks with God." You can be sure you are headed in the right direction when you walk with God and faithfully serve Him.

One of our favorite passages of scripture is Psalm 100. The last verse tells us that His loving kindness is everlasting and His faithfulness is to all generations. We serve an awesome God and He deserves our faithfulness in serving Him because He gave His life for us. God's faithfulness to us is never ending. He is faithful in all He does (Psalm 38:4) and His faithfulness endures forever (Psalm 117: 2).

TODAY'S WORD FOR JANUARY 5

WISDOM

For the Lord gives wisdom; From His mouth come knowledge and understanding. Proverbs 2:6

Wisdom is much more than just knowledge and information we acquire from being educated. The most educated people in the world are not necessarily the wisest. Solomon asked God for wisdom because he recognized that wisdom comes from God as he tells us (above) in Proverbs 2:6.

As small children we thought our parents knew everything. We felt that they were the wisest people in the world. As we grew older and became more independent we decided that they were not that wise. As teenagers we thought we had all the answers but as we grew older we come to realize how wise our parents really were. Solomon's advice to us in Proverbs 1:8 is to listen to what our father and mother teach us and then not to forget it. This is because experience brings wisdom.

If God were to come to you and say, "Ask for whatever you want me to give you," would you ask for wisdom? Solomon did in I Kings 3:5 when he defined the wisdom he needed as "a discerning heart to govern your people and to distinguish between right and wrong."

In the Old Testament the word used to express the concept of wisdom occurs over 300 times. The concept of wisdom is demonstrated in the Old Testament through the results of Godly choices versus ungodly choices. The lessons of the Old Testament focus our attention on the importance of wisdom in our approach to life in the choices we make concerning our values and commitments.

The person who desires to be wise will seek to know God, submit to Him, and apply God's guidelines when making daily decisions. Because God is the source of wisdom, God is able to provide us, as believers, needed discernment so that we will know what is evil and turn away from it and do what is right and just and fair. Knowledge of God brings wisdom that will guide us to live a life that honors God.

We gain knowledge of God by studying (which requires more than just reading) God's Word. Anyone who desires wisdom can ask God for it, just as Solomon did. As James advises in James 1:5, "If any of you lack wisdom, he should ask God, who gives generously to all without finding fault and it will be given to him."

As Christians we need to have wisdom in order to live a godly life. The wisdom we need to have is the wisdom that only God can give. In order to have wisdom from God we must first have a relationship with God and put our trust in Him and acknowledge Him in all we do (Proverbs 3:5-6).

The first three chapters of Proverbs deal with the importance of God-given wisdom and its benefits. As you seek wisdom, these chapters will be helpful to you if you read them and think about how you can apply them to your life. In I Corinthians 3:19 the apostle Paul writes that the wisdom of the world is foolishness in God's sight. This is why God has given us His Word to teach us godly wisdom

TODAY'S WORD FOR JANUARY 6

TRIALS

Dear friends, do not be surprised at the painful trial you are suffering as though something strange were happening to you. I Peter 4:12

Consider it pure joy, my brothers, when you face trials of many kinds because you know that the testing of your faith develops perseverance. James 1:2

God did not promise us that we would live in a "rose garden" when we became Christians. In this life we will have trials. Everyone does, but Christians have God's promise that He will go with us through the trials.

Paul suffered many trials on his missionary journeys. He was beaten and was thrown into prison. While preaching in Macedonia and testifying to the Jews, the Jews became so abusive to him that Paul just gave up on them. It was then that the Lord appeared to him and said: "Do not be afraid; keep on speaking; do not be silent, for I am with you" (Acts 18:9-10). God did not want Paul to give up. He wanted him to persevere through his trials. As a result Paul stayed there for a year and a half continuing to preach the Word of God.

Peter warns us (I Peter 4:12) not to be surprised when we are faced with a trial as if it were strange. Trials are a fact of life. James also teaches us (James 1:2) that it is not a question of "if" we will face trials but "when?" He also tells us to have a positive attitude in the midst of our trials and turn our suffering into a time of learning. It is through tough times that we learn perseverance and patience.

We do not know how stormy today will be but we do know that we will face trials. But one thing we are certain of is that if we have Jesus in our lives, we can persevere through our trials with the strength that Jesus gives us. In Christ we will be victorious and our future is secure. Jesus has not failed us in the past and He will not fail us today or in all our tomorrows.

Perhaps your world has collapsed. It may be a deep personal loss, a tragedy in your family, a loss of a job, a financial setback or even a family spat. Jesus is bigger than any crisis you might face today. He can rebuild your life. God can turn any trial into an opportunity. Reading God's Word and praying are the keys to conquering trials.

No trial is too large for God not to intervene and no person is too small for God to give His attention to. When we put our trials or difficulties in God's hands, God often does what would be considered impossible by us.

Happiness keeps you sweet, TRIALS KEEP YOU STRONG, sorrows keep you human, failures keep you humble, success keeps you glowing, BUT only GOD keeps you going.

TODAY'S WORD FOR JANUARY 7

ATTITUDE

And whatever you do, do it heartily, as to the Lord and not to men. Colossians 3:23

In Proverbs 23:7 it reads: "As a man thinketh in his heart, so is he." Our thought process affects our attitude. We need to think like a servant of God because we are what we think we are. But we are not always the way we think because our attitude precedes our actions. Our attitude is what often makes a lasting impression on others. Our attitude will motivate us to be the person others see us to be. It can become the thing that identifies us. There are all kinds of attitudes. We can be cheerful or grumpy, humble or boastful and short tempered and patient just to name a few. It is a choice that we have.

Our six children were quick to notice when one of their siblings had a bad attitude. Their reaction usually was to complain about the bad attitude.

The apostle Paul advises us how we can have right attitudes. In Philippians 2:5 he wrote, "Let this mind be in you which was also in Christ Jesus." The King James Version of this verse reads that we are to let the mind of Christ be in us. The NIV Version reads that your attitude should be the same as that of Jesus Christ. The apostle Paul tells us in Ephesians 4:23 that we are to be made new in the attitude of our mind.

Our attitude is a matter of choice. We can choose to let our attitude be controlled by our old sinful nature or we can choose to think and act as Jesus did. Sinful actions begin with wrong attitudes. We have examples in the Bible of those who had attitudes that led to evil actions.

Cain's jealousy of Abel led to hatred and hatred to murder. Saul sought to kill David because of his attitude of jealousy and hatred for David. It was the jealous attitude of Joseph's brothers that caused them to devise their evil plan to get rid of him.

When we let the Lord have control of our life, He will change our attitude for the better and right actions will result. Have you thought about your attitude and how it affects others? Have you thought about how your attitude affects your daily life? Attitude motivates us to do what we do and to be the kind of person that we are.

Attitude has a great deal to do with our success or failure in life. Our attitude can affect whether we keep a friend, get a promotion and almost everything else in life. Because our God is great, we need to think with an attitude of confidence, but with humility, recognizing that God is the one who enables us and that our thoughts can never be greater than God's. The Apostle Paul said: "I can do all things through Christ who strengthens me." Philippians 4:13. We can do all things through Christ if our attitude is right. God did not call us to live a life of failure but to a life of success.

TODAY'S WORD FOR JANUARY 8

HUMILITY

Humble yourselves under the mighty hand of God, that He may exalt you in due time. I Peter 5:6

Humility does not come naturally or easily. If we are doing what we consider "right" when others are not, or if we have had more success than another person, it is easy to think that we are the better person. The Apostle Peter cautions us against that idea by saying that we are to consider others better than ourselves. As Christians we are Christ's representatives to the world so we are to be kind, humble, meek, patient and peaceful, as Christ was, in order that others will see Christ in us.

As Christians what we are and what successes we have are because of what Christ has done for us and through us. The credit must go to Him. Success and glory in this world can be fleeting and we can only take pleasure in it for a time. If we get conceited and gloat over our success, God can take it away from us and humble us very quickly. In Mark 10, James and John, two of Jesus' disciples asked Jesus for the highest positions in His kingdom. They asked for one to sit on His right and the other to sit on His left. Jesus denied their request and explained that greatness was not achieved by being in a high position but by serving others.

There are two issues concerning humility as it relates to our lives. We should be in awe of God. The awesomeness of His power, His love, His Sovereignty, and His blessings, should humble us. If being humble is our desire we should not be concerned about having a position that brings recognition. What God thinks of us is more important then what others think of us.

It is amazing what can be accomplished when we do not care who gets the credit. Paul told the church at Corinth, "I planted, Apollos watered but God gave the increase" I Corinthians 3:6-7.

The second concern must be how we look to our family, friends and neighbors. Are we arrogant, proud and boastful? There is a huge difference between confidence and arrogance. We can be confident without being boastful. When one knows the Lord and has a daily relationship with Him, a humble spirit should radiate from one's life. Our family, friends and associates should see the spirit of Christ in us through all of our words and deeds. We are to be humble so that others can see Christ through us.

We all have moments when we are successful and we want everyone to know about that success. Can you stay humble while enjoying that success and at the same time honor and glorify God?

TODAY'S WORD FOR JANUARY 9

INTEGRITY

The man of integrity walks securely, but he who walks crooked paths will be found out. Proverbs 10:9

In my integrity You uphold me and see me in Your presence forever. Psalm 41:12

It is very difficult today to find a person with integrity. Some say that you cannot be successful in life unless you cut corners. Being a person of integrity is one of the most important characteristics one can have. It says in Proverbs 10:9, when we have integrity we can walk securely because we do not have to worry that we will be found out and our dishonesty will be revealed. When a person loses his or her integrity it is almost impossible to build it back.

Children today make their choices in life based on what they see their parents do. They are perceptive. They can see when a parent short-changes a friend. If a parent compromises his or her integrity, the first to see it is a child. The prevailing attitude seems to be if it benefits "Me" what does it matter if I compromise my integrity? Our integrity matters to God. To be truly successful we must be successful by God's standards of integrity.

God's standards are given to us in the Ten Commandments. They are to convict us of our sins and keep us from doing evil. If we are to be a person of integrity and live a life pleasing to God we must keep His commandments. These were given to us so that we may know what God expects of us. When any of these commandments are broken, the integrity of the one that broke that commandment is in question. And that is where the Lord comes in as He needs to be an intimate part of our daily routine because God honors those that honor Him. Psalm 41:12 (above) is a reminder to us that God rewards integrity. The Bible gives instance after instance of God's blessing on the lives of people who serve the Lord with integrity. Look at the story of Job and be reminded how God protected Him because of his integrity through probably the most difficult series of testing that any one has gone through.

In Genesis 39, we are given an example of integrity as seen in the life of Joseph. Potiphar had put Joseph in charge of his house and all that he had. Then Joseph was approached by Pontiphar's wife who put him in a compromising position. Joseph refused to sin against God or his master. He knew God's standard and chose to stand for right. That is integrity.

In Psalms 15:1-5, David gives us guidelines as to how to live a life of integrity. These are to walk uprightly so that you are blameless, do what is right, speak the truth and be honest, do not speak evil of others, treat your neighbors kindly, be accountable for your actions, honor those that love the Lord and do not be greedy for money.
NO LEGACY IS AS RICH AS ONES INTEGRITY

TODAY'S WORD FOR JANUARY 10

CARING

If anyone does not provide for his relatives, and especially for his immediate family, he has denied the faith and is worse than an unbeliever. I Timothy 5:8

Pure and undefiled religion before God and the Father is this: to visit orphans and widows in their trouble, and to keep oneself unspotted from the world. James 1:27

These scriptures remind us that we have a responsibility to care, both physically and spiritually, for those in our family. We are also instructed to care for the orphans, the widows, the hungry, the poor and needy.

After Saul and his sons were killed in a battle with the Philistines, David became King and asked in II Samuel 9:2, "Is there anyone still left of the house of Saul to whom I can show kindness for Jonathan's sake." David was told that Jonathan's son, Mephibosheth, who was crippled in both of his feet still lived.

Mephibosheth was called before David and he came with great fear because he knew that his grandfather, Saul, was jealous of David and had sought to kill him. After reassuring Mephibosheth to not be afraid, David said, "I will surely show you kindness for the sake of your father, Jonathan. I will restore to you all the land that belonged to your grandfather, Saul and you will always eat at my table" (II Samuel 9:7). All the rest of his life Mephibosheth sat at David's table like one of his sons. David showed he cared by his action. When we truly care we will act upon it.

God instructed the children of Israel under Moses, when they were wandering in the desert, that they were to take care of their families, and not only their families but also the widows, the fatherless and their neighbors. Caring for others does not come readily for most people. God does care about each one of us and has given us the responsibility to care for others as His representatives.

It has always been those who love God who have done the most to care for those who are lonely, hungry and needy. The closer you are to God, the more you will have a heart for others and the greater will be your desire to care for others.

As those who love the Lord, loving and caring for others should be our major life's work and caring for those of our "own house" is our highest priority.

All of our lives we have had the privilege to work with missions where we have been able to help care for the poor and needy. It began over 55 years ago when we were in Korea with the assignment to set up over 140 orphanages for World Vision to take care of the "GI" babies after the Korean War.

In later years we helped care for the children living in the slums and in refugee camps in Africa. And then our hearts were broken when we saw children in Honduras dying with cancer with no medical equipment or medicine. We have experienced great joy in caring for others and being able to do something to make their lives better. The blessing is always ours when we help someone else.

TODAY'S WORD FOR JANUARY 11

DEPRESSION

An anxious heart weighs a man down, but a kind word cheers him up. Proverbs 12:25

Just hearing the word depression probably brings to mind a time of depression that you have gone through. Depression becomes part of a person's life by the reaction to a "thing" that happens in life and it brings on a feeling of failure. It begins with anxiety and worries over "things" which soon leads to depression.

It may perhaps surprise you to know that great men of God have struggled with depression. One of them, which we read about in the scriptures, was so depressed that he prayed that he would die. Can you guess who that was?

This man was totally committed to God. He lived during the reign of Israel's most wicked King and Queen, Ahab and Jezebel. Under their rule, they led many of the Israelites to forsake God and to worship Baal. God chose this man to confront the King and Queen concerning their terrible sin and tell them that the judgment of God on them would be a terrible drought. Perhaps you have guessed that the man was Elijah, God's great prophet.

There was great famine in the land and Ahab blamed God's prophet Elijah for the lack of rain. It was in this setting that Jezebel, who was very wicked and anti-God was committed to kill Elijah. She sent a messenger to Elijah telling him that by the same time the next day his life would be over.

Elijah ran away because he had great fear and was in deep depression. Elijah tried to run away from his emotions but running away left him outside of the will of God. He reacted to his feelings and concern and seemingly lost his focus on God who had been with him in his victories in the past.

Being depressed in life always seems to bring isolation. This is what happened to Elijah. He took what the scripture tells us was a day's journey into the wilderness. He felt alone, rejected and abandoned. He felt life wasn't worth living. He was at such a low point in his life that he prayed, "I have had enough, Lord. Take my life" (I Kings 19:4).

We need to remember that Elijah was a man of God and a prophet. Through these hours and days of depression God never left Elijah but Elijah seemed to think that He had. It was at Elijah's lowest point that God sent an angel to where Elijah was sleeping in the wilderness. The angel told him to get up and get going. This is how God works. In times of need God provides just what we need. The angel brought Elijah food and water for two days to strengthen him for his journey.

In life today we as believers are going to have moments when we feel that everything is going wrong. We will have to make a choice. Elijah chose to run, but that was not the will of God. We can't run away from ourselves. Our choice must be to run to God and let Him strengthen us and put us back into action. Anxiety can make us depressed but only the Word of God can make the heart glad.

TODAY'S WORD FOR JANUARY 12

FORGIVENESS

He does not treat us as our sins deserve or repay us according to our inequities. For as high as the heavens are above the earth so great is His love for those who fear Him. As far as the east is from the west so far has He removed our transgressions from us. Psalm 103:10-12

For those who love God and have come to Him for forgiveness of sins, God forgives so completely that He separates us from it. The Psalmist says that God has removed our sins as far from us as the "east is from the west." God's forgiveness means not only that He takes our sins away but that He also forgets them.

How different God's forgiveness is from our forgiveness. We will say that we forgive others, but we just do not forget what they have done. We seem to love to bring up what was done in the past, especially when it serves our purpose.

Through the shed blood of Jesus Christ, all those who have accepted Jesus as Savior have received God's forgiveness for their sins and they are made a new creation. They are changed people with changed hearts and changed attitudes. Christians must put their faith into action so that they are more like Christ. A Christian's conduct should validate Jesus' transforming power in his or her life.

The apostle Paul understood the challenges Christian's face in living a life that is Christ-like. Forgiving others is a difficult challenge. In Colossians 3:13. Paul tells us, "Forgive as the Lord forgave you." Paul knew that God's forgiveness is perfect and complete because he experienced it. There is no better example of true forgiveness than God's loving and complete forgiveness toward us. If we consider how much He has forgiven us how can we not forgive the little wrongs others do to us.

We want others to forgive us, when we ask, but we find it difficult to forgive others. When we do not want to forgive someone, we need to heed Jesus' warning about forgiveness. In Matthew 6:14-15, He said: "If you forgive men when they sin against you, your heavenly Father will also forgive you. But if you do not forgive men their sins, your Father will not forgive your sins."When we are unwilling to forgive others, it means we are putting ourselves in God's place to decide who should be forgiven and who should not.

During the Revolutionary war a pastor learned that one of his worst enemies was going to be hanged for his crimes. He walked 60 miles to ask General George Washington to intercede for this man's life. The General said that he was sorry but he could not pardon his "friend." The pastor said that he was not his friend, but his worst enemy. Seeing the preacher's forgiving attitude toward his staunchest enemy, General Washington signed the pardon. The pastor took the signed pardon and walked 15 miles to the execution site of his enemy. He arrived just as the condemned man was trudging toward the scaffold to be executed. The pardon arrived just in time to save his life. What forgiveness! Yet Christ did much more for us. The scripture says in Romans 5:8 that "while we were yet sinners, Christ died for us."

TODAY'S WORD FOR JANUARY 13

KINDNESS

Love is patient, love is kind. I Corinthians 13:4

Be kind to one another, tenderhearted, forgiving one another, as God in Christ has forgiven you. Ephesians 4:32

But if you love those that love you, what credit is that to you? For even sinners love those that love them. And if you do good to those who do good to you, what credit is that to you? For even sinners do the same. So love your enemies, do good, hoping for nothing in return; and your reward will be great, and you will be sons of the most high. For He is kind to the unthankful and evil, therefore be merciful [kind], just as your father also is merciful. Luke 6:32-33, 35-36

As you read the above scriptures, did you notice that when you show love you show kindness? But you must not only love those that love you but you must love your enemies. That makes it much harder, doesn't it? Jesus said, "These things I command you, that you love one another" (John 13:34).

Our actions and our words need to reflect the heart of the One who paid the ultimate price to show us love and kindness when we needed Him the most. Our unkind words may stick with the hearer for decades. Unkind words once spoken can never be taken back.

Emily Dickinson once said: "Some say that a word is dead when it is said. I say it just begins to live that day." Nothing can hurt more than a harsh word. The words we say may have long term consequences. As Christians we need to constantly ask God to give us words of kindness for every situation in life, even when we are angry. Kindness is expressed by our words but we also need to show kindness by our actions, even to those who wish us harm.

Recently I (Ken) was having lunch with a Christian leader who was President of a ministry. We were talking about the past when he reminded me that we had met over 50 years prior and we had had a lengthy conversation about the value of investing our lives in Christian ministries. He thanked me several times during our visit, for being so kind to listen to him and to respond to his needs. Kindness sometimes is just giving some time and listening. He went on to say that the conversation that we had at that time made a lasting impression on his life. I took the time to be kind to him not knowing that it was a time in his life when he was searching for God's will.

Words of kindness and encouragement may not seem much when given, but so many times kind words are never forgotten. On the other hand harsh words are difficult to forget. We need to make sure our words are at all times words of kindness and encouragement. Take time daily, each morning when you pray, to ask God to help you to show kindness to every person you communicate with that day. If you do your day will be blessed by our Lord.

TODAY'S WORD FOR JANUARY 14

CHARACTER

To be esteemed is better than silver or gold. Proverbs 22:1

The other day we went to see one of our grandsons play baseball at his little league field. There were signs on all the screens protecting the spectators from foul balls. The signs all read: YOUR CHILDREN ARE WATCHING! What does this say about the character of parents today? These signs have been placed there to remind the adults to watch their language, eliminate their harsh criticism of umpires, coaches and even players.

It is next to impossible today, with all the pressures of our culture and society on a person, to live a life that is honest, exemplary and shows character without knowing Jesus. God has given us many promises in His Word and the key that unlocks these promises in our life is character. The believer has a responsibility to live the kind of life that reveals his or her good character. This sets believers apart from the rest of the world.

Our character is the sum total of our personal values and qualities. Character is a large factor in determining the life we lead here on earth. In Genesis 49 we find Jacob gathering all of his twelve sons together to give them his blessing before he died. He made a prediction on their future based on the way they had lived and the character they portrayed to others.

Of the twelve sons of Jacob only Joseph was described as having a commendable character. Joseph was the only son that Jacob predicted would have the blessing of God on his life in the future.

The Bible also tells us about other great men of virtue and Godly character. They included such men as Abraham, Enoch and Noah. All of these were known to walk with God. It is very important for us as believers to understand that good character comes only from walking with God.

The Apostle Paul encouraged the Christians at Galatia to be concerned about their character. Paul said that if our lives are controlled by the Holy Spirit, God will produce in us the characteristics of love, joy, peace, longsuffering, kindness, goodness, faithfulness, gentleness and self control [Galatians 5:22-23]. As you look at these character traits that Paul outlines in these verses, do you need to improve on any of them in your life?

Some of us need to show a little more gentleness and love to our family, or possibly, a little more kindness to a neighbor. It is not what you say you are, but it is who you are that is most important. We become known by what we do. If you are a Christian and are of good character, it will be evident by your actions. It is our actions that give us a good name. Solomon with all his wealth said a good name is more to be desired than riches. Do your friends and family see you as a person of good character who stands for what is right and does what is right in God's sight even when no one is watching?

TODAY'S WORD FOR JANUARY 15

ABUNDANCE

Then Jesus said to them, Watch out! Be on your guard against all kind of greed; a man's life does not consist in the abundance of his possessions. Luke 12:15

When God gives any man wealth and possessions, and enables him to enjoy them, to accept his lot and be happy in his work, this is the gift of God. Ecclesiastics 5:19

Abundance means different things to different people across our world. The definition is affected by our cultures and our living standards. But looking at the word abundance from a spiritual perspective we must view our possessions, whether large or small, as a gift from God.

In the book of Ecclesiastics, Solomon reflects back on his life. Solomon had it all. He had wealth, power and fame. He knew what it was like to have abundance. Solomon had asked God for wisdom. Through his wisdom he recognized that the abundance of "things" is not the source of joy. We are to rejoice and be happy because every good "thing" comes from God. Solomon reminds us that it is God who enables us to enjoy what we have and "accept our lot" and be happy.

In Luke 12:15 (above), Jesus tells us that our life does not consist of the abundance of our possessions. The worth of anyone's life has nothing to do with being wealthy, powerful or wise. Jesus warns us to watch out against getting greedy. Often the more we have the more we want. If God blesses us with abundance, that is a good thing and we should be thankful to Him for the blessings. Our perspective in regard to the abundance that God has blessed us with is important. If our perspective is to accumulate abundance for ourselves with no concern for helping others we will not be truly rich and will not be happy in the Lord.

Most people think of abundance based on the "things" they have in life such as possessions and money. The standard of abundance is different to the family living in the mountains of Appalachia compared to the family living in Beverly Hills.

The secret of abundance is not in what we have but what we enjoy and are thankful for every day. Abundance does not mean happiness. Some of the unhappiest people in the world today have, by worldly standards, everything. We have seen that the very opposite is true. People with very little are overflowing with joy because of all that God has given them. This is true with families living in the slums of east Africa, families living on the top of garbage dumps in the Philippines and families that live in poverty in America.

Jesus said in Matthew 5:8 that our Father in heaven knows what we need. We may not have all that we want, but God has promised to give us what we need. If we are obedient and remain faithful to Him He will bless us even in the direst of circumstances. When God blesses you with abundance, whether it is large or small, thank Him for His blessing to you. You have a responsibility to use your abundance for the glory of God.

TODAY'S WORD FOR JANUARY 16

RESPECT

Let all the earth fear the Lord; let all the people of the world revere Him. Psalm 33:8

We must first and foremost respect God and, unfortunately, most people do not feel that respecting God is important. It is not that they say that they do not respect God, but it is through their words and deeds that they show no respect to God.

Just think about how often you hear God's name used in a disrespectful way. The way a person uses God's name reveals how they feel about God. Those who use God's name disrespectfully have never considered who God is. He is the God who created us and all that is in the world. He is the one and only true God. He is Holy, and He is all powerful. The essence of all that God is should put us in awe of Him.

Beyond that, as you read in the verse that we have put above from Psalms you will see that you have no choice but to respect God. It is a Biblical command. If you still have any doubt read the Ten Commandments. The first four of the Ten Commandments (Exodus 20) addresses our relationship to God and what is required of us to show respect to God. The other six deal with our relationship to others and how we are to show respect to them.

Respect for God changes us. Before Paul met Jesus he had no respect for Jesus or anyone who believed in Jesus. After his conversion, Paul's respect for God changed him completely. Paul came to not only respect Jesus and His believers but to work side by side with those he once disrespected and sought to persecute.

The apostle Paul practiced showing respect to those that ministered with him. He praised Timothy for his unselfishness and proven character as well as being a true son who served with him in the gospel. (Philippians 2:20) Paul also commended and showed respect to Epaphroditus when he said, "my brother, fellow worker, and fellow soldier who risked his life for the work of Christ" (Philippians 2:25, 30).

Respect for God results in obedience to God. In Genesis God tells Abraham to take his son up to the mountain and offer him as a sacrifice. Abraham had respect for God and responded in obedience to do as God directed him, however God intervened and stopped Abraham just in time. God provided a ram for the sacrifice. When we revere God and do as He asks, God provides for us just what we need.

The root problem causing the lack of respect in our world today is our sinful nature. Many parents and children have little or no respect for God, their families, their neighbors or the people they meet daily. This lack of respect means that their sinful nature is controlling them. If children can't respect their human fathers how can we expect them to respect their heavenly Father?

To respect God is a biblical command. When that command is not kept our sinful nature takes control. Those who do not respect God will not respect anything or anyone else. Where do you stand as to showing respect to God and others? Where does your family stand? All of us need to realize that God expects us to show respect first of all to Him and then to those we live with.

TODAY'S WORD FOR JANUARY 17

HONESTY

The integrity of the upright will guide them, but the perversity of the unfaithful will destroy them. Proverbs 11:3

I have walked in my integrity. I have also trusted the Lord; I shall not slip. Psalm 26:1

The lack of honesty in people today is prevalent world-wide. It is hard to know whom you can trust. The newspapers and television news remind us how dishonest people are. Governments cannot be trusted. Businesses give dishonest financial reports and deceive investors. Taxpayers cheat on their taxes. Students cheat to get better grades. Spouses cheat on one another. Children lie to get out of trouble.

We are given the godly advice in Proverbs 11:3 to let honesty guide us. Honesty keeps us on the path of uprighteousness. Dishonesty leads us to destruction.

In the book of Acts, chapter 5, we read about the dishonesty of Ananias and Sapphira. Peter asked Ananias, "Why has Satan filled your heart to lie to the Holy Spirit?" Peter then rebuked Ananias saying, "You have not lied to men, but to God." Satan had planted in their hearts a very deceitful plan. Ananias and Sapphira were active church members but even church members are not immune to Satan's temptation. They sold a piece of property and brought a portion of the profit to the apostles as their gift to God, inferring they gave all the profit to the Lord.

Their sin was not about keeping some of the money but that they were not honest about it. They lied to the apostles to make themselves seem more generous than they were. It was not just that they were dishonest to the apostles and the church but they were also dishonest to God and themselves. It reads in: "Why have you conceived this thing in your heart? You have not lied to man but to God" (Acts 5:4). For this they paid a terrible price, death.

Ananias and Sapphira knew that what they were doing was dishonest but they felt that no one would know. But nothing is hidden from God. God knows our every dishonest thought, every lie we tell, and every dishonest thing we do.

Parents have the responsibility to set standards of honesty for their children. Children must see these standards of honesty upheld in the lives of their parents. And as parents we need to be well aware that we teach our children not only by our words but by example.

If a child is raised in a home where their parents and siblings are not honest and upright, then dishonesty becomes a way of life. Someone once said that being honest means that you will never have to look back over your shoulder. This is true because when one is dishonest one almost always will soon get caught with a conflicting story. It seems that there is always someone that surfaces that knows the truth. We may be able to deceive others but we can be certain that our heavenly Father knows the truth and we will have to sooner or later answer to Him.

TODAY'S WORD FOR JANUARY 18

GOALS

I've got my eye on the goal, where God is beckoning us onward to Jesus. I'm off and running and I am not turning back. So let's keep focused on that goal, those of us who want everything that God has for us. If any of you have something else in mind, something less then total commitment, God will clear your blurred vision. We are on the right track, let's stay on it. Philippians 3:14-15 Message translation.

Other than Jesus Himself, no man has made a greater impact on the development and spreading of the gospel than the Apostle Paul. He wrote thirteen books of the New Testament and these books, all inspired by God, still have an impact on the lives of people today. The verse that we have put above is from the Message Translation and spells out clearly the commitment that Paul had to reach his goal of serving Jesus with every ounce of energy that he had. He was focused on his goal.

Enoch was another man that had a clear goal to serve God. There are only 9 verses in the Bible referring to Enoch but what these verses said was that he was a man dedicated to walking with God every day. The scriptures only state that two men "walked with God." The other man was Noah.

Even before we were married we set a life-time goal. That goal was that our hearts would be broken so that we would be able to see the world as a world in need and that God would use our lives to be a witness to a lost and needy world. God honored our request in ways that we would never have dreamt. We learned at a very young age that when we asked God for something that if it was in His will He would honor it. We also learned that most of the time our goals, in God's mind, were small and He wanted us to be involved in something bigger. We learned clearly and very quickly that any project we attempted, whether large or small, would fail unless we allowed God to take over.

It was just a few weeks after we were married that we were off to Korea. We went with the goal of letting the Lord use us as He saw fit on a mission field. We were committed to establish orphanages for World Vision. Thousands of orphans had no home and no one to care for them. Establishing these orphanages allowed God to touch our hearts so that we had a lifetime concern for children.

Our time in Korea lasted only about five months. But in those five months God took over and used us to establish 145 orphanages, build a five story office building for World Vision, hire and train over 100 translators and set up and run a 22 day city wide evangelistic crusade in Seoul Korea which was attended by over 350,000 people with thousands coming to find Jesus as their Savior. We were young, dedicated and ready to be used of God. We were willing to attempt whatever door God would open for us. It has been our experience that when our goal is to serve the Lord, God works in marvelous ways in our lives.

TODAY'S WORD FOR JANUARY 19

ABIDE

Then Jesus said, If you abide in my Word, you are my disciples and you will know the truth, and the truth will set you free. John 8:31- 32

Families, today, need to be committed to Judeo/Christian principles similar to what America was founded on years ago. Parents need to teach these principles to their children by using the Bible as their guide book. Reading the Bible together daily as a family will allow each family member to make proper and positive choices for their daily walk. Unfortunately, sitting down as a family and reading the Bible together and then discussing what was read is no longer prevalent in our homes.

The Bible is God's instruction book to us. Jesus tells us to abide in His Word. Abide means to obey and hold fast to His teachings. Some translations of the Bible use the word "continue" for "abide." "Continue" means to habitually abide. Reading God's Word and obeying His words is to be a continuing habit in our life, not just now and then.

The above scripture says that if we abide in the Bible we will be a disciple of Jesus. The first step for true discipleship is to believe in Jesus Christ as your Savior and Messiah. The second step is to abide in the Word of God, the Bible, to develop your progress in becoming a true disciple of Jesus.

Disciples live by the instructions given by their leader. Jesus has given us in His Word principles and standards to live by on a daily basis. Abiding in God's Word prepares us to endure every situation in life without yielding to opposing views that conflict with the Biblical principles.

It is by abiding in God's Word that we know the truth. We know the truth by reading and studying the teachings that Jesus brought to His followers. The Bible never changes or is it ever out of date. It is as true today as it was when our parents read it and taught it to us as children.

Parents are responsible to teach the truth of God's Word to their children and lead them by example, setting guidelines and boundaries that honor God. You need to teach your children to have listening ears and compliant hearts.

Your child's future depends on this action on your part. The scripture is very clear in admonishing us to "train a child in the way he should go and when he is old he will not depart from it" (Proverbs 22:6).

Do you spend time daily abiding in His Word, the Bible? This is the only way we can teach the principals that lead us to be a disciple of Jesus. Make it your prayer today to be diligent in your study and then straight forward in your teaching others to know and understand the Word of God.

TODAY'S WORD FOR JANUARY 20

ASHAMED

For I am not ashamed of the gospel of Christ, for it is the power of God unto salvation for everyone who believes. Romans 1:16

Yet if anyone suffers as a Christian, let him not be ashamed, but let him glorify God. I Peter 4:16

Recently, we have noticed what seems to be a fear among people who know the Lord to communicate to their friends and neighbors about their faith. As a result of the influence of the liberal media and the pressure of being "politically correct" there is a moving away from the Judeo Christian principles that our country was founded on and many Christians are drawing themselves into a so called "shell."

They do this because they do not want to cause conflict and be ridiculed for their faith and beliefs. It seems they are ashamed to let others know that they are a Christian. Being ashamed of our faith is not of God and dishonors Him.

Peter in I Peter 4:16 instructs us not to be ashamed of our faith and if any of us do suffer as a result of our faith we can give glory to God through that suffering.

Paul was imprisoned in Philippi, chased out of Thessalonica, smuggled out of Berea, laughed at in Athens, regarded as a fool in Corinth, and stoned in Galatia. But even after these events Paul was eager to preach the gospel in Rome even though it was the seat of contemporary power and pagan religions. In Romans Paul tells us that it is important for believers to understand that the reason we are not to be ashamed of the gospel message of our faith in Christ is because it is, "the power of God unto salvation for everyone who believes" (Romans 1:16, above). It is through us that God brings His message of salvation. Neither ridicule, nor criticism, nor persecution could curb the enthusiasm to preach by Paul.

More than at any time in history God is expecting us, as Christians, to stand up for what we believe. God has not promised us that it would be easy and that we would not run into those who disagreed with what we believed, some even violently.

All we have to do is look at the life of Paul and the apostles in the book of Acts to see that this is true. God has promised that if we stay true to Him and keep, "PRAYED UP," God will empower us to unashamedly declare the gospel to others.

A few years ago one of our grandsons had his appendix removed. It was emergency surgery at about three in the morning. He was seven years old and had been in real pain for several hours. He had gone through the necessary tests to make sure the right diagnosis had been made and was in the operating room ready to be put to sleep. The doctor came in and asked our grandson if he had any questions. He responded by asking the doctor, "Are you a Christian?" The doctor responded saying that he believed in Jesus. That was all he wanted to hear so he relaxed and fell asleep for the surgery. This seven year old grandson was not ashamed to talk about Jesus and what he believed. Sometimes children set the example for us.

TODAY'S WORD FOR JANUARY 21

FAITH

For as the body without the Spirit is dead, so faith without works is dead also. James 2:26

I say to you, if you have faith as a grain of mustard seed, you will say to this mountain, move from here to there, and it will move. And nothing will be impossible for you. Matthew 17:20

We live by faith every day. It is easy to believe in things we can see or touch. It is much harder to believe in things that are unseen. We accept the unseen things by faith. We cannot see air but we take air into our lungs every time we take a breath. We cannot see the air but the evidence is there because without it we die.

When it comes to spiritual things, we enter a relationship with God by accepting by faith, His saving grace and forgiveness by believing on His Son Jesus as our Savior. This faith cannot be seen or touched but it is evidenced by the effect it has on our life. Faith in Jesus literally changes us and our outlook on life.

When God comes into our life we are made a new creation by His transforming power. We are changed from the inside out. Inside we are cleansed from our sin and made righteous. Our desires will not be for the things of this world, but for the righteous things of God. The evidence of our new life in Christ will be seen in our desire to serve God and do what is right and by the good works we do.

James 2:26, above, tells us that faith without works is dead. As believers our faith in God should be evidenced in our lives by our actions or else our faith is not much more than an intellectual acknowledgement of God. We must live our faith everyday so that our actions verify the reality of our relationship with God.

In the Old Testament we see in the lives of the great heroes of faith the validity of their faith by the way they lived and by their actions. These are some of them:

By faith Enoch walked with God and did not experience death.

By faith Noah built the ark.

By faith Abraham moved to the Promised Land.

By faith Moses led the Israelites out of Egypt and to the Red Sea.

By faith Joshua brought down the walls and conquered Jericho.

By faith David killed Goliath.

These faithful believers put their faith in action.

Those who live by faith desire to know God's will for their life and to do God's will. Faith gives us the confidence to do what God wants us to do even when it is difficult and seems impossible. Do you have the faith as small as a mustard seed? If you do Jesus says you can move mountains. We all have mountains in our lives to move. These mountains may seem insurmountable. It is possible to move these mountains by faith even if our faith is small. We can have assurance that it can happen because Jesus said nothing is impossible to those who have faith.

TODAY'S WORD FOR JANUARY 22

PRAYER

If you believe, you will receive whatever you ask for in prayer. Matthew 21:22

I tell you the truth, my Father will give you whatever you ask for in My name. Until now you have not asked for anything in my name. Ask and you will receive, and your joy will be complete. John 16: 23-24

Prayer is the key to a close relationship with God. Without communication it would be hard to develop a relationship with anyone. It is no different with God. Prayer is communication with God and absolutely necessary to strengthen our relationship with Him.

Prayer is one of the pillars of the Christian faith. If you find it hard to know how to pray, consider these six lessons from God's Word on prayer:

First, we must pray as the Lord prayed. He gave us an example with what we familiarly call the Lord's Prayer (Luke 11:1-4. Take time to memorize the Lord's Prayer and pray it daily until it becomes a vital part of your daily life.

Secondly, we are to pray in the Spirit. In Jude 20 we are reminded to "pray in the Holy Spirit." To pray in the Holy Spirit means to pray in the power of the Holy Spirit because He will guide and assist us in our prayers. Paul tells us in times of great need that "the Spirit Himself intercedes for us with groans that words cannot express" (Romans 8:26).

Thirdly, we are to pray according to God's will. In Romans 12:2 we are told that God's will for the believer is good, acceptable and perfect. We learn what God's will is by reading the scriptures, and by the leading of the Holy Spirit within us and by the circumstances which God allows to occur in our lives.

Fourthly, we are to pray without ceasing. In I Thessalonians 5:17-18, we are told to pray without ceasing and with thanksgiving. God desires your fellowship. He desires for you to have His forgiveness, peace, guidance and His rest in your soul. Praying without ceasing means having an attitude of prayer in all you do.

Fifthly, we are to pray believing. In Matthew 21:21-22 we are told to believe in God's almighty ability and desire to answer our prayers from the evidence He has given us in the scriptures. We can ask in prayer and we need to ask "believing." If you still do not feel God is answering your prayers then you need to ask yourself, "Do I really believe that God can answer my prayers?"

Sixthly, we are to pray in Jesus' name. Christ teaches us in John 16:23-24 to pray to the Father in His name. Before Jesus died on the cross to atone for our sins people could only pray to God through the priests. Jesus death and resurrection made it possible to come to God directly. We pray in Jesus name because Jesus is our high priest who has made us acceptable to God. Jesus assures us that if we pray in His name, He will answer.

TODAY'S WORD FOR JANUARY 23

TREASURE

Lay not up for yourselves treasures upon earth, where moth and rust corrupts, and where thieves break through and steal; but lay up for yourselves treasures in heaven, where neither moth nor rust corrupts and where thieves do not break through and steal. For where your treasure is, there your heart will be also. Matthew 6:19-21

In these verses from Matthew, Jesus was teaching about the desires of our heart. The heart is the central part or core of something. Our heart is the innermost core of our emotions. In this scripture, Jesus is in essence telling us to give ourselves a heart checkup. Things that are nearest and dearest to our heart are the things we treasure and most desire. There are earthly (material) treasures that are subject to destruction by moths, rust and can be stolen by thieves. There are heavenly (spiritual) treasures that will benefit us for an eternity and cannot be taken away from us. They are eternal and are the treasures that God wants us to develop in our daily walk with Him. We must examine our hearts to see what it is we treasure.

Someone once said, "What I hoard in this life, I lose; but what I give in this life, I keep." We cannot take our earthly treasures with us when we die, but we can send them ahead by sharing and caring for others and supporting kingdom work.

If your riches are here on this earth, your heart will be bound to this world's system. If your riches are in heaven, you will seek those things which are above and use the things of this world to the glory of God.

In Matthew 6:24 Jesus warns us that we cannot serve both God and money. When money and possessions become all consuming we will have no time for serving God. What Jesus wants is for us to accumulate or store up our treasures in heaven.

The Apostle Paul adds to these thoughts from Matthew when he writes to the church in Colossae, "If then you were raised with Christ, seek those things which are above, where Christ is, sitting at the right hand of God. Set your mind on things above, not on things on the earth" Colossians 3:1-2.

When we were children we were blessed with godly parents who not only taught us to build up our treasures in heaven and not on this earth, but also practiced what they preached. Earthly riches basically were never in our vocabulary. Our parents worked hard and God provided all we needed, and at the same time they invested their time, talents and treasures in heavenly things. We store up treasures in heaven by being obedient to God, serving Him, and seeking His will for our life, telling others about Christ, and helping others.

We continued this practice with our children and God has blessed us abundantly with all we ever needed on this earth. Our prayer for you is that you will invest your time and talent to build your treasures in Heaven. Everything we do in life that is obedient to God and His Word is a treasure that we store in our account in heaven.

TODAY'S WORD FOR JANUARY 24

WORRY

Therefore do not worry, saying, what shall we eat? Or what shall we drink? Or what shall we wear? For your Heavenly Father knows that you need all these things. Matthew 6:31

The above verse from Matthew 6:31 is part of what we know as the Sermon on the Mount. Many people listening to Jesus speak this sermon truly believed that they had reasons to worry. Jesus started out His lesson on worry by telling them "not to worry about the necessities of life such as food, drink, and clothing."

When Jesus said, "do not worry" He was not suggesting that one does not prepare for life. He is not saying that one is to be lazy and thoughtless with a no care attitude. God will not pamper slothfulness. He expects us to look after our responsibilities, work to eat and take care of our families and to work extra to have enough to give to others.

What Jesus is talking about is being so wrapped up in securing the things in life that we become anxious, disturbed, without sleep and then worry. Instead we need to be consumed by thinking about and working for the Lord. Worry is not necessary when we are trusting God.

These words are relative for today. A recent survey of doctor's tells us that worry is the underlying cause of about 73% of illnesses. Worry leads to emotional turmoil in family relationships. People also worry about major problems that more than often will never happen. Worry is non-productive. Time spent worrying is time wasted. In Matthew 6:27, Jesus says to us, "Who of you by worrying can add a simple hour to his life?"

Why do people today worry so much? Possibly they do not feel good about what they are doing or something they have done. Whether someone is a Christian or not a Christian they know the difference between right and wrong. Their own actions give them cause to worry. They are living with a weight of guilt and in fear that their world could come crashing in on them.

If you are carrying a heavy load of guilt it is time to confess your sin and get right with God and whoever you sinned against.

Real life happenings are often the cause of worry. A loss of a job, a home foreclosure, expenses running higher than the income being received or even a breaking family relationship, all cause people to worry. These are serious reasons for concern. There is a difference between concern and worry. Worry immobilizes us. Concern motivates us to action. God wants concern to motivate us to trust Him and bring our concerns to Him.

The Apostle Paul said in Philippians 4:6, "Do not be anxious (worry) about anything, but in everything by prayer and petition, with thanksgiving, present your requests to God."

TODAY'S WORD FOR JANUARY 25

ACCOUNTABILITY

Why did you despise the word of the Lord by doing evil in his eyes? You struck down Uriah the Hittite with the sword and took his wife to be your own. Thus says the Lord: Behold I will raise up adversity against you from your own house, for you did it secretly, but I will do this thing before all Israel. II Samuel 12:9-12

So that every mouth may be silenced and the whole world held accountable to God. Romans 3:19

Today, more than any other time in history, we believe people do all they can to avoid taking responsibility for their actions. When caught in a wrong doing, they do not want to be held accountable so they blame someone else. It began in the Garden of Eden when God confronted Adam for his sin of eating the forbidden fruit. Adam blamed Eve for giving the fruit to him. And then Eve blamed Satan for deceiving her.

In II Samuel (above) David tried to get away with the sin of killing Uriah by doing it in a deceptive way. David thought he had gotten away with it until he was challenged by Nathan, a prophet sent by God, to face his sin of taking Bathsheba and killing her husband Uriah.

These are two examples as to how easy and natural it is to want to avoid taking the responsibility for our own actions by finding a way to place the blame on someone else. Unfortunately, it often works and then an innocent person gets the blame. However, there is someone we cannot fool and He does hold us accountable. Hebrews 5:7 tells us, "nothing in all creation is hidden from God's sight. Everything is uncovered and laid bare before the eyes of Him to whom we must give an account."

No one likes to admit that they were wrong, especially if there are consequences, which is usually the case. Human nature makes us eager to accept accountability when the issue is favorable, right or positive. But since we all are of a sinful nature when a situation is negative or breaking a rule we are quick to want to pass the blame to someone else who is usually innocent.

It begins early in a child's life. Many times we could just look into the eyes of one of our children and see guilt. Then often we could watch our child do all he or she could to make someone else accountable for what he or she had done. How often when children are caught having a fight have we heard: "but he [or she] started it." Then the other one responds by saying: "did not."

The apostle Paul in Romans 3:19 says that God holds all of us accountable for what we do and none of our excuses or arguments are acceptable.

God wants us to be accountable for our actions. David did the right thing. When confronted with his wrong doing he confessed it and asked God for His forgiveness. This is what God wants us to do.

TODAY'S WORD FOR JANUARY 26

DISCOURAGEMENT

O Lord, how long shall I cry, and You will not hear? Even cry out to You, "VIOLENCE!" and You will not save. Habakkuk 1:2

Habakkuk, in the verse above, expresses his heart just like many believers do today. He was frustrated and baffled as to why God had not corrected the corruption in Judah? God was working but Habakkuk could not see it because it was not God's time to answer Habakkuk's prayers. Habakkuk was discouraged and could not understand why God was delaying.

It is difficult for believers today, as well, to see the injustice and evil that abounds in our world and not be discouraged and wonder if God is paying attention.

Do you feel stuck in discouragement? If so, you are not alone. At some point everyone experiences a disappointment which is an emotional response to a failed expectation. Disappointment is the normal initial reaction to a failed expectation but if you allow it to linger it will turn into discouragement.

The circumstances that bring on disappointment may be unavoidable but we have a choice how we can respond. We can either let it overwhelm us or bring it before the Lord who can help us through it.

Living in constant discouragement can divide the mind, making it hard to focus on anything but our pain. Then anger comes and we look for someone to blame, whether it be God, people around us, or yourself.

Frustration that isn't handled well may develop into depression, which will turn others away from us. This leads to a low esteem and then we make poor decisions. Choosing this self-destructive path is not God's best for our lives. Instead of sulking in self-pity we can choose to put our faith in God and bring our discouragement to God as Habakkuk did.

By the end of the book we find Habakkuk rejoicing in the Lord because God assured him that although the wicked may prevail for a time, eventually they will be judged and God will triumph.

Nehemiah is another great example (Nehemiah 2:1-8). He had every reason to feel defeated, because his people were in trouble. The city wall had been destroyed but he did not allow himself to stay in the low place of discouragement. Instead he cried out to God for direction. Even though Nehemiah knew that sadness in the presence of royalty was punishable by death, the Lord went ahead of Nehemiah and led the king to notice his servant's sadness and asked what he could do to help.

This miracle led to the rebuilding of the wall and the redemption of God's people. The Lord can work in our discouraging situations, just as He did for Habakkuk and Nehemiah if we cry out to Him for help. Even though we cannot see how God is working and we feel we have been praying long enough we do not need to be discouraged. God is doing His work even when we do not understand.

TODAY'S WORD FOR JANUARY 27

PATIENCE

But when you do good and suffer, if you take it patiently, this is commendable before God. I Peter 2:20

Rejoicing in hope, patient in tribulation, continuing steadfastly in prayer. Romans 12:12

But those who wait upon the Lord shall renew their strength; they shall mount up with wings like eagles, they shall run and not be weary, they shall walk and not faint. Isaiah 40:31

Many people miss out on blessings in their lives because they are inpatient and unwilling to wait for His timing. The scriptures encourage believers to be patient but most of us just by our human nature want answers today.

David exhibited great patience in waiting for the Lord's timing. David had been anointed King but he chose not to use violence to take the throne that he knew would someday be his. King Saul had become envious of David's success in battle and his popularity with the people so he planned to murder David. During the time Saul and his men were pursuing David to kill him; David was close enough to Saul to kill him on two occasions (I Samuel 24:4 and 26:12).

The first time David cut off a piece of Saul's robe. On the second occasion David took Saul's spear and water jug while he was sleeping. Although David had a reason to kill Saul to keep from being killed himself, when he had the opportunity he knew it was wrong to kill the Lord's anointed. In both instances he was willing to wait for God's timing and not take matters into his own hands.

David was patient. His attributes included having a strong faith and he believed that God would gain His victory at the right place, the right time and with the right method. David had values that helped him wait on God. Killing the King would violate his conscience and he would be out of the will of God. David's first desire was to do God's will and to have God's direction on his life.

In real life we encounter frustrations and situations such as the slow driver, a mischievous child or an uncooperative co-worker. As God's children we are called to live a life worthy of Him characterized by humility, gentleness and patience (Ephesians 4:1-3). The scripture tells us to be tolerant with one another and to do this we need to be patient. We are to bear one another's burdens and respond with kindness. In Romans 12:12, above, Paul tells us to be joyful in hope and patient in affliction. When we quietly endure our suffering or frustrations, we find favor with the Lord (I Peter 2:20).

When you are frustrated waiting upon God for a direction or an answer, always seek His wisdom and remember that "those who wait upon the Lord will gain new strength" (Isaiah 40:31 above).

TODAY'S WORD FOR JANUARY 28

COMMIT

Commit yourselves to the Lord and serve Him only. I Samuel 7:3

Commit to the Lord whatever you do and your plans will succeed. Proverbs 16:3

There are numerous times every day when a commitment to or for something is necessary. The most important commitment that one can make in a lifetime is a firm commitment to God. This is the first step in living a life that is pleasing to God. Making a commitment to God is more than going to church, reading the Bible or even praying. A commitment to God is having a relationship with God's Son, Jesus Christ. This is what makes Christianity meaningful, unique and different from all other religions. When we are in a close relationship with God, He will be able to work in and through us. It is when we commit ourselves to God that we can experience God's blessings.

Commitments are important to make in life. A commitment to your spouse and your family is very important. They are vital for one to live a rewarding and fulfilled life. It means more than just a promise. A commitment requires action.

Jesus warned His disciples in Luke 14:25-27 that making a commitment to follow Him would come at a cost. He told them that nothing, even their love for their father or mother could take precedence over loyalty to Him. When the disciples committed to follow Jesus they had to be willing to leave their home, their family, and their former life behind. Our love for Jesus today demands this same commitment.

Committing to follow Christ does not mean we will live a trouble-free life, but it will be a care-free life because we can cast all of our cares on Him (I Peter 5:7) and because we have the assurance that we have eternal life (I John 5:13).

The nation of Israel was the fulfillment of God's promise to Abraham, "to make him into a great nation" (Genesis 12:2). The Israelites were God's chosen people and God promised Moses that He would deliver the Israelites from slavery under Pharaoh. God also promised that all who would commit themselves to loving and serving Him and keeping His commandments would be brought safely to the "Promised Land." The Old Testament covers the history of Israel and vividly portrays how the times of commitment to God brought God's blessing of protection and victory and how disobedience brought suffering and defeat.

God is faithful and wants to bless us abundantly but we cannot expect Him to bless us when we are not committed to Him. The world offers many distractions that interfere with our commitment to the Lord. It takes conscious effort on our part to be faithful to keep our commitment to the Lord. The Lord deserves our full commitment, not a half-hearted one. 11 Chronicles 16:9 tells us, "The eyes of the Lord search the whole earth in order to strengthen those whose hearts are fully committed to Him." The Lord knows all about each one of us. We cannot hide anything from God anymore than Adam and Eve could hide their sin from God.

TODAY'S WORD FOR JANUARY 29

LONELY

No one stood with me, but all forsook me. But the Lord stood with me and strengthened me. II Timothy 4: 16-17

Look to the right and see; no one is concerned for me. I have no refuge; no one cares for my life. I cry to You O Lord; I say You are my refuge, my portion in the land of living. Psalm 142:4

How many times in life have you really felt lonely? When David wrote Psalm 142 he was hiding in a cave to escape from Saul's men who were seeking to capture him. He felt that he was totally abandoned by everyone and that no one was even concerned whether he lived or died. He was truly alone. Saul had been chasing him for years and was seeking to kill him so that he would not become King of Israel.

David had to live on the run, fleeing from one place to another. There was no one he could trust for fear that they would betray him. But despite being so extremely lonely, David knew there was someone he could trust and confide in. He was confident that God loved him and cared for him and that he could call on him at his time of need. He knew that God was there with him and heard his prayers. David trusted God to keep him safe and to protect him. God had chosen David to be the next king after Saul. David trusted that God would fulfill His plan for his life.

The verses from II Timothy were from the letter that Paul wrote while he was in prison and feeling lonely. In the Roman legal system of the day a person had two hearings. The first hearing established the charge and would rule if there was evidence enough for a trial. This is when Paul told Timothy that no one came to stand with him and testify for him. This was a very lonely time for Paul because he needed support from his friends and they were not there.

But Paul says that the Lord was there with him. (Verse 17) The Lord fulfilled his promise, given in Joshua 1:5, when He said that he would never leave or forsake those who belong to Him. That promise is good for us today and in our moments of loneliness we must remember, as Paul did, that our Lord will never leave us or forsake us if we are His child and have our complete trust in Him.

There are many situations in life that bring on loneliness such as the separation from a spouse or a problem with a child. When these moments come people look to other "Things" to keep their mind off of the problem. This will not get rid of the loneliness because these are mere distractions, not solutions.

Think about the lonely time that Jesus had in the Garden of Gethsemane just hours before His death on the cross. On the cross Jesus cried out to God, "My God, My God, why hast thou forsaken Me." He understood that He alone would pay the penalty of sin so that all humanity could have the blessed hope of spending an eternity with God. He knew how it is to feel lonely and He has compassion for us when we feel lonely. If you are feeling alone and feel that no one is near, talk to God.

TODAY'S WORD FOR JANUARY 30

WORSHIP

Because He is your Lord, worship Him. Psalm 45:11

Oh come, let us worship and bow down, let us kneel before the Lord our maker. Psalm 95:6

Worship is our way to show that we honor and reverence God. He is all powerful and all knowing but more than that He is a loving and just God. He loved us so much that He was not willing for us to die in our sins so He sent His only Son to suffer and die for our sins. Because of this alone, He deserves our worship.

We worship the Lord with praise and thanksgiving for who He is and for the salvation He provided for us through Jesus Christ. We also worship Him for all the blessings He has given to us. James reminds us that every good and perfect gift is from above coming down from our father in heaven [James 1:7]. We have an awesome God, how can we not worship Him?

We have been in Kenya several times representing our ministry. One of the highlights was visiting some of the 75 churches we sponsored. We learned from them what true worship was all about. These dear people filled their churches to capacity every time the doors were opened. Most of them walked for miles to get to their church. They had no cars and could not afford any city buses that may have been available. Many were standing outside looking in through the open windows. We never have heard such singing from the heart. They would sit or stand for hours taking in every word that was being preached.

And when the offering was taken we learned so much about worship through their giving. They worshipped God in the offering with a tithe of what God had given them. We saw chickens, vegetables and even clothes being given.

Many times we have compared the worship of these Kenyans with the church here in America. What a difference! These Kenyans understand true worship.

After we were first married and went to Korea for World Vision, one of the first things we experienced was the ringing of the Church bells for the early morning prayer meetings. At 6:00A.M. EVERY MORNING the churches were filled with those whose priority was to worship God. They had gotten up before daybreak to honor the Lord by joining with fellow believers in worship.

The South Korean people were a nation that showed their faith in God through prayer and worship. Over half of their population was classified as Christians. Our world today needs to make worshipping our Lord a priority in their daily lives.

When you are worshipping in the presence of God, this is a time for God to talk to you. A good indicator of our spiritual temperature is our eagerness to worship God. Our worship of God here on earth is only a prelude to the great worship services we will have in the future when we are in the presence of God. We encourage you to worship God daily and live for what you will not regret when you die.

TODAY'S WORD FOR JANUARY 31

ANGER

Let all bitterness, wrath, anger, clamor and evil speaking be put away from you. Ephesians 4:31

Anger is a strong and dangerous emotion. Anger motivates people to make bad decisions that often lead to violence. People do things in a fit of anger that they otherwise would never do and it has been going on since the fall of Adam. We read in Genesis 4:5, Cain was very angry and his anger led him to kill his brother Abel.

God does not say that we will not get angry but He teaches that we are to control our anger and handle it wisely and proper. The writer of Proverbs (29:11) tells us to be wise and keep our anger under control. Paul's advice to us in Ephesians 4:26 is to not allow anger to cause us to be evil and sin.

Yes, God himself gets angry but this does not justify our anger. What angers God is the godlessness and wickedness of people (Romans 1:18). In Numbers 32:13 we read that "the Lord's anger burned against Israel and He made them wander in the desert for 40 years, until a whole generation of those who had done evil in His sight was gone." God's anger is always justified and His punishment is always just.

Every family has to deal with times of anger between its members. It happens in the best of families. There is no perfect child that has never made his or her parents angry. When parents get angry with a child they need to stop and think if their anger is justified. Parents have the responsibility to demonstrate to their children how to deal with anger. If children see their parents yell and scream and rant and rave, they are sending a message to the children that it is OK to be angry. A mature person, one that lives by God's Word, always should exhibit self-control by keeping calm in a time of conflict.

In Proverbs 17:27 it reads, "He who has knowledge restrains his words." This means that we need to keep to ourselves words that we know could ignite anger in others. Certain personalities have trouble with this concept because just by their nature they want to stir up conflict. It seems to be inherent in all of us to want to get in the last word.

Words spoken in anger and things done in anger are really regretted after the fact. But then it is too late to undo the harm that was done. Angry words are rather like toothpaste; you cannot put it back into the tube.

In Proverbs 17:27 we read that, "A man of understanding is of a calm spirit." A man of understanding is someone who is truly wise. To be of calm spirit means to be even-tempered. To be a person of understanding and a calm spirit we need to follow Paul's instruction and get rid of all bitterness, wrath, anger, clamor and evil speaking (Ephesians 4:31).

The key to controlling anger is to stop when a conflict begins and ask God for a calm spirit and a cool head. Remember what Proverbs says in 15:1, "a gentle answer turns away wrath, but a harsh word stirs up anger."

TODAY'S WORD FOR FEBRUARY 1

BEATITUDES

Repent for the kingdom of heaven is at hand. Matthew 4:17

Crowds were following Jesus wanting to hear more about the kingdom of God and how to be part of it. When Jesus saw that there was a huge crowd following Him, He climbed a hillside, found a quiet place and sat down. From that hillside location he began to teach what came to be known as the Sermon on the Mount.

The Beatitudes, that he began His sermon with, define the character qualities that Jesus expects of those who would be part of His kingdom. The Beatitudes are the <u>ATTITUDES</u> that should <u>BE</u> evident in the lives of those who love the Lord. These attitudes are defined by the words that Jesus used to begin this sermon: Repent, for the kingdom of heaven is at hand. Repentance is His theme and our daily attitudes must be controlled by this theme that Jesus gave us.

The Sermon on the Mount is our King Jesus' manifesto of His principles. It has been known through the centuries as the greatest sermon ever preached. The disciples and the multitudes that listened were in awe.

Jesus followers wanted to make Him King, but Jesus had made it clear that the King could not establish His kingdom on earth because the Jewish people would not repent and accept the Messiah as their King. Thus we do not have yet the kingdom on earth but we do have the King's manifesto (proclamation) presented by Jesus in this sermon. We are to put into practice these principles of His manifesto as we live in this corrupt world because we are Christ's representatives to those who are lost.

The Beatitudes reveal the secret of true happiness to us as believers. We need to remember that our happiness is not found in the things we have but in what we are in Christ Jesus. We encourage you to study these Beatitudes with an open heart, a receptive mind, and a humble spirit, always being in prayer.

In these Beatitudes Jesus chose to teach reversed values. God's values contradict the world's values. In other words, instead of teaching about the rich he taught about the poor. He wanted to dispute the conventional wisdom of the time which said the wealthy and influential enjoyed more of God's blessings. Jesus wanted His followers to see that material things are only temporary and certainly not the only reality in life. He did not want them to think that their current situations were signs of God's blessing or judgment; instead He wanted the masses and the disciples to see that the materially poor can be spiritually wealthy.

Seldom in history have so few words been spoken with so much meaning as what Jesus spoke in these Beatitudes. The Beatitudes of our Lord, as they are known to us today, are powerful, holding before us and the world a descriptive picture of the true disciple of God. They are the King's manifesto, your guideline for a spirit-filled life here on earth. The Beatitudes cover the glorious hope and reward that the believer can expect not only now but in eternity.

TODAY'S WORD FOR FEBRUARY 2

POOR

Blessed are the poor in spirit, for theirs is the kingdom in heaven. Matthew 5:3

We need to notice that each one of the Beatitudes begins with the word "blessed." It must be understood what Jesus meant by "blessed." Blessed does not mean worldly prosperity and a life of ease. To be blessed means to experience hope and joy outside of prosperity and circumstances. It means to be happy, fortunate and blissful. Jesus was describing a divinely bestowed well being that only belongs to the faithful believers that believe in Him.

"Blessed are the poor in spirit" is the first Beatitude that Jesus taught in His famous Sermon on the Mount. The POOR IN SPIRIT are empty of all spiritual pride. A spirit of pride is the spirit of this age of which Satan is god. To be poor in spirit is to have a "contrite and humble spirit" as Isaiah wrote in Isaiah 57:15.

Being "poor in spirit" does not mean that a person must be poverty stricken and financially poor. Hunger, nakedness, and slums are not pleasing to God, especially in a world of plenty. Christ in this Beatitude is not speaking about material poverty.

First of all, being "poor in spirit" as Jesus was teaching, means for us to acknowledge our utter helplessness before God. It is the opposite of feeling self-sufficient. We must recognize our spiritual poverty and spiritual neediness. We are to be solely dependent upon God to meet our need and not to rely on our selves.

Secondly, it is to acknowledge our spiritual deadness and our inability to face life and eternity apart from God. The real blessings of life and eternity will only come from having a right relationship with God.

And finally, being "poor in spirit" is to acknowledge our lack of superiority before all others. This is acknowledging that we are no better, no richer, and no more superior than the next person, no matter what we have achieved in this world. We are to approach life with a humble attitude, contributing all we can to a needy world out of a spirit of appreciation for what God has done for us.

The message translation of this Beatitude says; "You are blessed when you are at the end of your rope. With less of you there is more of God." That says it very plainly, doesn't it?

The opposite of being poor in spirit is having a spirit full of self. There is a world of difference between these two spirits. There is a difference in thinking that we are righteous in ourselves versus knowing that we need the righteousness of Christ. Self righteousness dies but the righteousness that is of Christ lives forever.

A person that acknowledges his spiritual poverty turns his attention away from the things of this world and reaches out to God and seeks His kingdom.

The poor in spirit are weary of the deceptive enticements of this world and burdened for those who are lost. The poor in spirit receive from God the gift of life everlasting and eternal fellowship with God.

TODAY'S WORD FOR FEBRUARY 3

MOURN

Blessed are those who mourn, for they shall be comforted. Matthew 5:4

This Beatitude can only be understood by one who is a believer in Jesus as Savior. How can a bereaved person be blessed amid grief? Mourning means to have a broken heart. A believer understands what the Psalmist meant when he wrote in Psalm 30:5, "weeping may endure for a night, but joy comes in the morning." God has promised to comfort the mourner in this life and in the life to come. Sorrow lasts for a short time but God's comfort lasts for a lifetime.

Mourning is an action or emotion that comes upon one as a sorrow for sin, a broken heart over evil, or suffering. A mourner is so full of grief that he cries and weeps from within. Solomon tells us in Ecclesiastics 3:4 that there will be times in our lives when we will mourn, just as there will be times to laugh, weep and dance.

But Jesus, in this Beatitude, tells us that we will be blessed and comforted when we feel we have lost something or someone most dear to us because only then can we know what it is to be embraced by the One most dear to us, our Lord.

There are normally three types of people that mourn.

First is the person who is desperately sorry for his sins. He has such a sense of sin that his heart is broken. The second is the person who really feels the desperate plight and terrible suffering of others. It could be tragedies, sinful behavior or the evil that one faces in the world. And finally there is the person who mourns because of a personal tragedy, loss, or intense trauma.

Those that mourn shall be comforted. II Corinthians 1:3 says, "Blessed be the God and Father of our Lord Jesus Christ, the Father of mercies and the God of all comfort." God gives the one that mourns a settled peace from within. He receives an assurance of forgiveness and acceptance by God and a fullness of joy which is a sense of God's presence, care and guidance.

There is also an eternal comfort that God gives one who mourns. It is an assurance that one will pass from death to life and will spend an eternity with Him. It is an assurance that God will wipe away all tears and swallow up death into victory. There will be no mourning in heaven (Revelation 21:4).

The scripture tells us to mourn for lost souls. The apostle Paul in Romans 9:1-5 grieved for his "countrymen according to the flesh," and longed desperately for their salvation. When lost souls mourn their life of sin it brings them to repent and believe on the Lord Jesus Christ. Mourning comes before repentance. We are told in Luke 18:13 that when the publican (the tax collector) decided to repent he "beat his breast saying: 'God be merciful to me as a sinner.'" Mourning is part of true repentance. When you study this Beatitude, may you have a new sense of the comfort God will give to you as a believer in time of need.

TODAY'S WORD FOR FEBRUARY 4

MEEK

Blessed are the meek, for they shall inherit the earth. Matthew 5:5

In this Beatitude that Jesus taught in the Sermon on the Mount, Jesus was quoting from Psalms 37:11 that reads that the meek "shall inherit the earth." The philosophy of the world is the exact opposite of this Beatitude. People of the world consider the meek (humble and submissive) person to be weak, cowardly and even out of control. Meekness is the opposite of being out of control. It is having supreme self-controlled empowerment by God's Holy Spirit. What the world does not understand is that the most gentle, meek and humble person that ever lived on this earth was our Lord Jesus Christ.

Yes, the world may consider the meek to be weak, but meekness is not weakness. To be meek is to be in control of your actions and that takes God's strength and His power. Meekness is the opposite of being out of control. It is not weakness but total self-control empowered by the Holy Spirit in one's life. For a better understanding of this we need to read and study Ephesians 3:13-19. No, the meek are not weak; they are "strong in the Lord and in the power of His might" Ephesians 6:10.

The meek person is a quiet person. He is quiet before God, he surrenders to God and he communicates with God. A meek person is also quiet before men. He walks quietly before men and he is controlled in all things including his reactions, his speech and behavior.

A believer in Jesus, who is meek according to the standard of God, is blessed when he or she is content with who they are and what they have in the Lord. That is the moment you will find yourself the proud owner of everything that can be inherited from God on this earth.

When Jesus said that the meek would inherit the earth, there were two points to be stressed. The meek will inherit the earth now. They will enjoy the good things of the earth that God has blessed them with. The meek are comfortable with themselves. They know who they are and strong and confident in their faith. They know where they are going and are assured of victory, conquest and triumph over whatever confronts them. And they have peaceful souls because they have learned that whatever pressure or tension comes their way they will turn it over to Christ.

Secondly, the earth is the Meek's eternally for they will be part of God's kingdom in the new heavens and earth (Revelation 21:1-3). They have an inheritance of eternal life and dominion is promised for them, for they are joint-heirs with Christ.

Jesus wants us to be meek in spirit as we control our daily actions but strong in our faith relying daily on the strength that only God can give. A gentle, meek person is controlled and not undisciplined; humble and not prideful; gentle and not easily provoked; forgiving and not revengeful. Take a look today at your life and see if these qualities control your actions every day.

TODAY'S WORD FOR FEBRUARY 5

HUNGER

Blessed are those who hunger and thirst for righteousness. Matthew 5:6

We have often heard it said that the world is hungry for the gospel, but if this was true the whole world would be saved in a very short time. The truth is that the people of the world hunger and thirst not for righteousness, but to satisfy their lust of the flesh, lust of the eyes, and the pride of life. I John 2:16-17 tells us this. However lust and pride can never be satisfied.

The scripture describes two kinds of righteousness which men hunger and thirst after. One is legal or self-righteousness. This is man's own vain effort to establish his own righteousness by his own works, the works of the law. Titus 3:5 tells us that such "law works" cannot save a person from eternal damnation. These "law works" only produce self-righteousness which is like filthy rags, according to Isaiah 64:6.

The second kind of righteousness is the righteousness of God. This righteousness is what is right by God's standards.

Romans 10:4 says: "For Christ is the end of the law for righteousness to everyone who believes." And in Romans 3:22, Paul tells us that, "Righteousness from God comes through faith in Jesus Christ to all who believe." Faith alone brings righteousness and only believers who have received righteousness will know the blessedness of Salvation which brings peace and joy.

In Jesus teaching, to "hunger and thirst" is to have a starving spirit. It is a real hunger and starvation of the soul for righteousness. The word that Jesus uses here is translated from the Greek in the accusative case to mean all righteousness. When the word is used in the genitive case it means that a person sometimes feels a little hunger or thirst for a small bit of something. But Jesus says in this Beatitude, blessed are they that hunger and thirst for all righteousness, not for little tidbits.

It is important that we note that the person who hungers and thirsts to be righteous shall be blessed. Many just want bits and pieces of righteousness in their lives, just enough to make them comfortable. This gives a person false security and ultimately leads to loose living. You are blessed when you have worked up a good appetite for God. He is the food and drink that satisfies our hunger and thirst for righteousness.

Christ does not say, "Blessed are the righteous," because no one is righteous. He does say, "Blessed are they who hunger and thirst after righteousness." Man is born imperfect and has only one hope and that is to seek God who does not want anyone to perish for their unrighteousness but wants to make everyone righteous. That is just what God does and He does this because He loves us.

Righteousness is the only thing that will fill and satisfy man's innermost needs. In Galatians 5:22 it says that the fruit of the spirit is love, joy, and peace. In Psalm 63:1 it reads, "My soul thirsts for You." Do you have that hunger and desire to know and draw closer to the Lord?

TODAY'S WORD FOR FEBRUARY 6

MERCIFUL

Blessed are the merciful, for they shall obtain mercy. Matthew 5:7

This beatitude does not mean if you show mercy to someone that they in turn will show mercy to you. Some people may but in many cases people have been persecuted in return for them showing mercy. We should not expect to receive mercy from those who do not know our merciful Savior.

Jesus showed mercy throughout His earthly ministry. He healed the sick, cleansed the lepers, made the dumb speak and the deaf to hear. He made the blind to see and the lame to walk. He raised the dead and fed the multitudes. He never failed to show mercy. The Roman army, the religious leaders, and many of their followers joined efforts to put Jesus to death on the cross. They showed religious hatred not mercy.

We are to show mercy to others when they need mercy even when we know that the recipient may never show mercy in return. We are to show mercy in the name of our merciful Christ, who Himself will reward us not only in this life but in heaven.

Those who never show compassion or mercy have never acknowledged how great the mercy is that God has shown for them. Those who have not responded to God's great gift of mercy will not receive mercy on judgment day. The acts of loving kindness that are done for others give evidence of having received God's mercy.

Merciful means to have a forgiving spirit and a compassionate heart. It is a deliberate effort, an act of the will, to understand a person and to meet his or her need by forgiving and showing mercy. Remember two things: God forgives only those who forgive others and a person receives mercy only if he is merciful.

The person who is merciful has a tender heart. The merciful does not hold back any kind of help, no matter the cost, because they have the love of God dwelling in them. The merciful knows that it is more blessed to give than to receive.

You will be blessed by God when you care for others in their time of need. God expects us to care for others and at the moment that you do care for someone else you will find yourself being cared for by our Lord.

Jesus gave us an excellent illustration of mercy in the parable of the Good Samaritan (Luke 10:25-37). A lawyer asked Jesus, "Who is my neighbor?" To answer the lawyer's question Jesus told of a man travelling from Jerusalem to Jericho who was robbed, wounded, and left half dead by thieves.

A priest came by and saw the man but did not stop to show mercy. A Levite also came along, stopped to look, but continued on his journey showing no mercy. Not only did the priest and the Levite show no mercy, they walked by on the far side of the road to avoid the man. A Samaritan saw him, had compassion on him, and helped him without expecting anything in return. Jesus asked the lawyer, "So which of these three do you think was the neighbor to him who fell among thieves?" The lawyer answered, "He who showed mercy on him" Jesus said to the lawyer, "Go and do likewise." Jesus also says: Blessed are the merciful, for they shall obtain mercy.

TODAY'S WORD FOR FEBRUARY 7

PURE

Blessed are the pure in heart, for they shall see God. Matthew 5:8

Pure in the Greek means to have a clean heart, to be unsoiled, unmixed, unpolluted, cleansed, purged, forgiven, to be holy, and to have a single purpose, that of God's glory. Jesus taught this Beatitude on the Sermon on the Mount.

The person that is pure in heart lives a clean life. A clean life honors God. He keeps himself unspotted from the evils of the world. He obeys the truth found in the Word of God through the working of the Holy Spirit in his or her life. He keeps his hands clean and seeks to be at all times without spot and blameless.

Jesus tells us in this Beatitude that we will be blessed when we get our inside world, meaning our mind and heart, cleansed and purged of the pollution of sin. Then we will see God do His will in our outside world, our life.

A person's very best behavior is seldom free from some mixture of self. Because of our sinful nature it is questionable if we can be perfectly free from mixed motives. The believer is to constantly search his heart and cleanse it of impure motives.

There are two wonderful promises made to the pure in heart. On this earth, they shall see God by faith, and eternally the pure in heart shall see God face to face.

Man cannot have a pure heart as long as he rejects the Lord Jesus as his Savior. The natural (unregenerate) heart is deceitful above all things, desperately wicked and the things of God are foolishness to him (Jeremiah 17:9).

Who are the pure in heart according to the scripture?

- In Psalm 24:3-5 we read that they are void of hypocrisy.
- In Matthew 6:24 it reads that they have room for only one master.
- In Psalm 42:1 it says they thirst for God as a deer thirsts for the water brook.
- We read that they have a newly created heart in II Corinthians 5:17.
- The pure in heart forsake and confess all known sin. Proverbs 28:13.
- They are not free from sin but are not happy in sin. When they sin, they repent and seek forgiveness. I John 1:9.
- They are spiritually minded and discern what God's truth is because they have the mind of Christ. I Corinthians 2:15-16.

James tells us in James 3:17 that, "Wisdom is from above and it is first pure and then peaceable, gentle, willing to yield and without hypocrisy." In II Peter 3:1-2 we are told that if we obey God's Word we will keep our minds pure. In Psalm 24: 4-5 the Psalmist tells us that when our hearts are pure it will be evident because we will strive to live honest and moral lives that honor the Lord our God. If our hearts are pure our hands will be clean and uncontaminated by doing evil deeds. As believers we must always strive to have clean hands and a pure heart because Jesus said, "Blessed are the pure in heart."

TODAY'S WORD FOR FEBRUARY 8

PEACEMAKER

Blessed are the peacemakers, for they shall be called sons of God. Matthew 5:9

This Beatitude was taught by Jesus to the masses from the Mount of Olives. Seven was the number of perfection among the Hebrews and it may have been that Jesus placed the peacemaker as the seventh on His list because He was the perfect man and He wanted His life to be a model of peace in our lives.

To become a peacemaker we must first make our peace with God. To make peace with God we must be justified by God's grace through the redemption that is found in Christ Jesus. For God to declare us just, we must believe that Christ died on the cross to bear our sins, that He was buried in the tomb for three days and nights, and that He rose again on the third day according to the scriptures.

We cannot be peacemakers if sin and evil abound in our lives. If we even harbor thoughts of pride, greed, deceit, malice, jealousy, adultery and any other evil deed or thought we cannot be much of a peacemaker. We must repent of our sins and accept the Lord Jesus Christ as our Savior. Those who remain separated from God by their sin can never have peace with God.

Who is the peacemaker? A peacemaker is one that shares the gospel message of salvation through Jesus Christ to those who are lost, showing them how they can have peace with God. A peacemaker not only seeks to help the lost make peace with God, but seeks to make peace with others, seeking to solve disputes and erase divisions, reconcile differences and eliminate strife in relationships.

Jesus tells His disciples, and us, in this Beatitude that we will be blessed when we show people how to cooperate instead of competing or fighting. Nothing is more divisive than arguing. Wars begin with arguments.

As believers we are to become peacemakers, not troublemakers, because we are here to show God's love to the world. To become this kind of peacemaker we must first be, as Paul tells us in Romans 3:24 "Justified freely by His grace through the redemption that is in Christ Jesus." To be justified is to be declared Just by God because of the righteousness of God.

We are living in a world where we constantly hear the word peace. The world is constantly looking for ways to find peace. They try peace envoys, peace conferences and peace treaties. What they do not realize is that the only lasting peace that will come to this earth is the peace that Jesus will bring when He returns. Until that day or until God takes us home He wants us to be peacemakers, proclaiming the good news of the gospel to all who will listen.

Jesus closed this Beatitude by saying that the peace makers shall be called the children of God. As believers in Jesus and as peacemakers we are adopted into the family of God when we accept Jesus as our Savior and are now called a child of God. What a miracle and what a blessing. We do serve an awesome God.

TODAY'S WORD FOR FEBRUARY 9

PERSECUTED

Blessed are those who are persecuted for righteousness sake, for theirs is the kingdom of heaven. Matthew 5:10

This Beatitude is a beautiful and vivid description of mature Christians. They are reviled and persecuted because they love the Lord Jesus Christ and have been given the righteousness of God. Mature Christians are to respond to persecution by rejoicing and being exceedingly glad. God's truth is offensive to the world and Christians who are persecuted can rejoice because they know that a great reward awaits them in heaven where there will be no more persecution.

The Christian church was persecuted from its beginnings. The apostles were arrested and tried for preaching Christ and for doing miracles in His name. Some were close to being put to death, but instead were beaten and then released. But this did not stop them from preaching the gospel. Instead they kept preaching and rejoiced that they were counted worthy to suffer shame for His name. (Acts 5:33-42)

Jesus understood and knew persecution because He was persecuted. He knew that those who followed Him would endure suffering. Some of them would be mocked, ridiculed, criticized, ostracized, and treated with hostility and some would even be martyred. Others would be slandered, cursed and lied about. These are all forms of persecution and Jesus experienced them all.

The one who lives and speaks for righteousness and lives and speaks for Christ can expect to be persecuted for the sake of the gospel. Persecution is a paradox. The person who cares and works for the true love, justice and salvation of the world is actually hated and fought against. How deceived is the world that it rushes madly for nothing but earthly pleasures that last for maybe 70 years while persecuting those who offer a path to eternal joy.

Believers are forewarned that they will suffer persecution because they are not of this world. We are different and we are not part of the sinful behavior of the world; therefore, the world reacts against us as believers in Jesus.

The world is full of evil and sin but the believer is stripped away from this cloak of sin and the righteousness of God is revealed through the believer to the world. The world does not know God so they want no other god then themselves. The world conceives God to be the one who fulfills *earthly* desires only but believers know God as a supreme being and their Father who fulfills *all* of our desires.

The believer's attitude toward persecution needs to be one of joy and gladness, a feeling of special honor and a fulfillment of the Lord's presence in their life.

Count yourself blessed every time people put you down because of some word you spoke or deed you did in the name of Jesus. Count yourself blessed when you are persecuted or if people speak lies about you and your faith. All heaven will applaud when we stand up for what we believe and show others our belief in God.

TODAY'S WORD FOR FEBRUARY 10

CHOICES

Refuse evil and choose good. Isaiah 7:15

Every day we make many choices. Some of these choices we make are good and some are bad. We choose what we wear, what we eat and where we go. Parents choose how they lead and teach. Children choose how they respond. When facing life as we know it every day we have to make choices.

The greatest and most important choice we must make in our life is whether to serve God or not to serve God. If we choose to serve God we have made a good and positive choice and will spend an eternity in Heaven. If we choose not to serve God, we have chosen to spend an eternity in hell. Making no choice is the same as rejecting God. Your choice is not to serve God.

How can we determine when the choices we make in our daily lives are right or wrong? The right choice will not be in conflict with God's Word, the Bible. This is why it is so important to study the Bible because it is God's guide book for our life. The Psalmist said, "Your Word is a lamp to my feet and a light to my path" (Psalm 119:105).

Parents have a huge responsibility to train their children in how to make choices. If you as a parent have made or are making bad choices in your life it is going to be impossible for you to teach your children how to make right choices. You need to change now, with the help of God, and let your children know by your words and actions that you are changing.

There are pressures on children today that can affect the choices they make daily. There are many outside influences that have a profound impact on children's thinking. Three of the most harmful are peer pressure, music and television. Parents must be constantly on the alert, and that is why we encourage every family to have dinner together every night, so your children can talk and you can listen to what they are doing and how they are feeling.

Parents must make it a priority to spend time with their children so they know what is going on in their lives. Parents must begin teaching their children at a very early age that making the wrong choices can have a negative effect that will last for their life time. And the opposite is also true. Making the right choices affects one's life in a positive way for a life time.

Children are making choices today based on what they see their parents doing. With children, especially teenagers, what we do has a greater influence on them than what we say. That is why we parents must live a consistent Christian life putting God first in all we do and in all we say. If parents choose to live for sinful pleasure, that will affect their children and their grandchildren (Exodus 20:4-5). Parents who live by faith and honor God will have a strong influence for the positive on their children and grandchildren.

TODAY'S WORD FOR FEBRUARY 11

TRUST

Trust in the Lord with all your heart, and lean not on your own understanding; in all your ways acknowledge Him and He will direct your paths. Proverbs 3:5-6

The children of Israel wandered around the desert for forty years. Much of this long trek was because they often forgot to put their trust in God and because of this; God lengthened their time wandering in the dessert. He delayed their entrance into the Promised Land until He was sure that they would keep their trust in Him.

In Exodus 16:2-3 we read of one of the times that the children of Israel lost their confidence in Moses and in God. The whole congregation complained to Moses saying, "Oh, that we had died by the hand of the Lord in the land of Egypt, when we sat by the pots of meat and when we ate bread to the full." They went on to complain to Moses saying, "You have brought us into this wilderness to kill this whole assembly with hunger."

God told Moses that He would rain down bread from heaven and they should gather the food daily, taking only the amount they needed. On the sixth day He would provide double so they could observe the Sabbath as a day of rest. God said to Moses that the reason He gave such specific details about how the manna was to be gathered was to test their obedience and see if they trusted God.

Have you ever noticed the complete trust that young children have in their parents? When our children were young we saw how hesitant they were to take that first step. They were not sure if they would fall or keep standing. Our children would eagerly grasp our outstretched hand with complete trust that we would support them and keep them safe from falling. As they became confident enough to walk without falling, they outgrew their need to hold our hand.

This reminds us that God is holding out His hand to help us take every step. But the difference is that we will never outgrow our need to trust God and we will daily need Him to stand beside us and hold our hand through the turbulences of life.

We must learn as families to trust God daily and not to rely on self. This is a difficult concept to teach our children as they get older because they want to do everything their own way. They often do things because their peers say, "If it feels good just do it." Unfortunately doing something just because "we feel like it"' does not bring success in life. God allows us to go ahead and do whatever "we feel like" and then because of His great love for us, when we get in trouble, He is always available holding out His hand saying, "Trust Me, let Me help you and guide you."

Have you really given any thought as to what or who you have your trust in today? Proverbs 3:5-6 tells us we should trust in the Lord, with all our heart and lean not on our own understanding, and He will direct our paths.

We taught our children to trust the Lord daily because God is always trustworthy.

TODAY'S WORD FOR FEBRUARY 12

AGAPE

Whoever does not love does not know God, because GOD IS LOVE. This is how God showed His love among us; He sent His one and only Son into the world that we might live through Him. This is love, not that we loved God, but that He loved us and sent His Son as an atoning sacrifice for our sins. I John 4:8-10

Jesus said: "You shall love the Lord your God with all your heart, with all your soul, and with all your mind. This is the first and great commandment." Matthew 22: 37-38

Love must be sincere, be devoted to one another in brotherly love. Honor one another above yourselves. Romans 12:9-10

Agape is a true and genuine love between God and man. Agape love is not sexual love as between a man and a woman. Agape love is the very nature of God. Jesus talked about agape love in the verses above from Matthew 22. Jesus said this was the first and greatest commandment, loving God. He goes on to say in these verses that agape love was to love with all your heart, soul and mind. He said this to underscore the completeness of the kind of love that Jesus was calling for.

The ultimate expression of agape love is God giving His only son to die on the cross for our sins. This kind of love comes to us by God through His Son Jesus Christ. We have agape love in our hearts as a result of knowing that God loves us with no strings attached and that His love for us never changes. We show our love for God by the commitment of our heart, soul and mind to our Lord.

In I John 4, above, John tells us that believers should love with an agape love because God is the essence of love. He says that love is inherent in all that God does. God's judgment and wrath are always perfect at all times in harmony with His love.

How many times in life do we find ourselves in a position of just needing someone to love us? This is when we need agape love because we need the caring and comforting love that only the Lord can give. Remember, He gave His life for you. What greater love is there then this?

Agape love means that God first loved us and we are to love God first and then to love others. It is the love from Christ that compels us to act to share Christ's love to someone (II Corinthians 5:14). It is a love that never fails (I Corinthians 13:8). It is love that made Jesus say in John 21:7, "If you love me, feed my sheep."

Agape love is the love that a mother has for her newborn child or a man and woman have on their wedding day. In Romans 12:9-10 (above verse), Paul defines agape love as being sincere and being devoted to one another in brotherly love. When we have agape love we will honor others above ourselves. Agape love can only be felt by one that has a personal relationship with Jesus Christ. If you want to experience agape love then make that decision today.

TODAY'S WORD FOR FEBRUARY 13

LOVE

Love is patient, love is kind. It does not envy, it does not boast, it is not proud. It is not rude, it is not self seeking, it is not easily angered, it keeps no record of wrongs. Love does not delight in evil but rejoices with the truth. It always protects, always trusts, always hopes, and always perseveres. Love never fails. I Corinthians 13:4-9

In the Old Testament book of Ruth we have one of the greatest love stories in the Bible. After the death of her husband and two sons, Naomi decided to return to Bethlehem to her own country and kindred. Naomi thought that her two daughters-in-law should go to their home in Moab. Naomi was widowed and without money and family. She was in dire circumstances and in a state of emotional despair.

Orpah agreed to go back and Naomi urged Ruth to also go back. Ruth responded in her own beautiful words: for wherever you go, I will go; and wherever you lodge, I will lodge; your people shall be my people, and your God shall be my God. Ruth's willingness to stay by her mother-in-law's side to face a future of great uncertainty and a life of poverty reveals the depth of her love and loyalty to Naomi.

Centuries ago, God sent the world a LOVE LETTER, the Bible. God showed His love to us by sending His Son to this earth to pay the debt of our sins. There is no way we can completely comprehend the depth of God's love which would cause Him to do this. John describes God's love with these words in 1 John 4:10-11: "This is love; not that we loved God, but that He loved us and sent His Son as an atoning sacrifice for our sins. Dear friends, since God so loved us, we also ought to love one another." Today our lives need to be filled with the love that God has given us.

The love of Christ is unlimited and life-changing. When your life is filled with God's love you cannot hate and you cannot stay angry. When you love your neighbor you are honoring God's commandment that He has given us in His word.

In 1 Corinthians 13: 4-9 (above) Paul tells us about true Christian love. God's love to us never fails. In 1 John 2:5 it reads, "Whoever keeps His word, truly the love of God is perfected in him. By this we know that we are in Him."

From the moment each of our six children was born, we were committed to teach them to first LOVE GOD and then their family and neighbors. We endeavored to be consistent with them, expressing our love through our words and actions. God honored this commitment by blessing us with children that responded favorably and we are blessed to see them abiding in God's love today with their children.

We are called to love in deed and in truth. This means that we are to have compassion, LOVE, for those around us in need. To express true love as God has commanded, we need to demonstrate love by our deeds and actions.

If you want to grow in love than take time to think about how Jesus gave His life for you and the love that that took. Ask God to give you an understanding of His love and to teach you how to live that out in your relationships with your spouse, children, and family. As Christ's love grows in you, His love will flow from you.

TODAY'S WORD FOR FEBRUARY 14

LOVE

Go into all the world and preach the gospel to all creation. Mark 16:15

Today in America is a day, Valentine's day, when everyone shows love in a special way to their spouse, their children, their neighbors and their world.

John 3:16 tells us that God so loved the world that He gave His only Son so that anyone that believes in Him would not perish but would have everlasting life. There are very few people that are burdened to reach out to the world they live in to share their love and faith. How about you, can you see beyond your daily routine a world that needs Jesus? Are you willing to respond to their needs? As the writer of Hebrews tell us, we show our love for Him by helping others and God does not forget our good work of serving others.

God has blessed us to be able to see the world from a mission perspective. We have developed what one might call a world mentality. Many people cannot see beyond what they can see with their own eyes but God wants us to be concerned with a world that needs to know Him. We are to "Go" and "Preach" as it is written in the verse above, Mark 16:15, which we call "THE GREAT COMMISSION." It is brief, forceful and uncompromising.

Jesus made two critical points to those that love Him. First, it is the gospel that we are to preach. This infers clearly that we are not to preach our own thoughts, ideas, beliefs, religion or philosophy. We are to preach the gospel, the good news that Jesus came and died to pay the penalty for our sins, because the whole world desperately needs to hear it.

Secondly, Jesus says that the gospel needs to be carried "into all the world." The great commission was given to the whole church, every believer, and is a permanent commission to every generation.

The great commission does not allow for excuses like it is too hard, too far, too dangerous or there are too many barriers. God's command is uncompromising and as Christians we must reach out to the world we live in to share the good news of the gospel with every person.

As we have said before, begin at home, in your neighborhood and in your workplace. And even more important, as a parent you have the responsibility, as our parents did, to train your children to be compassionate to the world. You must lead by your actions and then using the Bible share with your children what God commands us to do concerning our world.

In 1 John 4:7-9 John put it this way: "Dear friends, let us love one another for love comes from God. Everyone who loves has been born of God and knows God. Whoever does not love does not know God because God is love. This is how God showed His love among us: He sent His one and only Son."

TODAY'S WORD FOR FEBRUARY 15

SERVICE

I beseech you therefore brethren, by the mercies of God that you present your bodies a living sacrifice, holy, acceptable to God which is your reasonable service. Romans 12:1

God sent His only Son, Jesus Christ, to buy our redemption at a great price. Jesus, our Lord and Savior, suffered and died on the cross to pay the penalty for our sins so that we do not have to pay that penalty. Is it not reasonable then that, in return for what He did for us, that we owe the Lord our God our loyal and faithful service (Romans 12:1) out of gratitude for what He did for us? To serve the Lord we must willingly give ourselves to Him, putting aside our selfish desires and in obedience submit ourselves to the Lord's guidance for our lives.

God has given each of us natural abilities that He expects us to use for His glory. He has given believers spiritual gifts for the purpose of doing His work here on earth. He has also given believers the responsibility of spreading the good news of the gospel message to all the world.

It is very important to recognize that God does not use the unwilling. He will not force us to serve Him but His desire is for us to be totally committed to doing His will. He will equip us (Ephesians 4:11-13) and will empower and prepare us for service. Our Lord possesses the power and authority to assign spiritual gifts to those believers that want to serve Him. Our part is to be faithful, obedient and available.

God gives us opportunities everyday to serve. The problem is that we seem to find ways to not respond to these opportunities of service. How easy it is to avoid serving the Lord using that wonderful excuse: "I am so busy." All of us make the time to do what we want to do. We urge you to look for opportunities that come your way and then act on them. Go to your church and assist in a Sunday school. Volunteer at a local food bank or a local mission office. When you decide to follow Jesus He will open the doors for you. The apostle Paul tells us in Colossians 4:5 to "make the most of every opportunity." The more we serve Christ, the less we will serve ourselves.

Be faithful in your desire to serve God and leave the results to Him. God uses ordinary people like you to do extra ordinary work. When you think of serving God, start with something you can do; but when it gets difficult do not stop because you cannot do it. Pray and ask God to enable you and then God will take over.

We are witnessing this truth with the FREE FAMILY DEVOTIONALS that we send out each day by e-mail. About two years ago a new friend, who found our devotionals while searching the web, asked if he could link these devotionals to his ministry link. Of course we agreed. Because of this dedicated evangelist in Pakistan, many hundreds of new Christians who can read English are reading these devotionals in far-away places where we cannot go. We started with something that we felt God wanted us to do and now God is using and blessing these every day.

TODAY'S WORD FOR FEBRUARY 16

RELATIONSHIPS

There was a man of the Pharisees named Nicodemus, a ruler of the Jews. He came to Jesus by night and said to Him: Rabbi, we know that You are a teacher come from God; for no one can do these signs that You do unless God is with Him. Jesus answered and said to him, Most assuredly, I say to you, unless one is born again, he cannot see the kingdom of God. John 3:1-3

People often confuse being religious with having a relationship with God. We cannot have a relationship with God through Jesus Christ by what we do. Keeping certain rituals that one feels are religion, such as doing good, being kind, helping a neighbor, feeding the poor and going to church, will not give one a relationship with God here on earth or eternal life in heaven.

Jesus said to Nicodemus (verse above) that unless one is born again he cannot see the kingdom of God. Being born again begins a relationship with God through His Son Jesus. We are born again when we acknowledge we are sinners and receive Jesus Christ into our heart as our Savior. Beyond a doubt we believe that this is the most important decision one can make in life.

The source of our salvation is Jesus. Ephesians 2:8-9 tells us that we are born again by faith and that not of ourselves. We are told that it is the gift of God, not of works, lest any man should boast. Thus it is clear that those who accept Jesus as their Savior, because He paid our penalty for our sins, have a relationship with God which is much different than being religious.

The Bible does make it very clear that whoever believes in Jesus will not perish but will have everlasting life (John 3:16). This relationship with God is guaranteed to all who accept and believe in Jesus, God's Son. Being religious or not being religious makes no difference in where one spends eternity. Our choice is simple, accept Jesus and have a relationship with God and spend an eternity in Heaven or be just religious without a relationship with God and spend an eternity in Hell.

We urge you today to accept Jesus as your Savior by simply praying and asking Him to forgive your sins and come into your heart. It is the same message today as it was when Jesus talked to Nicodemus some 2000 years ago.

We had the privilege working for the Billy Graham Evangelistic Film Association showing their films in churches. At the end of each film showing an invitation was extended to all who were attending to accept Jesus as Savior. We would sit down with the many that responded to the invitation each night and lead them one at a time to this new relationship with God through Jesus Christ. This was a life changing experience for each person. Have you had a relationship with Jesus that changed your life?

TODAY'S WORD FOR FEBRUARY 17

RELATIONSHIPS

As for me and my house, we will serve the Lord. Joshua 24:15

We are concerned because we do not see many Christian households practicing relationships with biblical principles. In Colossians 3:18-21 we have the words of the Apostle Paul instructing us concerning the roles of wives, husbands, children, fathers and mothers in a Christian home.

Briefly, Paul says husbands are to love their wives with a sacrificial love and be the spiritual leaders, and wives are to respect the leadership role of their husbands. Children must obey their parents. In turn parents must care for and love their children and not cause them to be bitter. There is a shared responsibility within a family to love one another and to work together, to be kind and fair to one another, and to submit in obedience. The foundation for a Christian home is reverence for the Lord and obedience to His Word.

Colossians 3:23-24 says, "Whatever you do, do it heartily, as to the Lord and not to men, knowing that from the Lord you will receive the reward of the inheritance".

As far back as we can remember, our parents taught us in our homes to love God and to honor our parents and our grandparents. We then taught our children the same and now we are blessed to watch our children teach their children the same. When standards are set with firmness, love and consistency they will be handed down from generation to generation.

Children look to their parents to be their role models and their example. Setting the right example is the responsibility of the parents, not the church, not the school and most definitely not their peers.

A child needs to learn that they have boundaries in life. Some call this having "gates" and "walls." Ancient cities all had walls to protect them from the enemy. When these walls (boundaries) have been set, then parents must be consistent in monitoring them and responding when the child goes beyond the established boundaries. Children need to be warned about the enemies in life and to understand that boundaries are there to protect them.

Many parents today are afraid to say "NO." They seem to be fearful that children will stop loving them and turn against them. Often the parents just do not want to deal with the issue at hand but in most cases the bond between children and their parents is strengthened if boundaries are set reasonably, clearly, firmly and then enforced with love. Children need to know that parents care enough about their safety and future to want to do something to help them. They need to know that it is just not words but a deeper love between children and parents. Home and family relationships can disintegrate as a result of a preoccupation with an occupation (such as a job, sports, hobby and television) and exclusion of family needs.

TODAY'S WORD FOR FEBRUARY 18

GRATITUDE

Although they knew God, they did not glorify Him as God, nor were thankful, but became futile in their thoughts, and their foolish hearts were darkened. Romans 1:21

Here in America many people do not understand what the word gratitude really means. Many people do not seem to be grateful for the things they have. Possibly we are spoiled and expect much more or possibly it is because of the so called "ME" generation that we live in where we feel we deserve whatever we want. We have taken our prosperity for granted. We really do not know how blessed we are.

In the above verse found in Romans, we read that the apostle Paul was saying that those that lived before him, the unrighteous, even though they knew God they were not thankful and showed no gratitude toward God for all that He had done for them. They did not glorify God and thus their foolish hearts were darkened. God expects us to be grateful for what He has given us and glorify His name at all times.

We in America have had so much given to us by God and we neglect to show Him the gratitude that He deserves. Here are several examples of places where we have visited. These were people that knew how to share their gratitude with God.

We visited a large garbage dump in Manila, Philippians where over 100,000 people lived. These people search through garbage scraps every day, dumped by the garbage trucks, for food just for survival. They live in shacks that look like they will collapse with any wind. We were walking on this dump, being led by a missionary that we worked with and came upon this lean-to shack with an open front and saw a little 10 year old girl sitting by a box, the only thing in the room, and on that box was a Sunday school daily vacation Bible school picture booklet.

We were introduced to her and soon we asked about the book. Her eyes lit up as she told us that someone had given her that book about a year before and since then she had read through the pictures every day. She said that she had never had a gift before and this was the best thing she ever owned. Her gratitude for the book and for God moved us to tears because we knew that this was one of the books we had sent to local missionaries to distribute several years prior.

There was the mother sitting with her child in a hospital's children's ward in Honduras. She was sobbing because we gave the hospital some cancer medicine that the doctor's felt could save her child's life. Her tears were expressing her gratitude to God for meeting the need of her child just in time.

Do you express your gratitude to God for all that He has given you? Do you express gratitude to your spouse, your children, your parents, your family and your friends for who they are? And do not forget that God expects us to show gratitude to Him for His blessings to us. How do you respond?

TODAY'S WORD FOR FEBRUARY 19

REJECTION

He came unto His own and His own did not receive Him. John 1:11

My God, My God, why have you forsaken me? Psalm 22:1 and Mark 15:34

It is one thing to be rejected by friends and associates, but quite different to be rejected by family. Any type of rejection hurts no matter where it comes from. Some rejection is brought on by one's own actions but for others it may be because of their beliefs or just because of jealousy. When a family rejects one of their own it is usually based on a major conflict between right and wrong. Rejection is painful because it results in separation and abandonment. Children who are abandoned feel the pain of rejection for a lifetime.

While Jesus lived here on this earth He experienced rejection. Jesus truly knew the meaning of rejection. First, his own people rejected Him. Secondly, it was the rejection and abandonment of His Father, when He took our sins upon Himself that brought Him to His knees in the garden of Gethsemane beseeching His Father to take that cup from Him.

We cannot begin to imagine the agony of the physical pain that Jesus endured as He hung on the cross. There is no more painful death than death by crucifixion. But it was the rejection and abandonment of His Father that caused Jesus to cry out, "My God, My God why have You forsaken Me?" It is because Jesus went through that suffering of rejection by His Father that we do not have to endure the rejection of our heavenly Father for our sins.

"Why does nobody care?" was the question that rings so clear in our minds from a young girl fighting hunger here in America. She had not eaten for three days and the hunger pains were devastating to her. She came to the backdoor of our warehouse with her mother asking for food. She did not care if it was bread, vegetables or fruit but she desperately asked for food. This young girl and her mother felt so rejected, desperate and so alone. Did anyone care? We assured them that help was on the way and within minutes she tore open a loaf of bread we gave her and began to eat. We saw the biggest smile of gratitude on her face that you could ever imagine.

Our organization did respond and thousands of children since have been helped because this one girl moved us to increase our outreach to inner city children here in America. Her feeling of rejection was used by God to enable many other children to get the help they need.

All of us have days and times that we feel rejected. It may be because of a spouse, a parent, a child or a friend. When these moments of rejection come our way we must look to the Lord for special strength that only He can give. You must remember that at the lowest times of your life when you feel rejection, God loves you and He will never reject you.

TODAY'S WORD FOR FEBRUARY 20

CONSIDERATION

Now therefore says the Lord of hosts: "Consider your ways." Haggai 1:5

To speak evil of no one, to be peaceable, considerate, gentile, showing all humility to all men. Titus 3:2

In his letter to Titus (above verse), the Apostle Paul instructs Titus to remind those who believe in Jesus of the Christian principles that should be evident in their lives. Paul reminds the believers of their previous state as non-believers lost in sin. Now, as believers, they need to learn to be considerate. Christians need to exemplify godly virtues in their dealings with everyone they meet and talk to daily. Paul tells Titus that this applies when dealing with believers and with non-believers.

Do you live life having consideration for others, both those that believe in Jesus and those that are unbelievers? We are living in a "ME" generation and most people today, especially young people, give very little consideration to others.

We have developed generations of people that are only concerned about themselves and care very little about other people's concerns. Let us share one example that every one of us experiences every day. We see someone and ask, "How are you?" But do we really care how they are doing? Most people do not care. All they are doing is recognizing someone they meet. Think about this!

Take a moment today and evaluate how considerate you are to others. The prophet Haggai (above) tells us to, "Consider our ways." At the time he wrote these words, Haggai was in the process of building the second temple. The people were mostly against this and Haggai was telling them to be considerate and consider their attitudes and actions. The people's self indulgence, hypocrisy and misplaced priorities were clouding their understanding of their economic and social distress along with their falling away from God. They needed to reconsider their ways.

In light of this verse we need to look at our ways. Look back to yesterday. Were you considerate to your spouse, children and those you met? When faced with an issue, did you take into consideration what may have been involved in that issue?

Before you react to an issue or concern, take a moment and think about how Jesus would have responded. Think of ways how you can be more considerate to your spouse and children today. Consider your attitude, your thought process and your decision making style. If you will work on these issues today, your day will be blessed of God. The scripture is clear in telling us that we are to consider others.

Our genuine concern and compassion for others is a true measure of the depth of our relationship with our Lord. Our good works cannot save us but if our faith is genuine we will reach out to others. In Isaiah 58:7, he tells us what truly honors God: "It is to share your food with the hungry and to provide the poor wanderer with shelter. When you see the naked, clothe him and do not turn away from your own flesh and blood."

TODAY'S WORD FOR FEBRUARY 21

ACHIEVEMENT

For we dare not class ourselves or compare ourselves with those who commend themselves. But they, measuring themselves by themselves, and comparing themselves among themselves, are not wise. We, however, will not boast beyond measure, but within the limits which God appointed us. II Corinthians 10:12-13

When one thinks of achievement, they think of successfully accomplishing a goal in life. It might be achieving a certain level of education, getting a job, obtaining a position of leadership, finding a marriage partner or owning a new home. From the world's perspective these achievements are more important than from God's perspective. God's goal for each of us is to have a personal relationship with Jesus Christ, to live for Him and to strive to achieve all that He wants us to be. He wants us to achieve things while we are on this earth to bring honor to Him. We need to strive daily to achieve the success that God expects of us in our marital, family, and friend relationships.

In II Corinthians 10: 12-13 (above), Paul warns that it is not wise to compare ourselves to others because we would be taking pride in feeling we had achieved more than someone else. God holds us to a higher standard.

Here are four steps to achievement that honors God:

PLAN PURPOSEFULLY: You have a responsibility to plan for yourself, for your family and for your future. In all of your plans you need to have a purpose to achieve success both spiritually and intellectually.

PREPARE PRAYERFULLY: When you plan you need to pray that God will guide your thinking so that your plans will honor God. You cannot achieve success if God's hand of blessing is not upon you and your plans.

PROCEED POSITIVELY: You need to plan your actions so you can achieve your goals with a positive attitude and have a positive completion.

PURSUE PERSISTENTLY: You must not become discouraged if you have setbacks. If you do not succeed at first you must try again. You must be persistent in all of your efforts and not give up if your first attempt fails.

As you look at your life you must first evaluate your achievements with what you have accomplished for your Lord. Have you set high spiritual standards to live by each day? Have you led your family in their relationship with Jesus? If you are right with the Lord, He will bless you and enable you to achieve success.

As we trained our children we put strong emphasis on their spiritual achievements but also worked to have them understand the importance of achievement in their daily activities. What are your spiritual goals in this life? Think about what you want to achieve while God has you on this earth and then compare that to what you have accomplished.

TODAY'S WORD FOR FEBRUARY 22

GENTLENESS

What do you want? Shall I come to you with a rod, or in love and a spirit of gentleness? I Corinthians 4:21

But you, O man of God, flee these things and pursue righteousness, godliness, faith, love, patience, gentleness. I Timothy 6:11

One of the characteristics of Jesus when He was on this earth was that He was gentle. In Matthew we read about His triumphal entry into Jerusalem and it reads that He came as a gentle king.

In Matthew 11:29 Jesus told us, "Take My yoke upon you and learn from Me, for I am gentle and lowly in heart, and you will find rest for your souls."

In Isaiah 40:11 the prophet tells of the coming of the Lord and describes Jesus by saying that, "He will feed His flock like a shepherd; He will gather His lambs with His arms and gently lead those that are young."

Gentleness is a characteristic missing from lifestyles today. Rarely will you meet a person that is gentle. The apostle Paul tells us in II Timothy 2:24, "And a servant of the Lord must not quarrel but be gentle to all, able to teach and be patient."

At times in our everyday lives there seems to be a conflict in our minds as to how we are to respond to situations. We must consciously work on responding as the scriptures tell us by being gentle, mild and tender.

In the verse above from I Corinthians Paul makes it very clear to us that he has the option to approach the church at Corinth with a rod or in love. He is explaining that a spiritual leader can use the rod of correction if the people persist in sin. One who sins, Paul infers, cannot live a gentle life and he is asking the church at Corinth how he should come to them, hoping he can come in love and with a spirit of gentleness and not with the rod of correction.

Paul tells Timothy in I Timothy, (above) to flee from the things that bring ruin and destruction and pursue a life that constantly shows righteousness, godliness, faith, love, patience and gentleness. Paul reminds Timothy that he is a man that officially speaks for God and as a man of God he needs to flee from such things as the love for money and pursue righteousness, faith, love, patience and gentleness.

God wants us to be gentle to those we meet. Again in the verse from I Timothy Paul makes it very clear to us that we have a choice. We can follow the Lord and be gentle or we can be harsh but we cannot be both. When we follow God the Holy Spirit will bring things such as gentleness and kindness into our lives. When Paul talks about righteousness he is saying to do what is right to God and man.

In Proverbs 15:1 it reads that a gentle and kind answer turns away wrath, but a harsh answer stirs up anger. Consider responding today to every situation that comes your way with gentleness and see what God does for you.

TODAY'S WORD FOR FEBRUARY 23

SORROW

I am weary with my groaning; all night I make my bed swim; I drench my couch with my tears. Psalm 6:6

The psalmist in the verse we have put above really spells out how many people feel when they are in deep sorrow. He is saying here that sleep has eluded him because of his severe sorrow. Today sorrow comes to us, just as it did to the psalmist, as a result of distress, sadness or grief that one feels when they experience a great loss or bitter disappointment.

Sorrow can be the result of many things. We have talked over the years with many people that have had dreams and plans to accomplishing something big. They invested their time, effort and money into a project feeling assured that it would be successful. And many times something would happen and the bottom would fall out of their carefully laid plans.

When this happens deep sorrow comes to that person. They lose their personal confidence and live a defeated life. The reality of crushed expectations takes a toll on a person and leaves them with a sense of loss and hopelessness.

There is another type of sorrow. This is a sorrow felt when a friend or family member comes down with a serious sickness or has an accident. The sorrow is even greater when that person passes away. The death of a loved one leaves a void in a person's life. Many are never able to overcome the loss of a loved one and their sorrow causes them to fall into a state of deep depression.

The psalmist, David, experienced hopeless despair as he struggled with his own failures, the attacks of others, and the disappointments of life. The depth of his sorrow drove him to heartache but in his grief he turned to God. David's crushed and broken life gave way to an assurance of God's care, prompting him to say, "The Lord has heard my supplication; the Lord will receive my prayer" (Psalm 6:9). We can be assured that God hears our prayers and answers them if we call upon Him in our time of sorrow.

In times of sorrow and disappointment people often look to other people for comfort and support. People do not usually understand our need and let us down. If you have a relationship with God daily and sorrow comes your way, you can call on Him and He will hear you and comfort you in your time of sorrow. Friends and family cannot give you what God can give you. When you have a relationship with God it is a heart relationship and He will touch your heart as no one else can do.

In our seasons of disappointment and sorrow we can learn from David and we too can find comfort in God, who cares for our broken heart. Remember, as someone once said, "God's whisper of comfort quiets the noise of our sorrow."

TODAY'S WORD FOR FEBRUARY 24

BURDEN

Cast your burden on the Lord, and He shall sustain you. He shall never permit the righteous to be moved. Psalm 55:22

For My yoke is easy and My burden is light. Mathew 11:30

When Jesus gave this invitation (verse above from Matthew) to come to Him, it was an open invitation to all that would hear. However Jesus knew that only those people that were burdened by their own spiritual bankruptcy and laden with the weight of trying to save themselves by keeping the law would respond.

In today's society we see the stubbornness of man's sinful rebellion is such that without a spiritual awakening, all sinners refuse to acknowledge the depth of their spiritual poverty. Jesus is calling out to all that will listen to bring their burdens to Him and He will take the load of those burdens away from you.

Several years ago we were privileged to go back to China and we saw where Ken was born. One of the things that stood out to us was the heavy burden that men and women would carry on their bikes. We saw items stacked dangerously high and some of the women even carried their young child in a sling as they rode a loaded bicycle to their destination.

Over the years we have seen many times; in many areas of the world, people carrying heavy loads on their heads, on their backs or in hand pulled carts. This has given us a real understanding of the word "burden."

When we think of burden we think of two definitions. In the prior paragraphs we have talked about physical burdens. There is also the burden of carrying a load spiritually, and being a burden to someone else. Most people we meet today are carrying heavy burdens in their hearts. It may be a spousal concern, a parent/child problem, a family issue, a problem at work, financial stresses or much more. These are spiritual and emotional burdens that are too heavy for one to carry alone.

All those who have not accepted the Lord as their Savior are carrying the heavy spiritual burden of their sin. Jesus does not want us to bear this burden so He took our burden of sin upon Himself and carried it to the cross. Jesus experienced all the hardships and burdens of life that we experience. Not only does Jesus care about our burden of sin but He cares about our burden of hardships in life.

A person that does not know Jesus has no one to help carry his or her burden. The person that knows Jesus can give that entire burden to Him. The verse from Psalms (above) says to, "Cast your burden on the Lord, and He shall sustain you." Sustain means to support, bear the weight of or keep from giving way. When David wrote this psalm, he was pouring out his heart to the Lord because a former close friend had betrayed him. What a comfort to know that God wants to bear the weight of our burdens and keep us from giving way under the heavy load.

TODAY'S WORD FOR FEBRUARY 25

EXCUSE

If I had not come and spoken to them, they would have no sin, but now they have no excuse for their sin. John 15:22

When He spoke the verse we have put above, Jesus did not mean that if He had not come, the people would have been sinless. His coming incited the severest and most deadly sin, that of rejecting and rebelling against God and His truth. Many in Jesus' day used every excuse possible to be able to reject the gospel.

How many times have you heard someone give an excuse for something not completed or not done? Even ones age does not seem to make a difference. Excuses for our actions seem to be the normal way to act. Most excuses are given to justify laziness. We do not know how many times we have heard the excuse; "I just did not feel like doing it," whatever "it" was that should have been done.

We also use excuses to justify our inaction. You have often heard, "I was just so busy that I could not get around to doing it."Most excuses are what we would call "lame." They are a lot like the child that tells his teacher that he cannot turn in his home work because, "the dog ate it."

In John 15, Jesus was teaching His disciples the gospel message and what to expect when they would be the ones teaching others. Just as Jesus and His message were rejected by many, He told them that they also would have their message rejected. This is still true today. As believers we must continue to tell all those we can, through our words and deeds, of Jesus' love and plan of redemption knowing that at times our message will be rejected. Those who accept Jesus will be saved, but those who reject Him will "have no excuse for their sin" when they meet God.

In Luke 14:15-24 Jesus shares what is called the parable of the great supper. The master invited most of his friends and neighbors to a great feast. They all gave excuses as to why they could not come to the supper. All the excuses smacked of insincerity. Jesus likened their excuses to all the excuses that are given when people are invited to know Jesus as their Savior.

Many people give excuses as to why they cannot accept Jesus. Some just do not want to change their ways. Others say they do not have to worry about it now but want to wait until later in their lives. These excuses are not acceptable to God. Rejecting Jesus leaves the one who rejects with no excuse in God's sight.

In Romans 1:18-20 the writer talks about the end-time judgment, when the wrath of God will come against all the ungodliness and unrighteousness of men. At that time it will be too late for excuses. He goes on to tell us that since the creation of the world God's invisible attributes are clearly seen, even His eternal power and Godhead so that mankind is without excuse. In the universe we see His intelligence, His beauty, His power, and His provisions. Those who reject God have no excuse. Salvation is available to all for the asking and excuses are not acceptable.

TODAY'S WORD FOR FEBRUARY 26

INSTRUCTION

Take firm hold of instruction, do not let go. Proverbs 4:13

All scripture is given by inspiration of God, and is profitable for doctrine, for reproof, for instruction in righteousness. II Timothy 3:16

Think of all the times in your life when you faced the necessity of receiving some instruction. When you were a child you needed instruction from your parents. When you went to school you received instruction from your teachers. When you went to Sunday school you received instruction about the Bible from your Sunday school teacher. When you had a new job, you received instruction as to what your responsibilities were. In your job you needed to be open to instruction every day in order to do your job well.

We learned at an early age from our parents the value and importance of instruction. As children we did not always like the instruction that was given to us. Children often rebel at instruction but if it is given consistently and in love soon the rebellion will be overcome. As we grew older we realized the value of the instruction given to us by our parents.

We also learned at an early age the value of the instruction we received in school. Our teachers and our parents taught us to study and to accept instruction as to how we were to study and learn. Without proper instruction how can a child learn? Today many children do not receive this kind of encouragement and the result is seen in the quality of education received.

The scripture verse found in II Timothy reminds us that the Bible was given to us as God's inspired word for instruction as to how we are to live our lives in this world as believers. God's Word provides for us positive training information in godly behavior. The instruction that we receive as we read God's Word at times seems hard to understand and many wonder if it is even realistic in today's culture. But when one accepts Jesus as his or her Savior a change in life style is expected and the instruction we receive from the Bible can be understood. We must understand that the instruction in the Bible has never changed through the centuries, only people and cultures change.

The above verse from Proverbs tells us to take hold of the instruction that God gives us. In this Proverb the father is commanding his son to acquire wisdom and instruction and guard it carefully. We encourage you to use discernment about what others do or what others say if it conflicts with the instruction given to us in God's Word.

As parents we must instruct our children in the ways of the Lord and as children we must learn from the God-given instruction that our parents give us. Remember, others learn from our words and our deeds. Make sure that what you do and say today is consistent with the instruction in God's Word.

TODAY'S WORD FOR FEBRUARY 27

DESTINY

Having predestinated us unto the adoption of children by Jesus Christ to Himself, according to the good pleasure of His will. Ephesians 1:5

Beloved, now we are children of God. I John 3:2

People are continually coming into this world and continually leaving. It is the destiny of us all. We are born; we live out our lifespan; and we die. Many people are asking the questions today to friends or more often to themselves: What is my destiny? Who am I? Why am I here? How did I get to where I am? Where am I going? Are you perplexed by these same questions? Earlier in our lifetime we faced these questions. The good news is that the Bible, God's Word, has answers for us.

God created each one of us for a purpose and with a destiny. Long before He created the world, God, because of His love for us, planned that our destiny was to be adopted as one of His children through Jesus Christ (Ephesians 1:5).

In 1 John 3, the writer John calls those who are believers "children of God." The first question that may come to your mind is, "How do I become a child of God?" The scripture tells us in John 1:12 that we become His children by receiving Jesus as our Savior. At an early age we had that question answered when we accepted Jesus as our Savior. We understood that Jesus died to pay the penalty for our sins.

You may ask the question, if we are children of God, where are we going? In John 14:1-6 we are told in the words of Jesus that one day He will receive us, who have accepted Jesus as our Savior, into a home that He is now preparing for us in heaven.

The story is told about a philosopher named Arthur Schopenhauer who lived in the 1800's in Berlin Germany. Day after day he walked through the museum constantly asking questions about his origin and destiny. He continued to look for answers in the museum but could never find any.

One day a park keeper walked up to him after seeing him daily looking depressed and lost. He asked the philosopher, "Who are you and where are you going?" The philosopher responded by saying, "I do not know. I wish somebody would help me." You see, philosophy has never been able to answer those questions.

Our maker is not only the author of science and history but He has written the story of every member of Adam's family since the beginning of time. This includes the philosopher, you and me.

We have no control over our coming into this world. Where and when we are born is in God's hands. However, we are in control of where we are going. God has given us a free will. We choose our final destiny. The choice is heaven or hell. If we choose to spend eternity in heaven, all we have to do is accept Jesus as our Savior who paid the penalty for our sins. The philosopher was searching, but no one helped him find his way to the saving grace found through Jesus Christ. When you know Jesus, you know who you are and where you are going.

TODAY'S WORD FOR FEBRUARY 28

FAMILY

And God said to Abraham, and in your seed all the families of the earth shall be blessed. Acts 3:25

To Timothy, a beloved son: Grace, mercy, and peace from God the Father and Christ Jesus our Lord. II Timothy 1:2

We have a large family with six children and twenty grandchildren. As God has blessed us with our family, He has also given us responsibility and wonderful experiences and knowledge as to the do's and don'ts in raising a family.

Nothing has been more important to us over the years, except our relationship with God and our Lord, than our family. Our lives have been built around them and today we are reaping the benefits. We learned that the little things made major differences for us. For example, we insisted on having dinner together with the entire family every night. This gave each one in the family an opportunity, every night, to share their activities and concerns with the family. Some may say that this is not that important. Frankly, it is very important for all families but very rarely seen today. It gave us as parents an opportunity to listen. This is when we could hear situations beginning and could talk about them before they became a problem.

Dinner was also a time when we could read the Bible and pray together as a family. We also memorized a verse from the Bible together each week.

It was important for us to put our children's schedule ahead of ours with very few work related exceptions. We always tried to go to their school activities and their sport activities so that our children knew that we were there for them.

One of the reasons that many families are considered dysfunctional is because they do not communicate and spend quality time together. In many families both parents work so children come and go as they want. Parents become too busy to do things with their children. When problems come up concerning relationships with spouses and children the issues are not dealt with because everyone thinks they will go away with time. They do not. They only grow to be major concerns.

In Genesis and again in the book of Acts (above) we are reminded that God promised Abraham that all the families of the earth would be blessed. This blessing comes to those of us that put our Lord first in our lives. As parents we must teach our children to live a Christ honoring-life. God blesses us when we honor Him.

The Apostle Paul in the verse above talks about his relationship with Timothy as that of a father and son. Paul was in prison in Rome when he wrote II Timothy. He was writing to Timothy, a young man, whom he had mentored in life, in faith and in ministry. They had developed a relationship that was strengthened by the spiritual bond of their mutual desire to serve the Lord. Timothy came from an incredible spiritual family heritage. His grandmother Lois and his mother Eunice taught him the scriptures and were involved in leadership at the church at Lystra.

TODAY'S WORD FOR FEBRUARY 29

CONVICTION

And Saul, still breathing threats and murder against the disciples of the Lord, went to the high priest, and asked for letters from him to the synagogues at Damascus, so that if he found any belonging to the way, both men and women, he might bring them bound to Jerusalem. Acts 9:1-2

Before anyone can come to know Jesus as their personal Savior, they must be personally convicted, realizing that they are a sinner. Then they must ask for forgiveness and ask Jesus to come into their heart.

Most non-believers do not understand what we mean by conviction. The scriptures give us one of the clearest explanations of conviction with the illustration of the life of Saul. Saul, later known as Paul, was a Jew, not a foreigner. He was born in Tarsus but was raised in Jerusalem because his parents wanted him to be educated in the Mosaic Law by Israel's greatest teachers (Acts 26:4).

Saul became a Pharisee and was committed to keeping the Law and was zealously dedicated to persecute the Christians and the Christian church. He had this zeal because he believed that he was pleasing God (Acts 9:1-2).

Saul actually hunted down believers and slaughtered them. He volunteered to the high priests and the Sanhedrin to go all the way to Damascus to arrest believers, both men and women, and bring them to Jerusalem for trial.

It was while Saul was walking down the road to Damascus that God reveals His plans for Saul. A bright light shone all around Saul and the men that were with him. It appeared suddenly from heaven, out of nowhere and totally unexpected. It was supernatural and miraculous, totally outshining the sun.

It was a confrontation between Saul and the Lord. He experienced Jesus in His glory and heard a voice speak to him. The men with Saul heard the voice but not the words and they saw only the light. The Lord was delivering a personal message to Saul, charging him with a terrible sin, opposing and persecuting Jesus Himself.

How many times have you seemingly heard an inner voice trying to convict you of your sin? Jesus called his name twice: "Saul, Saul," showing tenderness, love and concern. God was rebuking Saul for his past behaviors and it was an appeal from God for Saul to listen and obey. Saul now realized that it was Jesus he was opposing.

Saul was stricken down, humbled, convicted, and frightened with his encounter with God. He cried out in desperation, "Who art thou, Lord?" He knew that it was the Lord that he was supposed to know, but he did not personally know Him. He cried out, "Tell me Lord, identify yourself, and let me know You."

Can you imagine the guilt and conviction he felt? Paul had been doing what he sincerely believed was right but he was sincerely wrong. He was lost and separated from God, bound for an eternal hell. All this happened in a few short seconds on the road to Damascus. Have you had your personal encounter with God?

TODAY'S WORD FOR MARCH 1

DANIEL

So the governors and satraps sought to find some charge against Daniel concerning the kingdom; but they could find no charge or fault, because he was faithful; nor was there any error or fault found in him. Daniel 6:4

Daniel was a man of strong faith and godly character. Our goal in life should be to have a godly character like Daniel, so that others may see similar characteristics in us as those traits used to describe Daniel in verse 4 (above). Daniel was so faithful and upright that no fault could be found in him. As we read about Daniel, we can learn many things from his life that can help us understand what it means to be faithful to God and the importance of having a godly character.

If Daniel had flaws in his character the scriptures do not reveal them to us. However there are four character traits of Daniel that we can apply to our lives.

Daniel was a man of purpose. In Daniel 1:8 we read that Daniel resolved in his heart that he would not defile himself with the portion of the king's delicacies or wine. Although Daniel was living in exile as a captive of Babylon, he had found favor with the king and was offered the privilege of eating from the king's table.

He would not allow himself to be tempted with the meat and wine of the king, because it was an offering to Babylon's false gods and Daniel knew if he ate the meat and drank the wine he would be disobeying God. God gave him wisdom and strength to say "NO", and Daniel resolved to stay true to his convictions and always be faithful to God. We need to learn to say "no" to all of the temptations that Satan presents to us in order to prevent him from drawing us away from the Lord.

Daniel was a man of prayer. He recognized the importance of having communication with God. Daniel had been taken captive to Babylon and even though he lived in a pagan country, he continued to pray to his Lord even when he faced death for praying to his God. Daniel not only prayed when he was in danger, but he had a pattern of prayer; which was praying three times a day. We need to develop that kind of prayer pattern. We need daily communication with God.

Daniel was a man of power. King Nebuchadnezzar bestowed honor, gifts and great power on Daniel. He received power from the king, but Daniel knew that his real source of power came from God, and he continually gave God the glory in all that he did and always put his total trust in God's power, not his own. If we want to be men and women of power that God can use, we need to follow Daniel's example.

Daniel was a man of faith. He showed his faith in God even in his times of great distress and anxiety. For example, he was forced to spend a night in a den of hungry lions because of his loyalty and trust in God. The scriptures tell us in Daniel 6:23 that King Darius came to the den the morning after Daniel's night with the lions, and found Daniel alive and well, ("and no injury whatever was found on him, because he believed in God"). God will be with us as we go through our times of difficulty and will work miracles through our life just as He did in the life of Daniel.

TODAY'S WORD FOR MARCH 2

NOAH

So God said to Noah, I am going to put an end to all people, for the earth is filled with violence because of them. I am surely going to destroy both them and the earth. Make yourself an ark of gopher wood; make rooms in the ark, and cover it inside and outside with pitch. Genesis 6:13-14

Can you even begin to imagine how you would respond if God gave you a message like he gave Noah in Genesis 6:13-14 (above)? We are told how Noah reacted. "Noah did everything just as God commanded him." (Genesis 6:22). God made it clear to the people that they needed to repent from their evil ways, but they did not respond.

We can learn from the life of Noah how God wants us to respond to Him when He speaks to us. When God speaks to us, it is a command not a suggestion. We are to trust in God's Words that He speaks to us because God's Word is truth.

There are three ways that God revealed to Noah the gospel of the grace of God and God's will for Noah's life.

God spoke to Noah by word of mouth. In Acts 3:21 we read that God spoke to Noah by the mouth of his predecessors. Noah probably received God's Word from Methuselah, who probably was taught by Adam. Methuselah was 253 years old when Adam died and lived 600 years after Noah was born. He was Noah's grandfather and Noah found grace in the eyes of the Lord through his grandfather. God continues today to speak to us by word of mouth using person to person communication.

God spoke to Noah through written records. Adam must have created a language and a vocabulary that he reduced to writing because the scripture says that Adam gave a name to all the birds of the air and beasts of the field that God created. Adam created this language and vocabulary to express every thought and Noah must have had access to that information. Today, we have the Bible, the Word of God which is God's communication to us.

God spoke to Noah through revelation. God clearly revealed His will to Noah through the verse we have written above. When the ark was ready, He spoke to Noah and told him to enter the ark. When the flood ended and the land was dry, God told Noah to come out of the ark.

God clearly spoke to Noah and He speaks in many different ways to men today. He speaks to us through His Holy Spirit and through the Word of God. In the past 6000 years God has spoken to men through dreams or even a voice from heaven. God will speak to you if you are in daily communication with Him. The key to the kind of relationship that Noah had with God is that He honored God and communicated with Him daily. In Noah's case, as in ours, he was ready and listening when God responded to him and we need to do the same today. Are you ready and listening for God to talk to you?

TODAY'S WORD FOR MARCH 3

PAUL

For I am not ashamed of the gospel of Christ, for it is the power of God to salvation for everyone who believes, for the Jew first and also to the Greek. Romans 1:16

Paul was heading down the wrong road thinking he was on the right road until Jesus stopped him "dead in his tracks." Being confronted by Jesus completely changed the direction of Paul's life. Paul then became a tireless worker for His Lord, a fervent preacher of the gospel, a great apostle, and a spiritual warrior.

Paul wrote 13 of the New Testament books of the Bible. He won the first European convert to Christianity (Lydia in Macedonia). He was a great missionary founder of churches and suffered much for his belief in our Lord.

There are five important examples that we can learn from the life of Paul. First, he said that he was a debtor to the Greeks and the barbarians, the wise and the unwise (Romans 1:14). What Paul is saying is that he had an obligation to share the good news of the gospel which was the great sacrifice Christ had made for him.

Secondly, he was eager to preach the gospel to all who would listen. Paul did not know how much time he might have to preach, so he felt an urgency to preach so he could take all Christ had given him and pour it out to anyone who would listen. We should have that same urgency to share our faith with others.

Thirdly, Paul was not ashamed of the gospel. He lived in a day of moral degeneracy just as we do today. Paul took the gospel to pagan and immoral Greeks and Romans. Rome had become a moral sewer under Nero. The depravity of their lives was the exact opposite to the moral righteousness of the gospel that Paul preached. Paul's message was not well received. Paul was a Jew, a race thought by many in his day to be a despicable sub-human race, worth only to be cursed ill-used and enslaved. Even in this kind of surroundings and culture Paul, was not ashamed of the gospel, so he continued to preach everywhere he went. Paul was often rejected, not only by a few people, but by whole communities.

Fourthly, Paul was appointed to defend the gospel (Philippians 1:16). Some of the preachers of the gospel in Rome were very jealous and envious of the results he was having from the social circles and society of the community. They were envious of the support and loyalty that fellow believers were giving Paul. They felt threatened because he was gaining daily, as the leader of the Christian community in Rome. Paul was not affected by these feelings. Many preached with the wrong motive. Paul had only one motive and that was to preach the gospel and to defend it from false teachings. By preaching as he did, he was defending the gospel and God honored him. Much of the same jealousy and envy is seen today among believers and our churches. As believers, we must be like Paul and continue to preach the gospel with the motive of bringing the lost to a saving knowledge of our Lord Jesus Christ.

Finally, Paul labored more abundantly than others (1 Corinthians 15:10). God wants us to be the hardest worker in our church, community and in our home.

TODAY'S WORD FOR MARCH 4

ABRAHAM

I will make you a great nation; I will bless you and make your name great; and you shall be a blessing. I will bless those who bless you, and I will curse him who curses you; and in you all the families of the earth shall be blessed. Genesis 12: 2-3

Abraham was God's chosen vessel through whom He would reveal Himself to the world. Abraham could never have imagined how significant a role he would have in the future of all mankind. When God promised Abraham to make of him "a great nation" (Genesis 12:2) he had no idea what God was saying to him.

The key to the fulfilling of God's plans was Abraham's obedience. In Genesis 12:1, Abraham was told by God to, "Get out of the country, get out of your father's house and go to a land that I will show you." In order to accomplish what God had commanded Abraham to do, there were five stages of journeys Abraham took over a period of 600 years that showed his growth in obedience to God's will.

First, he travelled from Ur of the Chaldeans, where his father's house was, to Haran. We are told that his father, Terah, and his nephew, Lot, traveled with him. He only obeyed God in part. He left his father's house, but not his father.

Secondly, he travelled from Haran to Shechem which is in the center of Canaan with Lot (his father had died in Haran). He left his country, obeying God's command, but still not separating himself from his father's family. At Shechem, the Lord appeared to Abraham and promised He would give the land of Canaan to his children. Abraham then built his first altar to the Lord to worship and honor God.

Thirdly, Abraham moved from Shechem to Bethel which is known as the house of God and he built his second altar to the Lord.

Fourthly, he moved from Bethel to Egypt because there was a famine in the land of Canaan. This was the way that God was testing the faith of Abraham. He disobeyed God by going to Egypt and by not building an altar to God in Egypt. God wanted him in Bethel not in Egypt. It is only when one is in the will of God that he can truly worship the Lord and Abraham was out of the will of God. It is better to endure trials and accept the will of God, than to attempt our own limited solution.

Fifthly, Abraham left Egypt and went back to Bethel. He went back to the house of God (Bethel), worshiping at the altar of God. Lot was now separated from Abraham, and for the first time since the Lord called Abraham he was fully obeying God. He now was separated from his country, his family and his father's house.

TODAY'S WORD FOR MARCH 5

DAVID

And now, O Lord God, You are God, and Your words are true, and You have promised this goodness to Your servant. Now therefore, let it please You to bless the house of Your servant, that it may continue before You forever; for You, O Lord God, have spoken it, and with Your blessing let the house of Your servant be blessed forever. II Samuel 7: 28-29

Above we have written David's prayer from II Samuel. In this prayer, he indicates he fully accepted by faith, the extraordinary irrevocable promise of God that was made to David as king, and to Israel as a nation.

David served God in many capacities. He went from being a simple shepherd boy to a heroic ruler. We want to look at the various stages of his life so we can clearly see how his deep devotion to God allowed the Lord to use him mightily. It is our prayer that each one of us will learn from the life of David. David was not perfect and neither are we. As we learn from David's life we will soon realize God can use us even though we are not perfect, just as he used David.

As a shepherd boy, David learned how to protect the sheep. It was a job he took serious. He even killed a lion and a bear to protect his sheep. As a shepherd, he became strong and brave in order to take care of creatures weaker than himself. He had an early obedience to his earthly father who taught him how to be a shepherd and the humility he would need in order to depend on God.

David's writings reveal his hunger for God. He was open about issues such as fear, depression, defeat, loneliness and sorrow. David provided glimpses of himself for us to see that showed he knew God intimately. He described valley experiences so vividly and how he went to God for His leading and protection.

David was a commander and King. These positions were ones of privilege and power. He lived a life plagued by heartache, pain, suffering, and conflict. In his times of despair he turned to God who David knew was the source of comfort and mercy. From a young age, David had come to understand that the Lord was his strength, his shield and his help just as he wrote in Psalm 28:7, "The Lord is my strength and my shield; My heart trusts in Him, and I am helped."

In spite of his deep devotion to God, David committed great sins in his life. David acknowledged he sinned and sought the Lord's forgiveness. God forgave him and continued to use him. His restoration teaches us about the consequences of sin, but more importantly it shows us the limitlessness of the grace of God and how great His mercy is toward us. No matter what the circumstances were in his life, David never ceased to honor God and give Him praise and all the glory.

The record of David's life in the Bible continues to impact every follower of Christ down through the centuries. Have you been challenged by David's example of obedience and service to the Lord? He is a great example of what God can accomplish through us if we yield our life to Him.

TODAY'S WORD FOR MARCH 6

BEGINNING

In the beginning God created the heavens and the earth. Genesis 1:1

In the beginning was the Word and the Word was with God and the Word was God. John 1:1

This world and everything in this world has a beginning. In this verse from Genesis, we read that in the beginning God created the heavens and the earth. In the beginning God was there. In this verse from John, we read that Jesus (the Word) was also there in the beginning. Our triune God (God the Father, God the Son and God the Holy Spirit) has always existed.

When John uses the verb, "was," he is expressing the eternal pre-existence of the Word, Jesus Christ rather than selecting the verb that meant, "came into being" to establish the fact of Jesus Christ's existence even before the time-space-material universe. Jesus was in intimate fellowship with God in all eternity.

We all begin life by being born. Birth is a process by which each of us has our beginning. God in His Word speaks of our need to be "born again." There are many people that do not understand what it means to be "born again."

These words, "born again," were spoken by Jesus when He was talking to Nicodemus. Although he was a devout Jewish Pharisee, he did not understand what "born again" meant. He asked how one can be born more than once. Jesus said, that the first birth is a birth of the flesh, but the second birth is the birth of the Spirit. Our first birth gives us earthly life and our second birth gives eternal life.

In order to be "born again" we must go through the process of realizing that we are sinners and ask God for forgiveness. We then need to ask Jesus to come into our heart and accept Him as our Savior. By our first birth we are all born into this world as sinners because of the fall of Adam and Eve. As a result, we need to pay the price for our sins. However, God has provided a way by paying the price for us, to have a "New Beginning" when we accept Jesus as our Savior. In this life when we have our "New Beginning" with Jesus, we will have to deal with many changes.

First, we must be ready to expect the unexpected. Your own plan for your life is limited because of who you are. You do not know the future or even what will happen later today. God has His own plan for your life and a "New Beginning".

Secondly, we must be prepared to believe the unbelievable. Jesus did die on the cross to pay the penalty for our sins. Jesus was buried in a tomb. Jesus rose from the dead and Jesus wants a relationship with you, so you can spend eternity with Him.

Thirdly, in our "New Beginning" with Jesus we must discover the undiscoverable. As one who puts his or her trust in Jesus you will discover that you can experience joy at the moment you are afraid. You can express worship to God at the same moment you are most vulnerable to the evils around you. And you can express purpose at the same moment you are most confused about any situation in your life.

TODAY'S WORD FOR MARCH 7

CHILDREN

How great is the love the Father has lavished on us that we should be called the children of God. And this is what we are beloved, now we are children of God; and it has not yet been revealed what we shall be, but we know that when He is revealed, we shall be like Him, for we shall see Him as He is. I John 3:1-2

As a believer in Jesus Christ, you are part of a family. John reminds us in this verse that we are children of God. God is our Father and He sacrificed His Son to die on the cross in order to pay the penalty for our sins.

In Ephesians 6 as well as in Colossians 3 we are told children are to obey and honor their parents. In Proverbs 22:6 we are told as parents to train our children in the way they should go and when they grow up they will not turn away from God. In Psalm 127: 3 we are told that children are our heritage. When John the Baptist was a boy we read about him being a joy and delight to his parents. (Luke 1:14-15)

These same attributes can be related to us as believers in our relationship to God as children of God. We are to obey our Father. We are to honor our Father. We are to read the Bible so that God can train us through His Word. God, our Father considers us as His heritage and wants us to be a joy and delight to Him.

Child rearing today is a tremendous responsibility to parents. Children are being buffeted by so many outside forces that today's parents never experienced as children. Self will is the root of most sin and misery and if checked at an early age in a child, it promotes future happiness. Children, who are allowed to do as they please, will most likely live a life that leads to their destruction.

As any parent knows, children do not come with instruction manuals, and no two children are alike. Some parents are afraid to discipline their children at all and then others are too harsh to the point of being cruel and abusive. We are instructed in Proverbs 23:13, "Do not withhold discipline from a child, if you punish him with a rod he will not die." Just as God disciplines us, we are to discipline our children.

As children, both of us received a few well deserved "spankings" along with other forms of discipline including a loss of a privilege. The threat of the spanking was worse than the spanking, but it did get the point across to us. The spankings stung our pride and it made us understand the seriousness of our misbehavior.

Parents seem to be fearful if they "spank or hit" their child, that they would be accused of child abuse. This causes parents to refrain from using any discipline. Children need just and fair discipline to help them become responsible adults.

As Children of God we face many forces of evil in our lives, but the good news is that He will be always there for us. Jesus loves His children. In Matthew 19:14, we are told the disciples tried to shield Jesus from the children. However, Jesus responded by saying: "Let the little children come to Me, and do not forbid them, for of such is the kingdom of heaven." Yes, Jesus loves the little children and as a child of God, we can be assured that He loves us.

TODAY'S WORD FOR MARCH 8

EVIL

Do not be overcome by evil, but overcome evil with good. Romans 12:21

When we consider the evil in our world today, it is so bad that sometimes you might ask, "Is there any good at all in our world?" You can look at the newspapers, read the news magazines, listen to the radio or watch television and all you hear about is the bad (evil) things in our world.

The victim of evil is goodness. The goodness we are talking about is the goodness God designed for us to experience when He created our world for everyone to enjoy.

You can talk to friends and neighbors and you will find no shortage of opinions as to what is wrong in our world. From the day Adam and Eve ate the fruit of the "tree of the knowledge of good and evil," we have had to contend with evil. Beginning in the book of Genesis, the Bible traces the ongoing struggle between good and evil

God alone is good. Psalm 94:15 declares that "The Lord is upright; there is no wickedness in Him." The Psalmist goes on to tell us in verse 16, "Who will stand up for me against evildoers? Who will take his stand for me against those who do wickedness?" Of course in verse 15 he says God alone is good and we will be with him. Satan is God's enemy and adversary. He is completely evil. Satan is called the evil one, the deceiver, a murderer, a liar, the tempter and the ruler of demons.

Sometimes it seems that Satan has the upper hand and we are powerless. When the terrorists brought down the World Trade Center on 9/11, we felt paralyzed and helpless. We could only watch the TV coverage in unbelief.

Those of us that have our faith in the Lord do not feel powerless in times of evil. Most of us feel evil on a smaller, but more personal scale. In Romans 12:21, the apostle Paul tells us the proper response we should have towards evil. He says we are to abhor evil and not to repay it with more evil. More importantly we are not to be overcome by evil.

In John 3:20, the apostle talks about everyone who does evil, hates the light, and those who do evil do not come to the light for fear their evil deeds will be exposed. That is a classic illustration for us today. We see so many evil things being said and done by children, youth and adults. These people are captivated by the pleasures of the world which are evil, and stay away from the light as much as they can, which is righteousness and the gospel of Jesus Christ.

For us as believers, Paul wrote to the church at Thessalonica (11 Thessalonians 3:3), who were concerned about the evil they were facing, to remind us the Lord is faithful and He will strengthen and protect us from the evil one, who is Satan.

A final thought about evil is the use of our tongue. In James 3:8 it says that no one can tame the evil tongue. It is a restless evil and full of deadly poison. We need to always be aware of what we say and how we use our tongue. God will help us if we are daily communicating with Him.

TODAY'S WORD FOR MARCH 9

INHERITANCE

In Him also we have obtained an inheritance, being predestined according to the purpose of Him who works all things according to the counsel of His will. Ephesians 1:11

Did you know that you are an heir to unimaginable wealth that will never go away? If you believe in Jesus Christ and have accepted Jesus as your Savior you are known as a child of God. God has for His children an inheritance reserved for us in heaven. In the verse above the apostle Paul is making it very clear to the church at Ephesus that Christ is the source of the believer's divine inheritance, which is so certain that it is spoken of as though it has already been received.

Do you need to be reminded that He owns the cattle on a thousand hills? He has reserved for us in heaven an inheritance far beyond what our minds can comprehend. Our inheritance is so certain because it was sovereignly determined by God's will and guaranteed by the blood of the Lord Jesus Christ. It is the will of God that every one of us, no matter how vile a sinner, might be made righteous by believing in Christ and receive the inheritance God has prepared for us.

In I Peter 1:4, Peter tells us that if we belong to Christ, we are one of His children and our inheritance is incorruptible, undefiled, does not fade away and is reserved for us in heaven. Peter tells the believers to look past the persecution they receive being believers and to look towards their eternal inheritance. Life, righteousness, joy, peace, perfection, God's presence, Christ's glorious companionship, rewards and much more, is our inheritance in heaven. No one can take our inheritance from us because God has guaranteed it by sealing us with His Holy Spirit of promise.

Naturally, we all want to know what we are going to inherit. Much of our inheritance is far beyond our human comprehension, but the scripture gives us a few hints. Part of our inheritance will be the transformation of our body and soul. We will be conformed to the likeness of His Son (Romans 8:29 and I John 3:2). Our weak perishable bodies will be changed into strong, glorious ones that are free from sin and death. Not only will we live forever, but we will live in the glorious presence of our Heavenly Father and our Lord and Savior Jesus Christ.

In Ephesians 2:7 we are told that God will show us "the surpassing riches of His grace in kindness toward us in Christ Jesus." As we live our days on this earth let us show love and gratitude to our Father for such amazing goodness. Let us devote each day of our lives to living for Him.

We encourage you to make the words of Colossians 3:23-24 a part of your daily life. "Whatever you do, do it heartily as to the Lord, and not unto man; knowing that of the Lord you shall receive the reward of the inheritance. For you serve the Lord." Jesus has promised us a just and eternal compensation for our spiritual efforts here on earth. Again, whatever you do, do it heartily unto the Lord.

TODAY'S WORD FOR MARCH 10

MEDIATOR

For there is one God and one Mediator between God and men, the Man Christ Jesus. I Timothy 2:5

Mediation is not without a price. Just ask someone who has hired a lawyer. Literally millions of dollars are spent on mediation by two parties when they face some sort of disagreement.

Has it ever occurred to you that you have a most important case pending? It is YOU versus GOD. Romans 3:23 tells us that "all have sinned." God is perfect and without sin and our sin separates us from God. In Isaiah 59:2 it says that "your iniquities have separated you from your God." This is a universal truth applying to all men and women, sin separates people from God. We are in disagreement with God and our relationship with Him is broken. Therefore we need a mediator.

A mediator is someone who intervenes between two parties to resolve a conflict or radify a covenant. Jesus Christ is the only mediator who can restore peace between God and sinners. God sent His Son to die on the cross to cover our sins in order that we could be reconciled to God. Mediation comes with a price and Jesus paid dearly by dying on the cross to cover our sins. In 1Timothy 2:5, Paul not only instructs Timothy, but reminds us that Christ Jesus is the one and only mediator between us and God. There is no other way to salvation.

We cannot come to God except through Jesus. Jesus said this to us in John 14:6: "No man comes to the Father except through Me." Jesus declared here that He is the way to God because He is the truth of God. The message here is exclusive and emphatic that Jesus is the only approach that man has to God. There is only one way. We ask you the question, "Have you met with your mediator today?"

Our children, like all children, did not always see eye to eye on issues so they would get into verbal fights with each other. Each one thought they were right and the other was wrong. Once in a while they would come to us to plead their cases. Sometimes the disagreement was serious enough that their usual loving relationship between them was broken. They needed us as a mediator to reconcile them.

Children are not the only ones who need a mediator to reconcile broken relationships. Most problems in our world are related to broken relationships over issues. Mediators are necessary to resolve the issues of these broken relationships.

We could not get along it seems, without a legal system of lawyers and judges who serve as mediators in settling disagreements between two parties. Even in churches today, pastors become mediators for those who come for counseling to settle their disagreements. Governments and political leaders have disagreements which are usually solved when a third party mediator comes on the scene.

We are constantly in a position where mediation is necessary. The most important mediator is the mediator that God has provided, His Son Jesus Christ.

TODAY'S WORD FOR MARCH 11

DEFEAT

And He began to teach them that the Son of man must suffer many things, and be rejected of the elders and chief priests and scribes, and be killed, and after three days rise again. Mark 8:31

For I am convinced that neither death nor life, neither angels, nor demons, neither the present or the future nor any powers, neither height nor depth nor anything else in all creation, will be able to separate us from the love of God that is in Christ Jesus our Lord. Romans 8:38-39

Do you find it difficult at times to believe that your situation can ever be better or that something good can come from it? Even the disciples who walked with Jesus were completely devastated, filled with doubt and defeated after the crucifixion. The Savior had told them, in Mark (above), what was going to happen with Him.

They simply could not see past their human perceptions or expectations of what was happening. Their expectation and hope was Jesus had come as a conquering Messiah to defeat their enemies and free them from Roman rule. Now their Messiah was defeated and put to death by the Romans. The disciples were brokenhearted, despondent and absolutely helpless. They believed it was all over because they had seen Jesus suffer and die on the cross. All of their hopes and dreams had gone.

How often do you get caught up in this same attitude of defeat? Do you get overwhelmed by your circumstances and focus on your limited comprehension instead of focusing on God's awesome purposes for your life. You need to see past your imperfect understanding of what is happening in your life, to our extraordinary Lord and Redeemer and then your heart will be filled with joy.

Look at the disciples after the resurrection of Jesus to see what they discovered. First, they were able to realize that God always succeeds in carrying out His plans. Jesus did come as the conquering Messiah, but not to conquer the Romans, but to conquer death. Jesus promised to pay the penalty for our sins and deliver us from the penalty of death and He did. (Luke 24:46-48)

Secondly, the disciples learned that nothing can separate us from God. Paul assures us in Romans 8:31-39 no matter what hardship or defeat we may suffer, it is impossible for those who trust in the Lord to be separated from God. God's love will always reach us no matter where we are or what circumstances we face. As Christians, we will face hardships in this life, but not one thing can separate us from the love of God. The disciples thought they had lost Jesus through the crucifixion, but the resurrection assured them they would never be without Him again.

Thirdly, the disciples discovered any adversity we experience is temporary because Jesus has given us eternal life. You may feel you are facing defeat because your situation is so grave, but do not give up hope. Cling to the promise that God acts on behalf of those of us who wait upon Him.

TODAY'S WORD FOR MARCH 12

POPULARITY

"For what will it profit a man if he gains the whole world, and loses his own soul? Or what will a man give in exchange for his soul? Mark 8: 36-37

What was Jesus really saying to us through these words recorded in Mark? When He asked what it profits a man, He was bringing to our minds the simple equation of profit and loss. This basically states that one's soul is worth more than all the popularity, all of the riches, and all of the pleasures of this world. No matter how much you have what the world offers, if you do not have salvation in Jesus Christ you are eternally bankrupt. The soul is eternal and therefore worth more than anything this world has to offer.

To have all the world has to offer, yet not have Christ, is to be eternally bankrupt. All the world's goods, the apostle Paul reminds us, will not compensate us for losing one's soul eternally.

Popularity is not a bad thing if it comes for the right reasons and from the right actions. It is when popularity becomes an obsession it is dangerous, because it often leads to compromising one's character. The desire for popularity is one of Satan's tools. Many have sold their souls to the devil to gain popularity.

Jesus gained His popularity on this earth because He was God. His loving compassion, Godly wisdom, consistent teaching and healing touch made Him someone special and the crowds came to listen to Him.

He was popular because His teachings, His healings and His miracles (such as feeding the 5000) changed people's lives. He was consistent and had high standards and many were convinced to believe in Him as the Son of God.

Popularity is very important to young people. A young person wants to be liked and popular. However, one finds out quickly that popularity comes and goes quickly. This is why parents need to help their children get their eyes off of the "things" of the world, such as popularity, and onto the "things" that count for eternity. This is very difficult to do because of peer pressure and the mindset young people and adults get, when "everyone else is doing it." People want to be accepted and worry about what others may think.

When Jesus hung on the cross dying, His popularity was disappearing and even His disciples began to doubt. While He was dying on the cross paying for our sins and the sins of all mankind, there was doubt and sadness across the land. Jesus did not come to earth to be popular. He came to do the unpopular thing, to show us we are sinners and to provide an escape for us by paying our penalty for our sins. Popularity is not what God wants us to strive for in life. Popularity will last for a short time and then what happens? We need to daily work on our relationship with Jesus and then allow Him to work through us. He will satisfy everything we need and want when we put our trust in Him.

TODAY'S WORD FOR MARCH 13

GRACE

But Noah found grace in the eyes of the Lord. Genesis 6:8

And He said to me, My grace is sufficient for you, for My strength is made perfect in weakness. II Corinthians 12: 9

But to each one of us grace was given according to the measure of Christ's gift. Ephesians 4:7

In Ephesians 2:8 we read, by grace we are saved through faith and that not of ourselves, but it is the gift of God. Simply stated, grace is God's unmerited favor. We do not deserve God's favor nor can we earn it. It is a gift from God that He offers us because of His goodness. It is because of God's grace that He gave His only Son to die on the cross so that we would not perish in our sin, but have eternal life.

Our salvation is a free gift. We should not become complacent in our faith. In II Peter 3:14-18 we are told we need to be growing in our faith. In verse 14 we are to be doing what is right. In verse 15-16 we are to be confident in the truth of God's Word. In verse 17 we are to be on our guard against false teaching and in verse 18 we are to grow in the grace and knowledge of our Savior.

The Hebrew word for grace is CHANAN. It is used in Genesis 6:8. In this passage of the scripture concerning Noah we are told that Noah found grace, the goodness of God, in the eyes of the Lord. Noah found grace because he was a righteous man who walked with God. By God's grace Noah and his family were saved from the flood.

In the verse above from II Corinthians, the apostle Paul reminds us the grace God gives us is sufficient to meet all of our needs. Paul relates to the people in the church at Corinth that he had a "thorn in the flesh." In verses 7-8 he was constantly fighting the problem of exalting himself. God did not remove the thorn, but assured Paul He would supply him with grace to endure it. What a wonderful promise.

In John 1:17 we are told from where grace comes. It reads: "For the law was given to us through Moses, but grace and truth came to us through Jesus Christ." Before Jesus came to this earth one lived under the law. The law could not save. It only demonstrated our need to be saved. God designed the law as a means to demonstrate the unrighteousness of man in order to show him the need for a Savior. The law was preparatory in nature, but the reality of the full truth came to man through the person of Jesus Christ. When Jesus came everything changed because of the cross that Jesus died on and now we live under grace, the goodness of God.

In the verse above from Ephesians we are told grace is given to each one of us who believe in Jesus according to the measure of Christ's gift. Remember, we are saved by putting our faith in Jesus and by the grace (goodness) of God. Then after we have found the Lord, we are given individual gifts to use to spread to the world we live in, the good news of the gospel message of God's grace.

TODAY'S WORD FOR MARCH 14

TRAINING

When I call to remembrance the genuine training and faith that is in you, which dwelt first in your grandmother Lois and your mother Eunice, I am persuaded that it is in you also. II Timothy 1:5

Train up a child in the way he should go, and when he is old he will not depart from it. Proverbs 22:6

The verses above are reminders to us about the importance of the training we received from our parents. It is also a reminder to parents today about their responsibility to train their children in the way that they should go. This means to use the scriptures as your guide in the training of your children. To start with, the Ten Commandments given in the Old Testament and the two great commandments that Jesus gave us in the New Testament, are vital to proper training.

The commandment that Jesus gave us in Matthew 22:37 is that we "Love the Lord your God with all your heart and with all your soul and with all your mind." Jesus said this was the first and greatest commandment.

In the training of children, a parent's first priority and greatest responsibility is to teach their children to love the Lord their God. Training is a vital ingredient in making a happy family. God has given us the Bible as His training manual. Parents have the responsibility of reading it by themselves and to their children.

Most adults need to retrain themselves in some of the basic Biblical principles needed to keep a marriage together and in raising a family. You cannot keep doing and acting the same way you did before your marriage and before you had children. You have God given responsibilities to both your spouse and to your children.

The world would be very confused without training. One needs training in almost everything they do. We train people in new jobs, we train people to drive cars, we train people how to live on a budget, we train armed forces personnel, we train bus drivers, and we train our pastors and teachers. Without training children can become very confused and are easily enticed into harmful lifestyles.

Training children can become very difficult at times. When it does, read Proverbs 3:5-6: "Trust in the Lord with all your heart, and lean not on your own understanding; in all your ways acknowledge Him and He will direct your paths." It takes Godly wisdom to raise children which requires lots of prayer, along with spending time in God's Word.

In Proverbs 22:6 it tells us clearly we are to train our children in the way that he or she should go and then when he or she grows up they will not depart from it. Today's children are tomorrow's leaders and they will lead only as parents have trained them. That is why today we have so many poor leaders. They came from a generation that neglected training and this present generation may be worse.

TODAY'S WORD FOR MARCH 15

IMPOSSIBLE

For with God nothing will be impossible. Luke 1:37

But without faith it is impossible to please God. Hebrews 11:6

How many times have you faced situations you felt were impossible to conquer? What is your first reaction when you encounter a difficult circumstance that looks impossible? Some people start searching for an answer or even a way out of the circumstance; others curl up in defeat and try to avoid the circumstance totally.

As believers, we need to remember if we face circumstances we feel are humanly impossible to conquer, we need to ask the right question:

We may ask, "O Lord what am I going to do?" Is this the right question to ask? The problem with asking this question is, even though we are seeking the Lord's guidance, the focus is on our actions. Therefore, we limit our response to our abilities, resources and understanding. All too often our minds will start to devise plans and soon we will resort to manipulation and maneuvering to fix the problem.

We should ask, "God, what are you going to do?" Do you see the difference? Now you have changed the focus to the omniscience and omnipotence of Almighty God. God blows out the sides of any box that confines us, He untangles any situation that baffles us and He has the power to carry out His plan which is perfect and will bring Him the Glory.

God's Word is a treasure available to us. It is practical and contains answers for every concern we may encounter. Impossible situations for us are opportunities for the Lord to teach us valuable lessons we would never have learned any other way.

God's supremacy trumps all human resources, and remember, that God often requires our participation to achieve His purpose. In John 6 we read where Jesus asked Philip to get bread to feed the multitude. From a human perspective, it was an impossible situation. Jesus knew where the bread was and He knew how the multitude would be fed but He wanted Philip to see how God did the impossible.

Jesus called on Philip to do what Jesus knew Philip would think to be impossible. Right away Philip began calculating the cost. Philip concluded it would take over eight months of wages to pay for enough bread. Therefore, what Jesus asked of him was in his mind impossible. Philip assumed what is or what is not possible based on his limited resources. Limited resources are more than sufficient when given to Jesus. Jesus took five small barley loaves and two fish and provided more food than was needed to feed everyone.

When God asks us to do what seems impossible we must not let our estimate of our own resources hold us back from doing what God wants us to do. We must remember that "with God nothing will be impossible." It takes faith to believe that with God all things are possible and without faith it is impossible to please God.

TODAY'S WORD FOR MARCH 16

FOCUS

For I know the thoughts that I think toward you, says the Lord, thoughts of peace and not of evil, to give you a future and a hope. Jeremiah 29:11

What then? Notwithstanding in every way, whether in pretense or truth, Christ is preached; and in this I rejoice, yes, and will rejoice. Philippians 1:18

In Acts, chapter nine, we are given the account of the Apostle Paul's conversion. Before Paul was converted to Christianity, his focus had been on the persecuting of Christians. God confronted Paul on the road to Damascus to change his focus. God had temporarily blinded Paul physically so he could see spiritually. Paul was like an out of focus camera where the true picture cannot be seen clearly.

When Paul met Jesus he had a clear vision of his out-of focus life. From that point in his life, Paul changed his focus. He focused on Jesus alone and on spreading the message of Jesus' love and forgiveness that brings salvation to all who believe.

Despite times of great physical discomfort and emotional trials, he was consistently focused on the fact he was under God's sovereign hand. His focus on the Lord kept him from being resentful and walking away from his faith. He faithfully continued throughout his life to be focused on the Lord and preaching the gospel.

Paul learned early in his walk with the Lord to focus on God's sovereignty rather than his own will. It is easy to become bitter or feel frustrated with situations that come our way in life. When our focus is not on the Lord and we start thinking our enemies and difficulties are in control of our circumstances, we are defeated.

Psalm 103:19 reads "God has established His throne in the heavens, and His sovereignty rules over all." He is in absolute control and our focus in life needs to be on Him at all times. We may not understand His reasons for permitting hardship or pain in our lives, but His plan is always for our good and His glory.

Read the verse we have put above from Jeremiah and this will become clearer to you. Jeremiah is giving this message to the exiles and making it clear that God intends to bring blessings to Israel's future. The key for the Israelites to receive the blessing of God is for them to keep their focus on God.

We can learn from Paul. He was focused on his godly purpose rather than on personal gain. For example, pain, whether in the body or the heart, often absorbs all of our attention. Paul's words and life style reminds us there is no victory to be had when we dwell on our hurts. For example, Paul rejoiced when the guards that were guarding him while he was in jail, found Christ. That was where his focus was, not on his situation in that jail. Paul's joy was not tied to his circumstances. He was constantly focused on God and circumstances and critics would not sway him. Paul was so in focus with his Lord that he rejoiced when the gospel was preached no matter who was involved and taking credit for anything was not in his vocabulary.

TODAY'S WORD FOR MARCH 17

WAITING

Those who wait upon the Lord shall renew their strength; they shall mount up with wings like eagles, they shall run and not be weary, they shall walk and not faint. Isaiah 40:31

God is the one that formed us. He knows our talents and abilities as well as our weaknesses. He knows every detail of our decision making and the potential results of every decision we make. He knows what is best for our life. And when we have our faith in Him, He has a plan for us motivated by wisdom and love and He will execute what He has for us in His perfect timing.

This at times can be difficult for us to accept especially if it involves waiting. God wants patience to be part of His plans for us. He wants to teach us to trust and yield our longings to Him. We demonstrate surrender and humility to God when we submit to His timetable. And for most believers this is very difficult.

God gave us another option, the free will to choose His plan or do it our way. So many times when life does not go just the way we want, we will try to make things happen in our power. However, very rarely does this work and it always leads to disappointment and difficulty which causes us to miss God's best for our life.

The verse we have put above from Isaiah contains rich promises that we can claim throughout life. God always keeps His Word so as believers we are to believe with faith, anticipate with hope and wait quietly with patience.

Isaiah in this verse above is dealing with a basic principle. Believers who wait upon the Lord and who communicate to God through prayer develop patience. The result is being blessed by God with strength through their trials in life. The Lord also expects us to be patient and wait for His soon return to earth.

Waiting on the Lord takes patience especially when waiting means enduring hardship. David had to endure much hardship waiting on the Lord. While David was just a young boy, God directed Samuel to anoint him to be king after Saul. David had to wait many years before taking the throne. During those years David had opportunity to kill Saul and speed up God's time table. David chose to wait on the Lord. In Psalm 40:1 David said, "I waited patiently for the Lord."

The apostle Paul in writing to the church at Galatia (Galatians 5:5), tells them to wait for the completed and perfected righteousness that is to come when we are glorified with our Lord. There are so many times in the scripture we are told to be patient as believers and wait upon the Lord.

We encourage you to embrace whatever situation you are in today. If it is a time for waiting, choose to learn patience, trusting that His plan for your life is always going to be better than your own. Walking in His will requires us to remain sensitive to His voice. He will protect us from making mistakes when we wait upon Him and are ready to listen to Him in His perfect timing.

TODAY'S WORD FOR MARCH 18

ACCEPT

Accept one another, just as Christ accepted you, in order to bring praise to God. Romans 15:7

When Jesus was here on this earth the Jewish people despised the Samaritans and did not accept them. In John 4, Jesus met a Samaritan woman at the well and began to talk with her. When Jesus asked for a drink she was surprised and wanted to know why He was talking to her because no Jewish man would ever talk to a Samaritan woman. Jesus continued to talk with her and she believed and accepted His gift of "living water."

She went back to her village and led many Samaritans to become believers in Jesus. The good news we can learn from this, is Jesus came to this earth for all of us, and He accepts all who come to Him in faith believing for forgiveness of their sins.

In Romans 15:7 we are told to accept one another just as Christ accepted us in order to bring praise to God. As Christians we are to accept and encourage other Christians. We must be willing to accept others who do not know the Lord, without condoning what they do, so we can introduce them to Christ. Children need to know the difference between accepting someone and accepting someone's actions when that person is doing things that are against Biblical principles.

Jesus knew the Samaritan woman was an immoral woman. He did not shun her for her race, social position or her sins. He accepted her as someone who needed His saving grace.

People today are hungry for acceptance. Children in school do everything they can, including lowering their standards, to be accepted by their peers. Adults are much the same. They want to be included in "THE GROUP" just as children do. Paul tells us in Romans 14:1, "Do not refuse to accept someone who is weak in faith. And do not argue with him about opinions."

We, as Christians, need to make people feel important and needed. This way they will feel accepted and will more than likely be open to hear about Jesus.

In an ethics class, when we were in college, we had a discussion about a small group of students who were not living up to the standards set by the college and as a result they were not being accepted by many of their peers. We began praying for this group and soon communication began.

The one thing we remember was they communicated to us that as a group or as individuals they did not feel accepted, so why should they change their life style? They had all come from home situations where living a much looser life was acceptable. Our prayers and acceptance of them soon resulted in several of their lives being changed. Fellow students approached them with love and not with criticism and the result was soon they all felt accepted.

TODAY'S WORD FOR MARCH 19

LIFESTYLE

My son, hear the instruction of your father, and do not forsake the law of your mother.
Proverbs 1:8

When choosing our lifestyle we are dramatically affected by what we were taught and learned beginning in our childhood days. As a child we begin to learn all of the positive and the negative values in our parent's lifestyle. What a child witnesses in their parents' lifestyle has the most influence on them. A parent's influence has a major role in determining the kind of person a child becomes.

Lifestyles are learned by what a person sees and hears and decisions are then made by what interests the person the most. Children need to develop positive work ethics at a young age. When they do they will usually continue to have good work ethics throughout their life. Good work ethics are needed in order to succeed. The choosing of friends plays a vital role in shaping one's lifestyle. Again children are affected by what they see and hear.

In the verse above, the writer begins a lengthy section featuring parental praises of wisdom. A parent should read the first eight chapters of Proverbs often. In fact there are 31 chapters in Proverbs and we suggest you read one chapter a day. This would be spiritually rewarding for parents, non-parents and children.

In Ezekiel 18:5-9, Ezekiel says that the word of the Lord came to him and gave him some thoughts on what God wants in a lifestyle. The MESSAGE translation puts it in words that we can all understand today. "Imagine a man with the lifestyle of living well, treating others fairly and keeping good relationships." He then goes on to explain what God does not want in a person's lifestyle.

"Who doesn't eat at pagan shrines, doesn't worship idols, doesn't seduce a neighbors spouse, doesn't bully anyone, doesn't pile up bad debts, doesn't steal, doesn't refuse giving food to the hungry, doesn't refuse giving clothing to the ill-clad, doesn't exploit the poor, doesn't live by impulse and greed, and doesn't treat one person better than another."

Then Ezekiel tells us what makes a good lifestyle. "But lives by God's statutes and faithfully honors and obeys God's laws. This person who lives upright and well shall live a full and true life." That is the lifestyle God wants from us. Ezekiel, in these verses proposes two scenarios to clarify for the reader the matter of personal guilt as it relates to one's lifestyle. As believers we are to have a lifestyle that is characterized by love, imitates Christ, demonstrates true faith, gentle in behavior and is governed by truth which is God's Word.

From early on as young parents we wanted to guide our children to lead a lifestyle that was pleasing to God. When they did something wrong we corrected them and endeavored most of the time to explain why it was wrong. We taught them to live by God's standards. But what we realized to be the most important influence on them was our own lifestyle. They witnessed daily how we talked and what we did.

TODAY'S WORD FOR MARCH 20

STANDARDS

What does the Lord your God require of you but to fear the Lord your God with all your heart, to walk in all His ways, to love Him, to serve the Lord your God with all your heart and with all your soul and to observe the Lord's commands and decrees. Deuteronomy 10:12

God has set standards for us who love Him to keep. Setting human standards that ignore God and His commandments have no lasting effect. It is important for the believer to know the standards God has set for us and then to live by them daily. Unfortunately non-believers set for themselves standards for themselves that are made to be broken.

For those who know Jesus as his or her Savior, a standard has significant importance. God first gave the children of Israel His standards He expected them to live by. We read in Deuteronomy 10:12-13, there were five things God expected of them. These standards were preceded by the words, "What does the Lord your God require of you?" They are: 1. Reverence God. 2. Walk in all His ways. 3. Love Him. 4. Serve Him with all your heart and soul. 5. Observe His commands.

Jesus, when He was here on earth, lived by and taught these same standards. God does not change. His standards for us are the same as they were for the children of Israel and as they were some 2000 years ago when Jesus was on this earth and taught them personally. Standards are essential in every person's life. Are you living the way God expects you to and are you keeping God's standards?

Here is an additional list of standards for you to evaluate. Do you set a time daily for reading the Bible? Do you spend time praying to God? Do you spend time communicating about spiritual things with your family and with your spouse? At the workplace, do you set yourself a standard of excellence in your work? Do you complete your work? Do you communicate to the people you work with both in words and deeds a life that exemplifies the Lord?

Do you set examples and a standard for your family, friends and neighbors by your attendance at church? Do you attend Sunday school and take your family? Are you involved in a home Bible study group? Do you volunteer to help in some area?

We all need to set standards in our lives that honor God. Standards are necessary in life so that we can build our life on a base.

God has given us in the Old Testament ten standards to build our lives on. We know them today as the Ten Commandments. We urge you to read these today and then print them and put them in a prominent place in your home so you have to read them daily. If you choose to do this and then choose to live by them your life will change dramatically over night. Take time today to set some standards for your life. The TEN COMMANDMENTS are a good beginning and they cover every area of life. We also suggest that you add to the Ten Commandments the two commandments that Jesus gave us in Matthew 22:37-40.

TODAY'S WORD FOR MARCH 21

BOUNDARIES

Jesus said, You shall love the Lord your God with all your heart, with all your soul, and with all your mind. This is the first and greatest commandment. And the second is like it: You shall love your neighbor as yourself. Matthew 22: 37-39

Jesus put it right on the line for all believers when He gave us His standard to love the Lord thy God and love our neighbors. This sets up the boundary we need if we are going to honor Him and serve Him. When we love Jesus and our neighbors it puts us in a position of honoring God in all that we do. Webster defines boundaries as rules to enforce standards. The boundaries we have are what God has given us, the Ten Commandments, His Word and our personal experience with Him.

The prophet Nehemiah was governor of Jerusalem after he returned from exile. God spoke to him and directed him to rebuild the wall around Jerusalem. He responded because he knew God knew that the Jewish people needed a boundary around them to protect them from their enemies. (Nehemiah chapters 3-4)

Just like those that lived in Jerusalem during Nehemiah's time needed a boundary in the form of a wall to protect them from invaders, we as believers need a boundary of protection to protect us from the invasion of sin that we face daily.

We live in a culture that basically ignores God and thus we face evil influences everywhere we turn. When we live out our faith we face times when our faith is questioned. We are asked such things as "How can you believe that there is a God when all these bad things are happening?"

We face temptations daily. How many times a day are you tempted to do something that is not honest or at least borders on being dishonest. This is Satan at work in your life and in this world. The temptations we face begin with little things and then they get bigger and bigger and soon God is forgotten.

Our children face the evils of drugs, alcohol, sex and plain dishonesty and a philosophy of living for self glorification. Just sit down with a young person and get them to talk to you about the things they face in life and you will be appalled.

In the Christian life, it is like a line dividing right from wrong. When we cross the line and do what is not pleasing to God, it is wrong and a sin and we have breached the boundary the Lord has set for us. So often we make excuses like what is wrong if it is only a little white lie, or it will never be missed if I steal it.

How many drug addicts became addicted because they thought it would never hurt to try an illegal drug just once? How many drunkards started with just one drink? Once the boundary between right and wrong is breached it is like a tiny crack in a dam that soon expands until the floodgates are let loose and causes a disaster. This is why we need boundaries for our families that will protect us from the evils of this world. We need support systems. We need family communication daily. We need time daily to pray and read the Bible alone and as a family.

TODAY'S WORD FOR MARCH 22

NEGLECT

Therefore, to him who knows to do good and does not do it, to him it is sin. James 4:1

How shall we escape if we neglect so great a salvation? Hebrews 2:3

Many people we talk to justify neglect by excuses like, "I am too busy" or "later." In the work place today, many neglect doing a job intentionally and again use excuses to justify their action. In the world we live in today, neglect is commonplace. Parents need to train their children, beginning at a young age, that just not doing something they do not want to do is not acceptable. It is just plain neglect and done on purpose.

James says in the above verse when we know something is the right thing to do and we do not do it, it is a sin. This is called a sin of omission. It is as much of a sin as a sin of commission, like lying, stealing and committing adultery, in God's sight.

The Bible has a lot to say about neglect as well. The verse we have put above from Hebrews is very relevant for today. Many people just keep turning down opportunities to accept Christ as their Savior. They always have excuses. Some simply say they will accept Jesus later when they get older. Some just do not care about the consequences even when they are told. It all boils down to where one wants to spend eternity. God has made it so clear in His Word that salvation is only available through the acceptance of His Son as their Savior. The verse above says, HOW SHALL WE ESCAPE IF WE NEGLECT SO GREAT A SALVATION?

There is no excuse in God's sight for neglect. One may only have one opportunity in life to accept God's salvation. We do not know what tomorrow holds. What we do know is God will not accept any excuse or neglect.

In I Timothy 4:14 the apostle Paul exhorts Timothy and other believers not to neglect the gift that is in you, which was given you by God. We all have been given gifts that God expects us as believers to use for Him. However, so many never use their gifts as God expects them to do so. Again, God will not accept excuses from us for not using our gifts as He directs us to use them.

It is up to us as parents to, first of all, teach our children about God and Jesus so they can have the opportunity to accept Jesus as their Savior and not to neglect such a great salvation. Parents, also, must teach their children the difference between right and wrong. Children need to be taught so they know without any doubt what is good so they understand that neglecting to do the right things in life is as much of a sin as doing the wrong thing.

TODAY'S WORD FOR MARCH 23

ESCAPE

But Jonah rose up to flee into Tarshish from the presence of the Lord, and went down to Joppa. Jonah 1:3

When we think of the word escape for some reason Alcatraz, the prison in the bay of San Francisco, comes to our mind. This prison was reserved for the worst prisoners in America. They would be sent here to serve their time because the system felt they could not escape. If a person would try to escape from Alcatraz it would be a very long swim to land and most thought it was humanly impossible.

Today it is a museum and a few weeks ago one of our grandchildren went there to tour the museum. He told us they reported one or two prisoners may have tried to escape, but if they did, they would have drowned in their attempt to swim to land.

The scripture above tells us about the time God told Jonah to go to Nineveh and preach the Word of God. He did not like the assignment and decided to escape God's presence by running away to Joppa to get on a boat headed to Tarshish.

It was foolish for any person in the prison at Alcatraz to think they could escape by jumping off the Island into a vast sea expanse of water like the San Francisco bay. It was even more foolish for Jonah to think he could run and escape from God, who is all powerful, all knowing, and all present everywhere.

Just as trying to escape from Alcatraz could only lead to disaster so would Jonah's attempt to escape from God's presence. Jonah was hurled into a raging sea and as he was about to drown he cried out to God and even in the midst of a stormy sea God was present. God provided a great fish to swallow Jonah and saved him.

In trying to escape from doing what God wanted him to do just think about what Jonah lost. He lost not only valuable time he could have spent preaching God's Word, and he lost his peace of mind. He had lost the blessing of God's presence, God's provision and God's comfort in his life. God still had His way with Jonah. Jonah brought suffering on himself and he still ended up going to Nineveh.

There are occasions when we as believers fall away from our duty by not doing what God wants us to do. The result is always the same. We lose the presence and comfort of the Lord in our lives. Just like Jonah, we may find ourselves in the midst of a raging sea. The moment we run off to seek our own inventions, without God's blessing, we are at sea without a pilot. Then we cry out to God asking Him where has He gone? God has not left us, we have left Him. By this time in our life we are at the same place that Jonah was, on the run and with no peace of mind. Sin destroys a believer's comfort. Jonah found out it is harder to try to escape from doing what God wants you to do than to yield to His will.

When you put your trust in God and communicate with Him daily, you will not flee from what He tells you. It is hard to contend against God when you try to escape doing His will. When you trust Him, He knows what is best and will be with you always giving you His assurance of His faithfulness and the comfort of His presence.

TODAY'S WORD FOR MARCH 24

ABANDON

At my first defense no one stood with me, but all forsook me. II Timothy 4:16

Jesus said, I will never leave you nor forsake [abandon] you. Hebrews 13:5

Some years ago when we were involved in a large feeding program for inner city families in Los Angeles, we met a dear woman, Mae Raines. She lived in a poor area of south Los Angeles and was known as "God's Angel" to her community. She came to our warehouse center two to three times a week and filled her car to the roof with food. She then distributed this food to the neediest people in her community.

I remember when she came to our warehouse to pick up food and had in her arms a little 3 day old baby. This baby was what they called a "druggy" and had been abandoned. Mae could not allow this baby to die so she took him in and began the process of making him well. The baby was constantly shaking as his body was going through withdrawals from the drugs his mother had used during her pregnancy.

We watched this boy grow. It was the love of a Christian mother, Mae Raines, over several years that soon brought him to the place where he could live a normal life. Yes, this baby was abandoned, but a loving lady, "GOD'S ANGEL," saw to it that this boy could live and today he is living a normal life.

We can also remember watching TV reports about 20 years ago about the babies who were abandoned in Romania under the dictatorship of their former leader. When freedom came their way the terrible situation of these orphan children became international news. Soon many of these abandoned children were adopted and began to live a normal life because someone loved them. The lives of hundreds of children were literally saved. Their stories of how love and care changed the course of life for these abandoned babies are heart-warming and inspirational.

Just think how abandoned the disciples and the followers of Jesus felt when they saw Jesus crucified and His body lay in a tomb. They had put all of their trust in Jesus and now their hopes had vanished. Jesus appeared to two of His followers walking on the road to Emmaus in His resurrected body and they did not recognize Him. Jesus asked them what they were talking about. With saddened faces they explained they were talking about the crucifixion of Jesus. They said they had hoped Jesus was the one who was going to redeem Israel.

Jesus then explained to them from the scripture why He had to suffer and die. He explained also all the references in the scripture beginning with Moses and the prophets concerning Himself. As Jesus was talking to them, the scripture says that soon their eyes were opened and they saw their Messiah, the resurrected Christ. He had not abandoned them. He was right there walking beside them.

When you feel abandoned the Word of God is always the best place to look for comfort. We have a promise that Jesus will never leave us nor forsake us. Others may abandon us, but Jesus never will. He continues to walk beside us daily.

TODAY'S WORD FOR MARCH 25

CROSS

Greater love has no one than this, than to lay down one's life for his friend. John 15:13

Easter is one of the most significant and meaningful weekends of the year for Christians. The heart of Easter is the cross. Even though Easter is at a different time every year we want to share with you today several thoughts on this special weekend.

Good Friday is the day we remember the death of Jesus. He died to pay the penalty for our sins and every believer should be grateful for what He did for us.

Three days after Good Friday is Easter Sunday. This is the day we celebrate <u>the resurrection of Jesus</u>. Without the resurrection, Jesus would be just another great teacher and we would not be experiencing eternal life through Him.

It is our prayer that you will make Easter a weekend of celebration. Just think, where would we spend eternity without the Easter experience? What comfort would we have in our daily living on this earth without the Easter experience? For us it is the greatest weekend of the year and we hope you will celebrate with us.

The good news about Easter is that out of love for us, the Father has provided a place of safety for us. He sent His Son Jesus to die so we would not have to be separated from Him forever. Because of the death of Jesus on the cross and three days later His resurrection from the dead that place of safety is available to us. The big question for you today is, "Have you run to the cross?" To escape sin's curse you must run to the cross.

In the verse above we read about one laying down his life for another. To give your life so another person can live is the ultimate proof of love and the ultimate sacrifice. Jesus told His disciples that His purpose in coming into this world was to lay down His life for all mankind. This was for every man, woman and child ever born. He set the ultimate example of self-sacrifice by going to the cross.

Have you ever given any thought to the fact that Jesus did that for you? When He died in your place, He not only proved His love for you, but made it possible for you to be forgiven of your sins and to have an eternal home in heaven.

The song writer George Bernard, who we met personally many years ago, wrote these words in his song, "The Old Rugged Cross:"

" On a hill far away stood an old rugged cross, the emblem of suffering and shame; And I love that old cross where the dearest and best for a world of lost sinners was slain."

Christ's sacrifice was what God desired and our sin required. If you are not a believer accept Jesus into your heart today and make this day the greatest day of your life.

TODAY'S WORD FOR MARCH 26

HAND

Let Your hand become my help, for I have chosen Your precepts. Psalm 119:173

I can still remember when our children were trying to learn to walk. They always were reaching out to hold our hand. When they gained confidence they no longer would reach for our hand and almost without fail they would fall and sometimes even hurt themselves. Their over-confidence taught them a lesson that a strong helping hand could have kept them from falling and help them gain confidence.

Many times, we are sure; you have been in situations where you needed to take someone's hand to help walk on a slippery path. As we get older we often welcome having someone's hand to keep us from slipping or even falling.

We were in Panama and had the opportunity to visit a remote Indian tribe. We took a bus to a remote area and then walked down a steep hill to get into a dugout canoe. The mud was very slippery and there was no railing to grab. We were not the least bit confident we could get from the river bank into the canoe safely. There were no steps and the river bank was very uneven, muddy and rocky.

A teenage Indian boy, standing near the canoe with both of his bare feet planted firmly on the ground, reached out with his one hand to grab ours and with his other hand he grabbed our arm. With these helping hands we felt more confident that we could make it into the canoe. We got into the canoe, went down the river, met the tribe and returned knowing we had a very special day. We also knew that without the helping hands of this teenage Indian boy we may not have made it.

We look back through the years and remember when we were the ones reaching out with the helping hands. We both remember holding the hand of a young child who lived in the slums of Nairobi Africa. We also remember holding the hand of children living on the garbage dump in real filth in Manila Philippians.

In the verse we have written above the psalmist tells us, "Let Your hand become my help, for I have chosen Your precepts." God is holding out His hand every moment of everyday for us to hold, and when we live by His precepts He has promised to lead us according to His will.

In life, we all have been in difficult situations, both physically and spiritually, where we have overestimated our feeble abilities. Those are the times we reached out for help. The Psalmist tells us (Psalm 139:10) that "Your hand (God's) shall lead me, and your right hand shall hold me." In Psalm 89:13 we read, "You have a mighty arm; strong is Your hand and high is Your right hand." You can call out to God and say, "Give me a hand' and He will rush to your side.

We were so grateful for the strong and steady hand of the Indian boy on that river bank in Panama, but we are so much more grateful we have God's hand leading us and supporting us on the slippery slope of life. When adversity begins to strike you, remember God is ready to stretch out His hand to strengthen you.

TODAY'S WORD FOR MARCH 27

DETERMINATION

Never be lacking in zeal, but keep your spiritual fervor, serving the Lord. Romans 12:11

Some people have a great deal of determination in running their lives and others have very little. You can see different levels of determination in the same family. One's level of determination stems from the intensity of one's desire. One of our deep concerns is the lack of determination people have to serve the Lord.

This was a concern Paul had for the Christian's in the church at Rome when he wrote them and instructed them to never be lacking in their zeal to serve the Lord. In the verse above, Paul was encouraging the believers in the church at Rome whatever is worth doing in the Christian life is valuable enough to be done with enthusiasm and care. He also cautioned the believers that sloth and indifference in doing the Lord's work not only prevents good, but allows evil to prosper.

Paul, when he says "spiritual fervor," is suggesting we are to have plenty of heat to produce adequate productive energy to accomplish what our mission is for the Lord, but not so much heat that one goes out of control.

The story is told of a student in the late 19th century, Mary McLeod Bethune. She spent two years training at Moody Bible Institute in Chicago to become a missionary in Africa. After she graduated, no mission board would take her as an African-American woman to serve under their mission.

Unable to fulfill her dream, and seemingly what was a calling from God, she did not give up because she was determined to serve Jesus. She went to Florida and started a small school for African-American girls. This small school, because of her determination, became Bethune-Cookman College and she became a powerful force for change, not only here in America, but world-wide in the status of women.

Mary's legacy came about because of her determination to serve her Lord. Her dream of going to Africa did not become a reality because God had something better for her. Her determination, to think big, allowed God to do His work in her life. Can you learn from this dear woman? God truly did bless her for her determination.

In our recent travels we have often commented on the fact we do not see near the amount of determined people than we saw even 25 years ago. People are satisfied with the status quo. Worse yet they seem to want everything given to them.

We as parents and as believers need to develop a new determination to give all we have to serving the Lord. We need more believers outwardly showing the world that they are serving Jesus. We need to stand and to speak out about our faith and for the moral standards God has given us in His Word.

The world needs people with a new and vibrant determination to do the unusual and impossible. Many believers today are sitting back doing nothing when God wants them to move into action for Him. Let God do His work through you.

TODAY'S WORD FOR MARCH 28

CONDEMNED

They perish because they refused to love the truth and so be saved, all will be condemned who have not believed the truth but have delighted in wickedness. II Thessalonians 2:10 b and 12

How will you escape being condemned to hell? Matthew 23:33

The message of the Bible is we are all sinners as a result of Adam and Eve's fall in the Garden of Eden and as sinners we are condemned to spend eternity in hell. God, because of His love for us, sent His son, Jesus, into the world to die for our sins.

People who have not accepted Jesus as their Savior do not want to hear about condemnation, or about hell. It takes them out of their "comfort" zone. Preachers today shy away from preaching about hell because church attendees would rather hear a message that makes them feel good rather than face the fact they are sinners in need of a Savior.

This is nothing new. Jeremiah was a prophet chosen by God to bring a message of condemnation to Jerusalem because they had rejected God and had turned to worshipping false Gods and doing all kinds of evil. They did not want to hear it. At that time Jerusalem had already been besieged by King Nebuchadnezzar, who ransacked the temple and carried off to Babylon all the valuable temple articles. In addition, he took all, but the poorest people as captives to live in exile in Babylon.

Now Jeremiah was warning that greater disaster was coming unless they repented and came back to God. The people chose to listen to the more encouraging message of the false prophet Hananiah who told them within two years Nebuchadnezzar's power would be broken and the temple articles would come back to Jerusalem.

Choosing not to listen to a message we do not want to hear will not change the truth. The encouraging message of the false prophet proved to be a lie. Jerusalem did not repent and Jeremiah's message of condemnation was fulfilled when Nebuchadnezzar again besieged and completely destroyed Jerusalem, the temple, the palaces, and even the walls of the city were torn down.

God's word is truth. Paul tells us in Thessalonians that all will be condemned who do not believe the truth. Satan's influence is limited to deceiving the unsaved who will believe his lies. In the last days God will seal the fate of those who persist in following Satan and his Counterfeit christ. Those who reject the truth will be judged by God being left with the consequences of their sins.

The question Jesus asked in Matthew, "How will you escape being condemned to hell?" is answered by Jesus in John 3:18. "Whoever believes in Him is not condemned but whoever does not believe stands condemned already because he has not believed in the name of God's one and only Son." The believer has more than an intellectual belief in Jesus but a trust and commitment to Christ as Lord.

TODAY'S WORD FOR MARCH 29

SPEECH

But I tell you that men will have to give account on the Day of Judgment for every careless word they have spoken. Matthew 12:36

You can usually judge a person's character by listening to his or her speech. We were talking with one of our grandsons and asked him how he liked his new school. He responded very favorably, but went on to say that he had a mean girl in his class. Soon it was made clear the reason he regarded the girl as mean was because she was calling him degrading names and they were hurtful.

Children's behavior is a reflection of what they are taught in the home. Parents have a great responsibility to teach children how to speak with kindness and humility. In today's world the speech adults and children hear is mostly degrading. A lot of what we hear would be R-rated in the movies. The problem is what we hear on the street becomes part of us and influences how we ourselves speak.

As Christians we must be concerned about our speech. Paul instructs us in Colossians 4:6 to "Let our speech always be with grace, seasoned with salt, that you may know how to answer each one." We must always be gracious and respectful in what we say. To speak with grace is spiritual, wholesome, fitting, kind, sensitive, purposeful, complimentary, gentle, truthful, loving, and thoughtful. The speech of the believer should be a blessing to others and also a purifying influence within the decaying society of the world we live in today.

In Ephesians 5:4 Paul further admonishes us about our speech telling us, "Nor there obscenity, foolish talk, or coarse joking, which are out of place, but rather thanksgiving." Most importantly, Jesus holds us accountable for our speech as we read in Matthew 12:36 (above).

What kind of speech do your children hear around the house? Is God's name taken in vain? Are friends, family and neighbors talked about in a negative and degrading way? What is taught about speaking to God?

Jesus was speaking to the devil, as recorded in John 8:45, when He said, "But because I tell you the truth, you do not believe Me." In verse 47, He goes on to say to Satan, He who is of God hears God's Words; therefore you do not hear, because you are not of God. God speaks to the hearts of believers daily through His Word and we hear Him only if we are in tune with Him.

Our Lord wants to speak daily to those of us that believe on Him. Are you talking to Him daily, if not, why not? The only way we are going to grow in the Lord is to listen to Him speak to us. And more importantly, if you are not communicating to God daily, how can you survive this world and the evils we face daily?

Remember one is known by their speech. Words communicate much about a person. Take a good look at the words you use and the attitude that you show when you speak those words. Are they hurtful, profane, egotistic or kind and loving? Your speech can drive people to the Lord or drive people away from the Lord.

TODAY'S WORD FOR MARCH 30

LABOR

Six days you shall labor and do all your work. Exodus 20:9

Do not labor for the food which perishes, but for the food which endures to everlasting life. John 6:27

How many people will recognize it is not the labor of good works that will qualify them for eternal forgiveness? One who believes that good works alone is all one needs to have eternal life with our Lord is really attempting to buy forgiveness on credit. This is the philosophy of many religions. We all want to go to heaven. We all want everlasting life. Sin is the barrier that keeps us from heaven. So many people today believe the more good works they do will earn their way to heaven.

God has sent His Son to this world and He died on the cross to pay the penalty for our sins. We are all sinners and we all need to pay the debt for our sins, but doing good works and hard labor will not get one into heaven. We need to realize we are sinners, ask God to forgive us of our sins and then ask Jesus into our hearts. Working or laboring hard will not achieve forgiveness of our sins.

God has pre-paid our sin-debt in full so He has no need for our feeble good works, no matter how hard and diligently we labor. So what did Christ mean when He said in John 6:27, "Do not labor for the food which perishes, but for the food which endures to everlasting life?" The crowd Jesus was speaking to asked the same question. They wanted to know what they had to do to do the work God requires. Jesus answered, "The work of God is this: to believe on the one He has sent."

In Deuteronomy 10:12-13 we read that He requires of us is "to fear the Lord your God, to walk in His ways and love Him, and to serve the Lord your God with all your heart and with all your soul and to keep the Lord's commandments."

God expects us to labor and work hard representing Him in all we do. When you go to your work place, you go not only to earn the funds to live on daily, but to represent Christ to those you labor with. Your work place is your place of ministry.

Paul reminds us in 1 Corinthians 15:58, "Therefore, my beloved brethren, be steadfast, immovable, always abounding in the work of the Lord, knowing that your labor is not in vain in the Lord." If your prime purpose every day is not laboring for the Lord, then take a good look at your relationship with your Lord.

The author of Hebrews reminds us in Hebrews 6:10 that "God is not unjust to forget your work and labor of love which you have shown toward His name, in that you have ministered to the saints, and do continue to minister." Remember Paul's words encouraging us to always give ourselves fully to the work of the Lord because we know that our labor in the Lord is not in vain. I Corinthians 15:58.

One of the Ten Commandments tells us to labor six days and then rest on the seventh. Our seventh day should be dedicated to worshipping and praising God.

TODAY'S WORD FOR MARCH 31

POWER

But you shall receive power when the Holy Spirit has come upon you; and you shall be witnesses to Me in Jerusalem, and in all Judea and Samaria and to the end of the world. Acts 1:8

The machines and mechanized devices we use today in our daily lives make life so much easier for us. All of these devices have something in common. They need a power source. They come equipped with a fuel tank, an electrical plug or a solar cell. And these devices are useless unless they have power. A vacuum cleaner needs to be plugged into an electrical outlet and an airplane cannot fly without fuel.

People today are searching for a power source for their lives. Some look to money and others look to education or a political office. These sources of power are acquired by our own methods. Political leaders want power to control their governing policies. Parents want power to control their children. However this kind of power, when a person relies on himself, is doomed to failure over time.

God is all powerful and has provided a power source for us greater than all other sources because it comes directly from Him. Jesus tells us in the above scripture the Holy Spirit is that source for our power. It is important for all believers to remember for power in our lives we need to be controlled by the Holy Spirit.

Jesus was speaking to His disciples shortly before His ascension into heaven when He was commissioning them to be His witnesses. He knew the disciples could not do this in their own power so He tells them they would receive power when the Holy Spirit would come upon them.

This power is freely given to us today, but we must be willing to plug into the source. Unfortunately most people face life with all its issues and problems relying on their own abilities. When we have the Holy Spirit within us we have strength and a power that a non-believer does not understand and we do not have to face our day to day issues, both negative and positive, alone and in our own strength.

The apostle Paul fully understood the power of the Holy Spirit in his life. Paul wrote to his churches giving them and us much information concerning the power of the Holy Spirit. In Galatians 5 he tells us the Holy Spirit gives us the power to overcome our sinful desires and the evils we face every day. In Romans 8 Paul tells us we must be controlled by the Holy Spirit and He will give us power to please God.

In Galatians 5:22 Paul lists the results of what the Holy Spirit has the power to do for us: love, joy, peace, patience, kindness, goodness, faithfulness, gentleness and self-control. God gives us power through His Holy Spirit to allow us to accomplish things for Him that we might think are humanly impossible.

We are to be a witness of Christ in our own Jerusalem, our family, our home and our work place. Then we are to reach out beyond our home and workplace to our Judea and Samaria, our neighborhood and city. Finally we are to reach out to the end of the world and be involved in world mission programs.

TODAY'S WORD FOR APRIL 1

AFFECTION

Love each other with genuine affection and take delight in honoring each other. Romans 12:10

For God is my witness, how greatly I long for you all with the affection of Jesus Christ. Philippians 1:8

Genuine affection is demonstrated by selfless kindness that causes a person to put aside their own interests for the good of another. When we think of "genuine affection" we think of the relationship between David and Jonathan. In I Samuel 18:1 we are told that when they met, an immediate bond developed between them. Jonathan showed his affection for David by giving him his robe, his tunic, his sword and his bow and his belt.

Jonathan was Saul's son and David was his son- in- law. Saul became jealous of David because of his successes in battle and wanted to kill him. Jonathan interceded because of his brotherly affection for David. Jonathan remained loyal to David and helped him escape Saul's attempts to kill him.

Jonathan and David affirmed their bond of affection to each other with a covenant. Jonathan would keep David informed of Saul's plots to kill him. David promised to always treat Jonathan's family well after he became king.

Why would Jonathan's affection for David be stronger than his affection for his own father? Jonathan saw David's faith in the Lord and saw that David tried to do what was right in the eyes of the Lord. Jonathan did not allow his affection for his father blind him to the fact that his father's desire to kill David was wrong. Sometimes in order to stand for what is right we have to make difficult choices. Both Jonathan and David understood the meaning of the genuine affection that Paul spoke of later in the New Testament in Romans 12:10 (above).

In Psalms 136, the Psalmist expressed that the affection God has for us endures forever. In Jeremiah 31:3 we are reminded of the Lord's affection towards us when it is written that God has loved us with an everlasting love. And because of this love, He reached out to us with loving kindness. God's goodness to us flows from His deep and genuine affection for us.

God wants us to have the same genuine affection for others that He has for us. He wants us to exemplify the mutual love and commitment of true affection in our relationships with family and Christian friends.

Paul describes his affection for the Christians in Philippi as being like the affection of Jesus Christ. Paul used the Greek word for affection in Philippians 1:8 because it best expressed compassionate love. Christ Jesus affection for us was most certainly compassionate love. When we truly love the Lord we will, like Paul, be able to love others with the affection of Jesus.

TODAY'S WORD FOR APRIL 2

VICTORY

But thanks be to God, who gives us the victory through our Lord Jesus Christ. I Corinthians 15:57

For everyone who has been born of God overcomes the world, and this is the victory that has overcome the world, even our faith. I John 5:4

In the verse from I John, John defines who will overcome the world: Believers in the Lord. The Greek word for "overcome" means to have victory, to have superiority or conquering power. Because of our union with Christ as believers, we have continual victory, over-whelming success, over the evils of the world.

God first spoke of victory in Genesis when He was talking to Cain. Cain was very angry at his brother Abel because God had accepted Abel's offering and rejected Cain's. In Genesis 4: 6-7, God said to Cain, "Why are you angry? Why has your countenance fallen? If you do well, will you not be accepted? And if you do not do well, sin lies at the door. And its desire is for you, but you must have victory over it."

Cain did not celebrate a life of victory in God because he could not handle a moment of failure. He allowed anger to enter and rule in his heart which led him to kill his brother Abel. Cain lost the victory. Every day we have the challenge in our lives of being victorious over sin or losing the battle to Satan. When we sin, Satan wins and in that moment has victory over us.

Victory over Satan's temptations to sin is what we as believers must continually strive for. As Paul reminded us in I Corinthians 15:57, we can be thankful that we do not fight the battle alone and that through our Lord Jesus Christ we can have the ultimate victory over Satan. We need to be reminded that we as believers can claim victory over all the "things" in life we face because evil (Satan) was conquered by Christ when He died on the cross and three days later rose from the dead.

As we look at the state of our world today it would seem that Satan is winning the battle. Through Christ and His gift of salvation, we as believers have the power to overcome the world by our faith in Him. (I John 5:4) On the cross Jesus defeated Satan and his power. Jesus is the victorious Lord and ultimate ruler of this world. Satan has only temporary rule of those who choose to follow him.

All six of our children played several sports while in school. They always strived for victory and we were there to encourage them. After several years we made the decision to coach our younger children. When we coached, we shared with the children how easy it is to celebrate victory and how difficult it is to accept defeat.

We taught the children that in daily life there are times of victory and times of defeat and we had to learn how to win and how to lose. Teaching children to be gracious in losing is much tougher than teaching them to be gracious in winning.

Whether in victory or defeat we should reflect the love of Jesus in our lives and take courage knowing that, through Him, eternal victory will come.

TODAY'S WORD FOR APRIL 3

BATTLE

For You have armed me with strength for the battle; You have subdued under me those who rose up against me. Psalm 18:39

For the battle is the Lord's and He will give you into our hands. I Samuel 17:47

Our "word" today is BATTLE. Probably the first thing that crosses your mind is a battle among countries or cultures. Maybe you may think it is a battle among politicians or even neighbors. Our concern is the battles that are happening in our homes. Every day there are battles happening in homes.

It is a serious issue that must be discussed. These are not battles with guns or weapons but battles with words, attitudes and actions. In most cases these are verbal battles and there are no winners because ill spoken words are hurtful and can do irreparable damage to family relationships. Words between spouses and between parents and children often concern commitments, standards and choices. Children in these homes take sides or are forced to choose sides in these conflicts.

When home has become a battleground filled with constant verbal warfare, it may feel like there is no solution and cause families to give up in despair. In these circumstances the situation must be placed into God's hands and we must let the battle be the Lord's. The key is a willingness to turn to Him in faith and submit to His will and His direction.

We have said it so many times and we repeat it now. The first and foremost responsibility that a family has, beginning with the spouses on their wedding day, is to make a commitment to God. Without a commitment to God families will sooner or later become dysfunctional and they will fall apart.

In the verse above from Psalms we read that David made a commitment to God and as a result God armed him with strength for the battle he was set to face. The same can be true for us if we have our faith and trust in God. Our Lord will guide us through every battle we face if we put our trust in Him.

In I Samuel 17 we read about one of the most famous battles ever. It was the battle between David and Goliath. David fully understood what this battle was all about. The chief issue was that the Philistines were challenging the Lord by confronting the Lord's people. We all know the story, but what we can learn about this battle today is that David prayed to God, asked for His protection and then proceeded with confidence knowing God would give him victory.

We can have the same confidence that David had, but we must be prepared. In our lives Satan seeks to destroy a family's relationship with God. We need to prepare by reading the Bible daily and communicating to God daily through prayer. The result will be that each day we will grow spiritually and God will answer our prayers and go before us in everything we do.

TODAY'S WORD FOR APRIL 4

UNITY

Behold, how good and how pleasant it is for brethren to dwell together in unity. Psalm 133:1

Psalm 133 is David's Psalm of praise for brotherly unity. As King of God's chosen people, the Israelites, David desired that his people live in unity as true children of God. David recognized and praised unity as being good and pleasant. While David may have used the Psalm to call for national unity, that could only happen with a foundation of spiritual unity. This Psalm was sung by the Jewish pilgrims as they traveled to one of their three great feasts each year.

In John 10:30 John quotes Jesus in saying, "I and My Father are one." In this verse Jesus is emphasizing that while He was here on earth, He had unity with God the Father. Jesus often referred to those that believed in Him as sheep. In this verse Jesus was explaining that the Father and Son are unified in their commitment to the perfect protection and preservation of Jesus' sheep.

Jesus' great desire for His disciples was that they would become one, like the Father and the Son are one, so that through their unity they would be a powerful witness of God's love. In Jesus' prayer for His disciples, He prayed for all future believers that, "all of them may be one, Father, just as You are in Me, that they also may be in us, so the world may believe You sent me." (John 17:21)

The whole world is in turmoil and divided. The same is true for many of our homes. We need to recognize that this is not of God. He is not the author of turmoil and confusion. This is Satan doing his work in our homes and in our world. It is God's desire that we dwell together as believers in Him and in unity.

Bringing unity into our homes is a real challenge to parents because of all of the many outside influences. Unity begins with Christ-like love. A family must stand together and put the Lord first in their individual lives and in the family or unity cannot be attained. No one can overcome the evils of the world without God. Many individuals and families try, but without God they fail.

Christ-like love produces an inward heart of unity. Unity requires a God-given desire to work together for common goals. There is no room for selfishness if there is to be a spirit of oneness in the family. The philosophy of one living with a "ME" attitude is that it is all about "ME" and what "I" want. This is the exact opposite of Christ's example and teaching.

The apostle Paul in Philippians chapter 2 verses 1-2, challenges those who love Christ to be of the same mind, show the same love, be united in spirit and show humility in all they do. Paul is describing people here that are knit together in harmony, having the same desires, passions and ambitions. He is suggesting that believers in Jesus come along side of others and be encouragers, comforters, counselors and exhorters just like Jesus does for His own. This is a formula that works if you are truly seeking to restore unity in your home.

TODAY'S WORD FOR APRIL 5

APPRECIATION

Now to God and Father be glory forever and ever. Greet every saint in Christ Jesus. The brethren who are with me greet you. Philippians 4:20-21

Paul is closing his letter to the church at Philippi (above verses) and has one more item to cover that we can learn from. He expresses his appreciation to God and to his fellow believers. It is interesting to note that he says, "Every saint," referring to individual saints, rather than to all as a group.

This doxology in verse 20 is Paul's praise in direct response to the great truth that God supplies all the needs of the saints. This is Paul's praise to the character of God and His faithfulness. Paul wants to remind us that God is to be praised as God, the Creator and Sovereign ruler of the universe. Secondly, Paul wants to remind us that God is to be praised because He is our Father. By praising God we show Him our appreciation for all that He does for us.

As believers, God has adopted us as His sons and daughters. In spite of this, so many believers find reasons to criticize, grumble, and complain about how God does things. Where is the appreciation for God and what He has done for us?

There is so much that we as believers need to be thankful for. We need to show our appreciation for who God is and all that He has given us. In I Chronicles 16:25 we read, "For great is the Lord and most worthy of praise." Praise is how we show our appreciation toward God. When we truly appreciate God we will give God all the glory as Paul did. Appreciation for God and for others changes our attitude and our outlook on life and the way we treat others.

In the world today very few people show appreciation to anybody or for anything. In fact, when you even suggest to certain people that they should try to be an encourager they look at you in a way that seems to say, "Are you serious?" There is an even greater concern. Children show very little appreciation to their parents. This is because they are not taught appreciation. Spouses show very little appreciation to one another and this is what the children see and follow.

In the workplace hard work and a job well done often go without a word of appreciation from a superior. A worker needs to be encouraged and encouragement typically results in more and better work. Instead, most workers strive to do only what is necessary to make themselves look good.

As a child of God you should always be mindful to show your appreciation to others and not take what they do for you for granted. When we appreciate others it changes their attitude toward us.

The Apostle Paul, in his letters, sets an example for all fellow believers, teaching them to show appreciation first and foremost to God. This appreciation is for God because He has provided for us all that we have and all that we need in spite of the fact that we are mere sinners saved by grace and unworthy of His great love.

TODAY'S WORD FOR APRIL 6

WORD

Faith comes from hearing and hearing by the Word of God. Romans 10:17

Word is a term for the sounds that come from one's mouth. It also is used as a name for the Bible and what the scripture uses to refer to Jesus.

The Bible is called the Word of God because it is God's written Word to us. In II Timothy 3:16 it reads, "All scripture is God-breathed." This means that it was written by believers as God revealed His person and His plan to them.

It is important to note that this inspiration applies only to the original writings of scripture, not the Bible writers. There are no inspired scripture writers, only inspired scripture. The Bible is not a collection of stories or myths of human ideas about God. It is the Word of God.

God gave us His Word, the Bible, to teach us, correct us, rebuke us, and to train us in righteousness (II Timothy 3:16). We can be sure it is true because it is the Word of God. We need to realize that when words from the scripture speak to us, it is God speaking. Proverbs 30:5 says that God's Word is pure and flawless. This clarifies for us, if we had any doubt, that God's Word does not contain the uncertainty of human speculation, but the certainty of divine revelation. John 17:17 clearly says that God's Word is truth.

Jesus is also called the "Word." In Revelation 17:13, John writes, "His name is the Word of God." John 1:1-2 reads, "In the beginning was the Word, and the Word was with God and the Word was God. He was in the beginning with God." The Word is the first of all words from God, and secondly the Word is God, His Son Jesus Christ.

So there are many different meanings for the term "Word." We have talked about the Word being God, and His Son and the Words of God. But there are also the words that come from our mouths. Sometimes these words are good and at other times they are considered bad. Words do speak volumes about the person that says them. Thus, it is so important for parents especially to watch what words they use in their conversations because their children are watching.

In James 3:2-8 we are reminded that the tongue can be a wicked weapon. James says in verse 10, "out of the same mouth come praise and cursing." One of the 10 commandments clearly states that we are not to take the name of the Lord in vain. When children hear their parents using foul language and disrespecting the name of God, they will feel it is acceptable for them to do the same.

The tongue can also serve a very useful purpose. We can use our words to praise our Lord and Father in heaven. This is what children need to hear from their parents. In Ephesians 4:29, the apostle Paul advises us to let no corrupt word proceed out of our mouth, but to only use the words that would be helpful for building others up according to their needs. Just stop and think how many times you have been hurt because of words that have come out of someone's mouth.

TODAY'S WORD FOR APRIL 7

CONSCIENCE

How much more shall the blood of Christ, who through the eternal Spirit offered Himself without spot to God, cleanse your conscience from dead works to serve the living God! Hebrews 9:14

But sanctify the Lord God in your hearts, and always be ready to give a defense to everyone who asks you a reason for the hope that is in you, with meekness and fear; having a good conscience, that when they defame you as evildoers, those who revile your good conduct in Christ may be ashamed. I Peter 3:15-16

Have you been concerned about whether you can trust your conscience? After all, we often base our decisions in life on feelings of right or wrong. Our conscience does give us a sense of right or wrong and it is good to listen to our conscience.

In the verse above the writer of Hebrews reminds us that we need to cleanse our conscience from dead works. In other words, make sure that we have removed from our lives and our thinking the evil ways and thoughts of this world we live in.

Peter reminds us in the verse above, that when we speak to others in defense of our faith, we must be sure that we can speak with a clear conscience. Non-believers look for any opportunity to point out misconduct in the life of a believer so they can criticize the believer's faith. That is why every believer must be sure that they are living according to God's ways and not the sinful ways of the world. Our words will carry no weight with others if the way we live contradicts what we say we believe.

The first and foremost requirement that one must meet in order to trust your conscience is that you believe in Jesus and call Him your Lord and Savior. Secondly, the Word of God must be the basis of all of your conduct in life. This can only be a reality if you spend time daily not only reading the Bible, but applying it to your life.

You can trust your conscience when you have made it your daily desire and priority to obey God. As you read God's Word you will hear Him talking to you and you need to use your conscience to guide you in obedience. God will also use your conscience to warn you when you are not following His will. When your conscience sounds an alarm you need to respond immediately. When you feel guilty it is important to reverse your direction and get back on track. Your conscience is often a warning system and you know it has been activated if you feel guilty.

God uses your conscience to compel you to repent for your disobedience. It is the work of your conscience that makes you aware of sin and leads you to repentance. When you have experienced God's forgiveness and are seeking to follow Him, you can trust your conscience to cause you to do what is right.

When you put your faith and trust in the Lord and communicate daily with him, you will be able to walk with the confidence that God will use your conscience to keep you on the path of righteousness.

TODAY'S WORD FOR APRIL 8

SUCCESS

This Book of the Law shall not depart from your mouth, but you shall meditate in it day and night, that you may observe to do according to all that is written in it. For then you will make your way prosperous, and then you will have good success. Joshua 1:8

In the verse above God has given us the key to how we, as believers, can have success in our lives. It refers to the Book of the Law, God's Word and we must read it and study it daily so that we may know it and put it into practice.

It is not enough just to know God's Word; we must observe it and apply it to our life so that what we say and do is based on the words and lessons we have learned from it. Joshua writes that we need to meditate on God's Word day and night.

The end result of following God's instruction is that "you will have good success." You will not have just "success," but "good success." It is only through our obedience to God's Word that we will have success as God defines success.

Solomon advises us to commit our plans to the Lord if we want success. "Commit to the Lord whatever you do and your plans will succeed" (Proverbs 16:32). When we commit our plans to the Lord we are putting our trust in God for His guidance and giving Him control of our lives.

Several thoughts come to our mind that will help us as believers have success in our lives as God wants us to have.

First, we must always take responsibility for our actions.

Second, we must be willing to work for what we want in life. It will not just come to us on a silver platter. God expects us to make good use of our time.

Third, do not waste your time fighting for something you cannot change.

Fourth, admit when you are wrong and accept the consequences. A successful person always admits wrong and God always honors that decision.

Fifth, do not nurse a grudge and refuse to give forgiveness or to ask for forgiveness. Holding grudges with people will always hinder success.

Sixth, always be generous to those in need. So many people today show no generosity but only think of themselves. God will honor those who are generous to those in need.

Seventh, let your mouth always be used to give a word of kindness. Being kind to others is honored by God and appreciated by the one you show kindness to.

Eighth, refuse to wallow in self pity. When you are wronged or something does not go your way, look at the bright side and move on with a positive attitude.

Ninth, always be willing to listen. Put aside your own agenda when you are talking to people and listen to what they are saying. God will honor you with success when you listen to others, show concern for their needs and seek to help them.

Finally, God keeps His promises and He will bless you beyond anything you could ever imagine. God expects us to work as if everything depends on us, but pray knowing everything depends on Him.

TODAY'S WORD FOR APRIL 9

DEEDS

And whatever you do in word or deed, do all in the name of the Lord Jesus, giving thanks to God the Father through Him. Colossians 3:17

Sincere acceptance and belief in Christ as our Savior will bring about a change in our behavior and in our attitude. It is not enough to just say we believe. Our conduct should back up our words. As believers, when we become a new creation in Christ, it should be evident by our deeds. Many times we are judged according to our actions just as much as our words.

The apostle Paul speaks about what the heart of the believer must be like. He begins in verses 15-16 of Colossians 3 by saying that the believer's heart must be ruled first by the call of God to salvation, and then the peace of God which comes when we dwell on the Words of Christ.

With this in mind Paul goes on in verse 17 to tell us that as believers we are Christ's representatives and every aspect of our life reflects on the name of Christ. He is telling us that our words and deeds need to exemplify Christ at all times.

We as believers have a choice. No one speaks or acts for us. Whether we speak and act for Christ therefore is our choice. The command is made clear in the verse above, and that is that we are to, in our words and deeds, do everything in the name of Christ. The choice is ours.

Paul tells us that we are to act and speak in the name of Jesus. What does he mean? First of all, the name of Christ is the only name that God accepts in His presence. Therefore, we are to live with the sole purpose of bringing honor and glory to the name of Christ.

In Titus 3:1 we read where Paul tells Titus to remind the believers that they need to be subject to their earthly rulers, to be obedient and ready to do every good deed that they can. What Paul is saying is that being respectful and obedient to human authorities is part of their Christian testimony to the world. Christians are to exercise their Godly virtues, including doing good deeds, in their dealings with everyone.

To be what Christ wants us to be we must put all of our trust in the name of Christ and our total dependence on Him. We need to claim the name of Christ in all that we say and do. We must remember that non-believers are watching. We represent Christ in everything we say and do so we must do nothing to dishonor Christ. When we speak, Christ should fill our conversation. When we act Christ should be upheld and glorified by our behavior.

The bottom line is that as believers we need to glorify God with our words and our deeds. Non-believers watch carefully and are ready to criticize a believer's sincerity and love for the Lord if they see just one misstep.

TODAY'S WORD FOR APRIL 10

STUDY

Be diligent to present yourself approved to God, a worker who does not need to be ashamed, rightly dividing the word of truth. II Timothy 2:15

The law of the Lord is perfect, converting the soul; the testimony of the Lord is sure, making wise the simple. Psalm 19:7

We feel that there is a great need to a remind all of us that we need to do a better job of studying God's Word. Many sincere professing Christians are spiritually starving, or spiritually ill, because they have never thought seriously about the quality of their Bible study.

If our physical diet is not well balanced, or if our digestive systems are not functioning properly, our bodies will decline in health and eventually will starve. Someone that is starving spiritually must regularly eat nourishing spiritual food, which is the Word of God.

We would like to suggest several important basics for you to consider if you would like to have an effective Bible study. To begin, you must know what the Bible says about itself. In the verse above from Psalm 19:7 we are told that the law (the Bible) is perfect. It is the Word of God and without error. The Bible is clear that it was written for us by God. In the Old Testament alone the Bible asserts over 3000 times that God spoke what is written in it. God's purpose in giving us His Word was to reveal Himself to all mankind.

We need to know what God intended the Bible to do for us. The Bible is not only the book from God but is the book about God. In it we learn that He is our creator, our sustainer, our judge and our hope while we are in this world and for eternity.

We need to know that the Bible stands above all human options. It is the inspired Word of God so it saves us from listening to the babble of all human creations.

God's Word is truth. Perhaps the greatest lie that Satan gives us is that there is no such thing as truth. But the fact is, that Jesus is truth! When we study the Bible we need to understand that not only did every word in the Bible originate with God in heaven, but that most of its contents deal with how God's truth relates to the way we are to conduct our lives on this earth. As we study God's Word we need to pray that the Holy Spirit will illuminate the truth and how we are to apply it.

It is imperative that you develop a method of Bible study that is systematic and thorough (II Timothy 2:15). The Word of God will shape our opinions and give us direction for our lives if we allow God to work in us as we study.

Finally, Paul tells Timothy in II Timothy 2:2 to commit what he had heard from Paul to other faithful men who would be able to teach others. Thus the Gospel was passed from generation to generation. This is another reason why Bible study is so important. It equips us to teach others the truths of the Bible.

TODAY'S WORD FOR APRIL 11

CREATOR

Remember now your creator in the days of your youth, before the difficult days come, and the years draw near when you say, I have no pleasure in them. Ecclesiastics 12:1

There are many people today that question the fact that God created the world. The Bible is very clear on this. In the very first verse of the Bible, Genesis 1:1, we are told that in the beginning <u>God</u> created the heavens and the earth.

If we believe that the Bible is the Word of God and was written without error, you must believe that God created the world we live in. If you doubt this fact you are saying that the Bible may not be true, and it is not the Word of God, and you make Jesus a liar and not our Lord and Savior.

The Biblical record of creation asserts that the world was created recently. Recent means thousands of years and not millions. God created the world out of nothing. Even though God is eternal, His creation of the world marked the beginning of the universe and space.

God created this world in six days and the scripture tells us that He then rested on the seventh day. In six days he created the heavens and the earth, light and darkness, waters and the dry land, grass and trees, the moon and the stars, the fish of the sea and the living creatures on the land (animals). In addition to the fact that God created the heavens and the earth, He also created man. In Genesis 1:27, God's Word tells us that God created man in His own image; in the image of God He created both male and female. Yes, God is our creator and everything we have today is because of God.

As parents we need to teach our children about creation as outlined in the Word of God. It is the responsibility of parents to teach creation to our children so they are well prepared for the onslaught of evolution theory they will face in school and later in the work place.

Solomon advises in Ecclesiastics 12:1 to acknowledge God as our creator in our youth. Honoring God as our creator and Lord early in life can make a real difference in the direction of one's life and will help a person avoid "difficult days." Also, Solomon is reminding us that we are God's property so we should serve Him from the start of our years, not wait until the end of our years when our service would be very limited.

Creation is a very critical issue for families today. The world and everything in it is evidence that God exists. We ask, "How does anyone look upon the wonders of creation and not believe there is a God who created it just as recorded in Genesis?"

We do not have the option of picking and choosing what we want to believe or disbelieve in the Bible. We urge parents and children to study the Bible and study what the Bible says about our creator and how He created not only the heavens and the earth, but each one of us.

TODAY'S WORD FOR APRIL 12

SUPPLY

And my God shall supply all your need according to His riches in glory by Christ Jesus. Philippians 4:19

Paul wrote the book of Philippians from prison. He was often in great need and the church at Philippi had generously and sacrificially sent support to him. In Philippians 4:19 (above) Paul is assuring the church that God will supply all of their material needs. Their material means had no doubt been depleted because they had given so heavily to the church and Paul was encouraging them.

When Paul says, "God will supply all your need according to His riches" he is assuring the church that God would give increase to them in proportion to His infinite resources. God will supply not just what we need materially, but what we need physically (strength), emotionally (encouragement) and spiritually (faith).

We have everything we have because God supplied it to us. Parents need to teach their children that everything they have and see belongs to God. Children often see things they want as something they need and they should be taught the difference between "wants" and "needs." This is difficult because many adults do not discern between what is a "need' and what is merely a "want."

Fortunately, we have a wise and discerning heavenly Father who knows what is best for us. Jesus said that our Father in heaven knows what we need before we even ask (Matthew 6:8). It is important for us to learn that God will supply all of our needs but He will do it His way and in His timing.

When times are tough, when economies are slow and when financial concerns seem to flood our minds, many people start to complain. God does not want us to complain, but He does want us to present our needs to Him and He has promised to supply all of our needs if we put our complete trust in Him.

That word "IF" is the key word for those of us that believe in Jesus. God will supply our needs, but we must honor His commandments and honor Him. That is the "IF" that most people miss.

God has supplied so much for us. He sent His only Son to pay the penalty for our sins. He sent His Holy Spirit to comfort us as we serve Him. He supplies us with health, talents and abilities to serve Him. And He provides us with the certainty of spending eternity with Him in heaven.

There are several verses we need to memorize and apply to our daily lives. In Luke 6:38 it reads, "Give and it shall be given to you; good measure, pressed down, shaken together, and running over." In Matthew 21:22, "Whatever things you ask in prayer, believing, you will receive." In Luke 11:9 it reads, "Ask and it will be given you, seek and you will find, knock and it will be opened to you."

Jesus gives us key words in these verses. Each word demands action on our part. If we act as He suggests, just think what God will do in supplying all our needs: GIVE, ASK IN PRAYER, BELIEVE, SEEK and KNOCK.

TODAY'S WORD FOR APRIL 13

ETERNITY

That whoever believes in Him should not perish but have eternal life. John 3:15

For the wages of sin is death but the gift of God is eternal life in Christ Jesus our Lord. Romans 6:23

Have you ever tried to imagine what eternity is like? It is very difficult for our finite minds to grasp the concept of life going on and on with no end. On earth, things have a beginning and an ending. When we have to stand in a line we say it seems like an eternity, but really it is relatively short and it has an ending. Our life on this earth has a beginning and an ending, but when we leave this earth we have an eternity ahead of us with absolutely no ending.

"Where will you spend your eternity?" This question demands the most important decision you will have to make during your entire lifetime. We answered that question before we were ten years old. The two verses above gives us a choice to make and gives us all we need to know about eternity.

The first choice you can make is to accept Jesus as your personal Savior and receive God's gift of eternal life. God freely offers this to you because Jesus died on the cross to pay the penalty for your sins and now He is in heaven preparing a place for you for eternity.

The second choice you have is to do nothing about Jesus and ignore the issue. Ignoring it does not make the issue go away. A non-decision about Jesus is still a decision, a choice to spend an eternity in Hell. We hear it said over and over again, "I will make that decision later," but later may be too late.

And the third choice is to reject Jesus and God. This choice comes with a price, as the verse above says, "the wages of sin is death," so without that personal relationship with God you will spend an eternity in Hell.

You do not hear many sermons in church today about Hell. It is not a popular subject and pastors are fearful it would turn people away from church. People just do not want to face the fact that their unforgiven sins will bring condemnation. It is impossible to preach the gospel message of salvation through Jesus Christ and ignore the fact that there is a real Hell. Many pastors do preach on Heaven and Hell and their churches are growing. The message of Heaven or Hell stirs people to make a decision for Jesus and then stay in the church so they can grow in Christ.

People are searching for real hope and peace in their lives and the only way to have real peace and joy is to know where one will spend eternity. The decision of accepting or rejecting Jesus is the most vital decision one can make. Nothing is more relevant than eternity. Our question to you today is: "Have you made that choice?" Your eternity is at stake. Will you spend eternity with Jesus in Heaven or with the devil in Hell?

TODAY'S WORD FOR APRIL 14

GUIDANCE

Show me Your ways, O Lord; teach me Your paths. Lead me in Your truth and teach me, for You are the God of my salvation; on You I wait on all the day. Psalm 25:4-5

Who is the man that fears the Lord? Him shall He teach in the way He chooses. Psalm 25:12

When David was writing these verses in Psalms he was dealing with the heavy issues of life, avoiding denial and affirming dependence. He was reminding us to put our trust in God and rely on His guidance when we face trouble or troublemakers.

When you need to make a decision, big or small, it is important to wait on God for His guidance, direction and timing. We want to share with you four ways that you can take an active role in the process while you wait on God.

First, as we wait, we need to examine our heart, asking the Holy Spirit to expose any wrongs in our life. If the Holy Spirit brings anything to you it is important that you take care of that sin immediately. You accomplish this by confessing, repenting and doing whatever is necessary to correct the situation. We cannot expect God to work in our lives if we allow sin to remain. In order to receive God's full blessing, we must deal with the sin in our life.

Second, when we seek direction, we need to learn how to listen patiently and attentively for the Lord to give us the guidance we are praying for. Patience takes a great deal of strength especially when you feel time is of the essence. We can also find it very difficult to wait on the Lord because we want quick answers and a quick fix. Our timing, however, is not the Lord's timing and if you rush ahead of God, you may not only miss His will but miss a special blessing that He has for you.

Third, be open to alternatives. Sometimes we miss God's guiding hand because we want the Lord to do it "our way." We cannot allow ourselves to be tempted by our feelings and our own logic. God will give us the guidance we ask for and we can be sure it is the best for us because it will be in accordance with His perfect will.

Finally, the answer to our request for guidance sometimes requires our involvement. For example, if you are out of work and trusting God to provide a job for you, God expects you to actively look for a job. Just don't sit back and pray reminding God of your need. Waiting is not an excuse for inaction or laziness.

How can you be sure that you are making right decisions? What do you need to do to hear the voice of God responding to your need for guidance? We need to clear the pathway. We already mentioned the need to get rid of the sin in our life, but we also need to be willing to make our desires secondary to His.

You need to search the scriptures. Many people take time to pray but how can God communicate to you if you do not read His Word? The Word of God has an answer for every need and the Holy Spirit will always point us in the right direction if we seek and wait on Him.

TODAY'S WORD FOR APRIL 15

POVERTY

He who oppresses the poor reproaches his Maker, but he who honors Him has mercy on the needy. Proverbs 14:31

One who is gracious to a poor man lends to the Lord, and He will repay him for his good deed. Proverbs 19:17

He, who shuts his ear to the cry of the poor, will also cry himself and not be heard. Proverbs 21:13

Do you understand that it offends God, our creator when we neglect the poor? This is because they are part of His creation and He cares for them. It is God's will that believers show concern for the poor. It is His desire that all believers do all they can to help the poor. This would include praying for them, helping them through a need and providing spiritual and physical food for them.

Read the three verses above and notice that when we do not help the poor we "reproach our Maker." Also notice that if we are gracious to the poor we will be repaid by our Maker. And finally look at what will happen if we shut our ears to the poor, our Maker will not hear us in our time of need.

All of our married lives we have had the privilege of working to help the poor. We had our first contact with really poor children just several months after we were married. It began for us in South Korea after the Korean War where we set up over 140 orphanages for World Vision. These orphanages were needed to house and care for the poorest of the poor children. They were the victims of the war and many of them were known as GI babies. We knew that God loved them and needed us to make sure they had places to live so He could care for them. These few short months in Korea affected us so much that for over 55 years we have been doing all we can to help the poor, both physically and spiritually.

Statistics help demonstrate the problem we face in our world today. We are told that last year over 16 million people, mostly children, died from hunger. Also last year, over 10 million children died before their fifth birthday.

These are the numbers, but they are much more than numbers. Each number represents one child loved by God. This is why there are so many verses in His Word that tell us to reach out and help the poor.

As you read the verses from Proverbs again, do you wonder, "What can I do about this?" Most people will react by saying something like, "I am too busy," "I do not have any time." Or "I do not have the money." But God says we must help.

We can show mercy by volunteering at a church feeding center or a community soup kitchen. Maybe you can help a father find a job. How about taking a meal to a family that you know is hurting? Ask a few friends, and someone will lead you to a family who needs a helping hand. Accepting this responsibility honors God.

TODAY'S WORD FOR APRIL 16

FOLLOW

Do not follow the crowd in doing wrong. Exodus 23:2

The Lord said to Moses, Speak to the Israelites and say to them: I am the Lord your God. You must not do as they do in Egypt, where you used to live, and you must not do as they do in the land of Canaan where I am bringing you. DO NOT FOLLOW THEIR PRACTICES. Leviticus 18:1-3

Whosoever serves me must follow me. John 12:26

By definition, to follow means to accept someone as a guide or a leader and to do as they do. People can choose to follow many different leaders but tend, most often, to follow the crowd. There is a real danger in following the crowd. Just because "everyone" is doing something doesn't make it right. Following the crowd will lead us to think as they think and it can cloud our judgment concerning God's standards of what is right and wrong.

God called Moses to the mountain top at Sinai to give him the Ten Commandments. Moses then brought God's instructions to the Israelites to teach them how God wanted them to live their lives. One of God's instructions was, "not to follow the crowd in doing wrong" (Exodus 23:2). Although Moses spoke these words so long ago (1445 BC), this instruction still applies to us today. We must not follow the crowd when they are doing the wrong things. This means we often find ourselves standing all alone.

One of the major issues parents have to deal with in raising their children is their children's desire to follow the crowd. Teenagers want to be like everyone else, dress like everyone else, style their hair like everyone else, do what everyone else does, and on and on the list could go. Teenagers are very vulnerable to pressure.

What does a parent do? Start by evaluating themselves. Are they following the crowd? That is not how God would have them live. Children will follow the example of their parents and will begin to follow their own peer crowd. As parents our actions always speak louder than our words.

God created us to love and serve Him. Jesus said whoever serves Him must follow Him (John 12:26). When Jesus chose His disciples He instructed them to, "Come, follow Me" (Matthew 4:19). When we follow Jesus we must follow Him completely. When Jesus called the two brothers, James and John, they were fishing with their father. Immediately, they left the boat and their father and followed Jesus (Matthew 4:22). They left everything to follow Jesus. We must also follow Jesus according to His commandment to us, "Love the Lord your God with all your heart and with all your soul and with all your mind" (Matthew 22:37). Are we following the crowd or following Jesus?

TODAY'S WORD FOR APRIL 17

PARENTING

Children, obey your parents, for it is right that you should. Honor your father and mother, is the first commandment with a promise attached, in the words: that it may be well with you and that you may live long in the land. You fathers (and mothers), again, must not goad your children to resentment, but give them the instruction, and the correction, which belong to a Christian upbringing. Ephesians 6: 1-4 N.E.B

From the time God created Adam and Eve it was His plan and purpose that children be raised in a family. Sadly, many people have children today but have neglected their parenting responsibilities. Parenting is the rearing of children, which means taking care of them, training them and supporting them to maturity. Proverbs 22:6 tells us to "train a child in the way he should go." Training means developing or forming the habits, the thoughts and the behavior of a child. If it came down to a priority for us, a ministry, a job, a social event or our children, the children always came first. Today only a few families will make that commitment.

Look at the four verses above and you will see several important principles that we need to adhere to as parents and as children. Children have a responsibility to obey and honor their parents and this does not come naturally to a child. They must be taught to be obedient and respectful. Even as adults, we are still someone's child. How do we treat our parents? How can we expect children to obey and honor their parents if they are not taught to do so and do not have Christian role models?

In order to be an effective parent it is necessary to discipline justly and fairly. Parents are advised in Ephesians not to cause resentment in their children but to instruct and correct them in love and with consistency.

Parenting is a daily job and requires time, not just time but scheduled quality time. We learned from our parents that dinner was a good time to keep clear for parenting. It gave our family a time together every day to get to know each other and to build a bond. The result, we believe today, is that they are all very close and communicate regularly with one another. They are a support system for each other.

Being together every night for dinner gave each person a time to talk. We always asked each child to share with us the events of the day, and they did. They shared the good and the bad and asked for prayer concerning troubling issues. It gave us a chance to listen. As parents we became aware of concerns and issues and we could talk further, one on one, with that child when needed. Our children listened to each other and thus became a support system for each other through their crises and issues in life. Even as adults when there is a need, they are there for each other.

Every night we spent time reading the Bible and memorizing scripture. This allowed us to learn to listen to God daily through His Word. The Bible became relevant for each of us and a habit was developed to read God's Word. We closed every dinner with a time of prayer. By doing this we could take to our Lord our concerns and needs and we learned as a family to thank God for all He gave to us.

TODAY'S WORD FOR APRIL 18

FINANCES

Bring all the tithes into the storehouse, that there may be food in My house, and try Me on this, if I will not open for you the windows of heaven and pour out for you such blessing that there will be not room enough to receive it. Malachi 3:10

As we look back on the years before we were married and these 56 years of marriage, we were taught and learned about tithing. What we experienced as a result of faithful tithing has been one of the great blessings of our lives.

We have had conversations with our children and grand-children where they have asked: "How did you make it on the amount of money you received?" We had times of concern as to how we were going to make it financially. We always made it because we always tithed a minimum of 10% to the Lord's work.

The world is full of disorder, but as believers we have the assurance that God is in control. He created the heavens and the earth. He had a purpose and a plan which He carried out with precision and order. We can be certain God has a plan for each one of us and every aspect of our lives is under His scrutiny and under His care.

If we follow God's plan for our finances, He promises to manage our money. That is quite a blessing and most believers do not take God up on His offer. He promises that if we give Him the first tenth of all that we receive, He will provide for all of our needs. This is what we have done consistently, without missing a day, and God has kept His promise and met our every need. It has been amazing to see how God has taken us through many valleys and over many mountains.

When you see the promise that God has made, the blessing that He promises us, and understand His unfailing faithfulness, what keeps you from obeying His command? The reason is unbelief. People ask, "What if God does not come through?" Or "What if I give it away and then do not have enough to pay my bills?"

God's response to this is, "Try Me." God challenges us to put Him to the test. Everything we have comes from God. God asks that we give Him a tithe to advance His Kingdom then put our trust in Him to provide for our needs.

We have been blessed to visit Israel including trips to the Jordan River and the Dead Sea. These two bodies of water serve as an example of two vivid financial plans. The Jordan is surrounded by trees and greenery but then around the Dead Sea nothing lives. When the water flows into the Dead Sea it stays there because there is no outlet. Soon the salts accumulate and poison the water. The Dead Sea can be likened to the world's financial system in which you accumulate and preserve all your wealth. The result is self-centered stagnation. Hoarding makes lives spiritually unfruitful and hinders the good works God wants to do.

The Lord's financial plan is like the Jordan, a river that moves continually. As God's provisions pass into our lives, we pass them on to others and God continues to give. God supplies enough to live and enough to give.

TODAY'S WORD FOR APRIL 19

MOTIVE

Do you know where your fights and arguments come from? Don't they come from your desires that battle within you? You want something but don't get it. You kill and covet, but cannot have what you want. You quarrel and fight. You do not have, because you do not ask God. When you do ask, you do not receive because you ask with wrong motives. James 4:1-3

We remember our children arguing or fighting over a toy that they wanted. The argument usually went: "I had it first." "No you didn't." "I was playing with it before you were." "No you weren't." "Yes I was." Does that sound familiar? When children fight over a toy we see it as the result of immaturity. Even if you do not have children and haven't experienced their childish ways, no doubt you can remember arguing and fighting with a sibling or a friend when you were a child.

Fighting and quarrelling is not limited to children. Fighting and quarreling is a major problem in our world today. It is causing over half of marriages today to end in divorce. Fighting often leads to killing. Many are in prison because they carried a quarrel too far. Wars between nations have been going on for centuries and most begin with a quarrel of some sort.

James asks a thought provoking question in the verses we have written above. He asks us what motivates us to fight and quarrel. Then he gives us the answer. James says that quarrelling comes from the evil desires that battle within us. We want something but do not get it.

Our sinful nature compels us to want more than we have. We want more money, more possessions, more power and anything else that we think will elevate our status in life. Unfortunately, there are people that, when they do not get the things they want, fight for them, even to the point of killing for them.

James does give us a remedy. He tells us that we do not have because we do not ask God and we cannot receive because we ask with the wrong motives. God is the remedy for quarreling and fighting because He is the only one that can help us get rid of our selfish motives and desires. God cannot help until we are willing to submit ourselves to Him and ask Him to change us, to conform us to His will for us. He desires that we ask Him to forgive our sins, that we accept Him as our Savior and that we trust Him to give us what we need. Only then can we pray and ask God for what we desire and expect to receive what we ask for.

The apostle Paul talked to the people in the church of Corinth about the believer's motives for helping others. There are situations when your help could be hindering or hurting the person you are trying to help. If you are concerned that you may be over stepping your welcome with someone consider your motives. Then ask God to help you show the kind of love that "suffers long and is kind, not puffed up; does not behave rudely or does not seek its own, is not provoked, thinks no evil" (I Corinthians 13:4-5). Does your motivation to help come from a pure heart?

TODAY'S WORD FOR APRIL 20

PREJUDICE

And He has made from one blood every nation of men to dwell on all the face of the earth, and has determined their pre-appointed times and the boundaries of their dwellings. Acts 17:26

Prejudice is a serious problem in our world today. Prejudice can be based on the color of one's skin, one's culture, one's social standing, one's financial status, one's talents, education, religious belief, or any number of things that set one person apart from another. God's Word has made it clear that prejudice of any kind is not acceptable. Prejudice grows out of pride and causes people to look down on others they consider inferior to themselves.

In the verse above we are reminded all men and women are created equal in God's sight since all descended from one man, Adam. This teaching was a blow to the national pride of the Greeks, who believed that all non-Greeks were barbarians.

Likewise the Jews thought they were superior to others. Jewish males recited this prayer every morning: "Lord, I thank You that I am not a gentile, a slave, or a woman." But this was contrary to what Jesus was preaching to His disciples and to the masses that came to listen to Him. Jesus came to make all believers one in Christ, because we are all joint heirs in Christ. No one is more privileged than anyone else nor is anyone better than anyone else.

In the verse above the writer of Acts says, "Having determined their appointed times and their boundaries of their dwellings." God's sovereignty determines when and where we are born and thus who we are.

We live a life of faith when we are a child of God. Prejudice and faith cannot coexist. Prejudice destroys faith and faith destroys prejudice. In James 2:1-6 he writes that there must be no partiality, no prejudice in a believer's life. If a person is prejudiced against another person for any reason he or she is not a true follower of Jesus. As believers we are to love one another.

We cause real sorrow when we dishonor others through prejudice or bigotry. Every human being is created in the image of God and worthy of honor. When, by our own prejudice, we demean someone, we are wounding another human being at the deepest level. We are all of the same family, the family of God. God expects us, as His children, to be treasured and cherished by one another. He desires we show respect to all people because everyone was created by Him and in His very image.

The sad fact about prejudice is that it is usually passed from parent to child. Children learn from their parents. As believers, we have the responsibility to make sure that we do not have prejudice against others. When we live our lives in this manner, our children will learn from our example and prejudice will not be a major issue in their lives.

TODAY'S WORD FOR APRIL 21

GOOD DEEDS

In everything set them an example by doing what is good. In your teaching show integrity, seriousness, and soundness of speech that cannot be condemned. Titus 2:7-8

Titus was a Greek and most likely was led to Christ by Paul. Titus was taught and nurtured in the truth of the gospel by Paul. Titus accompanied Paul on some of his missionary journeys. He worked with Paul in Crete and when Paul had to leave, he left Titus to oversee the church and to disciple the people in the church.

The degenerate culture and the crude conduct of the people had a bad influence on the believers. False teachers were undermining the church with false doctrine.

Paul knew that he had left Titus with a tough assignment. He was concerned about his churches and about the young pastors. He continued to support them with advice and admonition. The book of Titus was his letter of exhortation to Titus.

Paul was encouraging and instructing the young men (verse 6) to show integrity in their leadership role as teachers in the church. Paul was exhorting Titus that he had a special obligation to exemplify the moral and spiritual qualities of a true believer by being a model of good works. In other words, Titus first needed to live by the moral and spiritual qualities that he was teaching. This also applies to us. We need to live by the standards that we teach and by our example our children learn.

The words "Good Deeds" appear five times in the book of Titus. Paul was teaching Titus that he must be above criticism in how he taught the doctrine that he had learned from Paul. These words are a warning to him and to us as well.

Paul gives Titus a description in 1:16 of those who are "unfit for doing anything good." They claim to know God, but by their actions they deny Him. In chapter two Paul tells Titus to set an example by always doing good. If he preaches sound doctrine it is meaningless if it is not backed by good deeds. Paul then, several times, exhorted Titus to communicate to the believers their responsibility to do good deeds, as Christ did and as the Word of God commands us to do.

As members of a civilized society we keep trying, by our own power, to change people and the way we behave. Society tries to effect change in people. We set tougher laws and boundaries, but people are people and human nature is the same. Someone once said that you can bring a pig into your house but it will not change the pig however it will certainly change your house.

And that is the problem. You cannot within your power change the behavior of your spouse, your children, your friend or anyone at all. You have to change the heart and this can only be done by God. If you want someone to act a certain way you must lead by example. Our good deeds give our words greater impact. People judge the integrity of our words by our deeds. We can't change people but by our example, we can be a witness of God's love and saving grace. In God's perfect timing a heart will be changed.

TODAY'S WORD FOR APRIL 22

PLEASURE

Therefore we also pray always for you that our God would count you worthy of this calling, and fulfill all the good pleasure of His goodness and the work of faith with power. II Thessalonians 1:11

There will be terrible times in the last days; people will be lovers of pleasure rather than lovers of God. II Timothy 3:1-4

We are spending an increasing amount of money each year on pleasure. Statistics tell us that Americans give $35 billion a year to churches and spend $150 billion on pleasure. That is over 4 times more on worldly pleasure than income to churches.

Now we understand that there is nothing evil or wrong with relaxation and recreation, but there is something wrong when the pursuit of pleasure becomes an obsession for a person or a family. It is so easy to get caught up in the frenzy of this life and forget that heaven will be a place of "pleasures forevermore."

Personally, we enjoy the time we set aside for pleasure. Sometimes we are with family and other times it is just the two of us. These are always important moments in our lives because it gives us time to relax, regroup, and get to know family and each other better. It is also an opportunity to look clearly at our priorities and reevaluate them. We also enjoy meeting new people, seeing new sites and going to new places. These are all very important to us personally but at all times we make sure that our relationship with God is not affected by what we are doing.

We are reminded of the account in the book of Nehemiah of the building of the wall around the city of Jerusalem. Nehemiah was a common man who led a comfortable and secure life. He was the cupbearer to the king of Persia. His position gave him the opportunity to take advantage of all the pleasures of the world, but that was not his desire. He was a man who wanted to be used by God. When he heard that the walls and gates of Jerusalem had been broken, it distressed him.

Nehemiah was a man of action and vision and when he saw a need he did something about it. The first thing he did was go to the Lord in prayer. Then he went to the king and asked for permission to go to Jerusalem to rebuild the walls. With the king's approval he went to Jerusalem. He organized the people and assigned them specific sections of the wall and completed the project in just 52 days.

Nehemiah is known as a man of prayer. Eleven times in the book of Nehemiah, we find him praying for direction and guidance. His pleasure was doing the will of God. Later, in Nehemiah 8:9-10, it is written that Nehemiah was governor and Ezra was the priest and scribe of that day. After the people had the scriptures read to them and explained by Ezra they were told to go eat, give portions to those that had nothing prepared and then have pleasure by rejoicing in the Lord.

We should learn that when we communicate with God by reading His Word and praying, we will have pleasure and rejoice in what the Lord is doing through us.

TODAY'S WORD FOR APRIL 23

ADVERSITY

O Lord, how many are my foes! Many are saying to me, God will not deliver him. But You are a shield around me, O Lord; You bestow glory on me and lift up my head. Psalm 3:1-3

Adversity is a fact of life. All of us have often faced difficulties or misfortune in our lives. Sometimes we cause our own troubles, but many suffer adversity through no fault of their own. You have read the story of Joseph in the Old Testament. He knew what it was like to suffer adversity.

Joseph's family moved to the land of Canaan when he was 6 years old. He had 10 older brothers who tended their father's flocks. Joseph's father, Jacob, had made it obvious that Joseph was his favorite son and the brothers were jealous. They hated Joseph. It was 11 years later, when Joseph was 17 that he came home from being with his brothers and shared with his father a bad report. This added fuel to the smoldering fire of animosity toward Joseph.

Joseph, in his immaturity, was not sensitive to his brother's feelings. He was boastful and his brothers could not interact with him without conflict and hostility. The brothers totally rejected Joseph and conspired to sell him into slavery. He was not only cut off from his family and his financial security, but he was taken to a strange land with a different language and strange customs. This was truly adversity for Joseph because he had lost control of his own destiny and was at the mercy of others.

Joseph had lost everything, but he did not lose his faith in God. This was the one thing that he could still control. We read in Genesis 39:2-4 that Joseph kept his faith and his relationship with God. As a result, the Lord was with Joseph and he prospered in spite of his adversity. As the story of Joseph's life unfolds there is no doubt that God was in control and working to fulfill His plan and purpose for Joseph's life.

Joseph did not let adversity keep him from being the man that God wanted him to be. Joseph worked hard and was diligent even in the lowliest jobs. As a result of his integrity and faithfulness the Lord was with him and gave him the success that only God could have given him. Joseph found favor with his master because the master saw that Joseph's God was blessing him. He wanted the same success that Joseph had.

Like Joseph, David knew what it was like to face adversity (Psalms 3). He also kept his faith in God through the adversities he faced in life. God protected David from all of his enemies and continually lifted him above his adversities.

When we face adversity we can learn from Joseph and David. We must remember that God never forgets us nor does He leave us. In the times of our deepest adversities, we need God and we must never lose faith in Him.

TODAY'S WORD FOR APRIL 24

FAILURE

Simon Peter said to the disciples, I am going fishing. They responded by saying that they were going with him. They went and got into the boat and that night they caught nothing. John 21:3

This fishing experience by Peter and the disciples was a total failure. In John 21:3-17 we read about this failure. When the disciples returned from their fishing experience they saw Jesus standing on the shore. (They did not know it was Jesus.)

Jesus asked if they had any fish. They responded saying they had none. Jesus told them, in their time of failure, to cast their nets on the right side of their boat and they would find fish. They followed the instructions and caught so many fish that they were not able to draw in their nets for the weight. That was when John recognized Jesus and said to the others, It is the Lord (John 21:7).

As soon as they came to land they saw fish and bread cooking. Jesus said to the disciples, Come and eat breakfast (John 21:12).

One of the things we felt important to teach our children was that there would be times of failure in their life. No one likes to fail but there can be value in failure. Failure can show us our mistakes. We sometimes learn more from our failures than from our successes. It isn't so much about the failure but how we handle the failure.

Our children had to learn that they might not get 100% on every test at school, they might not win every game in sports and they would not be successful in everything they tried. We admonished them not to let fear of failure keep them from trying and encouraged them when they failed to work harder and try again. We let them know that we supported them in all their endeavors and whether they were successful or they failed we would love them and be there for them.

The disciples fishing venture was a complete failure. This was a low point in the lives of the disciples because although they knew Jesus was risen from the dead and alive, He was no longer with them on a daily basis. The disciples were unsure as to what the future held for them.

It was in that moment of failure that Jesus appeared to Peter and the disciples. He commanded them to try again. When they obeyed and did as Jesus said, they had success. Their net was filled with so many fish they could not haul it into the boat. Jesus fed them and told them to go and, feed my sheep (John 21:15).

We can learn from this lesson how we should respond to failures in our lives. We typically fail because we endeavor to do things all on our own. When we involve the Lord in everything we do, He will lead us so that we will accomplish what He wants.

The good news for us is that Jesus is willing to forgive our failures and calls us back into service with Him. We are not perfect and Jesus knows that. If only perfect people were qualified to serve Him, He wouldn't have anyone to choose from. Although we are imperfect and fail so often, the Lord can still use us if we are willing to be used. Are you willing and wanting to be used of God?

TODAY'S WORD FOR APRIL 25

COVETOUSNESS

And Jesus said to them, Take heed and beware of covetousness, for one's life does not consist in the abundance of the things he possesses. Luke 12: 15

On many occasions we have watched our children and other children playing. Children always seem to want the toy another child is playing with. It doesn't seem to matter there may be a dozen other toys or they could have chosen that toy long before the toy was taken by the other child. The child wants that toy and wants it now, so in most cases they just take it.

As parents we should intervene. Unfortunately, one of the problems with families today is a parent does not intervene at times like this and children develop bad traits that stay with them for a lifetime. It is so important for a parent to know and understand what is right and wrong as well as good or bad for their children. For the most part, parents either do not know or they just do not want to go through the effort of training their child.

Adults are often covetous just like children. We never think of wanting something until we see someone else has it. When we covet what someone else has we are breaking God's Tenth Commandment.

On the internet there is a web page called "The Law of Attraction." This is a popular idea floating around about how to get whatever you want. One must just think and feel what you want to attract. This positive thinking philosophy teaches that the energy of your dominant thoughts "attracts" your circumstances. The theory is the more desire you have for a thing, the greater will be the attractive force exerted toward its attainment, both within yourself and outside of yourself. This sounds like coveting. It seems to teach that you should dwell on the "things" in life that you "want" but do not have. This is certainly not what we learn from the Bible.

Do not get caught up in "Laws" like this because they will distract you from your Christian walk with the Lord. Look to the Bible for all the theories you need. And the Bible says, do not covet (Deuteronomy 5:21).

We are to use our God-given abilities and work to provide for ourselves. As believers, we have good reason to be positive in our thinking, but it is because our heavenly Father understands our needs and meets them. Because He cares for us, we do not have to be anxious (Luke 12: 29-30). In the verse we have written above we are reminded that life does not consist in the abundance of things that we possess, so we make it our aim instead to be rich in God (verse 21).

In this verse above Jesus tells us to, "Take heed and beware of covetousness" because one day, like the rich fool in Luke 12:16-21, we will leave all material possessions behind. When the day comes for us to go to our Heavenly Father we will have more than we ever dreamed. In the meantime, God promises to care for all our needs. We do not need to follow foolish ideas like "The Law of Attraction" when we are a child of God. He has promised to supply all our needs, not all of our wants.

TODAY'S WORD FOR APRIL 26

PAIN

You prepare a table before me in the presence of my enemies; you anoint my head with oil, my cup runs over. Surely goodness and mercy shall follow me all the days of my life; and I will dwell in the house of the Lord forever. Psalm 23:5-6

Growing older gives us aches and pains that we never had to deal with before. We learn to live with these, understanding they are part of getting older. We have, thankfully, not experienced the pain that some of our friends have experienced.

Pain, physical and emotional, affects us. It causes depression and anxiety. On the positive side, pain can make you more sensitive to the pain of others. Pain can help you grow in the Lord because it forces you to lean on Him for comfort.

Often in life when a person goes through a time of suffering and pain they refer to it as going through a deep valley. When everything is going well in a person's life they might refer to it as being on a mountain top of blessing.

In the Bible, valleys symbolize periods of hardship and suffering. In Psalm 23:4 the Psalmist evokes a particularly dangerous and painful image by referring to "the valley of the shadow of death." Spiritual valleys are inevitable in our lives. Even those of great faith in the Lord will experience them.

In times of great pain many feel like they would just as soon die rather than endure any more pain. Even though Job had strong faith in God, his great pain and suffering brought him to such a depth of despair that he said, "Why did I not perish at birth, and die as I came out of the womb?" Job 3:11

People rarely think of suffering or pain as profitable. But when one faces the difficulty and pain of a valley experience, we mature spiritually. We make discoveries about ourselves when we face pain and trials.

Valley experiences also reveal our priorities. God's purpose for us during our pain is to take away from us everything we depend on, our spiritual crutches included, until nothing competes with Jesus' reign in our lives. When we are down and out, the only way to look is up. Crutches and personal bravery that we usually depend on are replaced by a dependence on God. In the verses we have printed above, believers are encouraged to recall that He provides for our needs, "prepare(s) a table before me in the presence of my enemies (pain)", and heals our wounds, "anoint(s) our head with oil."

A good shepherd, in Jesus day, rubbed oil onto the scrapes on his sheep while in the fields. In doing this, the healing began before the animal left the valley floor. When we rely on our Shepherd, Jesus, we experience healing from our pain, a renewed intimacy and a sense of peace that only the Lord can give us.

Many people are facing pain in their lives today from various causes. It may be physical pain, the pain of a dysfunctional marriage or family, or the pain of a lost job, a lost home or some other material item. It could also be the loss of a close relationship with God because the "things" of life are taking priority in one's life.

TODAY'S WORD FOR APRIL 27

CORRECTION

A fool despises his father's instruction, but he who receives correction is prudent. Proverbs 15:5

Do not withhold correction from a child. Proverbs 23:13

As we look back on how we were corrected as children and how we corrected our children, one thing stands out above everything else. When standards and boundaries were set and discipline for breaking those standards or boundaries was made clear, it made correction so much easier.

Correction is needed for people of all ages. This is because we were all born into an evil world. Doing things right is difficult because others, who do not know Jesus, do not have a godly standard of right and wrong. Just because one calls himself a Christian it does not mean that everything that person does is perfect.

Children constantly need to be reminded about the difference between right and wrong. As parents we are not to withhold correction from a child (above verse). Teenagers, most of the time, know when they are doing things that deserve correction and they try to keep what they are doing from being discovered by their parents. They cave in to the pressures of their peers and continue to do what they know they should not be doing. The minute a parent sees one of their children being wrongly influenced by a friend, the parent must step in to rectify the situation.

Not everyone appreciates correction, but David did. He felt indebted to those who corrected him. In Psalm 141:5 he said, "Let the righteous strike me; it shall be a kindness. Let him rebuke me; it shall be as excellent oil; let my head not refuse it."

Correction is a kindness. David suggests that correction is an act of loyalty. Loyal friends will correct one another, even when it is painful and disruptive to relationships. It is one of the ways we show love and help one another to grow stronger in the Lord. Solomon wrote in Proverbs 27:6, "Faithful are the wounds of a friend." A true friend will give advice according to what a person needs to hear, not what they want to hear.

It takes grace, especially for a loyal friend, to give godly correction. But it takes even more grace to receive it. In II Samuel 12:13 David received correction from Nathan concerning his sin of adultery with Bathsheba. David immediately confessed his sin and repented. But for many of us, we would be inclined to refuse correction under similar circumstances. We resent interference and do not want to be found out concerning things we are ashamed of and do not want to be known.

Growth through grace for the believer sometimes comes through the kind but unpleasant correction of a loyal friend. Think for a moment of times in your life a loyal friend has corrected you. Did you admit that you needed to be corrected and allow the correction to be of help spiritually? We should never refuse correction even if it is painful. Correction brings wisdom.

TODAY'S WORD FOR APRIL 28

MATERIALISM

Do not lay up for yourselves treasures on earth, where moth and rust destroy and where thieves break in and steal; but lay up for yourselves treasures in heaven, where neither moth nor rust destroys and where thieves do not break in and steal. For where your treasure is, there your heart will be also. Matthew 6:19-21

The desire to have "THINGS" is prevalent in our society. In most cases the motive is wrong. It is important to note that there is nothing wrong with a person or a family having "THINGS" as long as one understands that material things last only for a short time and mean nothing for eternity.

Money is one "thing" that is considered materialistic. Money in itself is not evil, but it is the love of money that is "the root of all evil." (I Timothy 6:10) The love of money will turn us away from pursuing God and storing up our treasures in heaven.

In Matthew six (above), Jesus was delivering His Sermon on the Mount to the masses. He made it very clear that our first priority, as believers, while we are living on this earth is to spend our time building up treasures in heaven.

We are reminded of dear friends who God blessed with great wealth. The husband and wife had worked hard operating several businesses and God had honored them with riches. They had their priorities right because they invested their money in missions, Sunday schools, churches and spiritual things, not on the material things that would make their lives more comfortable. They had two cars; both more than 15 years old and they had lived in a small house for over 40 years. They chose to live frugally so they could do more of the Lord's work.

One of our children was reflecting back over the years in a conversation with us. She commented that she understood that we were involved in Christian ministries and thus had limited income. She went on to comment that none of her five siblings, when growing up, ever missed a meal and really had all their desires met. Yes, they may have wanted new clothes instead of having to wear hand me downs from the older child, but they were always clean and always looked appropriate. Dottie stretched the food budget by being very creative. Everyone one was happy and we all had the same goal, to store up our treasures in heaven.

Times have changed and many things we would have considered luxuries are now considered necessities. Advances in technology have made all kinds of new things available. Computers, cell phones, HD TV's, iPods, just to name a few. These are wonderful "things" to have as long as they do not become so important that we devote all of our time and energy to obtaining them and to using them.

Jesus tells us in Matthew 6:24, "No one can serve two masters. Either he will hate the one and love the other, or he will be devoted to one and despise the other." If we say we want to serve God, we must consider what occupies our mind, takes most of our time and is our highest priority. Is it materialism or is it God? Do we understand that treasures in heaven are far more valuable than treasures on earth?

TODAY'S WORD FOR APRIL 29

BUILD

Unless the Lord builds the house, they labor in vain that build it. Psalm 127:1

We can remember the Sunday school song that we sang when we were kids about the foolish man who built his house on the sand and it did not stand firm. The song went on to tell about the wise man that built his house on the rock and it stood firm in the storm.

This song came from the section of the Sermon on the Mount that Jesus preached while He was on this earth. (Matthew 7: 24-27) Jesus had just warned the crowd to watch out for false prophets. He then proceeded to give a warning to those who profess to belong to God but have no relationship with Him. He then used this illustration of the wise man and the foolish man to emphasize what He was saying.

First, Jesus says that whoever hears His words and does them will be like the wise man who built his house on the rock. The rock is Christ Jesus. Just as the house that was built on a solid foundation of rock was able to stand firm when the storms came and the winds beat against it, so will the man who builds his life on the solid foundation of Christ be able to stand through the storms of life. Jesus explained that when the rain comes down, the pressures of this world we live in, and the floods and winds come our way the house (our lives) will not fall because our foundation is built on the rock Christ Jesus.

He then goes on to say that those who hear what He says and do not put it into practice are likened to the foolish man who builds his house on sand. When the rain, floods and winds of life come and beat on the house, it will fall. And He says: "AND GREAT WAS THE FALL."

On what are you building your life? Are you building on the "things" of this world or are you building on the commandments that God gave us years ago through Moses His servant? Are you laying up treasures for yourself in heaven? Is your house, your life, built on the rock Christ Jesus or the sand?

In Psalms 127:1, Solomon, the author of this Psalm, warns us that unless we allow the Lord to build our house (our life), we are laboring in vain. Solomon was reminding us that God is central in our lives. God needs to be sovereign in our everyday life and in our family life.

In the first two verses of this Psalm Solomon talks about building our house, protecting a city and earning a living. In all three instances, the sovereign intention of God is far more crucial to the outcome of this building than that of our efforts. Unless we include God in our life and build on Him, our endeavors are in vain. We need to remember that prosperity, a good foundation to build on, comes from the Lord. No matter how hard we work to accomplish great things, only what is done for the Lord will last.

TODAY'S WORD FOR APRIL 30

OBSTACLES

Now Jericho was securely shut up because of the children of Israel: none went out, and none came in. Joshua 6:1

The Lord has a plan for the life of each believer. To thwart God's purposes, Satan puts obstacles in the path of believers. There are many different kinds of obstacles. They include a difficult boss, contrary family members and financial concerns. Anything that blocks a desired goal can cause anxiety and frustration. And these can derail what God wants from you. But remember, that no obstacle can touch you or be a concern to you without the consent of God.

Read the verse above concerning the Biblical account of Joshua and the city of Jericho. The strong fortress around the city of Jericho barred Israel's entrance into the land. The city was fortified by a double ring of walls, the outer one was six feet thick and the inner wall was twelve feet thick. Jericho was also built on a hill so there was a steep incline to even get close to the walls. This was an obstacle to God's plan for the Children of Israel and Joshua to conquer Jericho.

Satan will always put up obstacles, fortresses, to hinder our spiritual progress just like He did to Joshua and the Children of Israel. The conquest of Jericho seemed impossible to Israel but not so to God. Everyone knew that Joshua's army was no match for Jericho's military and the walls of Jericho were an impossible barrier to cross.

God had promised the Israelites the land and Joshua believed that God would provide a way for them to get into Jericho. Joshua was not deterred by what seemed impossible, but instead acknowledged God's power and sought His guidance.

Before Joshua even realized that God was at work, God was already preparing the city for destruction by instilling fear into the hearts of the kings in the region and the people in Jericho. God's direction was a very unlikely battle plan, but Joshua obeyed and God's people triumphed.

The apostle Paul understood how to handle obstacles. Even when he was in prison he kept his eyes and full trust on Christ. His days in prison were filled with joy. He wrote the book of Philippians from a jail cell and it is full of expressions of joy. In 1:18 he talks about his joy in Christ. In 2:18 he talks about rejoicing in the Lord. And in Philippians 3:1 he talks again about rejoicing in the Lord. Having joy in your life and rejoicing in the Lord will help you get over the obstacles you will face.

We overcome obstacles in our lives by focusing on Christ. This is neither a natural reaction nor an easy one. Our instinct is to dwell on the situation that we are facing. We search for our own solutions and stew over pain and difficulty. Our troubles look insurmountable and overwhelming, but fear and defeat cannot last long in the heart of a believer that has his or her trust in the Lord. The choice is yours, just as it was for the apostle Paul, Joshua and the Children of Israel. We must ask ourselves, "Where is our faith and trust?"

TODAY'S WORD FOR MAY 1

ABILITY

And to one he gave five talents, to another two, and to another one, to each according to his own ability. Matthew 25:15

Each one should use whatever gift he has received, to serve others, faithfully administering God's grace in various forms. If anyone speaks he should do it as one speaking the very words of God. If anyone serves he should do it as with the strength which God provides so that in all things God may be glorified through Jesus Christ. I Peter 4:10-11

God has given us different abilities and talents and He expects us to use our abilities in a way that will bring honor to Him. In the parable in Matthew 25:14-18 the amount of talents the master gave his servants was according to their ability. Each was given what the master thought the servant could manage. The lesson of the parable is not about how much we have, but how well we use what we have.

We have experienced, in working with people, that it wasn't those with the greatest ability who accomplished the most for the Lord but those with the most desire. One individual that worked with us was content just to come to work every day and do just enough to get by. He had great ability but never seemed to have the desire to take advantage of the abilities God gave him.

We have worked with several others with somewhat limited ability who worked hard at every task given them and not only did all that was asked of them but far more than was expected of them.

There were others who had the attitude that they could do anything and do it better than others. Most often they overestimated their ability and could not produce what they said they could.

We have shared with you three types of people. Those that have great ability and do not use what God has given them. Those who may have great or little ability but they always work over and above what is expected of them and excel in what they accomplish. And finally the person who talks big, but accomplishes very little.

It was very evident that in the parable of the talents Jesus knew there were those that had more ability than others. It is clear that He expects us to use whatever talents He has given us to the best of our ability. What counts with God is not how much we have to offer Him but about how well we serve Him with what we have.

Some people say they have no abilities or special talents that the Lord could use. This is not true. Everyone has some ability. In I Peter 4:7-11 Peter lists things that we all can do like showing love to one another, being hospitable, serving others and praying for others. What God wants from each of us is to be a good steward of what God has given you and use your abilities to serve and honor Him.

TODAY'S WORD FOR MAY 2

INVESTING

For where your treasure is, there your heart will be also. Matthew 6:21

Then He said to them, Watch out! Be on your guard against all kinds of greed; a man's life does not consist in the abundance of his possessions. Luke 12:15

Recently we were reading through a publication that had literally pages of reports, suggestions and recommendations about investing. Advice was given about good investments, shaky investments and bad investments. There was advice about investing in land, in real estate, in gold, in banks, and in the stock market just to name some of the possible ways to invest. The so called "professionals" gave varied opinions but very few agreed on what to invest in. There were reports on why some investments were successful in the past and why some failed. One thing that was certain to us as we read this publication was the uncertainty of all investments.

When you think of the word investment, what comes to your mind? Over the years we have met many people that live in cultures where the word investment would never be discussed and for most could not even be defined. All of their thoughts every day were centered in survival. They have nothing to invest materially but these people know that we all can make a spiritual investment that is certain and you will not lose.

The scripture gives us the best investment advice: Store up for yourselves treasures in heaven where moth and rust do not destroy and where thieves do not break in and steal (Matthew 6:20).

In the verse above, Jesus gives an investment alert when He said that where our treasure is, there will be your heart. In other words if you spend your time in investing your time in getting more money, being more popular or gaining a better position in life then that is where your heart is. Jesus advises that the desire of the heart of believers must be to invest our time, talent and treasure in spiritual things.

In Luke 12:16-21, Jesus told a parable of the rich fool to explain why investing in the things of heaven is wise. A rich man who already had plenty of material things, tore down his barns and built bigger barns so he could store up more of this world's goods. The parable has a sad ending. He died with his barns full leaving it all to someone else. He had put all of his effort in preparing for his life before death but had neglected to prepare for life after death.

This man was rich in possessions but he was not rich toward God. This is the warning that we read in Luke 12:15 (above). We must "WATCH OUT!" and be on guard that we do not make the purpose of our life be to obtain worldly possessions.

We become rich toward God when we invest our time, talent and treasures in serving Him. We store up treasures in heaven by our acts of obedience and faithfulness in doing His will.

TODAY'S WORD FOR MAY 3

SERVE

You have done all this wickedness; yet do not turn aside from following the Lord, but serve the Lord with all your heart. 1 Samuel 12:20

When the people of Israel insisted on having a king, despite the warnings of Samuel, the prophet reminded them that the Lord God was their King (1 Samuel 12:12). In spite of Samuel's warning, God allowed them to have their own way and they got a king. After they had chosen and insisted on having a king they realized the evil thing they had done and they asked for Samuel's help and prayers (1 Samuel 12:19). Samuel gave the following response to the Children of Israel, "Do not fear. You have done all this wickedness; yet do not turn aside from following the Lord, but serve the Lord with all your heart" (1 Samuel 12:20). Even when we do the wrong thing God does not give up on us. He wants us to return to following Him and to serve Him and will never reject us if we turn away from our evil ways.

When we fail to serve God as we know we should, remember we cannot undo what we did yesterday or the day before but we can act today. Samuel in verse 24 urged the Children of Israel to, "Only fear the Lord, and serve Him in truth with all your hearts; for consider what great things He has done for you." How many times have we read in the scripture of the Children of Israel coming back to God and God doing great things for them?

When we fail to serve the Lord we need to humbly ask for His forgiveness and acknowledge His faithfulness to us. He has promised to accept us back, just as He accepted back so many times the Children of Israel. God wants us to serve Him today and we cannot let yesterdays failures bankrupt tomorrow's victories.

Every believer knows in his or her heart that God wants all of us to obey His commandments and to serve Him. Yet all of us often decide we want to do things our way and we do not involve God in our decision making. This was the mistake that the Children of Israel made in I Samuel 12.

We can remember the great anticipation we experienced arriving in Seoul Korea for our new responsibilities with World Vision some years ago. We arrived with some fear but totally dedicated to serving Jesus with all of our hearts, minds and souls. Arriving in a country with, new customs, a new place to live, and a new language quickly reminded us that we could not do this on our own but in order to serve God we needed to rely on Him.

The certainty of the return of Christ is probably the greatest reason we need to serve the Lord daily. The anticipation really overwhelms our hearts with excitement and gives us a new desire daily to serve our Lord. Do you get as excited as we do just thinking about the soon return of our Lord and Savior?

TODAY'S WORD FOR MAY 4

FUTURE

If it is the Lords will, we shall live and do this or that. James 4:15

For I know the plans I have for you, declares the Lord, plans to prosper you and not to harm you, plans to give you a future and a hope. Jeremiah 29:11

Jeremiah was a prophet chosen by God to bring a message to Judah of the coming destruction of Jerusalem unless they repented of their sins. Judah rejected Jeremiah's warning and Jerusalem was destroyed and the people were taken captive to Babylon. The exiles had no hope for the future. The 29th chapter of Jeremiah is a text of Jeremiah's letter he sent to the captives. It was a word of hope from God assuring them of a future and that God had not forgotten them.

The God who controls the future had plans for them, plans to prosper them. God's plans for all who belong to Him are always good plans. He desires to prosper us. The exiles could see no hope for their future. Jeremiah's letter brought them the good news that God's plan was to bring them back from captivity (Jeremiah 29:14).

TIME magazine in a 1992 issue had an article titled "BEYOND THE YEAR 2000." In this article they wrote about the future and the new millennium and wrote: "The first rule of forecasting should be that the unforeseen keeps making the future unforeseeable."

James reminds us in James 4:13-14 that any view of the future that omits God is foolish and proud. We cannot be sure if we will be here from one moment to the next. It is God who determines the length of our life; therefore we can fulfill our plans only if God allows us to fulfill them. TIME magazine's article acknowledges that no one knows what the future will bring and that man has no control over the future. No one can foresee the future, but God's Word teaches us that we can know the one who not only foresees the future but controls the future.

Many people begin a statement that they may make about the future with, "The Lord willing." This is a clear and concise message acknowledging that God's overruling hand controls the future. James tells us that we should daily say that "If it is the Lord will, we shall live and do this or that." As we look ahead to the future as believers in Jesus we need to keep God firmly in view. We can face the future with confidence when we include Him in our plans. The true believer in Jesus submits all of his or her plans to the Lord. Our plans will disappoint us if we leave God out of them.

Those of us who know Jesus Christ as our Savior can face the future with hope and confidence because we know God controls the future and we know His plans are to prosper us and bless us.

We do not know what tomorrow will bring. James tells us in James 4:14 that "Our life is just a vapor that appears for a little while and then vanishes away." We need to be ready for that day when we go to spend a glorious eternity with our Lord.

TODAY'S WORD FOR MAY 5

FLAWED

My strength is made perfect in weakness. II Corinthians 12:9

In an interview with an actor, he said that he enjoyed playing "flawed" characters in movies because people relate to an imperfect character. This is true. People like to hear about flawed people. When you look at what makes the biggest headlines in the news it is stories about famous people, such as politicians, sports figures, or stars in the entertainment world who commit a scandalous act of wrong doing.

The media knows that the public loves to hear about other people's failures and flaws, especially those who are famous for some special ability and idolized by others. The reason we like to hear about other people's transgressions is that it makes us feel better about ourselves. We all know that we are flawed but we do not want others to know how flawed we are.

Most of us would agree that it is easier for us to understand people who are not perfect because we know that we are not perfect. Therefore they are like us.

There are many accounts in the Bible of people who were flawed and had weaknesses and yet God used them in powerful and mighty ways. Most of them faced times of decision or times of crisis that revealed their weaknesses. Jacob resorted to deceiving his father so that he would receive his father's blessing. Gideon was so unsure of God that he asked him twice for proof that He would be faithful to do what He said He would do. Peter was so fearful for his own safety that he denied knowing his friend and Lord.

When you read the rest of the stories of these men, you will observe that these people were able, with God's help, to overcome their shortcomings and ultimately were useful to God. They were all flawed but God made them useful because they put their trust in God. It was by first seeing that they were weak that they could see that they had to depend on God and not on themselves.

Just as the people who lived thousands of years ago, each one of us has flaws. By the grace of God we can overcome our flaws and imperfections by embracing "His strength which is made perfect in weakness" II Corinthians 12:9. When we forget to depend on the Lord, the Lord may make us weaker with the intention of making us realize we will do better when we rely solely on Him. By doing this we receive His strength.

God's strength and power is available to all who love Him and no one is so flawed that God cannot use them.

TODAY'S WORD FOR MAY 6

SOWER

And as he sowed some seed fell by the wayside; and the birds came and devoured them. Some fell on stony places, where they did not have much earth; and they immediately sprang up because they had no depth of earth. Matthew 13:4-5

The parable of the sower in Matthew 13:3-8 is easy to understand, because Jesus interpreted it for His disciples. The sower is the one who sows the Word of the Kingdom of God in the world. It is either the Lord Himself or a servant of His. The seed is the gospel of Jesus Christ, the Word of God. The ground onto which the gospel seed is sown is the heart of the men who are the hearers.

Jesus taught that a sower went forth to sow and a large number that listened did not allow the Word to take permanent root. Only a small number allowed the Word to take permanent root and only a few allowed the Word to bear 100% fruit.

In this parable not all of the seeds sprouted and not all of those that sprouted bore abundant fruit. The yield of the fruit depended on the soil it fell on. Christ did not teach that all the world would be converted even though that was His desire. God put the responsibility for the reception of the seed, which is the gospel message on the soil, which is the hearer. In this parable the four types of soil represent the four types of responses to the gospel.

The first response comes from a hard heart. The wayside soil is hard and unprepared for seed. The fowls that devour the seed that fell on the hard ground are Satan and his evil demons. Those whose hearts have become hardened do not want to hear the gospel and they reject it.

The second response comes from a shallow heart. Those who are shallow receive the gospel with joy but they do not let God's Word take root in their heart. They honor God for a while, but when tribulation or persecution comes their way they quickly fall away from their profession of faith. They are the ones who blame God when they have problems and life gets difficult for them. They say that they just cannot believe that God really cares about them if God would allow them to suffer. They are, what we might call fair-weather believers that only want to say they know God when all is going well.

The third response comes from a worldly heart. A heart that loves the world system is a heart that becomes easily alienated from God. The love of money, success, and the pleasures of the world choke out the influence of the Word of God in the life of the professing believer so that he becomes unfruitful. They choose fame and fortune over God.

The fourth response comes from an understanding heart. Only a few people allow the Word of God to take permanent root. They are the ones that have a tender and receptive heart. They hear the Word of God and understand it and they bear the fruit of God's Word in their own life. They will be faithful to God, obey His commandments and be a witness to the lost. Where do you stand?

TODAY'S WORD FOR MAY 7

TARES

Another parable He put forth to them saying, The kingdom of heaven is like a man who sowed good seed in his field; but while men slept, his enemy came and sowed tares among the wheat and went his way. But when the grain had sprouted and produced a crop, then the tares (weeds) also appeared. Matthew 13:24-26

Tares are known today as darnel, a type of weed that can hardly be distinguished from wheat until the head matures. At harvest time the weeds are separated from the wheat and burned. Sowing darnel in someone else's wheat field was a way for enemies to catastrophically destroy someone's livelihood. In this parable Jesus said that this depicted Satan's effort to deceive the church by mingling his followers with those who follow God.

Jesus explained this parable by giving us six comparisons to understand:

First, He tells us that the sower of the good seed (the wheat) is the Lord Jesus.

Secondly, the field represents the world. Jesus came to this world to sow the good seed in the hearts of man. Before He ascended into heaven, He commissioned those who received the good seed to proclaim it to the world, our mission field.

Thirdly, the good seed in this parable is not the gospel but the children of the Kingdom. Through His disciples Jesus has sown (scattered) the good seed (the children of God) first in Jerusalem, then in Judea and Samaria; and he continues to scatter His children into all parts of the world to spread the good news of the gospel.

When we are born into this world we have no choice as to what part of the world we are in. God puts us into the part of the world we live in for a reason. Wherever you live, you as a believer, are a "good seed," a child of God, and His ambassador.

Fourth, the tares are "the sons of the wicked one," Satan. Jesus said to the unsaved religious teachers of His day, "You are of your father the devil." Where Jesus sends His followers, Satan also sends his followers to promote false teaching.

Fifthly, the enemy that sows the tares is the devil. His aim is to destroy God's wheat field, Christ's church. In the world true believers must live side by side with false believers. Like wheat and tares it can be hard at times to see the difference.

And finally, the harvest is at the end of the age, when we will experience the final judgment after Christ's return. He will then send His angels to reap the harvest and separate the wheat from the tares. He will rapture the "wheat," the children of the kingdom, and burn the "tares," the children of Satan. The children of the Devil will be cast into "the furnace of fire," while the children of God "will shine forth as the sun in the kingdom of their father." Revelation 20:15

There are good and bad people in this world. God sows the righteous and Satan sows the wicked. We are not to judge who the wheat and tares are because only God is qualified to judge the hearts of man. God alone has the wisdom and authority to judge. We have the responsibility to proclaim the good news to the world.

TODAY'S WORD FOR MAY 8

MUSTARD SEED

Another parable He put forth to them saying: The kingdom of heaven is like a mustard seed, which a man took and sowed in his field, which indeed is the least of all the seeds; but when it is grown it is greater than the herbs and becomes a tree, so that the birds of the air come and nest in its branches. Mathew 13:31-32

The Palestinian mustard plants are large shrubs, sometimes growing to about 15 feet high. These plants are certainly tall enough for birds to lodge in them. These large shrubs grow from one of the smallest of seeds.

The mustard seed in this parable is the church, God's Kingdom in its very beginning. The Church began as the smallest of seeds but has grown into the greatest of movements. On the day of Pentecost, after Jesus ascended into heaven, the small kingdom began its phenomenal expansion. Like the mustard seed it continued to grow, branching out into other nations of the world. Today the body of believers, known as the church, reaches into every corner of the world.

God planted the seed, the Church, and His field is the world. In the parable the fowls of the air that lodged in the branches came to find rest and safety. Some interpret the branches to be a place of worship where many believers and non-believers come to seek help and safety.

The Church referred to here is the body of believers that believe in Jesus, not a building. The church began in the soul of one man, Jesus, a carpenter from the obscure village called Nazareth who was sent to this earth by His Father.

The message and work of the kingdom was carried forth by men without position and prestige. They were not mighty, noble or famous. They were common folk. They began with very little faith but continued to grow under their teacher, the very Son of God. The body of believers numbered only about 120 people when Christ departed from this earth.

The bush is all believers who believe in Jesus throughout the world. It has grown from small beginnings into the greatest of bushes. Not only did God grow His Kingdom through the early believers but God continues to grow His Kingdom through His faithful followers each and every day.

This parable is an encouragement to every believer that what we plant He will grow. It encourages us in our personal lives and ministries and to look forward to our hope in eternity where we will be rewarded for our faithful labor. It encourages us to reach out to the world around us and proclaim the good news of the gospel.

Just as the birds come to the mustard plant to nest in the safety of the branches, we are to come to Him to find safety in His outstretched arms which are reaching out to us to bring us into His Kingdom. He is waiting for you to come to Him. We are to come to Him first and then live and walk with Him. Where do you stand?

TODAY'S WORD FOR MAY 9

LEAVEN

He told them still another parable: The kingdom of heaven is like yeast that a woman took and mixed into a large amount of flour until it worked all through the dough. Matthew 13:3.

In this parable the kingdom of God is pictured as yeast that multiplies quietly and permeating all that it contacts. In other Bible passages yeast is a symbol of evil. Some say that the yeast represents evil that penetrates the Kingdom of God and His church. Most Bible scholars will say that the yeast symbolizes the Kingdom of God that penetrates and works silently to transform man and society.

The yeast cannot be interpreted to symbolize evil in this passage because it would twist the actual words of Jesus in this parable and violate the context of what Jesus is teaching His disciples and to the crowds that followed Him.

The message of this parable is to demonstrate the power of the Kingdom of God to penetrate a person's life just as yeast permeates the dough. Jesus is saying that the growth of the church will come as the believers permeate individuals and society with the gospel to do its transforming work.

In this parable, yeast is compared to the gospel. Yeast makes bread soft and no longer hard. The yeast of the gospel penetrates the heart of a man and softens the hardness of his heart.

Yeast makes bread moist and no longer dry. The yeast of the gospel penetrates the dryness of a man's heart and life. Yeast makes bread satisfying and no longer unfulfilling. The yeast of the gospel transforms the life of the unbeliever with no purpose in life, into one with meaning and significance.

Yeast makes bread nourishing. The yeast of the gospel nourishes our faith. The growth of our faith will prepare us and inspire us to feed others with the yeast of the gospel.

Jesus seemed to want believers to understand how the Gospel penetrates to the heart and soul of the unbeliever by comparing it to yeast. Yeast works quietly and silently until it permeates the whole batch of dough. The Gospel, like yeast, works silently and quietly in the soul of those who receive it causing the dough to grow. The Gospel works slowly and gradually in the believer causing him or her to grow spiritually. Yeast changes the quality of the dough and not the substance.

The Gospel leaves a new believer unchanged on the outside but on the inside he is a changed person. He has been made a person of perfect quality, a man of God. As you study this parable ask God to help you to learn the importance of sharing the gospel with those people you know that do not know Jesus as their Savior.

TODAY'S WORD FOR MAY 10

TREASURE

The kingdom of heaven is like treasure hidden in a field. When a man found it, he hid it again, and then in his joy went and sold all that he had and bought the field. Matthew 13:44

Jesus spoke this parable to His disciples who were alone with Him. The crowds had dispersed and Jesus wanted His disciples to understand the kingdom of heaven and its great value to them. In Jesus' day it was common practice for people to hide their treasures and valuables by burying them in the ground to keep them from being stolen. Everyone understood clearly when Jesus said the kingdom of heaven is like treasure hidden in the ground.

In this parable Jesus referred to a man who found a treasure in the field. The field represents the Word of God and the treasure would be Christ who is "hidden" in the gospel message of God's Word. A person cannot find the treasure, Christ, by just scratching the surface of the gospel but must dig and dig deep into Gods Word. The treasure of the Kingdom of heaven is hidden to the unbeliever.

This parable pictures salvation as something hidden from most people. Also in this parable it is inferred that salvation when found is so valuable that people who have it revealed to them are willing to give up all they have to possess it. We as believers today must understand this and apply the lesson of this parable when we are telling others how to find Jesus.

In this parable it says when the man found the treasure, so great was his joy that he sold everything that he had in order to buy the field so that he could possess the treasure. The value of the Kingdom exceeds the value of all earthly treasures and those who find it are willing to give up all they have to obtain it.

When any of us experience the joy of finding Christ, there are five results:

First, we will protect it by hiding it deep in our heart where it cannot be taken away.

Secondly, we receive God's mercy which we value as a great treasure.

Thirdly, we sell, that is we repent and get rid of the sinful ways of our former life.

Fourthly, we buy, that is we commit all that we have to possess all the riches of salvation we obtain through our Lord and Savior.

And finally, we rejoice in the completeness and satisfaction in the treasure we have found in Christ, who is Lord of Lords and King of Kings, and who reigns in the Kingdom of heaven and is preparing a place for us there for all eternity.

We as believers then experience an abundant life in Christ, a completed life in Christ, and have available to us the fruits of the spirit which includes love, joy, peace, longsuffering, gentleness, goodness, faith, meekness, and temperance. Have you found the treasure (Christ) hidden in the field (Gospel)?

TODAY'S WORD FOR MAY 11

PEARL

Again, the kingdom of heaven is like a merchant looking for fine pearls. When he found one of great price, he went away and sold everything he had and bought it. Mathew 13:45-46

Most ladies will tell you that if they were to receive a string of pearls, they would feel that they had received a most expensive and beautiful gift — and it would be. Good pearls are very valuable today and they were also valuable when Jesus was on this earth. So when Jesus talks about pearls you can be assured they are beautiful and accepted as a wonderful gift or possession.

When Jesus refers in this parable to the merchant He is no doubt referring to the God-man Jesus Christ. The merchant came seeking beautiful pearls and found one pearl of exquisite beauty. Jesus, our merchant, came into the world to seek and to save those who were lost and His magnificent pearl is the Church.

This parable pictures salvation as something hidden from most people, like a pearl is hidden. But Jesus says that salvation, the pearl, is so valuable that people who have it revealed to them are willing to give up all that they have to possess it.

The Lord has been adding to the church, which is made up of individuals that have come to find Jesus as their Savior. These believers are all children of God and each one is of great value to our Lord Jesus Christ.

This pure, pearl-like quality of the church may never be visible to us who are on this earth, during this age. It will be realized though, according to the scriptures, when the dead in Christ are raised and those who are alive are caught up to meet Him in the air. Then we will be perfect in mind and body and, as the parable states, "one pearl of great price" paid for by the death, burial and resurrection of Jesus, the merchant.

Just like the merchant in the parable, Jesus came to this earth to accomplish His purpose. He sells all that He has, giving all on the cross to pay the penalty for our sins. With His shed blood He buys the pearl, providing for us life eternal making us part of His eternal kingdom.

There is nothing more valuable that we could possibly have than the Kingdom of heaven. We should be willing to give up all we have to obtain it. How grateful are you that Jesus commended His love toward us so that while we were yet sinners He died for us. Jesus paid a great price for you. He is seeking you to be part of His Kingdom. Anyone who comes to Jesus in faith, believing in Him, will be a pearl of great value. In serving Him you can enrich His Kingdom by bringing others to know Him.

TODAY'S WORD FOR MAY 12

NET

Again, the kingdom of heaven is like a dragnet that was cast into the sea and gathered some of every kind. Matthew 13:47

In this parable Jesus was teaching that the net is the Kingdom of Heaven and the gospel is the message of the kingdom. The sea is the world in all the depth of its darkness and its unknown. The fisherman represents Christ.

Jesus continued teaching using this parable as an illustration by saying: When the net was full they came to shore and sat down and gathered the good into vessels and cast the bad away.

In those days, fisherman used large weighted nets which were dragged along the bottom of the lake. All kinds of fish would be caught in the net so it was necessary to sort the good fish from the bad. Jesus related the sorting of the fish to the sorting He will do on judgment day determining who will be part of His eternal Kingdom.

We need to note several things that Jesus was saying. First, they worked hard fishing. Jesus compares the hard work of these fishermen to the hard work needed to cast the gospel message of the kingdom into the world of unbelievers.

Second, Jesus reminds us that there is a mixture of good and bad that are drawn into God's visible kingdom here on earth just as there were good and bad fish caught in the net. There will be some people that will join the kingdom here on earth that are not sincere and have not genuinely accepted Christ as their Savior.

Thirdly, Jesus said in verse 49 that there will be an end to the world. There is a set time in God's plan when that climatic time will come. The net has a limit as to how many it will hold just as someday heaven will be full. Of course, only the Lord knows when He will draw the net.

Fourthly, Jesus makes it clear that the good, those who are true followers of Christ and obey His commandments, and the bad, those who are hypocrites and not true believers, will not be separated until the net is full. The Lord alone has the right to execute judgment when He casts away the bad at the last judgment. The unrepentant wicked will be cast into the furnace of fire and there shall be wailing and gnashing of teeth (Verse 50).

Yes, judgment day will be a tragic day for all those who come before Jesus still covered in their sins having never accepted Jesus and received His gift of cleansing atonement for their sins. (This will include some who were regular in attending church, but attending church does not get one into heaven).

After this parable Jesus asks the question, "Have you understood all these things" (Verse 51)? Having just warned of the coming judgment you cannot help but notice the urgency in Jesus' question. It is an urgent question for each of us.

Jesus warned us in Luke 12:40 that we must be ready because He will return at an hour when we will not expect Him.

TODAY'S WORD FOR MAY 13

HOUSEHOLDER

Then He said to them, therefore every scribe which is instructed concerning the kingdom of heaven is like a householder who brings out of his treasure things old and new. Matthew 13:52

After Jesus concluded His sharing of these parables with His disciples, He asked his disciples (verse 51) if they understood His teaching concerning the Kingdom. The new treasure we read about in Matthew 13:52 is the gospel message of Jesus and it was vitally important for the disciples to truly understand it as they would have the responsibility to spread the message of Jesus after Jesus returned to His home in heaven.

Jesus wants us to know and understand His Word so that as believers we are equipped and ready to help new believers understand the Word of God. Jesus reminded the disciples to understand that they had been unusually blessed, having been instructed in the Old Testament law just as the scribes had but now also they had been taught by the Messiah himself. They possessed the "old treasure" and the "new treasure." The new insights that they had gleaned from Jesus' parables were to be understood in light of the old truths they had learned under the law and vice-versa.

Just as Jesus told His disciples that they had the responsibility to share the whole counsel of God, both the old and new counsel, we have the same responsibility.

The Jewish Scribes were extremely devoted and studied the law so that they were knowledgeable and well versed in it. Jesus expects us to be like the scribes and study the Word of God, both the Old Testament and the New Testaments, with unswerving diligence. We who follow Jesus are to be a storehouse of His truth by letting the Word of Christ dwell in us. We are not to be like the scribes who perverted the treasure of God's Word and therefore missed the truth of God's Word.

Jesus also explained this parable further by using the householder as an illustration. The householder had two prime duties. He was to store and preserve the old food and obtain new food as needed. By this His disciples understood they were to store in their hearts both the old laws they had learned from the Old Testament and the new ones that Jesus taught them.

Jesus charged them with the responsibility of not only preserving Christ's teachings but also to teach what they had been taught about the Kingdom of heaven, both old and new, to others.

Today all believers are householders of the old and new treasures and we are responsible for the spiritual nurturing of those within the Kingdom.

TODAY'S WORD FOR MAY 14

DEPENDENCE

Who among you fears the Lord, let him trust in the name of the Lord and rely (have dependence) upon his God. Isaiah 50:10

Trust in the Lord with all your heart. Do not depend on your own understanding. Proverbs 3:5

In the verse above from Isaiah, Isaiah was giving a call to the unconverted to believe in God and be saved, along with a warning that those who tried to escape moral and spiritual darkness by depending on their own methods of self-righteous ideas, were to end up in eternal torment.

David went from being a shepherd boy to being the King of Israel. Throughout his life he was dependent on God. As a shepherd boy he had to kill a lion and a bear to protect his sheep. In each instance he gave the Lord credit for delivering him from harm.

When David told Saul that he would go and fight Goliath, Saul was against it because David was just a young boy. David answered Saul by saying "The Lord who delivered me from the paw of the lion and the jaw of the bear will deliver me from the hand of the Philistine" (I Samuel 17:37). This was the first of many battles that David had to fight in his life time, and through them all he never lost his trust in God. He was dependent always on his God.

David wrote many of the Psalms and in them he proclaimed how much he depended on God. For example:

"Find rest, O my soul in God alone; my hope comes from Him. He alone is my rock and my salvation; He is my fortress, I will not be shaken. My salvation and my honor DEPEND on God! He is my mighty rock, my refuge" Psalm 62: 5-7.

Just as a young child depends on his or her parents for almost everything, we as believers in Christ need to depend totally on God. As Solomon wisely advises us, in Proverbs 3:5, to trust in the Lord God and not on our own understanding. God has given us the ability to think and reason but when we trust in our own understanding or wisdom, we often find that we do not have all the answers. Our wisdom is limited but God's is not.

When we put our trust in God we will seek God's guidance and be willing to correct our thinking and actions when they go against God's Word. One needs to learn the independent side of dependence as one walks the Christian life. We need to show our independence in our day to day living by separating ourselves from the sinful activities the world entices us with. To resist the world it is absolutely necessary to put our trust in the Lord. We can depend on Him to guide us on the right path.

TODAY'S WORD FOR MAY 15

ZEAL

Then he said, Come with me and see my zeal for the Lord. II Kings 10:16

How many people do you know that show real zeal for what they are doing or how they feel? Do you know many people that show zeal concerning their personal spiritual beliefs day after day? If you are like us you will respond by saying, "Not too many."

We have often seen new converts express their joy with real zeal after their conversion. This might be in a church giving their testimony or even an entertainer on a television or a radio program expressing their new found faith in Christ. But so often after a few months their passion for the Lord begins to dwindle.

The Lord expects us as believers to show this kind of exciting zeal for our Lord every day of our life. If we are excited about our faith and looking forward to the soon return of Jesus to take us to heaven, it should be expected that we would show excitement and zeal in our daily walk?

In the verse from II Kings above, we read about Jehu who was anointed King of Israel by the prophet Elisha. After Elisha anointed Jehu to become king he gave him instructions from God that Jehu was to destroy all the household of Ahab, the wicked king of Israel. Jehu was chosen by God to fulfill the prophecy of Elijah that all of Ahab's descendants would be destroyed because of Ahab's many sins against God and because he killed God's prophets.

Jehu set out immediately to fulfill his commission. After killing all of Ahab's family in Jezreel he set out for Samaria to kill the rest of Ahab's family. On the way he met Jehonadab who was zealous in following the Lord.

Jehu asked him if he was in agreement with what Jehu had to do. He responded favorably so he was invited to ride in the chariot with Jehu. Jehu said to him, "Come with me and see my zeal for the Lord." When God directs us to do something it is important that we do it with zeal but more importantly to do it with His guidance.

As a result of Jehu being zealous in doing what God asked of him, we read in II Kings 10:30 that God said to Jehu, "Because you have done well in accomplishing what is right in my eyes and done to the house of Ahab all that I had in mind to do, your children to the fourth generation shall sit on the throne of Israel."

God always honors those that show their zeal for Him. Many Christians today are very lethargic about their faith in Christ. Many believers are content to just blend into the crowd in their workplace or at a social gathering. It is not that they are living sinful lives, but they have no zeal for their faith. So people do not see Christ in their lives. We should want people to see that we are different. This account about Jehu is an example that we can learn from. When we show our zeal for the Lord and honor Him in all we do, He will honor us.

TODAY'S WORD FOR MAY 16

AFRAID

Be of good cheer! It is I; do not be afraid. Matthew 14:27

Do not be afraid, for I am with you. Genesis 26:24

When I am afraid, I will trust in You. Psalm 56:3

Do you often feel afraid? If you do you are not alone. In times when we are afraid, God's message to us is the same message that He gave to Isaac when he feared for his life. God said to Isaac, "Do not be afraid, for I am with you" (Genesis 26:24). Great men down through history, in their time of fear, needed the assurance from God that they had no reason to fear.

When you read the scriptures you will see that Abraham, Moses, Isaac, David, Jeremiah, the disciples, Peter, Paul and others were all told by God not to be afraid.

In Matthew 14:27 is the account of a time when Jesus disciples were afraid. They were in a boat on the Sea of Galilee in a wind storm and being tossed about by the waves. Suddenly they saw what appeared to be a ghost, walking on the water toward them. They weren't just afraid, they were terrified (Matthew 14:26). It was Jesus and He immediately spoke to them saying "do not be afraid it is I."

Nothing causes greater fear than the threat of losing one's life. David's life was often in danger so David knew well what it was to be afraid. Psalm 56 was written by David at a time in his life when he was afraid of being killed by the Philistines. David's natural reaction must have been to panic but in this Psalm he demonstrates that the believers in God can replace anticipated terror with composure by putting their trust and faith in God.

In verses 1-4 David relates his fear and contrasts it with the confidence of his trust in God. His trust and faith in God gives him the victory he needs over fear. In verse 9, David says, "This I know, that God is for me." Being afraid is a result of the evil that engulfs us on every side, because of our unbelief and sinful nature and because of our lack of faith that God is greater than all our enemies. When God is with us those who are against us will never succeed.

We can remember our young children from time to time waking up in the middle of the night saying that they were afraid. What makes this happen? Most of the time it relates back to a time when they heard about something that was frightening and might do something to hurt them. There reaction, of course, is to run to someone they can trust. There is no place where a child feels safer than to be in the safety of their parent's protective and loving arms.

Remember our hope and strength is in the Lord and God is for us. When fear comes into your life put your trust in God. When we cast our cares, our worries, and our fears upon Him, He will take care of us.

TODAY'S WORD FOR MAY 17

RICHES

Command those who are rich in this present age not to be haughty, nor to trust in uncertain riches but in the living God, who gives us richly all things to enjoy. I Timothy 6:17

We began early in the lives of our children to teach them to be responsible with their money. We are grateful to our Lord that He provided just enough riches to us to provide our children what they needed. But we were not always able to provide the "wants" they would have liked to have. The end result was a positive one because our children developed a greater appreciation for what they did have.

We encouraged our children to spend their money on their "wants" after they gave their tithe to the Lord. One of our sons said that as a child he didn't always understand the principle behind what we were teaching but as he matured he came to understand the value of what we were teaching concerning money and tithing.

We also taught our children that 10% of all the money earned or even received as a gift belonged to the Lord. God has proven to all of our family over these years that He will bless us if we honor this commitment to Him. Although our budget was always tight, we tried to show our children by example the importance of sharing with others a portion of what God blessed us with.

The negative aspect of riches, as written in the Bible, is that they are referred to as spiritually valueless, inferior, fleeting, unsatisfying, hurtful, deceitful, choking, uncertain and corrupted. This is quite a list and should set off a warning light to one who has an obsessive desire for riches and wealth in this world.

Riches and money are powerful forces in the world we live in today. We work hard for money, we save money; we spend money for our longings and necessities and then desire more. Money can never completely satisfy.

Trusting in wealth and using it to gain power clogs our spiritual arteries and spiritual development. We are told in Deuteronomy 8:17 and 18, "You may say in your heart, my power and the might of my hand has gotten me this wealth. But you shall remember the Lord your God, it is He who has given you power to get wealth." Our hope is not to be put in riches but in the Lord.

The apostle Paul tells us in I Timothy 6:17 (above) that those who are rich in this world should not be conceited about their wealth because worldly riches are temporary and cannot be taken with us when we die. Paul also tells us not to put our trust in uncertain riches. He infers in this verse that it is very hard to have riches in this world without putting some measure of trust in those riches.

In verse 18, Paul tells us that if God does bless us with riches we should be ready and willing to give and share. You will be laying up rich and lasting treasures in heaven (verse 19). Riches are a blessing to those who make them a blessing to others. God does not want us to put riches first in our lives, nor to put our trust in riches.

TODAY'S WORD FOR MAY 18

CONFESSION

For it is with your heart that you believe and are justified, and it is with your mouth that you confess and are saved. Romans 10:10

Confess your faults (sins) one to another and pray for one another, that you may be healed. James 5:16

When we worked with Billy Graham years ago we witnessed at every church meeting where we showed a Billy Graham film and at every crusade meeting where Billy Graham preached, an invitation at the conclusion of his message for one to accept Jesus as their Savior. When one was ready to make that decision they were invited to come to the front of the stadium or building to confess their sins and make their decision to receive Jesus into their heart in front of witnesses. This is what Timothy is saying in the above verse. God wants us to tell the world about our confession of being a sinner and our new found faith in Him and we begin by making a formal decision in front of witnesses.

The scripture is also very clear that in order for us to have a relationship with Jesus, there are two requirements. We must believe in our heart that Jesus is Lord and Savior and then confess to Him that we are a sinner and ask for forgiveness. God's response is immediate, we are saved! (Romans 10:10).

The Bible is clear that we are expected to confess before men our decision to follow Christ. This is why we encourage you to get involved in a Christ honoring, Bible believing church that gives people the opportunity to accept Jesus as their Savior and to confess Him before those in the church. We encourage you to be part of such a church and then you will grow in Him.

Confession is also important in family life. All of us, parents and children, need to be willing to confess and apologize to family members when we do them wrong. Confession is hard and many people struggle to admit guilt or any wrong.

For us as parents we are so very thankful that we had the blessed experience of hearing each of our children make their confession of faith and ask the Lord to forgive them of their sins and to come into their heart. Although, we have not been with our grandchildren at the moment they made their decision to accept Christ we can't begin to tell you how thrilled we have been to get their telephone call saying: "Grandma and Grandpa, I asked Jesus into my heart today."

Nothing heals better then confession. Situations would arise with our children when an argument developed. When we got involved in the process of helping to solve the argument, blaming one another was very common. After we sorted out the problem we encouraged the guilty one to confess and say "I am sorry." Confession is good for the heart and allows both parties to get on with life and they will usually not carry a grudge. As Christians, when we need to confess a wrong doing it is important that we do not procrastinate. Get on with your confession and apology.

TODAY'S WORD FOR MAY 19

TROUBLE

Be not far from me, for trouble is near; for there is none to help. Psalm 22:11

In life we have a choice of two paths, the path of righteousness or the path of wickedness. Neither path is trouble-free. Even the righteous will have suffering and troubles in their life. In Proverbs 34:18-19 we read: "The Lord is close to the broken hearted. A righteous man may have many troubles but the Lord delivers him from them all." The believer who has chosen the path of righteousness has the promise of God that He will be close to him in the time of trouble and will deliver him from it. The wicked by their own sinful ways bring more and more trouble upon themselves.

David was no stranger to trouble and suffering. In Psalms 22:11 he said that God was the one who could deliver him from trouble and the only one he could call on for help. He called on God to be near him because there was no one else to help him.

There are troubles in life where God is our only source of help. This promise is in Psalms 60:11-12, "Give us help from trouble, for the help of man is useless. With God we will gain victory, for it is He who shall tread down our enemies."

In the third chapter of Daniel you can read about the trouble that Shadrach, Meshach and Abednego had because they refused to bow to the golden image that their King Nebuchadnezzar required all to bow to. The scripture tells us that the King was furious and in a rage and gave the command to bring Shadrach, Meshach and Abednego before him. The King asked them if it was true that they would not serve his gods or worship the gold image that he had set up.

The King told them to bow now or they would be thrown into a burning fiery furnace. Now it would seem that these men were in more trouble than they could handle. They had to choose the path of righteousness or the path of wickedness. They knew that as believers in God that they would not bow down to false gods.

They had to make a choice. They must either bow down or face death in the fiery furnace. They did not hesitate in giving Nebuchadnezzar their answer. They said, "The God we serve is able to save us, but even if He does not, we want you to know, O King, we will not serve your gods or worship the image of gold you have set up."

The King was full of fury and ordered the furnace to be heated seven times hotter than normal. The men were bound and thrown into the furnace. Then the King was astonished at what he saw. He asked his counselors if they put only three men in the furnace because he could now see four. The King said that the fourth man is like the Son of God. He ordered the men taken out of the furnace. When he saw that the fire had not harmed them in any way the King said; "Blessed be the God of Shadrach, Meshach and Abednego" and he decreed that no man should speak against the God of these men or they would be sliced to pieces. Nebuchadnezzar acknowledged that their God was the true God with these words: "for no other god can save in this way." If God could help these men He can be with us in our times of trouble.

TODAY'S WORD FOR MAY 20

FELLOWSHIP

God, who has called you into fellowship with His Son, Jesus Christ, is faithful. I Corinthians 1:9

Finally, all of you be in one mind, having compassion for one another; love as brothers, be tenderhearted, and be courteous. I Peter 3:8

God's purpose in creating Adam was so He could have fellowship with him. God saw that it was not good for Adam to be alone (Genesis 2:18) so He created Eve to be his helpmate so they could fellowship with one another as well as with God. When Adam and Eve disobeyed God their sin separated them from fellowship with God.

Today there are many individuals who live only for self and never develop many friends. We need fellowship with others today to keep our lives in balance. There are just too many "pressures" we face to live without friends and fellowship. Fellowship is sharing our time, our treasures, our thoughts, our concerns and our victories.

We need fellowship with our family. This includes daily communication with our spouses, our children and our parents. For many today communication (fellowship) is difficult to schedule. We use the word schedule but fellowship should come naturally, whenever we are together, as part of a healthy and functional family.

As believers the scripture tells us that we should fellowship with other believers. This is why we need churches, Sunday schools, Bible classes and small group studies. These all provide places and programs to stimulate fellowship with others.

Christian fellowship combines social and spiritual interaction. Fellowship among Christians is unique because it is made possible only through a true relationship with Jesus Christ. Believers in Jesus have a common bond. We are all His children.

But most important we need to have daily fellowship with God. As Paul tells us in I Corinthians 1:9, God has called us into fellowship with His Son, Jesus Christ our Lord. Sin broke the fellowship Adam and Eve had with God. Our sins keep us from fellowship with God. To have fellowship with God takes a commitment that includes reading His Word daily and communicating to Him through prayer daily.

Peter writes in I Peter 3:8 as believers we are to be all of one mind. This involves an agreement in doctrine but also in our purpose in life and attitude toward others. This is the opposite of the way the world thinks. We are not to render evil for evil but have compassion for one another, love one another and be courteous.

In Galatians 2:9 we read that James and John gave "the right hand of fellowship" to Paul and Barnabas as they were leaving on a missionary trip to minister to the Gentiles. This represented a pledge of support and partnership. They gave them their blessing and assurance of their prayers and support. As believers we need to extend our hand of fellowship to those who are ministering for the Lord by praying and giving them support.

TODAY'S WORD FOR MAY 21

BOLDNESS

Great is my boldness of speech toward you; great is my boasting on your behalf. I am filled with comfort. I am exceedingly joyful in our tribulation. II Corinthians 7:4

In the world we live in today it is becoming increasingly difficult to speak out with boldness about our spiritual convictions. One of the reasons for this is that one may feel that it would offend someone or possibly be "politically incorrect." Most Christians are timid about talking about their faith because they are more concerned about what the world thinks than they are about obeying God's command to be a witness to a lost and sinful world.

One of the most powerful passages of scripture in the Bible concerns the last journeys of Paul and his imprisonment. Paul's words are powerful because he wrote with conviction about what he personally had experienced. During this time Paul wrote to the church at Philippi that he was not ashamed to have been serving Jesus. Paul also wrote that it was a privilege to suffer for Jesus. Paul looked for every opportunity to speak with boldness about Jesus and sharing with others God's plan of salvation. He was not ashamed to speak boldly of his faith.

Paul knew the reality of persecution for the first century believers. Before his conversion he had been a persecutor of Christians. And then after he became a believer he was beaten, stoned and thrown into prison because of his faith. Paul did not let any persecution stop him from preaching with boldness. In prison, Paul spread the good news of the gospel by writing letters to the churches he had helped establish.

As he waited in a lonely place during his last imprisonment, he wrote the church at Philippi asking them to pray for him that as he stood trial he would in no way be less bold than he always had been for Christ. Paul's desire was to have a bold testimony whether he lived or died. In Paul's own words (Philippians1:20) he wanted Christ always to be magnified in his body, whether by life or by death.

There are not too many Christians today that are bold in declaring their faith in Jesus. Some of the boldest that we have seen are children. We have mentioned before in these devotionals about one of our grandchildren who was in the hospital waiting for an emergency appendectomy. Before they put him to sleep, the doctor walked in and asked if he had any questions. Our seven year old grandson said that he had one question. He asked. "DO YOU KNOW JESUS?" When the doctor said he did, our grandson had no further questions. Not many people are bold enough even to ask their friends whether they know Jesus. It is not easy to be outgoing and bold about our faith.

America was founded by men who were bold in their faith. They established America as a nation under God. Today there are those who desire to remove God from our society and silence the voice of Christianity. Now is the time that Christians must stand up boldly for their faith while there is still opportunity.

TODAY'S WORD FOR MAY 22

SACRIFICE

It came to pass, that God tested Abraham, and said to him, "Abraham!" And he responded, "Here am I." Genesis 22:1

But do not forget to do good and to share with others, for with such sacrifices God is well pleased. Hebrews 13:16

Let each esteem others better than himself. Let each of you look out not only for his own interests, but also for the interests of others. Philippians 2:3-4

When God asked Abraham to give Isaac back to Him as a sacrificial offering of worship, Genesis 22:1 calls it a test to see if there was anything in Abraham's life that he treasured more than God. Such a severe test must have made no sense to Abraham. Why would God want to take the life of Isaac who had been a fulfillment of God's promise to Abraham? It might seem that God was trying to cause Abraham to doubt God and be disobedient. God's purpose was to examine Abraham's heart and so strengthen his faith. God often tests us in ways that may not make sense to us.

There are times when God requires something from us that requires a sacrifice of our time or money in order to get His work accomplished. He may ask us to sacrifice portions of what we may call valuable time to advance His cause. He may ask us to share what we have with someone in need. He may ask us to sacrifice our pride and forgive someone who wrongs us. The way we respond to what He requires of us speaks volumes about how we really feel about God. When we do good and share with others God considers our acts of kindness as sacrifices of worship to Him and He is pleased. (Hebrews 13:16 above).

Years ago when I (Ken) was in Honduras I remember seeing a young boy with his mother, dying of cancer lying in a hospital bed. Our mission supplied medicines to this hospital. Even though I delayed our scheduled appointment with another mission leader it was crucial that I found out what the exact medicine was that this boy needed, as well as what was needed by other children in this hospital. It was also very important for this young boy and his mother, as well as for me, to spend a little time with them letting them know that God cared for them.

We are to do as Jesus did and do good to others. Each thing we do to help someone, no matter how large or small, is an offering in God's sight. The writer of Hebrews says we should "not forget to do good."

The apostle Paul reminds us with his words in Philippians 2:3-4 that as believers we are to look beyond ourselves and our own interests and look to the interest of others. It may demand a sacrifice on our part but look what Jesus sacrificed for us. No sacrifice should be considered too big for the One who sacrificed His all for us.

TODAY'S WORD FOR MAY 23

MORALS

Every way of a man is right in his own eyes, the Lord weighs the heart. Proverbs 21:2

All the ways of a man are pure in his own eyes, but the Lord weighs the spirits. Proverbs 16:2

God is the source of morality. In His Word he has given us His standard for morals. As a result of our sinful nature man likes to do what he wants to do. We can rationalize that almost anything is "OK" and then proceed in doing it with the feeling that it is all right and justified.

The writer of Proverbs in the verses above tells us that the way man sees it is, "every way of a man is right in his own eyes." and "all the ways of man are pure in his own eyes." The writer tells us that God sees it differently. God sets the standards of what is right and He will judge if what we do is right. We can be certain that if our way does not measure up to God's moral standard, as given in His Word, that our way is not right. God determines man's motives and whether they are moral.

We are living in a world where people live for their own self interests and could care less about their morals if they stand in the way of what they want to do. They prefer to be popular with the world than to be right with God. Integrity seems to be more and more lacking in the lives of people. There is a quote attributed to Abraham Lincoln that we would like to share with you. Compare this to what we seem to read and hear about our friends, neighbors and leaders.

"My desire is to so conduct the affairs of this administration that if at the end, when I come to lay down the reins of power, I have lost every other friend on earth, I shall have at least one friend left, the friend deep down inside of me. I do the very best I know how; the very best I can; and I mean to keep doing that until the end. If the end brings me out all right, what is said against me will not amount to anything. If the end brings me out all wrong then a legion of angels swearing that I was right will make no difference."

Abraham Lincoln was willing to do the right thing no matter what the cost, even if it meant he lost every one of his friends. He left us a heritage to build upon and as a people we have not built on this heritage. He always trusted God for the wisdom that God alone could give to make the correct moral decisions in life. In the eyes of many, slavery was all right. Abraham Lincoln recognized that in the eyes of God it was wrong and must be abolished.

An army officer recently told of his first night in a tent on the battlefield. Most of the troops were swearing and telling filthy stories. Finally the officer spoke and said to all in the tent; "I have heard your rough talk but now I am going to talk to God. Out of respect to Him I ask you all to please be quiet." The place grew quiet; the officer prayed alone and never again had to contend with immoral talk.

TODAY'S WORD FOR MAY 24

DESPERATION

We were burdened beyond measure, above strength, so that we despaired even of life. Indeed, in our hearts we felt the sentence of death. But this happened that we might not rely on ourselves but on God. II Corinthians 1:8-9

Have you ever felt as desperate as the above scripture says? Paul had endured many hardships in his life, and although he does not give us a lot of details, he does indicate that he and his companions felt they were going to die. Paul goes on to say that because they were helpless to help themselves they had to rely on God.

Sometimes we have to come to the point of desperation before we realize our need to completely trust in God. We have talked to many desperate people. Some have been facing a desperate situation in their marriage and others have a desperate situation with a child. Possibly you face a desperate health situation or financial crises. In many areas of the world people are desperate for food.

We have witnessed unbelievable desperation in third world countries. We have seen mothers crying because they have no food, milk or medicine for their dying child that they are holding in their arms. We have seen single parent families with no housing, no food and seemingly no one to help because the father had died or just left home. This is real desperation.

Closer to home, here in America, there are the same hunger problems but in addition we see parents that are desperate because of the actions of their children. Parenting is very difficult in today's society. Many times problems with children develop when parents have not developed a lifestyle that honors God in their homes and their lives for their children to see as they were growing up and they have not taught their children from God's Word how to honor God. Children need good role models beginning with their parents.

But we also have seen great desperation from what we consider wonderful Christian parents. There are so many evil outside influences on children today that even children raised in Christian homes can be led to make choices in their lives that are the opposite of the way they were raised. We have only one answer for parents facing that situation and that is to pray for that child, continue to love that child and continue to live your consistent Christian life. Even when we stray God still loves us. Prayer can do what we can't do.

The feeling of desperation results often from choices one makes in life due to circumstances which one has no control. With desperation comes a loss of hope.

But there is a solution for a person that is facing a desperate situation in life. The scripture says that we are to "cast all of our cares upon the Lord because He cares for you." Let us tell you and assure you that no situation is too hard for God to overcome. It is our lack of faith that causes us to doubt what God wants to do for us. When desperate situations get us down, the only way to look is up. God is waiting for you to bring your desperation to Him.

TODAY'S WORD FOR MAY 25

JESUS

No man ever spoke like this man! John 7:46

Jesus said, why do you call me good? No one is good but One, that is, God. But if you want to enter into life, keep the commandments. Matthew 19:17

Jesus encountered a wealthy man who called Him "Good Teacher." The young man was right, for Jesus is both good, completely perfect, and the Teacher. He is the only One who can make this claim.

Today we want you to see and understand who Jesus is. He is the Son of God. He was sent to this earth by God to pay the penalty for our sins, because we are all sinners. He truly is our Savior, our Lord and our salvation. Make sure you know Him personally and develop your relationship with Him.

At the end of the third year of Jesus' ministry here on earth, the chief priests and Pharisees sent their soldiers to arrest Jesus. When they found Him, He was teaching and they heard Him speaking and left without arresting him and returned empty handed. They had been emotionally, morally and spiritually stunned and reported to the chief priests and Pharisees (John 7:46) that no man ever spoke like this man.

Jesus, while on this earth, possessed qualities of moral integrity and divine righteousness that marked Him as being different than all men. His claims went far beyond the claims of any rabbi. His teachings radiated with the glow of truth and godliness. His compassion for the fallen was genuine and His understanding of the Law astonished all that heard Him.

He was a man, but He alone possessed and displayed the God given credentials of the promised Messiah. These credentials were the out workings of His perfect moral character. He was the Messiah and He had come into the world. Jesus came to do the will of his father. Jesus said, for I did not speak of my own accord, but the Father who sent me commanded me what to say and how to say it John 12:49 (NIV).

Jesus was unique in his mission. He was sent into the world to do what no one else could do. He came to die for sinful man, every man, woman and child that ever lived, so that they might be reconciled to God and have eternal life. In John 10:14-15, Jesus stated: "I am the good Shepherd and I lay down my life for the sheep."

The writer of Hebrews in the first chapter verses 1-13 clearly states that Jesus was spoken of by the prophets and was above the angels. He would be worshipped by all and would sit at the right hand of God in heaven for eternity.

Jesus was unique in His birth, His ministry, His death, His resurrection and will be unique in His second coming to this world. If you know this man they call Jesus, He is knocking on the door of your heart right now asking you to accept Him as your Lord and Savior. Now is the time for your salvation, tomorrow may be too late.

TODAY'S WORD FOR MAY 26

BIBLE

For the Word of God is quick (alive), and powerful, and sharper than any two-edged sword, piercing even to the dividing asunder of the soul and spirit, and of the joints and marrow, and is a discerner of the thoughts and intents of the heart. Hebrews 4:12

An online Bible resource "Bible Gateway" shows that the number one verse in the Bible searched for from their 8 million monthly visitors is John 3:16. As far back as we can remember we were taught that John 3:16 was the key verse of the Bible.

Born-again Christians, those that have accepted Jesus as their Savior, believe the Bible to be God's very Word from beginning to end. Nevertheless, many professing Christians are spiritually starving because they do not read or even open a Bible very often if at all, and certainly do not read it with serious thought.

The Bible is not simply a collection of sacred writings. The Word of God is alive, dynamic and powerful as stated in Hebrews 4:12. It penetrates to the very core of our soul, revealing who we are and what we are not. It makes us aware of the evil that is within us and it opens our eyes to the holiness of God. If you are going to understand the significance of the Bible you must know the following basic truths:

First, you need to know what the Bible says about itself. In Psalm 19:7 we read that "the law of the Lord is perfect, converting the soul; the testimony of the Lord is sure, making wise the simple." We need to understand that what we read in the Bible is perfect and sure. It is the Word of God. God's Word is truth and it does not change, however, God's Word will change us.

Secondly, you need to know what God intended the Bible to do for you. The Bible is our guide book for living. In Genesis 1:1, the very first verse in the Bible we read, in the beginning God. The Bible is God's Word and He wants us to know that He is God who has existed for all time. He created the heavens and the earth and we can be assured that God is in control of all that He created.

Thirdly, you need to know that the Bible deals with facts. In Colossians 2:8 the apostle Paul was talking to the Christians at the church in Colossae and preached that the gospel is not a philosophy based on human ideas and experiences but on Christ's life and His example. He then goes on to say that we are to beware lest anyone mislead us through philosophy and empty deceit, based on the human traditions of the world, and not according to Christ who is one with God the Father.

And finally, you are to understand the importance of knowing the Bible. The apostle Paul was teaching Timothy telling him to be diligent by presenting himself approved to God, a worker who does not need to be ashamed, rightly dividing the word of truth. The word of truth is the Bible, God's Word.

The scriptures are filled with truths for each one of us to search out and share with others. In Psalm 119:97 the psalmist shared his thoughts about the Word, the Bible, and his desire to search it and be taught by God when he said, "Oh, how I love Your law." The more you read the Bible, the more you will love the author.

TODAY'S WORD FOR MAY 27

SALVATION

How shall we escape if we neglect so great a salvation? Hebrews 2:3

Believe on the Lord Jesus Christ and you will be saved. Acts 16:3

Non-believers do not understand us when we talk about salvation. They do not understand the biblical meaning of the word and cannot relate to it. They do not know what they need to be saved from and why they need to be saved.

Salvation is the gift of God that He has given to us through His Son Jesus. This salvation is available to everyone. We are saved when we believe on the Lord Jesus Christ as our Savior (Acts 16:3). Our hearts are broken that so many people today have rejected any need for God and the salvation that He has offered everyone. America was founded as a nation under God but many people today have an agenda to take God out of our society. This is being done through our schools and decision makers in our government.

Jesus began His ministry on earth with a challenging message: "Repent, for the kingdom of heaven is at hand" (Matthew 4:17). He never gave us an option. His message was simple and clear — "REPENT."

When we realize our need to be saved we should seek salvation immediately as the jailor did in Acts 16:29-30. God caused an earthquake to open the prison doors of the jail for Paul and Silas to escape. The jailor was so frightened that he ran and fell trembling before Paul and Silas and asked, "Sirs, what can I do to be saved?" The answer was given clearly: "Believe on the Lord Jesus Christ and you shall be saved, you and your household."

The writer of Hebrews stated that salvation is "SO GREAT" because:

- It was from God and through His Son Jesus Christ. John 3:16 reads, "For God so loved the world that He gave His one and only Son that whoever believes in Him shall not perish but have everlasting life."
- It came at a great cost. I John 3:16 reads, "Jesus Christ laid down His life for us."
- It is complete and for all time. I Peter 3:18 reads, "For Christ died for our sins once and for all."
- It is the only way to God and eternity. John 14:6 reads: "I am the way, the truth and the life. No man comes to the Father except through Me."

The Philippian jailer never asked what he could do to be "LOST." He knew that answer: You do not have to do anything to be lost because we are all born sinners and are condemned because of our sins. The only way to receive eternal life in heaven is by the SALVATION that God has offered us.

TODAY'S WORD FOR MAY 28

MERCY

He saved us, not because of the righteous things we had done, but because of His mercy.
Titus 3:5

The dictionary defines mercy as one being compassionate toward an offender. We have all sinned against God so we are all offenders and in need of God's mercy. God is truly a God of mercy and of love.

In I Samuel 24 we read of David showing mercy to Saul. David was being pursued by Saul and his army and Saul wanted to kill David. Saul entered a cave where David and his men were hiding. David managed to creep up unnoticed on Saul and cut off a piece of Saul's robe. David could have easily killed Saul, but instead he showed mercy to Saul and let him escape. Later, David showed Saul the piece of robe and was made aware of David's act of mercy, Saul repented and reconciled with David. Like Saul, we should be so grateful for the mercy God has shown for us that we desire to repent of our sins and be reconciled to God.

Although we are undeserving, because we are all sinners, He showed His mercy to us by sending His Son to this earth to save us from death which is the punishment we deserve. He sacrificed His only son to die on the cross to pay the penalty for our sins and then Jesus arose from the grave and soon went to Heaven to prepare for us a place to live for eternity. God then showed His mercy to us by sending His Holy Spirit to guide us as we live on this earth.

In Genesis 18 we read of Sarah laughing at God's promise, to give her a son in her old age, because she doubted God. God had mercy on her, in spite of her doubt, and gave her the promised son. Time after time the people of Israel turned away from God and sinned against Him, but God had mercy on them and continued to love them and bless them. This was the unmerited mercy that God continued to give all the generations that followed. In Psalm 18:21 it reads that God gives mercy to the merciful. God wants us to be merciful to those our lives touch each day and He promises to be merciful to us. We as Christians serve an awesome God who shows mercy to us.

Our children loved to participate in sports. We coached several of their teams because it gave us a chance to teach important life values to our children and their peers. We taught them about teamwork, what it meant to win and lose. We taught how to play fair, the value of practice and hard work. And on a few occasions we even dealt with mercy. In youth sports there is a "MERCY RULE" which brings a game to an early ending when one team has such a big lead that it is evident the losing team has no chance to win. We taught them to think about how they would feel if they were the losing team so that they would understand that it was the right thing to show them mercy.

TODAY'S WORD FOR MAY 29

REVERENCE

Therefore, since we are receiving a kingdom which cannot be shaken, let us have grace, by which we may serve God acceptably with reverence and godly fear. Hebrews 12:28

All across our world today there is a lack of reverence for God. Many deny He even exists. The problem is simply they have their own god. It is a "ME" generation and their god is themselves.

On any given day you can hear the word "GOD" spoken irrevently rather than with reverence. The third commandment of the Ten Commandments is: "Do not misuse the name of the Lord for the Lord will not hold anyone guiltless who misuses His name." This commandment is broken on a regular basis by many and when broken they show irreverence to God.

When we understand who God really is then we will not misuse the name of the Lord. When we know God we cannot help but be in awe of Him and have reverence for Him. Even though we cannot see God, we can know Him through reading the Bible and having the Holy Spirit dwelling within us.

Moses asked God to show him His glory (Exodus 33:18) but God told him no man could see His face and live. It is God's glory that demands reverence. God's glory is His majestic splendor.

There are many words referring to God's character in the scriptures: God is Holy, Majestic, Pure, Just, Almighty, Merciful, All-knowing, All-powerful, Ever-present, Eternal and our Creator. When we stop and think about these attributes of God we can begin to comprehend who He is and we cannot help but revere Him with awe and Godly fear. The most fundamental description of God is "HOLY." God's holiness is more than just an attribute; it is the essence of who He is. Our response to God's holiness is reverential awe.

As believers in Jesus we should desire to worship Him with reverence and in awe, and serve Him with Godly fear and respect. Today we get caught up in the "things" of life and forget to daily revere and serve God with fear and respect as the scripture tells us.

With reverence for God comes obedience. Reverence for God will compel us to live our life with caution, carefully, with discretion and circumspection so that our life honors God. God is to be held in awe because He is Lord. We must serve Him in an acceptable way, bearing fruit of the Spirit (love, gentleness, joy, faith, goodness, peace, meekness and self control).

These acts of obedience that we have just mentioned: reverence, obedience, honor, service, bearing fruit and telling others about Jesus is a list that all of us must work at daily. Those who revere their Lord and Savior will desire to serve Him and honor Him with their life.

TODAY'S WORD FOR MAY 30

CONFIDENCE

For the Lord will be your confidence and will keep your foot from being snared. Proverbs 3:26

In today's society it is very difficult for a person to be confident about anything or even anyone. One of the reasons for this is that situations can change daily. For example a job that seemed secure two years ago can be lost overnight today. Homes are going into foreclosure at a very fast rate.

But even more important we are seeing families falling apart. The only way that a person can feel securely confident is to have their confidence in the Lord and not in people and things. This verse from Proverbs assures us that when we have confidence in the Lord, He will guide every step we take in life.

Today we look at the Children of Israel as an example of our word, "confidence." God had enabled Israel to easily overcome the city of Jericho so Joshua set about to conquer the city of Ai. Ai was strategically located to provide a foothold in the central highlands for Israel and was the logical next step for Joshua to proceed to conquer the land that God had promised for them.

Joshua sent spies to Ai to check out the military strength of the city. The spies returned confident that the city of Ai could easily be taken by Israel. They advised Joshua that it would be so easy that they would not need their whole army. They said to Joshua, "Send two or three thousand men to take it and do not weary all the people, for only a few men are there." Joshua took their advice and sent three thousand men against Ai. To their surprise they were driven out by the men of Ai and thirty six of their men were killed.

Joshua and the elders of Israel had become too self-confident. How quickly they had forgotten that it was God who had given them the victory over Jericho. That was their first mistake. Secondly, they did not consult God about taking the city of Ai. They rushed head long into battle relying on their own strength. The third mistake was that they did not prepare themselves spiritually. They had already forgotten that before they undertook the battle of Jericho, God had required that they prepare themselves spiritually.

Joshua and the elders could not understand why they were so easily defeated by the men at Ai. The Israelites were so grieved over the loss that they tore their clothes in mourning, fell down on their faces and cried out to God asking what went wrong.

Most of us are just like the Israelites and go about our daily routines confident in our own abilities to accomplish whatever we have to do. But for the most part it just does not work. We seldom seek God's help. We turn to God only when we have been defeated. There is a better way and that is for us to begin each day by getting ourselves prepared spiritually. Remember when you read the Bible; this is the way God speaks to you. When you pray; this is the way you speak to God. When we put our trust in God we can be confident that He wants to give us victory and not defeat.

TODAY'S WORD FOR MAY 31

TRUTH

Jesus said to the Jews who believed Him, "If you abide in My Word, you are My disciples indeed. And you shall know the truth and the truth shall make you free." John 8:31-32

Many times the question is asked, "What is truth?" The answers we hear are many but the verse found in John 14:6 gives us the one and only true answer. Jesus said in this verse, "I am the way, the truth, and the life. No man comes to the Father except through Me." These words from Jesus are true because Jesus is God's Son and is Holy and perfect and He cannot lie. God is the source of all truth and the only way we can come to God, the Father is through His Son Jesus.

There is so much deceit and deception in this world that it is very difficult at times to know if you are hearing or reading the truth. One of the most difficult situations in the lives of parents today is to know whether their children, their spouse or their neighbors are telling the truth. This is very unfortunate, but it is true because of the evil and sinful nature of the world we live in.

There is a way to build truth into your life. The one sure way is to become grounded in the scriptures. In other words to read the Bible daily, study the passage you read and then pray that God would make that portion relative to you.

A good illustration is comparing learning the truth from the Bible to learning the details of the job where you are working. When you begin a new job or a new project at home or at school, you are trained. You are given detailed instructions as to how you are to accomplish what is expected of you. You read the orders over and over, if necessary until you fully understand what you are expected to do.

The same is true when you study the Bible. To find the truth in the Bible read it over and over prayerfully until God makes it clear to you and it becomes embedded in your heart and mind. Some people that believe in the Lord Jesus as their Savior have accepted erroneous ideas of truth because they have not incorporated the truth that is written in the scriptures into their hearts and mind.

You need a real desire and a firm commitment if you are going to let God's Word shape you. Whenever you have an area of need turn to the Bible and find a passage of scripture that addresses that need. For example, if someone has hurt you look for verses on forgiveness. You can look in a concordance or in the subject section in the back of your Bible under the word forgiveness. As you read these verses look for instructions from God and then respond. The awesome thing about the Bible is that there is no area of life or human experience that the Bible does not address.

If we let the truths of the scriptures fill our minds, guard our emotions and influence our conduct, God will richly reward us with His blessings on our lives. By reading and meditating on His Word we learn to understand His ways. The more we know Him the more we will love Him.

TODAY'S WORD FOR JUNE 1

BITTERNESS

For I see that you are poisoned by bitterness and bound by iniquity. Acts 8:23

Get rid of all bitterness, rage and anger, brawling and slander, along with every form of malice. Ephesians 4:31

Years ago a famous boxer was convicted of murder and sent to jail for life. The boxer maintained his innocence and approximately 19 years later his verdict was overturned. When the boxer was released, he was asked if he was bitter. He responded Yes and stated sure anyone would be bitter under those circumstances. He also said he learned in prison that bitterness only consumes the life that allows it. That means a person who permits bitterness to control his or her life is allowing those who imprisoned him to take even more from him than his freedom.

Bitterness is like cancer. It eats away at us and keeps us from enjoying God's blessings. In Hebrews 12:15 it reads, Looking carefully, lest any root of bitterness springing up cause trouble, and by this many become defiled. Some of the Christians the author was writing to were considering returning to Judaism because of the persecution and injustice they were facing. The author tells them that bitterness could spring up in their hearts and overshadow their deepest Christian principles and relationships the same way a small root grows into a big tree.

When we are mistreated by others and have disappointments in our life it is so easy to let bitterness come into our lives. God does not want this to happen. Jesus can heal our concerns that cause bitterness so we must put them in His hands.

In the verse written above in Acts, Paul was talking about Simon who had practiced sorcery and claimed he was someone great. However Simon listened to the preaching of Philip and came to know Jesus and was baptized. Later, we are told about Simon meeting Peter and John and observed them placing their hands on new believers, and those people received the Holy Spirit. Simon asked if he could buy that same power. Peter told Simon he was poisoned by bitterness and bound by iniquity and could not have any share in their ministry. His heart was not right.

As Christians, we need to learn not to be bitter about "things." We need to learn to turn our disappointments and our concerns over to the Lord. Do not let them fester and grow in our minds allowing bitterness to control us. When bitterness is in our heart it is not right with the Lord. Paul tells us to get rid of all bitterness because it brings grief to us personally and it also grieves the Holy Spirit of God.

Bitterness and joy are emotions felt in our heart. A stranger cannot feel our bitterness as we feel it. If people see that we are bitter, we are not a testimony of the joy that comes from being a believer, and this grieves the Holy Spirit of God.

TODAY'S WORD FOR JUNE 2

FOOLISHNESS

But the natural man does not receive the things of the Spirit of God, for they are foolishness to him; nor can he know them, because they are spiritually discerned. I Corinthians 2:14

Foolishness is bound up in the heart of a child; the rod of correction will drive it far from him. Proverbs 22:15

Several times in our lifetime we have made decisions we looked back on and said to one another, "That was a foolish decision." We then tried to ask ourselves what were the reasons we made that decision. We asked ourselves if we saw any "red flags" or things that should have alerted to us to reverse that decision. We also learned from the decision so we would not repeat a similar mistake. If we evaluated foolish decisions properly after they had been made, we learned the evaluation process became a great learning experience for us.

Foolishness is a word Paul used several times in the scripture. In the verse above from I Corinthians, Paul reminds us the "natural man," one who does not believe in Jesus as Lord, feels the things of the spirit of God are foolishness to him. The natural man lacks wisdom and cannot understand spiritual truths. Only the believer can understand the things of the spirit.

Understanding God's message to us and to the world as given in His Word has nothing to do with one's intelligence. The message of God sending His Son into the world to die on the cross as a condemned criminal in order to save a world of sinners who rejected and denied Him, cannot be comprehended by the human mind, no matter how intelligent a person might be. The spiritual eyes of the unbeliever are blinded and cannot see the truth.

In I Corinthians 1:18-19 Paul said, "For the message of the cross is foolishness to those who are perishing, but to us who are saved (and have accepted Jesus as Savior) it is the power of God. For it is written: I will destroy the wisdom of the wise, and bring to nothing the understanding of the prudent."

In Proverbs 22:15 (above), the writer reminds us foolishness is *in* the heart of a child, but correction will drive foolishness *from* the child. The word foolishness in Hebrew means silliness, perverseness and carelessness of body. We want to make it clear this does not refer to ones sin nature, but it is the by-product of the fall of man. The rod of correction cannot change the sin nature, but it can subdue foolishness because it brings wisdom. Without correction, children will continue to do foolish things because wisdom must be taught which will drive foolishness from a child.

Foolishness is a form of sin according to Proverbs 24:9 and according to Mark 7: 21-23 because it originates in the heart. Ecclesiastics 7:25 tells us foolishness is a sign of wickedness. The consequence of foolishness brings sorrow to people and keeps us from knowing God which increases our spiritual blindness.

TODAY'S WORD FOR JUNE 3

PROSPER

If you do not obey the Lord your God, you shall not prosper in your ways. Deuteronomy 28:15&29

He sought God in the days of Zechariah and as long as he sought the Lord, God made him prosper. II Chronicles 26:5

Pray for the peace of Jerusalem: May they prosper who love you. Psalm 122:6

We all want to prosper and be successful in life. Even Moses was very specific in Deuteronomy chapter 28, telling the Children of Israel what they needed to do to receive God's blessings and to prosper in life. He told them they must obey the Lord their God and carefully follow all His commandments (Verse 1). In later verses he listed the blessings they would receive as a result of their obedience. However in verses 15-68, Moses detailed the curses they would receive because of their disobedience. Therefore, Moses warned them if they disobeyed God they would not prosper. Are you living in disobedience to God and wondering why everything is going wrong? Some people become envious and bitter when they see others more prosperous.

What does it mean to prosper? God has prospered you with specific talents to do His work. Are you using them as He would desire? However God may prosper you with time so you can help others in their times of need. If so, how do you spend your time? Finally, God may prosper you with wealth. Can He trust you with what He has given you? How do you respond?

Another thought for you to consider is God will only prosper you when you put Him first place in your life. You cannot, if you live for the Lord on Sunday and not on the weekdays. Also you cannot treat your friends kindly and your family unkindly and expect to prosper. God may prosper you with talent, time or even financially, how you respond is what makes a difference.

In II Chronicles 26, we read about Uzziah who became King of Judah at the age of 16. It is recorded when Uzziah was living under King Zechariah as a younger child, he continually sought God in all he did. When he became King, God said as long as he sought Him, he would prosper. Notice the 5th verse says "as long as." During the short time Uzziah was obedient to God he did prosper. Unfortunately, he became proud which led him to be unfaithful to God. God afflicted him with leprosy until the day he died.

Psalms 22:6 instructs us as Christians to pray for the peace of Jerusalem. The Psalmist says if we do, God will prosper us. Do you pray for this each day? Be aware God expects us to do this. God's chosen people have turned away from Him, but God has never turned away from them.

TODAY'S WORD FOR JUNE 4

SAME

Jesus Christ is the same yesterday and today and forever. Hebrews 13:8

Think about how quickly things become old and out of date and not much stays the same. Do you remember typewriters and carbon paper? Most young people today have no idea what these are. They know about computers and printers and the fact a printer will produce as many copies as needed. Therefore carbon paper is no longer needed to make a second copy.

We have a printer attached to our computer to help us edit devotionals. A few days ago the print head of the printer had what we called, a fast death. We called to see if it could be repaired or replaced. We soon found out we could purchase a faster printer with better technology for less money than repairing our dead printer. We were reminded again how things change and the fact not much stays the same.

Many things change faster today than most people can understand. Someone will get a new computer or a new camera and before it is out of the box, a better and more sophisticated one is in production. This is true in almost every area of our lives today. For example, think of how fast advances are being made in the medical field.

Everything man makes or invents will become old and obsolete. Often what man thinks is true with his limited wisdom is often discovered to be false.

For example years ago a relative had severe stomach ulcers. He was rushed to the hospital and the doctors did surgery on his stomach thinking that was the only cure. We now know, several years later, that ulcer problems can be cured with antibiotics. Continually new discoveries and inventions literally change the way we live and the way we handle sicknesses, diseases and accidents.

The writer of Hebrews reminds us Jesus does not change like everything else in life. Isn't this thrilling to know? He clearly and firmly states Jesus is the same yesterday, today and forever. (Hebrews 13:8) Yesterday Jesus created the world. The scripture tells us, "In the beginning, O Lord, You laid the foundation of the world." (Hebrews 1:10) Today, Jesus sits at the right hand of God, our Father in heaven. "He, having offered one sacrifice for sins for all time, sat down at the right hand of God." (Hebrews 10:12) Tomorrow, Jesus will still be creator, He will still be sitting at the right hand of God, and He will rule forever with us by His side. Hebrews 1:8 tells us God, the Father, declares about the Son, "Your throne O God, will last forever."

We have been in many churches that display these words, written by the author of Hebrews: "JESUS CHRIST! The same yesterday, today and forever." What a comfort to read these words when we enter the church.

Yes, we live in a world that is constantly changing, but the good news of the gospel will never change. What a blessed assurance we have because our faith is in a Savior, our Lord Jesus Christ, who is the same, yesterday, today and forever.

TODAY'S WORD FOR JUNE 5

ETERNAL LIFE

I have come that they may have life, and that they may have it more abundantly. John 10:10

And the testimony is this, that God has given us eternal life, and this life is in His Son. He who has the Son has the life; he who does not have the Son of God does not have life. I John 5: 11-12

Every day we wake up happy, rejoicing, and looking forward to another day to serve the Lord. The reason for this does not depend on the circumstances we are in or on how we are feeling physically or emotionally. The reason is not based on our feelings but it is because what we know. Because we have accepted Jesus as our Savior and we have put our total trust in Him, we know we will have eternal life with Him and our life here on earth is only temporary.

One of the most transforming truths found in the Bible is the truth spoken by Jesus as stated in John above. This is not just good news, it is *great* news! Jesus wants us to know our sins are forgiven by His shed blood and we as Christians are on our way to heaven. Additionally He wants us to experience joy, fulfillment, peace, and satisfaction here on this earth until the time He takes us home to be with Him.

John is telling us in this verse, Jesus as the Messiah and Son of God is the only way of being saved from sin and hell and the only way to receive eternal life. Jesus is the one source for the knowledge of God and for the one basis for spiritual security.

We do not have to struggle through this life making the best of bad situations, falling and failing, doubting and despairing, discouraged and defeated or barely hanging onto life until it is over. The good news is we do not have to go through these struggles and wait until eternity to find abundant life. We can have an abundant life while on this earth, with the assurance of Jesus as our Savior.

Who was this man Jesus who shed His blood so that we could have eternal life? He was the perfect human being, God's ideal for humanity, because He is the very Son of God. For thirty-three years He lived among us under the same pressures we face every day. Yet, He lived a perfect and sinless life. The abundant life Jesus offers us and wants us to live, does not mean our life will be filled with an abundance of things. Jesus offers every believer a rich and satisfying life. Out of His riches He fills the life of every believer with joy, peace, comfort and assurance.

Each of us can enjoy that kind of abundant life now. It begins when we ask Jesus to forgive us of our sins and accept Jesus into our heart. We then receive God's precious gift of spending an eternity with Him in heaven. What do you think when you hear the word abundant? As believers, we need to get our minds off of the "things" of the world and get our minds onto the "things" God has for us. Nothing is more rewarding than waking up every morning with joy, peace, comfort and the assurance you will spend an eternity with Jesus.

TODAY'S WORD FOR JUNE 6

COMMUNICATION

No man ever spoke like this Man! John 7:46

The greatest communicator of all time was Jesus. In the verse above from the book of John, the temple officers returned to the chief priests and the Pharisees and asked why they had not brought Jesus to them. Their response was, "no man ever spoke like this man." Therefore, the Pharisees asked the temple guards if they had been deceived the same way the crowds had been deceived about this man, Jesus!

The temple guards were Levites who worked in the temple to maintain order. They were religiously trained and knowledgeable and were sent by the chief priests and Pharisees with orders to seize Jesus. However something happened when they came face to face with Jesus and heard His powerful preaching. Jesus' words affected them so much they could not bring themselves to arrest Him.

Jesus was a great communicator, but more than just a communicator, He came to this earth with the greatest message ever given which was to save sinners like you and me from our sins. He had a message that needed hearing and there were those like the Pharisees who refused to hear the message and wanted Him killed. They were self righteous and arrogant because of their religious knowledge. They had closed their minds to the message Jesus was communicating. Communication requires listening. We must be willing to listen to what God is communicating to us.

Communication is basically taken for granted. We can call on the telephone, send an E mail, a text message and even a video and get connected immediately. With all of these communication aids, individuals do not use them to strengthen their faith.

A believer's first communication priority must be their communication with God by reading His Word and communicating to Him in prayer.

Our second communication priority is our communication with our family. The American family has very little communication with each other. They are missing the time needed every day in the home for communication on a one-on-one basis. Families do not eat together; they do not share concerns or problems nor even play together. Each day Dad goes one way, Mom goes another and the children go another way. Because both parents work to provide for the family and children are in daycare, families have a shortage of quality time together.

When we were growing up many families would take time to eat a meal each day together and would pray and read the Bible as a family. Today this is not practiced nor considered to be a part of the family's schedule. How can a family bond with each other without any kind of communication with one another? The answer is simple, it cannot! We wonder what is wrong with our society, our families, our schools, our churches and our leaders in government. The problem is God has been removed from each of those areas. We are living in a godless society. We need families to desire communication with God and then among themselves.

TODAY'S WORD FOR JUNE 7

REPENTANCE

Truly, these times of ignorance God overlooked, but now commands all men everywhere to repent. Acts 17:30

Webster defines repentance as deep sorrow or contrition for a past sin. It is true, repentance requires being sorry. However, true repentance requires more than just feeling sorry. It also requires a complete turning away from sin and a determination not to return to or repeat our sinful acts.

When we accepted Jesus as our Savior and became believers, we needed to repent of our sins. Do you remember doing this? God expects each of us to repent if we are to become one of His children. True repentance requires changing the direction of one's life from sin centeredness and self to God centeredness. If we are willing to renounce our sin filled way of life and turn to God, He will give us a new direction in life.

Take a moment now and evaluate your life. Is repentance necessary? How have you treated God? How have you interacted with your spouse, children and family? How have you acted at your workplace? Have you been honest and responsible? Have you honored God in all that you have done?

We are all born sinners into this world and cannot have both God and un-repented sin in our life at the same time. The only way we can have God in our life is to be willing to repent and turn from sin. Repentance opens the door to God's free gift of salvation through faith in Jesus Christ.

True repentance is always coupled with faith. It is impossible to have saving faith and not to be repentant. Faith without repentance is the ultimate result of hypocrisy, and repentance without faith is futile. When you asked Jesus to come into your heart you asked for forgiveness of your past sins.

Repentance is not merely sorrow for something done, nor penance or reformation brought about by our own efforts for self-glorification. However repentance is an intentional intellectual, emotional and spiritual change in ones life. The prodigal son first had a change of mind, then a change of heart and then a change of will. As we know the result was repentance.

We have many examples in the scriptures where repentance was preached. John the Baptist preached repentance. Jesus preached repentance. Peter and Paul preached repentance. Repentance is so important to God that He commands "all men every where to repent."(Acts 17:30) Jesus said the lost were to repent. Paul said the back sliders were to repent. Jesus said in Luke 13:3: "But unless you repent you too will perish." There are severe consequences for those unwilling to repent.

The proof of repentance in your life is threefold: Turning from sin; turning to God and then seeking to do what the Lord leads you to do.

TODAY'S WORD FOR JUNE 8

SATAN

So the great dragon was cast out, that serpent of old, called the Devil and Satan, who deceives the whole world; he was cast to the earth, and his angels were cast out with him. Revelation 12:9

Satan is a person. Yes, there is a personal devil. We read in the scriptures that he appeared before God, he talked with God, and he reasoned with Eve in the Garden of Eden, he tempted Jesus, he performed miracles and signs and he tempts both the saved and unsaved to commit sin. Only a person can take part in an intelligent dialogue and reason, therefore Satan is a person however, you must remember he is the chief evil spirit in the world.

He has been given many names and titles in the scriptures:

- Satan — "adversary" He does not have the capacity to love or to show mercy. He is called Satan 50 times in the Bible.
- Devil — "slanderer" this title is used over 100 times in the New Testament
- Abaddon — "destruction"
- Apollyon — "destroyer" Found in Revelation 9:11.
- Lucifer — "day star" or "morning star" he can transform himself into an angel of light. Isaiah 14:12

He is called "the god of this age" in II Corinthians 4:4, the "prince of the power of the air" in Ephesians 2:2, the "great dragon" in Revelation 12:9 and the "serpent of old" in Revelation 20:2. Jesus called him the ruler of this world in John 12:31. Remember he is not the ruler of creation but the ruler of the world system. God warns us: "Do not love the world or the things in the world." I John 2:15. Satan desires that we all be caught up in his system and be lost. God desires all of us accept Jesus Christ and be saved.

Satan fell from his original exalted position when he decided to put his self-will above God's perfect will. Five times it is recorded in Isaiah 14:12-15 that Satan said, "I will." He said, I will ascend into heaven, I will exalt my throne above the stars of God, I will sit on the mount of the congregation on the farthest side of the north, I will ascend above the heights of the clouds and I will be like the most high.

Two things you must be aware of concerning the devil. First of all, we are warned to be alert because the devil is our enemy and always looking to tempt us. I Peter 5:8 says to "Be self-controlled and alert. Your enemy the devil prowls around like a roaring lion looking for someone to devour."

Second, we have a defense against the deceitful ways of the devil. James tells us to: "Submit yourselves to God, resist the devil, and he will flee from you." Satan has power in this world, but God has power over Satan.

TODAY'S WORD FOR JUNE 9

AFFLICTIONS

My heart is in turmoil and cannot rest; days of affliction confront me. Job 30:27

This is my comfort in my affliction, for your Word has given me life. Psalms 119:50

A great concern for us has been to see children, young people and adults suffering afflictions in their lives. All of us react when an affliction affects one of our family members, but do we show concern for those in far off areas of our world who may have even greater afflictions? The definition of the word "Affliction" refers to the mental or body pain one may have in a sickness or a calamity.

When sin entered the world through the fall of Adam and Eve, affliction entered as well. Our minds and our bodies are now subject to suffering and pain. Some suffer greater afflictions than others. It is heart wrenching to see children born with physical and mental challenges as well as people suffering with cancer and with other diseases. It is also sad to see whole families living in poverty who do not have food to eat. This is affliction as well. No matter if the affliction is large or small it is so easy for the victim to fall into despair and, as Job said, the "heart is in turmoil."

As believers in Jesus we face affliction with a different attitude than those who do not know Him. We can look beyond our affliction with the hope of a life without affliction when we are in heaven. Our suffering in this life is only temporary.

It is usually the case when we are going through tough times in life with our greatest afflictions that God does His greatest work through us. Afflictions should increase our reliance on the Lord. This gives us an opportunity to share with others the strength of our faith and allows God to demonstrate His power through us.

Recently we had a dear friend who was afflicted with lung cancer. She used this time of affliction to testify to others of her faith and trust in the Lord. What a blessing and encouragement she was to us and many others. She is now home with her Lord and Savior and free from all suffering and affliction.

We have witnessed so many situations of affliction that it would be very easy for us to become immune to them. However we continue to ask God daily to make us sensitive to those who are going through a time of affliction. Do you have that caring spirit and attitude? Almost daily a situation comes our way, but we are limited, as many of you are, by our finances and even with the time to respond. One thing we can always do is pray and be a friend to that person who is hurting.

The afflicted one may be a relative or friend with cancer, a child without food, a man who lost a job or a family who lost their house and is now homeless. The list can go on and on, but remember, we can pray, we can love, and we can care.

When you are facing an affliction in your life, look for opportunities to let others see Christ in you. You will be surprised to see how much God will bless you and ease your affliction because you are thinking of others and not yourself.

TODAY'S WORD FOR JUNE 10

HEAVEN

This is what the Lord says: Heaven is My throne and the earth is My footstool, My hands have made both heaven and earth, they and everything in them are mine. Isaiah 66:1-2

For I have come down from heaven to do the will of God who sent Me, not to do My own will. John 6:38

When the Lord Jesus had finished talking with them He was taken up into heaven and sat down in the place of honor at God's right side. Mark 16:19

What do you think about when you hear someone refer to the word "heaven?" We get excited because we know we will be in heaven soon and we will see Jesus face to face. Won't it be wonderful to sing praises unto God by the hour with the angels? We do not have good singing voices now so we are very excited to know that God will take care of our voices so we can praise Him. Have you considered standing before God knowing that He is God? As many say today, what an awesome feeling that will be.

We will also see our parents, our family and friends who have gone to heaven before us. What a meeting that will be. In heaven there will be no more sickness, no more persecution, no more sin and no more earthly cares.

These verses from the Bible that we have listed above cover three major thoughts we would like to share with you. First, the verse from Isaiah reminds us God created the heaven and the earth and the entire universe which are His dwelling places. Secondly, the verse from John reminds us that Jesus came down to earth from heaven to do the will of God. Finally, the verse in Mark reminds us that Jesus ascended back into heaven when His work on earth was done to prepare a home for us in heaven.

Heaven, we know, is a place where God our Father dwells. In John 14:2 Jesus tells us that "In My Father's house are many mansions, I go to prepare a place for you." Heaven is as real as the place where you live. It is called a city whose maker and builder is God (Hebrews 11:10). In I Kings 8:23 we are told that heaven is above the earth.

Heaven is a place prepared for the "saints" of God. A "saint" is one whom by faith in the Lord Jesus Christ has been spiritually born into the family of God. As members of the family of God, the apostle Paul reminds us in Colossians 3:2, to "Set your minds on things above (heaven), not on things on earth." Faith in Jesus as our Savior changes our focus and our priorities away from temporal things on earth to heavenly things which are everlasting.

Our home on earth is only our temporary home. For us that know the Lord, heaven is our eternal home. Are you ready?

TODAY'S WORD FOR JUNE 11

HELL

The wicked shall be turned into Hell, and all the nations that forget God. Psalm 9:17

Then He will say to those on the left hand, depart from Me, you cursed, into the everlasting fire prepared for the devil and his angels. Matthew 25:41.

The verse above from Psalms says that the wicked shall be sent to Hell. It is most important for us to tell you, if you have not accepted Jesus as your Savior and Lord, then we can say with total confidence you are on the way to Hell. Hell is not fictional. Hell is a real place for real people who reject the only true God and Savior, the Lord Jesus Christ.

Making no decision about Jesus is the same as saying "no" to Jesus and to His gift of spending an eternity in Heaven with Him. The Bible in John 3:36 makes this very clear "Whosoever believes in the Son has eternal life, and whosoever rejects the Son will not see life." Unless you know Jesus as your Savior, you are headed for Hell. The decision is yours and yours alone.

In Acts 1:25 we are told that Hell is the sinner's own place of torment. After Judas betrayed Jesus and saw Him die on the cross, he was remorseful. He returned to the chief priests and elders and tried to make restitution. The scripture says after he threw down the 30 pieces of silver he received for betraying Jesus at the feet of the chief Priest, Judas went out and hanged himself. As a result of his own transgression, Judas went to "his own place."

In the verse above from Matthew we see Hell is an eternal place God prepared for Satan and his angels. They are anti-God and have no choice, but to go to Hell. We have a choice. We can choose Satan's prepared Hell or the Heaven which God has prepared for those who believe in Him.

The day before Jesus died on the cross He said to His eleven disciples: "Let not your heart be troubled, I go to prepare a place for you." The place He is preparing for us is His "Fathers house, Heaven." The choice we have is either Hell, which is prepared for Satan along with his angels, or Heaven, the place in God's house Jesus has prepared for those who follow Him.

Jesus said in Matthew 7:13-14, "Wide is the gate and broad is the road that leads to destruction (Hell) and many enter through it. But small is the gate and narrow is the road that leads to life, (Heaven) and only a few find it."

You have a choice either to follow the many on the broad way that leads to eternal Hell or you can join the few and follow Jesus on the narrow road that leads to eternal life in Heaven.

Hell is a place of eternal fire, a place of darkness and a place of torment. In Matthew 13:50 we are told those who are in Hell will weep and gnash their teeth. Hell is eternal and once someone is there, there is no escape.

TODAY'S WORD FOR JUNE 12

REVIVAL

If My people who are called by My name will humble themselves, and pray and seek My face, and turn from their wicked ways, then I will hear from heaven, and will forgive their sin and heal their land. II Chronicles 7:14

Many professing Christians today have never experienced a revival and probably never heard of one, or even know what a revival is. If someone asked you what we meant by a "revival," how would you respond?

A "revival" as we refer to it here, is a time when a single person or a group of people (believers in Jesus), decide they need to restore their faith in the Lord and get back to living by the fundamentals that God expects from us.

Today, we need a revival and it can begin with you. All that is necessary is one person who really is dedicated to live daily for God.

There are at least 12 revivals referred to in the Old Testament. There are four factors preceding each revival common to these Old Testament revivals. These factors are also relevant for us today. They are, a moral and Spiritual decline among the people of God; preceded by some kind of a righteous judgment from God; the raising up of an immensely burdened leader or leaders; and a common location for a beginning with a common burden.

God used Moses to bring revival to the Israelites when they rebelled against Him. It would seem after all the miracles the Israelites had witnessed that they would be forever faithful to God. Yet just within months, while Moses was receiving the Ten Commandments on Mt. Sinai, the Israelites turned away from God and made a golden calf to worship. Moses had to call his people to a revival of their relationship with God.

America was founded as a nation under God, but today as a people we have rebelled and sinned against God. Thus, we have witnessed a moral and spiritual decline, not only among the general population, but also among believers. Because of this we need a revival of individuals who will spread it to our families and finally to our churches. Perhaps you need a revival in your family. God desires believers to be leaders in our families and to call our family members to repentance in order to bring revival in our homes.

Our actions should be to bring our families together and have each one humble themselves before God; pray; seek God's face; confess their sins and then turn from their wicked ways. He will forgive their sins and heal their homes which will bring them into a right relationship with Him. Then God will open doors for others to be drawn near to Him because of our families.

When God moves into our homes and touches family members spiritually, a revival will begin. God is just waiting for us to humble ourselves; pray; seek Him, and turn from our WICKED WAYS. Then we will hear from heaven and when we repent, God will forgive our sins and heal our homes and land.

TODAY'S WORD FOR JUNE 13

TESTIMONY

This is the disciple who TESTIFIES of these things, and wrote these things, and we know his testimony is true. John 21:24

And I, brethren, when I came to you, did not come with excellence of speech or of wisdom declaring to you the TESTIMONY of God. For I determined not to know anything among you except Jesus Christ and Him crucified. I Corinthians 2:1-2

He who believes in the Son of God has the witness in himself; he who does not believe God has made Him a liar, because he has not believed the TESTIMONY that God has given of His Son. And this is the TESTIMONY: that God has given us eternal life, and this life is in His Son. I John 5:10-11

The word testimony is probably best known in the secular world as statements made in a court session. In the Christian world, a testimony usually refers to the words one gives concerning one's relationship with Jesus. A testimony usually contrasts one's life before accepting Jesus as Savior, with the life one is living now.

We can remember as children going to church and hearing moving testimonies of life changing experiences from familiar people whose lives had been completely changed because they had accepted Jesus as their Savior.

A testimony is of no value unless it is based on truth. A testimony given in a court of law, includes a person who must swear to tell the truth and nothing but the truth. In John 21:24 the Apostle John is speaking of himself as the one who is testifying Jesus was God. John's testimony is true because he was an eye witness and his account was based on his personal relationship with Jesus. John walked with Him, talked with Him, and worked with Him daily. John's words verify Jesus is the Christ and He is the Son of God.

In the passage we noted above from I Corinthians, Paul is writing to the church at Corinth verifying his testimony Jesus is Lord and Savior and available for them. Paul always looked for every opportunity to give his testimony and was a learned scholar who could preach with eloquence. In this passage, Paul says he preached a simple testimony of Jesus and wants us to understand, it is not the eloquence of the words of a person's testimony that brings others to faith and a relationship with Jesus, but it is by God's power. We should never fear to give our testimony. God will use our testimony no matter how eloquent or simple it is.

In I John 5:10-11, John tells us whoever believes and receives the testimony God has given us, will receive His promise of eternal life. If you ever doubt the certainty of your faith and your relationship with Jesus remember you have the testimony of Jesus, God's Son. You have the testimony of the disciples who walked, talked and lived with Jesus. You have the testimony of God's Word and those who were led by the Holy Spirit to write down the testimonies of those that were affected by Jesus.

TODAY'S WORD FOR JUNE 14

FEAR

The fear of the Lord is the beginning of knowledge, but fools despise wisdom and instruction. Proverbs 1:7

So we can say with confidence, the Lord is my helper so I will have no fear. What can mere people do to me? Hebrews 13:6

Oh fear the Lord, there is no want to those who fear Him. Psalm 34:9

The fear of the Lord, as referred to in the Bible means to revere and respect God and to be in awe of His power and majesty. Job tells us the fear of the Lord is wisdom, because it wisely brings us to revere and honor God and causes us to desire to live in obedience to His Word.

Solomon says fear is the beginning of knowledge and wise men store up knowledge [Proverbs 10:18]. Fear of the Lord, the scripture tells us, should cause us to run to Him and not from Him. In Proverbs 18:10 we are told the name of the Lord is a strong tower and the righteous should run to it. The awesomeness of the power of God that leads us to fear Him is also what causes us to run to Him. We are to run to God for our salvation and when we are saved we have no reason to fear.

Fearing the Lord is only one meaning of the word fear. There are also fears that many people have in their lives today. These fears could be family related such as fear of abuse, job situations, health issues or financial concerns. Many people today are fearful about the uncertainty of their national economy. The Lord has said in Psalms 27:1 "He is our light and salvation, whom shall I fear? The Lord is the strength of my life, of whom shall I be afraid?"

These fears arouse a sense of impending danger in our minds that could cause bodily harm or mental and emotional concerns. In II Timothy 1:7 Paul tells us God has not given us a spirit of fear, but of power and of a sound mind. When we put our trust in God, He gives us the power and courage to face our fears and the sound mind to calm our fears.

We have an awesome God and nothing is too big for Him. We need to put our complete trust in Him and He will take away our fear. But for those who do not put their faith in Jesus, life will be filled with fear. The unbeliever has no hope and no room for joy in your life. If your life seems hopeless today then study this verse: "So we can say with confidence, the Lord is my helper so I will have no fear. What can mere people do to me?" Hebrews 13:6.

You have a choice to make if you do not have your trust in the Lord. You can continue living a life controlled by fear, hopelessness, loneliness and the emotional anguish that accompanies fear, or you can run to God and put your trust in Him and ask Him to be your helper and take away your every fear.

TODAY'S WORD FOR JUNE 15

REWARD

Your Father who sees in secret will reward you openly. Matthew 6:4

Each one will receive his own reward according to his own labor. I Corinthians 3:8

But love your enemies, do good, and lend, hoping for nothing in return; and your reward will be great. Luke 6:35

It seems everything we do somehow involves us getting rewards in return. When you go to stores, they give you cash back or points so you can get something free.

When you fly on airlines they ask if you are going to use points. Every time you fly with that airline or use their credit card, you earn points. All of these are put into place to encourage business. These are better known as reward programs.

Children will do special projects for a parent when there is a reward involved. Students generally will go the extra mile to complete an assignment when there is a reward involved. In the work place, employees always do a job more accurately and with more speed when there is a reward involved.

God has a rewards program far better than everything offered to us here on earth. Believers seem to show very little interest in His program. Jesus often spoke of His Father's promise to reward us for loyally serving Him. For example, when we are persecuted for His sake, in other words for taking our stand for our Lord, Jesus tells us to rejoice for great is our reward in heaven (Matthew 5:12).

God wants us to give, pray and fast, not as the Pharisees' did in public for all to see but He wants us to do these things in private. "Your Father who sees in secret will Himself reward you openly in heaven." (Matthew 6:4, 6, 18). We are to serve from the heart unto the Lord and not for the praise of men.

Almost without exception when the scriptures mention reward, it is for those who are faithful in serving the Lord here on earth and whose reward will be received in heaven. What an awesome promise all believers should be committed to work toward. Luke tells us in the verse above, to help others without the need of a reward in return. Nevertheless, God still promises us a reward for being obedient.

We do not serve Jesus for the rewards we may get from serving Him. When He died on the cross, He did far more for us than we deserve. Loyalty to Him and our service to Him are to be done as an act of worship that expresses our loving gratitude for His love toward us. In return, He delights to encourage us with the assurance that ultimately His rewards will outweigh whatever we give up for Him. The apostle Paul tells us in the verse above from I Corinthians, we will receive our rewards in heaven according to our labor here on this earth. We need to commit to live for Jesus every day regardless of the cost or the rewards. We are assured whatever is done for Christ in this life, will be rewarded in our life to come.

TODAY'S WORD FOR JUNE 16

ASSURANCE

And we know that the Son of God has come and has given us an understanding, that we may know Him who is true; and we are in Him who is true, in His Son Jesus Christ.

This is the true God and eternal life. I John 5:20

Everyone that calls upon the name of the Lord will be saved. Romans 10:13

Faith is the confidence that what we hope for will actually happen; it gives us assurance about things we cannot see. Hebrews 11:1

People of all ages today constantly need assurance. When a child takes his or her first step he or she looks to the parent for assurance. They want you to know what they have accomplished and want to hear "good job, we are proud of you."

The same response is desired when a child enters new endeavors. They look for assurance when they have their first day of school. The same is true when they take their first test or give their first speech.

Likewise teenagers need assurance that only a parent can give when they start a new school or meet new friends. Adults also need assurance at their work places. If a boss never gives a pat on the back or says "good job," one gets very discouraged and soon loses interest in their job.

In the verse we have written above, the writer in closing his letter makes strong comments as to the assurance God gives to us as believers. What God has told us in His Word is true and unshakeable. What He has revealed to us is absolutely certain.

In three consecutive verses, I John 5: 18, 19, and 20, John begins with the confident phrase of assurance, "We know." John says we are of God; we possess the very nature and being of God; and the whole world is in the power of the evil one.

The world talks about love and hungers for love, but it does not understand the very thing it seeks. It lacks the power to practice it, because the world does not know the One who is love personified.

God is love. John writes since we are of God, He has given us the understanding to know Him and the power to experience eternal life. What a declaration this is and what assurance this gives to all of us who believe in Him.

We live in an age of moral relativism, where people claim we cannot know anything for sure, where uncertainties and confusion abound. But we, as believers in Jesus, have been given the assurance we are people who can stand alone in an unsecure world that is falling apart, because we have our trust in God.

The verses we have put above from Romans and Hebrews are the basis for the assurance believers have for the future. Read each verse carefully. Having this assurance in our lives give us hopeful anticipation of what God will do through us on any given day. If you are living with this assurance in your life you can wake up every morning excited to see what God is going to do through you that day.

TODAY'S WORD FOR JUNE 17

TEMPTATION

No temptation has overtaken you except such as is common to man; but God is faithful, who will not allow you to be tempted beyond what you are able, but with the temptation will also make the way of escape, that you may be able to bear it. I Corinthians 10:13

Temptation is a lot like an unexpected storm that sweeps in and causes damage to those who are caught unaware. A believer in Jesus must be alert to seeing the approach of a temptation and be prepared to ride it out. None of us, as believers, will reach a spiritual level of maturity at which we will no longer battle sinful enticements. The closer we walk with the Lord, the less enticing the sinful temptations and ways of the world will be to us.

Understanding our own weaknesses is an important part of being prepared for temptation. It is usually a multitude of little sins that cause most people trouble. We need to watch for these little sins and know when we are most vulnerable.

God has given us His guidelines in His Word for living a godly life that is pleasing to Him. The Bible clearly defines what sin is. We do not have the right to draw the line between what is sin and what is not. That is God's right.

God has given us a line, and as believers we must not cross that line. If we take one step over the line, soon there is an inducement to continue and then you find yourself totally estranged from the Lord and overwhelmed with guilt.

Building a defense against temptation you must understand that every temptation originates as a thought. If you hold onto that thought it becomes a fantasy. Fantasies become entangled with your emotions and then they become a desire.

At that point you will need to make a choice. This process is quite dangerous. The progression from a thought to a choice can be almost instantaneous. Wise believers determine to resist a temptation as soon as it enters their consciousness.

The verse we have written above gives us two assurances God has provided in our battle against temptation. First, God is faithful and we have a commitment as believers to obey Him. Secondly, we have the assurance He is in control and has limited what Satan can do against us, and He provides a way for us to escape.

Spouses need to talk about the temptations that come their way so they can pray with each other about their weaknesses. Parents need to teach their children what a temptation is and then how to properly deal with it. It is easier to overcome a temptation if you discuss it when it first comes your way. Families break apart because there is a breakdown of communication. If they do not talk about the temptations they face, the breakup will come quicker. Temptations not only affect family relationships but also each family member's relationship with the Lord.

When temptation comes your way take your focus away from the temptation and look at the bigger picture. Ask yourself these two questions: Is this choice I make a violation of God's Word? What are the consequences?

TODAYS WORD FOR JUNE 18

ENCOURAGEMENT

We sent Timothy, our brother and God's fellow worker in spreading the gospel of Christ, to strengthen and encourage you in your faith. I Thessalonians 3:2

The Apostle Paul on his second missionary journey established a church for new believers in Thessalonica. Paul knew the importance of new Christians needing encouragement so they would not be drawn away from their faith by the pagan society which they lived. Since he could not return, he sent Timothy to encourage and strengthen them in their faith.

People continually go through times of discouragement and need friends like us to give them a word of encouragement. Unfortunately many children never receive a word of encouragement from their parents. This was verified by a recent study released by UCLA that said the average father spent FOUR minutes a day talking to his child and FOUR hours a day watching TV. Children who receive no encouragement or affirmation at home will seek it elsewhere. Most likely it will be in the wrong places and from the wrong people without guidance. How then can that child feel encouraged to be successful in life and do what is right?

Children are surrounded today by a POP culture, with drugs and alcohol available to them wherever they go, including on their school campus. They have the trash on the internet and unless a parent filters what they can see, they see the worst. They are not allowed to read their Bible or pray at school. The Ten Commandments have been banished and now there is an attempt to remove the phrase IN GOD WE TRUST from our nation's money.

Our children live in an immoral society with their peers looking out for themselves and doing only what makes them happy. Most importantly we live in an anti-God and anti-religious society.

Communication is one of the most important elements of a successful marriage and family. Families today are breaking up because no one gives another family member any words of encouragement. We are so quick to criticize, but so slow to encourage. Stop and think right now — when was the last time you gave an encouraging word to your spouse, to your children, to your extended family or to your associates. No doubt there is someone you know right now who is going through a time of discouragement. What a blessing an encouraging word from you could be to that person.

Begin today by making it a point every day to call someone on the telephone and leave an encouraging message. Think about stopping on the street just to say "hello" and "how are you?" to someone. You will have scores of opportunities to be friendly and to give someone a word of encouragement. Those you talk to will feel so much better. When we encourage someone there is a positive result — we are united in love.

TODAY'S WORD FOR JUNE 19

RELIGION

If anyone among you thinks he is religious, and does not bridle his tongue but deceives his own heart, this one's religion is useless. Pure and undefiled religion before God and the father is this: to visit orphans and widows in their time of trouble, and to keep oneself unspotted from this world. James 1:26-27

Many people are very confused and defensive when we talk about religion because there are so many "religions" in our culture. A non-believer in Jesus does not know how to respond concerning their belief because they have only head knowledge. When we talk to someone about our "religion", we make it clear we are talking about a "relationship" and not a series of concepts of "do's and don'ts."

Very simply, we have a personal relationship with Jesus. This relationship began when we accepted Jesus into our hearts as our personal Savior. God sent His Son to this earth to pay the penalty for our sins and we accepted His offer of redemption. All other religions offer a series of rituals. The difference is the "RELATIONSHIP."

With Jesus we have a relationship grounded in love. God loved us so much He sent His Son. By believing in Him we could become children of God and joint heirs with Jesus Christ. There is a reason it was necessary for God to send His Son to this earth. Because of the sin of Adam and Eve, we are all born sinners. This is a fact and not a theory. God is entirely without sin and sin is what separates us from God. There is no amount of spiritual rituals that will cleanse us from our sins.

This is why God sent His Son to this earth; to pay the penalty for our sins by dying on the cross. In order to receive God's gift of Salvation we must be willing to admit we are sinners; confess our sins; ask for God's forgiveness; and then acknowledge Jesus Christ as our Savior and redeemer. The shed blood of Jesus cleanses us from all our sins and restores us into a right relationship with God. Therefore all who believe and receive Jesus as Savior, become children of God and will spend an eternity with God and His Son Jesus. Just think of all the untold and unseen riches that will be ours as joint heirs with Christ.

In the verses from the book of James, we read the fruit of our religion is in what we do and what we say. Our relationship with Jesus is a heart relationship and not a head religion. When we have a relationship with Jesus, we will watch what we say and our deeds will be a commitment to honor our Lord by helping those in need. When we have a relationship with Christ the people around us are able to see evidence of our relationship with Him by our actions. When we do not live by God's Word or practice what God teaches, James tells us "our religion is useless."

Is your "religion" just a series of rituals you do your best to try to honor? In your "religion" do you have a certainty you will spend eternity with God? Is your "religion" a relationship with Jesus that gives you hope for an eternity with God? You can know about God, but you cannot know God until you have entered into a relationship with Him and become a "child of God."

TODAY'S WORD FOR JUNE 20

ASK

So I say to you, ask, and it will be given you; seek and you will find; knock and it will be opened to you. For everyone who asks receives; he who seeks, finds; and to him who knocks, the door will be opened. Luke 11:9-10

In the verses above from Luke we are taught to ask and seek and then everyone who asks will receive. Why does God want us to ask when He already knows what we want and what we need? Jesus gives us these verses as a mini-sermon telling us to persevere and endure in prayer when we ask. He wants us to ask through prayer continually. If He does not provide by our asking then we are to seek Him so we will recognize He is the one who provides for us. He alone hears and answers our prayers.

In this verse Jesus tells us if we do not receive what we have asked for, then we need to knock and it shall be opened to us. The point He is making is we, as believers, need to pray continuously for what we are asking. Jesus uses three verbs of continuous action: ask, seek and knock. God assures us that an answer is coming in His perfect timing if we persevere and endure in prayer.

Many people just do not want to ask someone, let alone God, for anything because of pride. We should not let pride keep us from seeking God's help. Remember, Jesus says: "ask and it will be given you; seek and you will find."

There are many situations in life where we need to ask for help. Families need to be willing to help others in their time of need. Families also need to be willing to ask in their own time of need. Remember there is a difference between asking and demanding. When asking for help the response you receive is affected by the way you ask. Whether you ask favors of people or when you just ask questions for informational purposes, learn to ask kindly.

Today one of the most important lessons we can learn from the scripture is that God expects us to ask Him for help when we are in need so He can fulfill His plan through our life.

There is no request too big or so small that we cannot bring it to God. The Lord wants us to pray about everything. Paul assures us of this in Philippians 4:6 when he says: "Do not be anxious about anything, but in everything, by prayer and petition, with thanksgiving, present your requests to God."

Jesus own words to us are, "Whatever things you ask in prayer, believing, you will receive." Matthew 21:22. Can it be said any clearer? In James 1:5 and 6, we are told if we lack wisdom let us ask of God. Then it says we are to ask in faith with no doubting.

When we rely on our own wisdom we often fail and we limit God and what He will do for us. When we ask in prayer, ask believing and ask in faith with no doubting, then we will receive according to God's perfect will.

TODAY'S WORD FOR JUNE 21

VALUE

Look at the birds of the air, for they neither sow nor reap nor gather into barns; yet your heavenly Father feeds them. Are you not of more value than they? Matthew 6:26

What is valuable in God's sight? In the verse above from Matthew, Jesus teaches us if He feeds the birds in the air even if they do not sow or reap their own food, how much more valuable are we to God. He reminds us it is God who feeds them and it is God who feeds us.

God is all knowing and all powerful and has every thing He needs. He puts great value on our soul even though in comparison to God we are nothing. Sometimes we feel worthless and wonder how could we be of any value to God? God wants us to understand value from an eternal perspective.

Jesus often taught using parables. He taught the parable of the lost sheep in Matthew 12:12-14. He said if a shepherd owns one-hundred sheep and one gets lost, he will leave the ninety-nine to look for the one who is lost. Jesus said the shepherd is happier about the one sheep when found than the ninety-nine others. This is the way God feels about us. He places the same value on us as the shepherd with the sheep, and does not want to lose a single one of us.

Jesus has offered us an eternal inheritance that is ours if we ask. When we recognize the value of what God did for us by sending His son to this earth to pay the penalty for our sins and to give us eternal life, how can we reject such a valuable gift?

There are many things that are considered to be valuable in life. God talks about the value of His people; the value of life; the value of being rich or poor; the value of a lost sheep; the eternal value of a soul; the value of a widow's mite; the value of an eternal inheritance; and the value of our faith.

Most of us realize the value of a healthy life. If you need to be reminded how valuable a healthy life is, then go and visit your local children's hospital. God will do something special to fill your heart with concern for these children that are hurting and you will thank God for your good health.

Most of us understand the difference between being rich or comfortable financially versus poor. If you do not, then go and talk to a family living in the slums of the inner city or a homeless man sleeping on the street. God will again move your heart to compassion to help the hurting and you will thank God for the blessings He has given you.

Finally, when we think of the widow's mite, we realize how valuable it is to our Lord when one person gives whatever he has to further His work. We cannot out give God. It has been our experience when we give that God bestows blessings on us that far outweigh the value of what we have given.

TODAY'S WORD FOR JUNE 22

CALL

Seek the Lord while He may be found, call upon Him while He is near. Isaiah 55:6

As Christians we have a most wonderful and reliable source to call on every moment of every day. God has promised to be with us through every trial and tribulation we face as well as through all the good times. All we have to do is call on Him and He is there for us. He is near and He can be found. The word "CALL" in the scriptures has several considerations for us.

In 1 Samuel chapter three we read the story of when Samuel was called by God. From the time he was a young child, Samuel had ministered in the temple under Eli, the high priest. Samuel was awakened from a dream when he heard a voice calling his name. At first, Samuel thought it was Eli, who was very old calling him because he needed him. However Eli told him to go back to his bed.

God called Samuel three times before Eli realized it was the Lord calling. He told Samuel if you are called again, respond by saying: "Speak Lord, for your servant hears." That day Samuel was called to serve God as a prophet, priest and judge of Israel. When God calls are you ready to answer "speak Lord your servant hears?"

God blesses those who answer His call, as Samuel did, and He makes them a blessing to others. The scripture tells us those who reject God's call will be held accountable. In Isaiah Chapter 66:4 it reads: "Because when I called, you did not answer; when I spoke you did not hear." Then the Lord will bring judgment and "you shall cry for sorrow of heart, and wail for grief of spirit" (Isaiah 65:14). In Psalms 81:11-12 we are told when "My people would not heed my voice [call]; I gave them over to their own stubborn heart, to walk in their own counsels." Finally in Jeremiah 7:13 and 15 we read the Lord said: "but you did not hear, and I called you, but you did not answer, and so I will cast you out of My sight."

God is patient and gives us ample opportunity to respond to His call. When we continually reject His call, He allows us to continue in our stubborn ways satisfying our evil desires, but there are always consequences. We not only lose God's blessings on our life, but we bring God's judgment on our lives.

In contrast to those who do not respond to God's call, we read how the disciples responded [Mark 1 and 2] to the call of God. They did not ask questions. They immediately left what they were doing and followed Jesus. They were moved by the call of God and responded not knowing all Jesus had for them. They responded as Samuel did, "YES LORD, HERE AM I."

We are told in Acts 16:9-10 how Paul responded to the vision calling him to Macedonia to preach the gospel. Paul answered the call of God without reservation. When God calls, we can be sure "He is faithful and will do all that He has promised" (I Thessalonians 5:24). How we respond to God's call is a matter of our will. We can stubbornly cling to our will to do what we want or we can respond to God's call to follow His will for our life.

TODAY'S WORD FOR JUNE 23

HOLY

Holy, holy, holy is the Lord of hosts; the whole earth is full of His glory. Isaiah 6:3

Exalt the Lord our God and worship at His Holy hill; for the Lord our God is holy. Psalm 99:9

When people hear about something out of the ordinary, we often hear them say, "Holy smoke," or "Holy moley," or "Holy mackerel "to indicate they are surprised to hear it. We also have often heard the term, "Holy terror" to describe an out of control child. When these expressions are used there is really nothing "holy" about what is being referred to as "holy."

Only God is truly holy. God is perfect in goodness and righteousness and without sin. He alone is worthy of our worship and devotion. As the Psalmist says, we exalt the Lord our God and worship Him because He is our God and He is holy. In reality the word "holy" should only be used to refer to God Himself, His Holy Word and to those things that relate to God. This verse in Psalm 99 also says to worship God at His Holy hill. This is the hill in Jerusalem where the temple was and where it will be located in the future messianic kingdom.

In the verse above from Isaiah, the prophet was having a vision and he saw the seraphs speaking to each other in praise. They were saying Holy, Holy, Holy, three times implying God is three persons. He is God, His Son Jesus and the Holy Spirit. The verse continues and says, full of His glory. Isaiah saw the earth as the worldwide display of God's immeasurable glory, His perfections and the attributes as seen in His creations. However, fallen man refuses to glorify Him as God.

The word "HOLY" also means to be dedicated or set apart. When applying the word "HOLY" to places, persons or things, it means being set apart for the service of God and thus sacred and removed from the realm of ordinary. In the Old Testament everything associated with worship is set apart in this manner, and thus considered sacred or "holy." "HOLY" is God's realm and God is to be honored supremely. Therefore, everything associated with "HOLY" was to be treated with the utmost respect and care.

We no longer, since the death and resurrection of Jesus, worship God with the Old Testament rituals. The fact these Old Testament rituals were regarded as "HOLY" because of their association with God, should be a healthy reminder to us today about the holiness of God and the fact we must show Him our utmost respect.

So how do we who are unholy become holy? The believer in Jesus Christ becomes holy by being obedient to all of God's commandments and following Christ's example. As believers it is necessary to separate ourselves from the evil ways of the world. We should "stand out in the crowd' because our life exemplifies Christ-like qualities. As believers we are set apart from this world and should be totally dedicated to serving our "HOLY" God.

TODAY'S WORD FOR JUNE 24

MONEY

For the love of money is the root of all kinds of evil, for which some have strayed from the faith in their greediness, and pierced themselves through with many sorrows. I Timothy 6:10

A recent survey taken in America asked the question: "What is your greatest desire in life?" Over 74% of the people said money was there greatest desire. Only 14% of those people said having a happy family relationship. Probably the most concerning fact was only 6% wanted to have God in their lives. This is a strong reminder and indication how money has become the "god" for many people. These people are convinced money can buy happiness, success and popularity.

People, who have money and have acquired success and popularity, soon realize they are not truly happy. Money will only bring happiness if it is used to honor God.

We need to realize it is the LOVE OF MONEY that is the root of all kinds of evil. Timothy tells us in 1 Timothy 6:10 (above) it's not money itself, but the love of money that leads to greed. Greed leads to an all consuming desire to get rich by any and all means. People can be so driven by their love for money they will steal, cheat and participate in all manner of evil things. Timothy warns the believers the love of money can cause them to stray from their faith and bring sorrow in their lives.

We believe God blesses some people with money because He knows they will use it for His glory. For years we knew a man who served as a wonderful example for us concerning his use of money and we also learned many important life principles from him. This man and his wife were very wealthy financially but they lived humble and unpretentious lives.

They used their money to help others. They drove an old car that always ran well, but you wondered if it would make it to his next appointment. He converted an old school bus into a camper he could take his 7th grade Sunday school students on outings. They owned a printing press and did the printing for scores of Christian ministries at cost and many times for free.

We shared a need for a warehouse for our mission with them and several weeks later they found just the right building to meet our needs. They not only found the building, but they gave the necessary funds, as a loan, to purchase the building. God honored these people with money and they used what God gave them for His glory.

They were faithful stewards and by their overwhelming generosity, honored God with the blessings God gave them. We observed through the years, the more they helped ministries the more God blessed them.

God does not bless us all with financial wealth, but He does bless us in so many other ways. God does not promise to give us what we want, but what we need. We have not been blessed with financial wealth, but God has blessed us with certain abilities, talents and time He has given to us to use as we serve Him. All along the way He has supplied our every need because we have tried to be faithful to Him.

TODAY'S WORD FOR JUNE 25

CHRIST-LIKENESS

Put on the new man which was created according to God, in true righteousness and holiness. Ephesians 4:24

The process of becoming like Christ is most of the time painful, but it is always worth it. When we talk about becoming Christ-like, we mean our daily life should always show the spirit of Christ in all we do and all we say.

Becoming Christ-like is an ongoing process that requires us to do battle with our sinful nature. In Colossians 3:5-9 Paul gives us a list of the sinful acts that should no longer be part of the life of anyone who has accepted Jesus as their Savior. The list includes sexual immorality, impurity, lust, evil desires, anger, rage, malice, slander, filthy-language, and lying. In verse three, Paul says we must put to death all these things because they are actions that come from our old sinful nature.

To become Christ-like in today's society is very difficult because of the pressure to conform to the growing evil we face in this world. As we have often said, we live in a "ME" generation and if you are going along with the crowd and living for yourself, you cannot be Christ-like.

Receiving Jesus into our hearts, God's gift of salvation is a one-time event, but to become like Him is a daily event that often requires suffering and struggle. It involves putting off your old sinful habits and replacing them with new godly ones.

The apostle Paul wrote in Ephesians (above), "Put off, concerning your former conduct, the old man which grows corrupt and put on the new man which was created according to God, in true righteousness and holiness."

The renewal of your mind when you accept Jesus as your Savior brings not only a renovation of your character, but a transformation of your old self to your new self. The new self is created in the very likeness of God. This verse continues to remind us our new self must radiate the righteousness and holiness of God. Righteousness relates to our moral responsibility to our fellow men and holiness refers to our responsibility to God.

As a believer in Christ, have you put out of your life the evil and ungodly habits of your past? Look at the Ten Commandments and they will give you a checklist so you can grade yourself. Old habits are tough to eliminate, but God expects us to get rid of them and promises us help to do so.

What is troubling you today? God may be using the kind rebuke from a family member or friend or even a painful trial to prompt you to get rid of a sinful habit. By doing this God will replace that habit with godly character.

In I Peter 4:1-2 it reads: "Therefore, since Christ suffered for us in the flesh, arm yourselves also with the same mind, for he who has suffered in the flesh has ceased from sin, that he no longer should live the rest of his time in the flesh for the lusts of men, but for the will of God." The conversion of a soul is the miracle only God can do in a moment, but the growth of a soul is God's work of a lifetime.

TODAY'S WORD FOR JUNE 26

SATISFACTION

And My people shall be satisfied with My goodness, says the Lord. Jeremiah 31:14

The backslider in heart will have his fill of his own ways, but a good man will be satisfied from above. Proverbs 14:14

Receiving the feeling of satisfaction for a successful accomplishment is something that every person we know hopes to receive. Children, young people and adults are constantly looking for satisfaction.

A child receives satisfaction when he or she realizes they have taken their first step. When they put steps together and begin to walk, the satisfaction is expressed so clearly with their big smiles. When a parent cheers them on and shows how excited they are, the satisfaction is even greater.

For young people, satisfaction comes by being accepted by their peers and complimented for a deed done well. A good grade on a test, a good play in a game, and even being on a team that wins a game brings great satisfaction to a young person. Graduating from high school or college is a milestone in every student's life that is long remembered as a special time of satisfaction. We do not want you to forget or take lightly the love of a parent to a child through their entire life brings real satisfaction to the child.

Adults also look for satisfaction in accomplishments in their own lives. When a job or project is completed successfully, satisfaction abounds. When a spouse solves a family concern, satisfaction is felt by everyone.

But all the satisfaction we may receive on this earth is nothing like the satisfaction our Lord has when one person comes to find Him as their Lord and Savior. The scriptures tell us the angels will sing and rejoice when one person comes to Jesus.

The verse from Proverbs (above) says a good man will be satisfied from above. The only way anyone can become a good man is by accepting Jesus as their Savior and asking Him to forgive their sins. When we accept Jesus we are a child of God. Children depend on their parents to satisfy their needs. God will not only satisfy all of our needs, but will reward us from above if we are faithful to Him.

The writer of Proverbs 14:14 talks about the good man being satisfied from above and he is comparing this to the man who backslides who is a fool, wicked and disobedient.

In Jeremiah 31 God is saying through Jeremiah the prophet when Jesus returns, Israel's mourning's will turn to joy and they will have true satisfaction. Jeremiah says the Lord satisfies us with His "goodness" (Jeremiah 31:14). The Lord's goodness gives us true and lasting contentment, more satisfying than anything we receive from this world we live in. Make sure today your satisfaction comes from above and be assured your satisfaction comes from the goodness of God.

TODAY'S WORD FOR JUNE 27

BELIEF

God from the beginning chose you for salvation that came through the Spirit who makes you holy and through your belief in the truth. Therefore, brethren, stand fast and hold the traditions which you were taught, whether by word or our epistle. II Thessalonians 2:13, 15

He must have a strong belief in the trustworthy message he was taught; then he will be able to encourage others with wholesome teaching. Titus 1:9

Anyone who says he is a Christian is saying that he has a belief in Jesus Christ and follows His teachings. Webster defines belief as confidence in the truth or existence of something. Jesus said: "I am the way, the truth and the life." John 14:6. God and Jesus are the source of all truth and that is the basis of our belief. Therefore those who put their belief or trust in Jesus can have confidence in the truth of His teachings. The message of Salvation that Jesus gave us is trustworthy and we should have a strong, unshakeable and confident belief in what He taught us so we can encourage others.

In the book of Titus (1:5-9) Paul reminded Titus about the strong leadership qualities leaders in the Church must have. Paul gives us a list of what we must do. We must be hospitable, love what is good, self-controlled, upright, holy, and disciplined. The way we live our life is a testimony to our faith in what we believe. The keys for our lives are:

- TRUSTING GOD: This comes first. Our belief is in God and our faith is strengthened by trusting God. We must trust in the Lord with all our heart. (Psalm 37:3 and Proverbs 3:5 are good verses for you to read)
- DO GOOD: Our faith is demonstrated by the good we do by word or deed. Psalm 37:3 instructs us to trust in the Lord and then do good.
- RELY ON THE LORD: When we have troubles we are to "Cast all our cares on Him." I Peter 5:7. When we face a situation that is difficult for us, we are instructed to give it to the Lord. We do not have to walk through it alone. We can rely on the Lord to be a constant help.
- COMMIT OUR PLANS TO GOD: Every day when we begin our activities, our belief in God allows us to "Commit to the Lord what ever you do and your plans will succeed." Our problems arise because we have not committed our plans to our Lord.

Many people living in today's world really believe in nothing more than themselves. We do not know how we could make it even through one day without our faith in the Lord. With all the stresses and all the uncertainties of life in today's world, we are certain if we did not have our strong belief in God and Jesus, we would be in deep despair.

TODAY'S WORD FOR JUNE 28

MEMORIAL

In the future, when your children ask you, What do these stones mean? tell them that the flow of the Jordan was cut off before the Ark of the Covenant of the Lord. When it (the Ark) crossed the Jordan the waters of the Jordan were cut off. These stones are to be a memorial to the people of Israel forever. Joshua 4:6-7

Memorials are a way of preserving and perpetuating the memory of people or events that were important to us. Memorials are important to those who lost loved ones and to remember great events and people in public life. In the Bible, we read about memorials erected at locations where God had done something special. They are reminders of how God protected and blessed the lives of those who loved Him.

After crossing the Jordan River the first thing God instructed Joshua to do was to build a memorial. While the priests who were holding the Ark of the Covenant were still standing in the middle of the Jordan River, Joshua instructed one man from each of the twelve tribes to take a stone from the Jordan river at the spot where the priests were standing. These twelve men then carried the stones to the place, Gilgal, where they were to camp the first night in the Promised Land.

There, Joshua set up a memorial to remind the people of the miracle God had done in parting the Jordan River. Children who were born after the crossing of the river would see the stones and ask what the stones meant? Their parents would tell them the story and teach them about God and what He had done for them.

We took our children to Washington D.C. to see all the memorials and historical places in our nation's capital. We had the opportunity to teach our children about who these men were that had memorials, what they believed, and what they had done for our country. We shared with them the impact God had on their lives.

Reminders of God are rapidly being banned by our government leaders and this may cause the fall of our country. Prayer is no longer allowed in schools. The Ten Commandments cannot be displayed in schools or government offices. Parents, teachers and even churches are not teaching our children about the reasons America has been great. Children have not been taught the reasons for the memorials or the reasons for their locations. Frankly, it is up to us as Christian parents and grandparents, to teach our children and grandchildren to trust in God. We need to teach them to keep God in the center of all of America's activities.

Children love to ask questions and as parents we need to be ready to give an answer. Many questions can be answered by referring to our heritage here in America and the memorials that are standing to remind us of that heritage including the role God had in the founding of our country. We should not forget about the Biblical memorials built to show how great a God we have.

Do you teach your children about who God is and what He has done for you? Do you share with them how God has blessed this country, how He has answered your prayers, and how He continues to meet your needs?

TODAY'S WORD FOR JUNE 29

CHANGE

For I am the Lord, I do not change. Malachi 3:6

God, who is all wise, all knowing and without sin, never changes His mind nor withdraws His promises. He gave Moses the Ten Commandments and they are still valid today. God's plan for salvation has never changed and His promise for eternal life through Jesus Christ has never changed.

When we see someone make their decision to accept Jesus into their life, most of the time we see a dramatic change in that person's life. As a result of Adam's and Eve's sin, we are born with a sinful nature. God is without sin, so our sin separates us from God (Isaiah 59:2). God cannot change who He is, so we are the ones who must change if we are to have fellowship with God. Our righteousness must be changed into His righteousness (Romans 3:22). That change takes place when we come to Christ and receive His righteousness, which is a free gift.

The apostle Paul tells us when we come to Christ, we become a new person and the old person is gone (II Corinthians 5:17). Paul's life is evidence this is true. His life was completely changed when he met Jesus. His old life was filled with persecuting the Christians, and his new life was filled with preaching the gospel and being persecuted himself because of his faith in Christ. His life was completely changed. He considered the gift of life offered by God to be well worth any persecution he might have to endure. God does not change, but He does change us.

When we think of the word "change" another thought comes to mind we want to share with you. Many families today seem to be disintegrating because of many different reasons. Some of these reasons include:

- Preoccupation with an occupation to the point of exclusion of family needs. This goes beyond work. It can include watching TV, being with associates such as in a club, and many other activities. Family needs to come first.
- Refusal to face the severity of a child's action. A situation arises and you respond by thinking it is not that serious, or I am too tired to deal with that.
- Refusal to respond quickly and thoroughly to the warning of others. This could be a neighbor, a relative or a spouse warning you, and you just do not have time to see if it is a problem or you just do not care.
- Rationalization of a wrongful fact, therefore becoming part of the problem.

When things are not going well in your life, especially within your family, it is time for change, a change for the better. To change we must want something more than what we have now. We must be willing to give up our sinful ways. What is better than to make a change in how we live our life today and have assurance we will spend eternity in Heaven with our Lord? If you are willing to make a change, then God is waiting for you to come to Him and He will change you.

TODAY'S WORD FOR JUNE 30

WORKS

What good is it, my brothers, if a man claims to have faith but has no deeds? Can such faith save him? Suppose a brother or sister is without clothes and daily food. If one of you says to him, Go, I wish you well; keep warm and well fed, but does nothing about his physical needs, what good is it? In the same way faith by itself, if not accompanied by action, is dead. James 2:14

For by grace you have been saved through faith and that not of yourselves; it is the gift of God not of works, lest anyone should boast. Ephesians 2:8-9

We were taught as children and we taught our children that the most important decision that they would make in life is to accept Jesus as their Savior. We taught them that we were saved by grace through faith. (Verse above). After we accepted Jesus as our Savior then we were commanded by our Lord to "work" for Him.

Many people we talk to believe their good works will get them into heaven where they can spend an eternity with God. Most are very good people and live a clean life. They are the kind of neighbors you would love to have living next door. They are also the most difficult to convince they have a need for a Savior. They believe their good works, clean living and being kind to everyone will get them into heaven.

We remember several conversations we had with a friend who was very generous with his time and talent. When we talked to him about his relationship with Jesus, he always talked about his good works and told us not to be concerned about him because he would see us in heaven.

Some people find the two verses we have listed above from Ephesians and James contradictory. They ask us if salvation is received simply by grace through faith alone or does it have to be earned. Paul wants us to understand there is nothing we can do to merit or earn our salvation. Keeping all the laws in the Bible will not earn us salvation, it is only by the grace of God through faith that we can be saved.

Paul in Ephesians talks about salvation through faith. In James 2:14 James says faith without deeds, (works), is dead. They do not contradict each other, they actually complement one another. James would never argue against Paul's assertion that salvation is by faith. James presupposes we understand these doctrines that are so clearly stated in Paul's letters. James goes further by saying that a commitment to Christ is expressed through our actions. Our works are evidence of our faith.

Martin Luther puts it this way: A man is justified (declared righteous before God) by faith alone, but not by a faith that is alone. Genuine faith will produce good deeds, but only faith in Christ saves.

God is expecting us as believers to work hard until His return. God has put each one of us on this earth for a purpose. When we consider the great price God and His Son Jesus paid for our salvation, we are committed for a life time to work for Him.

TODAY'S WORD FOR JULY 1

CONQUERORS

Yet in all these things we are more than conquerors through Him who loved us. Romans 8:37

Most people are conquerors by nature. We like to be victorious in what we do. We all like to conquer a test we have to take in school. We like to conquer a job at work. We like to look back in our lives and evaluate circumstances and accomplishments.

The story of David and Goliath was one of the favorite Bible stories of our children. David proved he could conquer anything or anybody with God at his side. Being a conqueror for Jesus is life's greatest accomplishment for all of us.

David loved God and trusted Him to be his shield and defender. David went out to face the Philistine giant as a conqueror because he knew the battle was the Lord's and the Lord would deliver him. When Goliath taunted David because his only weapon was a slingshot, David's response was, "You come against me with a sword and spear and javelin, but I come in the name of the Lord Almighty."

Not only did David not have a sword or a spear, he had no shield. I Samuel 17:50 tells us, "So David triumphed (conquered) over the Philistine with a sling and a stone; without a sword in his hand he struck down the Philistine and killed him."

David fought many battles and God was the one who enabled him to be a conqueror. He gave God the credit and in Psalm 144:2 he praised God for being his "shield and defender." He praised God with these words "He is my loving God and my fortress, my stronghold and my deliverer, my shield, in whom I take refuge, who subdues peoples under me." We can be conquerors in all situations in our lives, but we must recognize that "the battle is the Lord's."

Christ will carry us through each situation as well as give us strength and encouragement. We cannot lose when we let the battle be the Lord's:

- He will give you rest. (Matthew 11:28)
- He will give you peace. (John 14:27)
- He provides for you an escape from temptation. (I Corinthians 10:13)
- He will comfort you through all trials that you may face. (II Corinthians 1:3-4)
- He will supply all your needs. (Philippians 4:19)
- He will deliver you through all persecution. (II Corinthians 4:8)
- He will enable you to overcome the world. (I John 5:4)
- He will deliver you from fear. (Isaiah 41:10)
- He will give you eternal life. (John 10:28-29)
- He will keep you from evil. (II Thessalonians 3:3)

In everyday life are you more than a conqueror? Do you let Satan and the world take away your Christian birthright? Realize anew today that you are a child of the King, the ultimate conqueror. Go out and act like it today in all that you do and say.

TODAY'S WORD FOR JULY 2

ETHICS

For this is the covenant that I will make with the house of Israel after those days says the Lord: I will put my laws in their mind and write them on their hearts; and I will be their God, and they shall be My people. Hebrews 8:10

You will be accepted if you do what is [ethical] right. But if you refuse to do what is [ethical] right, then watch out. Sin is crouching at the door, eager to control you, but you must subdue it and be its master. Genesis 4:7

Over the past few years the moral values of our country have steadily declined. The Bible cannot be read in public schools and the Ten Commandments have been banned from schools, government offices and many public places. We are living in a society that has chosen to put aside Gods standards of ethics.

Most people today have rejected Gods ethical standards of living given to us in the Ten Commandments, and choose to set their own standards of right and wrong. When we look in the Old Testament we see that man's sinful nature has not changed. In Judges 17:6 we read after the death of Joshua, all the people did whatever seemed right in their own eyes. This is exactly what we see today.

Have we forgotten God gave Moses the Ten Commandments for a reason? Laws and regulations are necessary to keep man's evilness in check. God created us and wants what is best for us. He knows how we should live and these commandments are a measuring stick to help us be what God wants us to be. These are the most complete and important list of ethics ever known to man. They cover every detail that one needs to live a Christ centered life. They are as relevant today as they were when God gave them to Moses. In the New Testament (Matthew 22:37-38) Jesus adds to this list two more commandments. They are:

"You shall love the Lord your God with all your heart, with all your soul, and with all your mind. This is the first and great commandment. And the second is: You shall love your neighbor as yourself."

God expects us to live by these standards of ethics. The scripture tells us in Proverbs 14:12 there is a consequence for doing things our way. "There is a way that seems right to a man but in the end it leads to death."

When we do not live by God's standards and we are unethical, we not only sin against God, but our sin affects how others see us. Sin (breaking God's ethical standards) always has consequences. We urge you today to make a commitment to read THE TEN COMMANDMENTS yourself and then with your family. We also suggest after you have read through them, follow this with a time of discussion with your family as to where you stand in relation to each commandment. Each of us must make a commitment to live daily by this set of ethics God has given us. Place the Ten Commandments in a prominent place in your house where it can be seen.

TODAY'S WORD FOR JULY 3

MESSIAH

You search the scriptures, for in them think you have eternal life; and these are they which testify of Me. John 5:39

The Jews, scribes, and Pharisees searched the scriptures, looking for keys to finding their Messiah. They diligently investigated the scriptures but they were spiritually blind to seeing their Messiah. They saw only the Law. They were so legalistic they searched the scriptures for only one purpose, to interpret the Law. They were so blinded by the Law they did not recognize the Lawgiver, who came to fulfill the Law and give us eternal life.

As believers, Jesus is our Messiah and our Jewish friends are still looking and waiting to find their Messiah, who is Jesus. Many of our Jewish friends today are realizing that Jesus is their Messiah and are turning their lives over to Him.

There are two important facts that prove Jesus is the Messiah, the Son of God. The first proof is Jesus' resurrection from death into life. The second is that Jesus fulfilled every prophecy made about Him in the Old Testament.

It was prophesied by Isaiah the Messiah would be born of a virgin. Micah prophesied Jesus would be born in Bethlehem. And Jeremiah prophesied Jesus would be a descendent of Abraham, Isaac, Jacob, and David. The Psalms foretold what Jesus would suffer and be betrayed and accused by false witnesses.

Even His death by crucifixion was prophesied although it was hundreds of years before crucifixion was being used. The most important prophecy Jesus fulfilled was the prophecy of His resurrection. Without the resurrection of our Savior, Jesus Christ, we would all be doomed to suffer eternal death and separation from God.

Today, as we discuss our Messiah, we want to share with you several Messianic Psalms. Psalm 8 is a messianic psalm that exalts the name of Jesus. In verse one you can sense the excitement of David when he says, "O Lord, our Lord, how excellent is Your name in all the earth, who have set Your glory above the heavens."

In Psalm 118 we read about the Messiah being rejected. In verse twenty-two it reads, "The stone which the builders rejected has become the chief cornerstone." The Jews rejected Jesus as their Messiah, but the Messiah has become the chief cornerstone of the body of believers, the church.

In Psalm 69, the Messiah is forsaken. In verse four the Messiah says, "Those who hate Me without a cause are more than the hairs of my head; they are mighty who would destroy Me, being my enemies wrongfully." In verse 8 the Messiah says, "I have become a stranger to my brothers, and an alien to my mother's children." In verse 9, the Messiah says, "Because zeal for Your house has eaten me up." He is referring to the Temple being desecrated with money changers and by those selling sheep, oxen and doves. This King of Kings is our Messiah, our Lord and our Savior. Our Messiah is the Lord Jesus Christ. Get to know Him now.

TODAY'S WORD FOR JULY 4

FREEDOM

It is to freedom that you have been called, my brothers. Only be careful that freedom does not become a mere opportunity for your lower nature (the flesh). You should be free to serve one another in love. Galatians 5:13 (Phillips translation)

When God created us He gave us a free will to choose whether or not to serve Him. With that free will comes the freedom to sin. Sin, however, is not free. It comes with a price tag which is death and eternal separation from God.

God sent His Son, Jesus, to pay the penalty for our sin. Those who accept God's free gift of salvation are set free from the penalty of sin. Salvation covers the penalty for all of our sins, but does not take away our freedom to sin. Just because all of our sins have been forgiven, it does not give us a license to sin. God will hold us accountable for our sinning. In Galatians 5:13, above, Paul warns us, "to be careful that freedom does not become a mere opportunity for your lower nature."

Various issues in life cause people to lose certain freedoms. For example, the freedom to go where you want to go if you were physically disabled or had some crippling disease. The freedom to do certain things if you lived in inescapable poverty lost your job, or your home. These circumstances affect your freedom.

America was founded by those who lost their freedom to worship God. We need to take a new look at what it means to have freedom in Christ. Reading God's Word each day is a privilege that many people around the world do not have.

The Bible has a lot to share with us about the freedom God has given to those of us who love and serve Him. God first shows us an example about freedom in Genesis (13:10-13). Abraham responded to the leading of God and gave Lot the freedom of choice as to the land that would be his. Lot chose the fertile land of the plains of Jordan and left the desert area of Canaan to Abraham. But as the scriptures tell us, the land that Lot chose caused nothing but problems for Lot while God blessed the land left to Abraham. The reason was very clear. Lot, with his freedom, chose not to honor and serve God. Abraham, with his freedom of choice, chose to serve God.

We are told to proclaim freedom to the poor in Isaiah 61:1. We communicate to many people the importance of helping the poor in their time of trouble. We have spent most of our lives dedicated to helping mission outreaches care for the poor. We will assure you God will bless those who reach out to help the poor.

We are promised freedom from our sins in Romans 6:14. The greatest freedom is given by God when He lifts our burden of sin. In John 8:32-36 we are told in God's Word; if you are faithful to the Lord and if you live according to God's teaching that He has given to us, "We shall know the truth and the truth shall make us free."

Finally, in 1 Peter 2:16-17 we are admonished as believers to "Live as free men; not however, as though your freedom were there to provide a screen for wrongdoing; but live as servants of God, honoring all men, love your brothers and fear God." Let Christ control your life; it is then you have true freedom.

TODAY'S WORD FOR JULY 5

SOVEREIGNTY

The Lord has established His throne in the heavens and His sovereignty ruled over all. Psalm 103:19 (NAS)

The Sovereignty of God is a theological term meaning our God has absolute authority and right of dominion over all His creation, because He is the self-existent creator. God has always ruled over all things and people from everlasting to everlasting from His throne in heaven. He has the sovereign right to do whatever He pleases. Sometimes we may think He is not acting as we think or want, particularly when we look at the evil and corruption in this world. We wonder why God allows it. The powers of darkness, sin, Satan, demons, and the wickedness of mankind cannot alter the purpose of our sovereign God.

Habakkuk, a prophet of God, questioned God's inactivity concerning the evil that prevailed in Judah in his day. He cried out to God with all his concerns. He said there is violence and evil deeds everywhere. People love to argue and fight. The wicked far out number the righteous. Justice has become perverted and there is no justice in the courts. He could have been describing the day and age we are living in today. Habakkuk felt God was not seeing or hearing what was going on.

In response to Habakkuk's perplexity and pleading, God broke His silence, informing Habakkuk He was not indifferent to Judah's sin but rather than seeing a revival among the people, He was sending the "dreaded and feared" judgment. (Verse 7)

In Habakkuk 1:5-6 God answered and assured Habakkuk that He was already doing something about it. God said: "I will work a work in your days which you would not believe, though it was told you." Judah's day of reckoning was coming. God was raising up the Babylonians who God would use to punish Judah. God is in absolute control of all things and of all people and not obligated to reveal "the what or the why" of His works.

Even these prophets of old found it hard to understand the sovereignty of God and the same is true of us today. But we do know God has unlimited authority over all things and He always creates and molds everything perfectly, even our lives when we put our trust in Him.

Most people in our world today do not comprehend the sovereignty of God. They seem to really believe what they do and say makes no difference to God. But as believers, we should know better and through our words and actions make sure our lights shine bright so that those who do not believe will see the sovereignty of God through us.

TODAY'S WORD FOR JULY 6

GOSSIP

A man who bears false witness against his neighbor is like a club, a sword, and an arrow.
Proverbs 25:18

A perverse man stirs up dissension and a gossip separates close friends. Proverbs 16:28

Gossip defined really is the act of someone sharing with another party information about a third party that is most often just a rumor and not true or at least stretching the truth. Most certainly it is not complimentary to the third party and is most often very hurtful.

Our sinful nature causes us to relish juicy tidbits of gossip. We love to hear about someone's rumored indiscretion and we can't wait to tell others. The most prevalent place for gossip is in the work place. In fact, it has become so bad that a person can get fired for gossiping in certain workplaces. According to a recent poll, the average employee gossips 65 hours a year. Notice this includes all employees — that is over ¾ of an hour each and every week if someone works 50 weeks a year.

There are some work places that take corrective approaches to gossip. They range from firing the one who gossips, to a group in the entertainment industry who takes the time to pray for a person who is making bad choices rather than spreading the facts or rumors to more people.

There is no place in the life of a believer for gossip. As believers it is clear what God wants from us concerning gossiping. Exodus 20:16 reads, "You shall not bear false witness against your neighbor." That is quite clear and simple to understand. In the verse we wrote above from Proverbs it is stated very strongly that the use of our words in a gossiping situation is like a club, a sword and a sharp arrow.

In this verse above the clubs, swords and sharp arrows are weapons that cause great pain and harm. Like a weapon, gossip causes pain and does great harm. The writer is saying that a man who stirs up dissension by bearing false witness is as destructive to one's reputation as those weapons are to the body.

The writer of Proverbs 16:28 tells us that gossip is harmful because it stirs up dissension and separates close friends. The word translated here, stirs up, comes from the same root word that was used for the release of flaming foxes in the grain fields of the Philistines. (Judges 15:4-5)

Gossip should not be part of a believer's life. It will always hurt someone and one cannot honor God by gossiping about other people, places or things.

Unfortunately, we have heard many people gossip in church. Of all places this is not a place for gossip. Gossip feeds into our natural desires to feel superior to others and to belong or fit in with the crowd. If you choose to love others and be concerned about others you will live in a gossip free zone. You can never justify gossip. It is better to pray for someone and then you will find it difficult to gossip about them.

TODAY'S WORD FOR JULY 7

VISION

When your eye is good, your whole body is also filled with light. But when your eye is bad, your body is also full of darkness. Matthew 6:22-23

Your old men will dream dreams and your young men shall see visions. Joel 2:28

Where there is no vision the people perish. Proverbs 29:18

When we think of the word "vision" two things come to mind. First, is the "vision" we have when we see things as they are. Secondly, we think of "vision" as it relates to things in the future we want to accomplish. In life today most people see things only as they are now and cannot, for the most part, see past today.

Living without vision is worse than blindness. Jesus said in Matthew (above) that inward blindness corrupts one's whole nature and affects one's whole being.

As we think back on our lives we have seen God do so much through our lives and many times because we had a vision to accomplish what sometimes seemed impossible. We did not allow blindness to over shadow our vision. We must remember the words of Jesus in Matthew 20:26, "With God all things are possible."

In the verse from Proverbs, above, the writer talks about the vision one must have to hide God's Word in one's heart and then to proclaim to the world the good news of the gospel. The lack of God's Word in one's life leads to lawless rebellion. In contrast, living with God's Word is living with joy and glory in a lawful society.

Life for most families today, with children, demands a series of prayerful visions, in order to accomplish their goals. For example, education here in America has become quite expensive. God gave us a program to challenge our children to do their best in school at a young age so that they could get the best education possible. Each one responded and they all excelled in school and went to college.

For us, life would have been unproductive and unsatisfying if we did not have a vision for our family or a vision for our ministry to a world that needed Jesus.

Columbus had a vision to find the new world so he set out on a course that was unknown to man and his vision resulted in finding this new world. We grew up in the 1940's and 1950's when there were many new ministries begun because of the vision of leaders who responded to the call of God. Our lives were affected because we saw first-hand God at work. Many of these Christian leaders had a vision for the impossible. Then God took over and those visions became a reality.

We challenge you and your family to ask God for a special vision to further His work here on earth. Whether your vision is large or small it is important to God. We can remember our prayer 56 years ago. It was simply for God to use us and give us a burden for a world that needed Jesus. Then we watched God open doors and we were ready to march through those doors as God led us.

TODAY'S WORD FOR JULY 8

ANCHOR

This hope we have as an anchor of the soul, both sure and steadfast. Hebrews 6:19

When we think of anchors, we think of ships or boats. An anchor is lowered to keep the ship in place so it will not float into a dangerous position. In Acts chapter 27, the apostle Paul gives us an account of the time he was on a ship as a prisoner being moved with other prisoners to their trial. He tells about a terrible storm when they had to put the anchor out to keep the ship wrecked vessel from being dashed to pieces on the rocks.

In Hebrews, above, the writer tells about the hope we have as an anchor for the soul. As believers we have the hope, assured, for the fulfillment of God's salvation promises which is the anchor of our soul. Our hope is embodied in Christ Himself who has entered into the presence of God in the heavenly Holy of Holies on our behalf.

Thinking of ships and boats, we remember going out in a small boat with an out board motor with Ken's mother and step father. We had our six children with us and we went out no more than a mile into the Pacific Ocean. All of a sudden we noticed the boat was slowly beginning to fill with water. Since we had young children on board my step father radioed the Coast Guard for help. We knew an anchor would not help and a bucket bailing the water out of the boat was not sufficient. We also knew that now was the time to pray. We all were praying and doing all we could to help get rid of the water at the same time, as we slowly tried to get the boat back to the safety of the shore.

Soon we saw a Coast Guard ship getting close. To say the least, it was huge. We thought the whole American Navy was coming. They responded quickly probably, because they knew there were small children on board. To make a long story short, the Coast Guard got us and the boat safely back to shore. That day, in our situation, a boat anchor was not what we needed. It was the anchor of our hope in Jesus Christ that we relied on by praying and believing.

As Christians, our hope in Jesus is the anchor for our soul and it is sure and steadfast so we will not drift away. In the storms of life we are like a ship at sea that is tossed and battered and in danger of being dashed to pieces. Our anchor, Jesus Christ, is always with us keeping us safe, stable and in a position not to float away into worldly problems.

It is impossible to live a happy and joyful life without an anchor that works. That anchor is Jesus. There is no other anchor that works. When you face each day in life, make sure your anchor of faith in Jesus is steadfast and sure. Seek the Lord daily to keep your anchor firm and put your trust in Him to keep you steady in the storms of life. He will be there with you every moment of the day.

TODAY'S WORD FOR JULY 9

LOYALTY

No one can serve two masters; for either he will hate the one or love the other, or else he will be loyal to the one and despise the other. You cannot serve God and mammon. Matthew 6:24

As believers we know that our loyalty to God, our creator, our Savior and our Lord must be a priority in our life. Then secondly we need to make sure we are loyal to our spouses, our children, our parents and even our friends.

Loyalty is a trait we admire in others and look for in a true friend. We all like to think of ourselves as loyal. Unfortunately the reality is that we do not see much true loyalty in our world today. It is easy to be loyal if it doesn't demand anything of us. It is when loyalty costs us something, that our resolve to be loyal crumbles. It is difficult to maintain because it often puts us in a position of having to choose sides.

Theodore Roosevelt, the former President of the United States, said in 1919: There can be no divided allegiance here. We have room for one God, one flag, one language, and for one sole loyalty and that is to the American people.

As children we were taught to be loyal and devoted to God and then to our country and our flag. Our parents taught us to be loyal to them and to our siblings.

Solomon was known for his God-given wisdom and devotion to God. In spite of his wisdom and his love for God he failed to remain completely loyal to God. In I Kings 11:4 we read Solomon's loyalty became divided. He allowed pressure from his pagan wives to compromise his devotion to God, As Solomon grew old, his wives turned his heart after other gods and his heart was not devoted to the Lord his God.

There are many pressures in this world that can cause us to compromise our loyalty to God. In Matthew 6:24 Jesus warned of this danger and compared it to trying to serve two masters. "No one can serve two masters; for either he will hate the one or love the other." Loyalty to the Lord our God requires making a choice. If we choose our Lord, He wants our loyalty without compromise.

Loyalty to the Lord may not be easy. Anyone who has lived under communism knows that devotion to God comes at a heavy cost. Many have paid with their lives because of their faith and loyalty to their Lord. In America we are often mocked for our faith, but we must stay strong and loyal to our faith and God will honor us.

Dan Crawford was a person that loved to go into new areas of our world and explore. He tells of a native guide who was leading him along a new trail. Being uncertain of his direction, he asked the guide just where they were going. You want to know the way? I am the way! smiled the native guide, pointing to his head where the knowledge was stored.

TODAY'S WORD FOR JULY 10

ROLE MODELS

Beloved, let us love one another, for love is of God; and everyone who loves is born of God and knows God. I John 4:7

We often hear people refer to another person as a role model. A role model is one who another person respects and imitates. Stop now for a moment and think of all the people you know and write down the names of the ones who are role models to you. When you look at the list then ask yourself the question, "Do you really know each one?" Many on your list could include movie, television, sports or even Christian personalities. But do you really know them or do you call them a potential role model because you have seen only the good from a distance.

As we were growing up we often had Christian leaders as our role models. Unfortunately, we found out that they were human also and had their faults. We have talked about several of these sad situation many times. They became a very real warning for us to watch who we considered to be role models in our lives and to teach our children the same.

Today's society feels it is important to have role models. Famous people talk about being role models, but do not seem to care if they have bad traits or fail. They still feel they are role models. Teenagers are influenced by role models and do not always use discretion in choosing their role models. Therefore, parents must be aware of who their children are looking to as role models. Just because someone is a big "star" and famous does not make them worthy of being a role model.

Only God and Jesus are worthy to be role models. Jesus is the perfect role model because He lived in our sinful world, was tempted as we are, yet He never sinned. Look at all He has given us to build on. First of all, He loves us, and gave His life for us. Then He lived His life as the perfect example of how to live our life.

He serves as an example showing us how to love one another. When you love, it is impossible to hate at the same time. The righteousness of God and Jesus should be the focus of our choosing our role model. Can you think of any living person better to imitate in life? God has given us His Son to pay the penalty for our sins. God has given us His Holy Spirit to lead us through life each day. God has given us time, talent and treasure to use for Him. God has given us His Word as a guide for living. What else can we want or hope for in a role model?

As believers in Christ we can still look to people as role models so we can learn how they live their Christian lives. We need to do this with caution and wisdom. We can learn from the positives we see in their lives, but we should always be alert to the possibility of failure in their lives.

We must remember they are human just like us and vulnerable to the devil's temptations. God and His Son alone are trust worthy. God never changes. When someone fails us we cannot blame God. God is faithful and He will never fail us.

TODAY'S WORD FOR JULY 11

ACCEPTANCE

Therefore I exhort first of all that supplications, prayers, intercessions and giving of thanks be made for all men, for this is good and acceptable in the sight of God our Savior
I Timothy 2:1

When Jesus was here on this earth the Jewish people literally despised the Samaritans. They did all they could not to meet or talk with a Samaritan. We read in John 4 that Jesus met a Samaritan woman at the well and began to talk with her. When Jesus asked for a drink she was surprised and wanted to know why He was talking to her because no Jewish man would ever talk to a Samaritan woman. However, Jesus continued to talk with her and she believed in Him and accepted His gift of "living water."

She went back to her village and led many Samaritans to become believers in Jesus. We can learn from this story that Jesus came for all of us and He accepts all who come to Him in faith believing for forgiveness of their sins.

The apostle Paul in the verse above was exhorting Timothy to urge the believers to pray for the lost. Evidently they had stopped praying because there were false teachers preaching that salvation was only for the elite and for the elected ones chosen by God. Paul was urging Timothy to make prayer for the lost, a priority again in the lives of the believers.

Paul was telling Timothy that the lost needed to feel acceptance from the believers and they have a great need for salvation. Believers, Paul said, should always be asking God to meet the needs of the lost.

In Romans 15:7 we are told to accept one another just as Christ accepted you in order to bring praise to God. We are to accept and encourage other Christians as well as accepting others who do not know the Lord, so we can introduce them to Christ. Jesus knew the Samaritan woman was an immoral woman. He did not shun her for her race, social position or her sins. He accepted her as someone who needed His saving grace.

People today are hungry for acceptance. Children in school do every thing they can, including lowering their standards, to be accepted by their peers. Adults are much the same. They all want to be included in "THE GROUP".

Paul tells us in Romans 14:1 "Do not refuse to accept someone who is weak in faith. And do not argue with him about opinions."

We need to make people feel important and needed. This way they will feel accepted and will likely be open to hear about Jesus. If we see a Christian weak in their faith, we should not argue about things in their life we disagree with, but lovingly encourage them to help them grow in their faith.

This is an example that should remind each of us to do all we can to make people we touch shoulders with feel accepted.

TODAY'S WORD FOR JULY 12

SCRIPTURES

All scripture is given by inspiration of God, and is profitable for doctrine, for reproof, for correction, for instruction in righteousness. II Timothy 3:16

It is important that we understand when we talk about the inspiration of the scriptures that inspiration applies only to the original creator not the Bible writers. There are no inspired Scripture writers, only inspired scripture. Sometimes God told the Bible writers the exact words to say, but more often He used their minds, vocabularies, and experiences to produce His own perfect infallible, inerrant Word.

Paul has told us how we could and should guard against the trials of life we face daily. We first learned that we should constantly be alert for all the evil influences we face and rejoice in the Lord always.

Paul tells us the scriptures are full of promises that we as believers need to heed in order to guard against the trials of life we face. The scripture is as powerful to us as a two edged sword and is our defense in the spiritual and moral battles we face.

Paul notes the scripture says that it was written to instruct us and to help us in pressing on for Christ. No person can press on and grow spiritually without heeding the scripture. If we fail to study and obey the scripture we will cave in either to the trials of life or to false teaching. Only as we obey the scripture which contains the commandments of the Lord, can we show our daily love and loyalty to the Lord.

Over and over in the scriptures we are told to obey the Word of the Lord and keep His commandments. It is so important that in just one chapter, John 14, Jesus said three times to obey His commandments.

In John 14:15 Jesus says, "If you love me, keep My commandments." In verse 21 Jesus said, "He that has My commandments, and keeps them, he it is that loves Me: and he that loves Me shall be loved by My Father, and I will love him, and will manifest Myself to him." And in verse 23 Jesus says, "If a man loves Me, he will keep My words, and My Father will love him, and we will come to him, and make our abode with him."

It is not only necessary to keep God's commandments, as written in the scriptures, to show we love Him. If we truly love Him we will want to obey His Word. We must read and study the scripture daily in order for us to put up our guard against the evil we face in our lives. God is identified through His Word and when scripture speaks to you it is God speaking to you. Scripture is called the oracles of God and cannot be altered. Scripture provides the comprehensive and complete body of divine truth necessary for all believers to live a life of godliness.

The scripture exposes sin. Scripture rebukes bad behavior and points the way back to godly living. Scripture provides positive training in godly behavior. Every believer needs to study scripture daily. It is our guide book for living a godly life.

TODAY'S WORD FOR JULY 13

DISCIPLESHIP

Go therefore and make disciples of all the nations, baptizing them in the name of the Father and of the Son and of the Holy Spirit, teaching them to observe all things that I have commanded you; and lo, I am with you always, even to the end of the age. Matthew 28:19-20

Jesus gave all believers the command to go and disciple new believers in the Word of God. The verse above is the commission of Jesus to His disciples and all believers after His resurrection and before He returned to heaven.

We are concerned that very few believers are truly committed to being disciples of Jesus here on this earth. In Mark 1:17-18 Jesus called men and asked them to follow Him. Follow me, and I will make you become fishers of men. These were mostly fishermen and they left their nets and followed Jesus. Some were tax collectors, business men and zealots and all were willing to give up everything they had to follow Jesus. Thus began their discipleship program.

These were ordinary men, just like you and me, simple lay people engaged in their personal affairs. They were not religious or political leaders of their day and were not students in schools of higher learning. They were industrious and hard working men. They were visionaries looking for their Messiah and ready to follow Him.

When Paul met Jesus, God knew he needed help from a very special believer to learn about Jesus. The believer God chose to disciple Paul was a simple unknown believer named Ananias. The traits Ananias possessed were exactly what Paul needed. We need to understand God is looking for people like each one of us to disciple new believers. He wants us to study and know God's Word well enough so we are prepared to help new believers.

Ananias was obviously a godly man and devoted to the Lord. Ananias was also very sensitive to the call of God because he communicated daily with God through prayer. When God called him, he knew the voice of God and was prepared to follow what God wanted him to do. God chose Ananias to disciple Paul because Ananias was spiritually prepared and submissive to the leading of the Holy Spirit.

God told Ananias what Paul needed to be taught and encouraged Paul to know that he was a chosen vessel and a chosen instrument of God. God has the same message for us. "You have not chosen me, but I have chosen you, that you should go and bring forth fruit, and that your fruit should remain" John 15:16.

Jesus is not content to just be our "fire insurance" saving us from eternal punishment and an eternity in Hell. He wants us to know who He is and then wants to connect with us on a deeper level so we can represent Him to the world. God wants us to apply them to our lives today so we can be vessels to be used by Him. Start preparing today to be a disciple of Jesus and get to know and love Him more and more each and every day.

TODAY'S WORD FOR JULY 14

REGRET

When Judas, who had betrayed Jesus, saw that He was condemned, he was seized with remorse and returned the thirty pieces of silver to the chief priests and the elders. I have sinned, he said, for I have betrayed innocent blood. Matthew 27:3

Most people could write a book about all of the times they regretted something they said or did. Let us assure you as we think about what to write concerning this word "regret," many incidents pop into our minds. Most often we regret what we say or do too late. The damage has already been done.

We think the best illustration in the Bible about regret is the deep regret that Judas must have had after he realized what a terrible thing he had done to Jesus.

Judas was seized with remorse. By this time the chief priests and the elders had made their decision to put Jesus to death. When Judas realized Jesus was going to be killed, he went to the chief priests and returned the money he had received to betray Jesus. He wanted to undo what he had done, so he confessed to the chief priests and elders saying, "I have sinned for I have betrayed innocent blood."

He hoped his confession and his profession that Jesus was innocent would change the minds of the chief priests and the elders. It was too late. His thoughtless act of betrayal had already set in motion the consequences of what he had done.

Who we are and what we are develops out of the decisions we make in life. Every day we make choices. We choose what we do, where we go, who we talk to, what we read and what we watch. All of our choices have consequences. Our choices will have a positive effect on our life or a negative one and our choices affect others.

On every decision we make, we should think before we act because it is our nature to want immediate gratification. When that is our motive, we will make bad decisions that we will regret later and generally too late to correct. Even an apology is really not effective because the damage is already done.

Any decision we make that is in disobedience to God's laws will bring consequences that will cause us to regret what we have done. We need to consider each day if our decisions are made in accordance to what God wants us to do.

Sunday schools have recently used the phrase, "What would Jesus do?" in teaching children how to make the right decisions. WWJD became the acronym for that phrase. Some of our grandchildren had bracelets they made with WWJD on them. It was a reminder to them to stop and consider what Jesus would do in the same situation that they were in. That is the question we should ask ourselves before we make decisions.

Judas regretted his decision to betray Jesus. Regret is never enough. He went to the wrong people to set things right. Judas confessed to the high priests he had sinned and betrayed an innocent man. Judas should have repented and sought forgiveness from Jesus. If there are things you have done or are doing that you regret, now is the time to repent and ask God's forgiveness.

TODAY'S WORD FOR JULY 15

ADOPTION

We are children of God, and if children, heirs also, heirs of God and fellow heirs with Christ.
Romans 8: 16b-17a

In ancient Rome, adoption was occasionally used by the emperors to pass on succession to competent heirs. Augustus Caesar was adopted by his great uncle Julius Caesar so he could be his successor. Emperors Tiberius and Hadrian did the same thing, adopting a capable person to succeed them.

Such Roman emperors had no entitlement to be emperor by right of birth. It was only because of the Roman law of adoption. Under Roman law, adopted children became an heir to their father's estate. Adopted children under the Roman laws had all the rights and privileges of the biological children. It was the Jewish practice for the inheritance to go to the first born.

Every Christian, a believer in Jesus, is an adopted child of the King of kings. Our adoption comes at a great cost. God brought us into His family through the sacrifice of His Son Jesus on the cross. We became a child of God when we asked Him for forgiveness for our sins and accepted Him as our Savior. Although we are adopted children, God has made us joint heirs with Christ as written in Romans 8.

In Hebrews 1:2 the writer tells us that God has appointed Jesus heir of all things. As children of God we have inherited eternal salvation along with everything in the universe. Think about what this means for us who believe in Him. Every believer is going to receive, by God's grace, the same inheritance that Christ receives by divine right. Earthly inheritances will perish, but we are heirs to God's eternal kingdom and its riches which will never perish.

Paul tells us "Our Lord Jesus Christ though He was rich, yet for your sakes He became poor so that you through His poverty might become rich." Do you realize that you are rich? We should feel great indebtedness to Him for all that he has done for us. There is no way to repay Him. In return for our being adopted into God's family, God wants us to live in a way that a child of God is expected to live.

In Colossians 3:5 the apostle Paul writes that we are to get rid of sin in our lives when we have been adopted by God. He writes, "put to death the sinful ways of are old life; sexual immorality, impurity, lust, evil desires, greed and idolatry."

These are to be replaced by activities and desires that show that we belong to the family of God. In Colossians 3:12, Paul writes for us to "put on tender mercies, kindness, humility, meekness and longsuffering."

TODAY'S WORD FOR JULY 16

LIFE

Jesus said to him, I am the way, the truth, and the life. No one comes to the Father except through Me. John 14:6

I call heaven and earth as witnesses today against you, that I have set before you life and death, blessing and cursing; therefore choose life, that both you and your descendants may live. Deuteronomy 30:19

God created us to live a life that is productive and full. Real life comes from a total commitment to God. It is not an easy commitment because it requires discipline and a willingness to yield oneself to God.

Many never find happiness because they look for it in obtaining possessions and material things they feel will make them happy. Things do not provide satisfaction, therefore, people always want more and their lives are filled with emptiness.

Contrast this with the life of one who has put his or her faith in the Lord. Even though we were born as sinners into an evil world with sinful influences all around us, God provided a substitute for us who paid the penalty for our sins. As believers, we can live a life of hope knowing we have God walking with us through all the ups and downs of life. God is with us wherever we go.

David recognized that God is life and the creator of life. God knew and loved David before He ever existed. He designed the person David was and brought him into being according to His predetermined plan. David was shaped by his Heavenly Father into a unique creation and David chose to live a life of obedience to God.

Moses in his last days just before he put Joshua in command of the Children of Israel urged the people to renew their covenant with God. They had spent 40 years wandering in the wilderness because they had broken their covenant with God. He gave them a choice of life and prosperity or death and destruction.

In the verse above from Deuteronomy Moses told the children of Israel to make the right choice and choose LIFE! In choosing life they were choosing to love the Lord, obey His voice and cling to Him. Moses told the Children of Israel that if they chose life, they were to be obedient to God and they would live longer and be able to dwell in the land God promised them through Abraham, Isaac and Jacob.

Jesus as God's Son is life as well as the giver of life. In John 4:46-54, Jesus was asked by a nobleman to come to Capernaum and heal his son who was on the brink of death. He came to Jesus believing He could give life. The crowd around them did not believe, so Jesus put him off by saying "unless you people are dazzled by a miracle you refuse to believe." But the nobleman would not be put off and he insisted, "Come down! It is life or death for my son." Jesus simply said, "Go home. Your son lives." The father chose to obey Jesus and went home and asked when the son got better. It was the exact time Jesus spoke to him that his son lived. As a result, the nobleman and his entire household believed in Jesus.

TODAY'S WORD FOR JULY 17

CONVERSION

Blessed be the God and Father of our Lord Jesus Christ, who according to His abundant mercy has begotten us again to a living hope through the resurrection of Jesus Christ from the dead. I Peter 1:3

As young people, we both can remember listening to adults, youth and even children tell about their conversion. They would say, "The greatest thing that ever happened to me was the day I met Jesus Christ." Neither one of us had a shattering emotional experience when we made our decision to accept Jesus as our Savior; even though it was an experience we have never forgotten. It was a response to the moving of God's Holy Spirit in our life. We look back on all that has happened to us during our lifetime and without a doubt, the decision we made to accept Jesus as our Savior stands out as the greatest decision of our lives.

Peter in I Peter chapter one deals with the subject of conversion. Peter reminds us the experience of the new birth is so important because it is part of God's provision for salvation for us. First, it gives us a new hope of heaven when we die, which will be eternal life. And secondly, our conversion gives us a living hope to carry us through our life here on this earth. This hope protects the believer in Jesus against the attacks of Satan and produces joy that we can rely on daily.

In the gospel of John, third chapter, Jesus had a conversation with Nicodemus who was a Pharisee and a ruler of the Jews. The Pharisees thought of Jesus as an enemy, therefore, Nicodemus went to Jesus by night so his fellow Pharisees would not know about his visit. He told Jesus he knew He was a teacher sent from God because no one could perform the signs He had done unless God was with Him.

Nicodemus had knowledge about Jesus, but knowledge alone does not save. Nicodemus was seeking to learn more, but did not know what he was seeking. Jesus who knows the heart of all of us knew what Nicodemus was seeking.

Jesus said to Nicodemus: "I say to you, unless one is born again, he cannot see the kingdom of God." Nicodemus and Jesus had a lengthy conversation about being born again or conversion (verses 4-15). In the 16th verse Jesus said what many feel is the most significant verse in the Bible. This verse concisely tells us of God's plan of salvation: "For God so loved the world that He gave His only begotten Son, that whoever believes in Him should not perish but have everlasting life." John 3:16.

We are all sinners, but God loves all of us and loves us so much that He gave His only Son, Jesus, to die for our sins so that we can have eternal life if we believe in Him. This is the only way we can have a spiritual conversion. It is God's act of spiritual regeneration in us whereby we receive eternal life. Where do you stand today? God is waiting for you to ask Him for forgiveness for the sins you have committed. Now is the time. Tomorrow may be too late.

TODAYS WORD FOR JULY 18

SEEKING

Behold, I stand at the door and knock. If anyone hears My voice and opens the door, I will come in to him and dine with him, and he with Me. Revelation 3:20

We will talk today about two kinds of seeking. The children of Israel began seeking to have a king like the pagan nations around them, so God allowed the Children of Israel to choose a king who would make their decisions for them. They were in the process of taking their eyes off God. They chose Saul and it turned out to be one of the great tragedies in the Bible because Saul continually made his decisions seeking human favor for himself.

God told Saul to kill all of the Amalekites, but he chose to save the life of their king because Saul felt it would grant him favor in the eyes of his people. Saul had a divided allegiance. He was quite content to serve God as long as it pleased those around him. The failure in the life of Saul was his continual hunger for the affection of people around him. Do you know people like that today? We all do.

Now we have the contrast of knowing a seeking Savior rather than one who is seeking the favor of others. In the third chapter of Revelation, John relates to us that the Christians at Laeodicea were self deceived, picturing themselves as rich and self-sufficient, when in reality, their spiritual blindness and self-righteousness had prevented them from seeing their true poverty.

They had closed the door between themselves and Jesus even though Jesus still was reaching out to them as their seeking Savior. Christ was seeking to enter this church that bore His name, but lacked a single true believer. He was knocking hoping that just one member would recognize his own spiritual bankruptcy and respond to God's saving faith, so Jesus could impact the church.

John describes Jesus reaching out to us as well through the verse above. First, He is standing at the door. Jesus takes the initiative and willing to seek us even when we have erected a barrier.

Secondly, He knocks at the door. He tries to get our attention through circumstances we might face, needs we have, pain, trials, conviction, sleeplessness, or even His Word. He patiently waits for us to respond.

Thirdly, Jesus invites us to open the door. Jesus seeks us and He is omnipotent, but never pushes His way into a relationship with us. We are the one who chooses to accept or reject Him, not Jesus.

Fourthly, Jesus enters through the door. If we open the door to Him He will come in. Through the indwelling of the Holy Spirit in our lives we will actually partake of Christ's divine nature and we will be transformed into His image. What a wonderful promise.

Finally, Jesus will dine with us inside the door. When we allow the seeking Jesus to come into our heart nothing stands between us and Jesus. We can begin to enjoy the benefits of an intimate relationship with Him and be nourished by His Word.

TODAYS WORD FOR JULY 19

FRIEND

Greater love has no one than this, than to lay down one's life for his friends. You are My friends if you do whatever I command you. John 15:13-14

A friend loves at all times. Proverbs 17:17a

A man who has friends must himself be friendly, but there is a friend who sticks closer than a brother. Psalm 18:24

People need friends today because human nature drives a person to need to communicate with someone. People learn quickly there are many types of friends.

We feel many people are "fair weather friends." They are with you as a friend as long as all is going well between the two of you or until another friend comes along. Many people keep friendships only as long as it benefits them. They are suddenly gone when you face a crises or situation when you really need a friend.

Where do you look for friends? This is a critical decision every person must make when looking for friends. One needs to remember where their heart is that is where there you will feel most comfortable. When you love the Lord you need to look for friends in places where like minded people who also love the Lord gather.

We developed friends with parents of children who went to the same school and church that our children attended. They attended a Christian school so there was a closer bond because of our mutual love for the Lord. Our best friends in our lives were the leaders we met in missions because our heart interests were the same.

Take a moment to read the book of Philemon. It is only 25 verses long Paul talks to his brother in Christ, Philemon, about Christian brotherly love. Philemon was a beloved friend and fellow laborer in faith.

Paul writes Philemon to intercede for Onesimus, Philemon's runaway slave. Onesimus had become a believer and developed a deep bond of friendship with Paul. Onesimus was helpful to Paul while he was in prison. Paul asks Philemon to be forgiving and welcome Onesimus back, not as a slave, but as a Christian brother.

Paul reminds Philemon they have a responsibility to love their friend Onesimus. We as believers have the same responsibility today to love our friends just as Jesus loves us. To love as Jesus does, we must be forgiving of those who have wronged us and are seeking our forgiveness and accept them back as a friend.

The three verses we have written above are reminders to us how we are to live our lives in a spirit of love and to be the kind of friend Jesus wants us to be. Do you show love to those friends who are counting on you for support and friendship? Do you show the love of Christ in your daily walk and talk? Do your friends see a difference in you compared to some of the other friends they may have?

It is important for us to remember the greatest friend we have is Jesus. He is with us through thick and thin. He never leaves us nor forsakes us.

TODAYS WORD FOR JULY 20

ACCOMPLISH

So shall My word be that goes forth from My mouth; It shall not return to Me void, but it shall accomplish what I please, and it shall prosper in the thing for which I sent it. Isaiah 55:11

After this, Jesus knowing that all things were accomplished, that the Scripture might be fulfilled, said, I THIRST. John 19:28

In the verse above from Isaiah, the phrase," it shall accomplish what I please," shows the power of God's Word. The Word of God will produce its intended results in fulfilling God's spiritual purposes in our lives. We, as believers must be willing and available for God to use us.

All of us want to be successful and accomplish things during our lifetime. We are successful in some of the tasks we attempt which gives us the satisfaction of accomplishment. However, we also fail in some tasks and our feelings are very different. Many times are failures are because we move ahead without involving God. All of us like to successfully accomplish what we start.

The Hebrew word in this verse in Isaiah for accomplishment is ASAH. In Hebrew, it makes the point that God is able to bring out of Himself the power, the victory, the solution to problems and the comfort needed anywhere and anytime. In other words, our God can accomplish whatever He desires and no one can prevent God from accomplishing His purposes. In this verse from Isaiah we are being reminded that the Word of God will produce its intended results in fulfilling God's spiritual purposes for His kingdom here on this earth.

God also accomplishes things from other things, not only out of Himself. He makes the tree yield fruit and He causes the sun to shine. He brings the rain. He gives man the power to create wealth. God can do wonders with His weakest child if His child will let Him work in his or her life.

In the verse we have given you from John, we need to comment while Jesus was on the cross He did not respond to His need until He knew all had been accomplished to fulfill what had been prophesized in the scriptures. It was at that point he said, "I THIRST." God will not discontinue working on us until he has accomplished all He needs from us.

The principle we want to share with you today is for you to make sure you do not limit God by your lack of faith. We learned by experience that if we truly wanted to accomplish something for God, we needed to step up, increase our faith, and ask God to do something special through us. When we felt God was finished using us in one project we would move fast and ask God to take us to the next plateau. There is nothing God cannot accomplish through your life. We need to wake up, step up and let God perform, in us and through us, whatever it is He wants to accomplish.

TODAYS WORD FOR JULY 21

DECEIT

He who works deceit shall not dwell within my house; He who tells lies shall not continue in My presence. Psalm 101:7

The meaning of the word deceit is the misrepresentation of truth and intentional concealment of a wrong. For many people today misrepresenting the truth and concealing a wrong is a way of life and they never consider this to be a sin against God. When you misrepresent the truth or conceal a wrong it is deceit and a sin.

Because of our sinful nature, deceit runs rampant in our society. Think about the things you see and hear that you know are not true. How does that affect your opinion of that person? Think about yourself and weigh every word and deed that you do. Is there cheating, misleading, untruthfulness or fraud in your life? And if so, do you think it affects people's opinion of you? Take the time to listen and watch your family, friends and neighbors. See how much deceit, cheating, misleading and untruthfulness comes from them. We all know when we are not being truthful so we must be aware that deceit is the result of a conscious effort in our lives.

When you watch television, read magazines and newspapers, much of what you see and hear is an undercurrent of lies, cheating and evil things. Parents lie to and mislead their children. Children lie and mislead their parents. Teachers, bosses and spouses lie to each other. Some say they do not lie, they just stretch the truth. Others say it is just a little white lie. Stretching the truth in God's sight is a lie.

Lying is deceitful and misleading. Basically it happens when one is either trying to cover up a mistake or a failure in life or just making oneself look good. People will do and say what they think is best for them with no consideration of anyone else. Thus, a lie or some deceitful comment in order to complete a task or to make one just feel better seems to be accepted and considered proper, until one gets caught.

There are those who call themselves Christians who are deceitful. They perform the same way as a non believer because they are not in tune with God. In God's sight this is sin and not acceptable. The Psalmist in the verse we have written above makes it very clear as to how God feels about deceit. God is truth and deceit and truth cannot dwell together in God's kingdom. When a person has a deceit problem they will not dwell in the house of the Lord and will not be in the presence of God. The Psalmist also tells us in Psalms 32:2, "Blessed is the man to whom the Lord does not impute iniquity, and in whose spirit there is no deceit."

Being deceitful in God's sight has very serious consequences. If we are deceitful we will not dwell in His house! This is serious because it affects one's whole eternity. We need to understand deceit hurts God and it is not acceptable in His sight.

It is also written in Proverbs 12:20, "Deceit is in the heart of those who devise evil, but counselors of peace have joy." As Christians we can have joy in our hearts if we do not practice deceit. It is impossible to live a life of joy and be deceitful. When we lie we have to live with stress because of our concern of being caught.

TODAYS WORD FOR JULY 22

OBEDIENCE

Train up a child in the way he should go, and when he is old he will not depart from it. Proverbs 22:6.

The verse from Proverbs (above) gives parents no option, but to train their children to be obedient. Realistically a parent does have an option, but if they want their child to live a God honoring and God fearing life, they have no option.

We can assure you from our experience that training our children in the way of the Lord does work. Children learn obedience and so many other traits in life not just by the teaching they receive, but also by the examples set by the parents. We need to walk and talk as honoring to God or the teaching can become meaningless.

The first reference to obedience we find in the Bible is the lack of obedience by Adam and Eve. They were told by God not to eat of "the tree of the knowledge of good and evil, for in the day that you eat of it you surely shall die." Satan, in the form of the serpent, tempted Adam and Eve and they were not obedient.

Then in Geneses 12:1-4, we are told of the obedience of Abraham. The Lord told Abraham to get out of his country and from his father's house and family. God told him if he obeyed, He would make him a great nation and would bless him and make his name great and all peoples on earth would be blessed through him. Abraham's response was immediate and he obeyed the call of God.

It was to Israel that God chose to send His Son, Jesus Christ. Jesus was sent into the world to pay the penalty for all the sins of everyone in the world fulfilling God's promise that all peoples on earth would be blessed through Abraham.

What a contrast! The disobedience of Adam and Eve brought condemnation to all. The obedience of Abraham brought salvation to all. Disobedience brings consequences and obedience brings blessings.

A famed children's specialist was quoted, "When it comes to a serious illness, the child who has been taught to obey has four times the chance of recovery than the spoiled and undisciplined child."

In order for Abraham to be obedient to God's will he had to be willing to give up what was dear to him. He had to walk away from his home and his friends. He had to step out of his comfort zone to receive greater blessings from God. Being obedient to God's will may require you to make difficult changes in your life. Teaching obedience to our children is difficult. When a parent says "NO" many things happen in the mind of a child. The child may be testing the parent to see where his or her boundaries are and how far they may be stretched. A child also is watching for consistency and wants to know if the "No" is really a "No."

Parents also must be consistent with what they are doing in front of their children. When an adult talks about obedience everyone is watching for honesty, consistency and seriousness in their words and deeds.

TODAYS WORD FOR JULY 23

RIGHTEOUSNESS

Not by works of righteousness which we have done, but according to His mercy He saved us, through the washing of regeneration and renewing of the Holy Spirit. Titus 3:5

Many people will tell you they strive daily to live a righteous life. When you ask them to tell you what they mean by being righteous, you will get many different responses. Some will say being righteous is living an honest life. Some will say being righteous is being kind to people or being helpful to others is living a righteous life.

Most people will also tell you it is very hard to live a righteous life and others will tell you it is impossible if you are going to be successful. Many people are trying to achieve righteousness by their own strength and actions, but it is impossible to overcome their evil desires because of the sinful nature we are all born with.

We cannot buy righteousness and we cannot earn it. Paul writes in Romans 3:10, "There is no one righteous, not even one." A person who does not know Jesus as their Savior cannot experience the righteousness we are talking about today.

The scripture above begins very clearly by stating, "Not by works of righteousness which we have done." It is because of God's mercy that He saved us and only through Him we can experience righteousness in our lives.

Salvation has never been available by one's deeds or works. Salvation brings divine cleansing from sin and the gift of a new, Spirit-generated, Spirit-empowered, and Spirit protected life as God's own children and heirs.

In Galatians 2:21 we are reminded that righteousness does not come through the law. If it had been possible to obtain righteousness by keeping the law and doing good, then Christ would have died in vain. Those who insist they can earn salvation by their own efforts and good works, undermine the foundation of Christianity.

Paul tells us in Philippians 3:9 we ourselves do not have our own righteousness from the law, but it comes to us through faith in Jesus. Paul was expressing to the church at Philippi and to us, that his union with Christ was possible only because God imputed Christ's righteousness to him.

In Ephesians 6:14 Paul tells us we are to put on the breastplate of righteousness, that only God can give us, in order for us to stand firm against the temptations of the devil. A breastplate was a tough, sleeveless piece of leather or heavy material with animal horn or hoof pieces sewn on, covering the soldier's full torso protecting his heart and other vital organs. Finally, Paul tells us in 1Timothy 6:11 we are to flee the things of this evil world and pursue righteousness, godliness, faithfulness, love, patience and gentleness. Look at the company Paul puts with righteousness. Are you practicing and growing daily in faithfulness, godliness, love, patience and gentleness? Each day we need to strive to be more like Jesus, but it is only because of His mercy we will be righteous in His sight.

TODAYS WORD FOR JULY 24

SHARING

But do not forget to do good and to share, for with such sacrifices God is well pleased.
Hebrews 13:16

Children, as well as adults today, do not understand what it means to share. They have not experienced the joy one can have in their heart when they learn to share. Children are not being taught to share in their homes mainly because their parents do not share things with others, including their words (feelings) or deeds.

When a child is not taught properly when they are young, how do we expect them to be any different when they grow up? The verse above the author of Hebrews wrote is so clear. It reminds us that sharing is doing good.

We began when our children were very young to teach them to share. We taught them to share their toys, not only with their siblings, but with friends who would visit them. We taught them to share their time when someone needed help. We taught them to share their resources (ten percent), which we referred to as tithe with our church. Sharing is tough to learn for children, but when you are consistent and lead by example they will learn. At the beginning, their response would be something like "that is mine and I want it."

When we taught our children to share, we constantly reminded them that sharing was a two way street. It was important for them to understand if one shared an item with another sibling then the other needed to be willing to share also. When children learn this, it becomes a life principle for them when they become adults.

When we think of the word sharing we need to think about how we share our faith with others. Very few believers today feel comfortable about talking about their faith with a non-believer. This type of sharing is almost non-existent.

It is thought that most people do not feel any kind of urgency or burden to share their faith with others. They feel that should be the responsibility of the pastor, the missionary or the evangelist who comes to town. They also feel unprepared to answer the questions they may be asked. If this is your problem, you will then want to study the Bible daily and pray daily and God will give you the answers.

In John 1, we read about Andrew who was one of the two first disciples picked by Jesus. He was a humble person, devoted and Christ like. His name means "manliness." After Jesus chose Andrew to be His disciple, he spent time learning from his Messiah and became a rugged evangelist known for his willingness to share Christ personally with all he came into contact with daily. When he first met Jesus, he shared with his brother Peter the good news that he had met the Messiah.

Part of sharing is also developing a compassion for others to the extent of being willing to share with them some of your possessions, time, and your faith.

Sharing should begin with sharing our faith with our family, friends and neighbors. We must be consistent and willing to share with others our time, talents and treasures including sharing our blessings with the poor.

TODAYS WORD FOR JULY 25

COMPLAINING

Do all things without murmurings (complaining) and disputing so that you may become blameless and harmless, children of God without fault in the midst of a crooked and perverse generation, among whom you shine as lights in the world. Philippians 2:14-15

Most of us have read about the blessings and the failures of the Children of Israel on their march to the Promised Land. Not all went well during their 40 year trek. Many scholars estimate that there were well over two million people walking together through the wilderness. During those 40 years, roughly 1.2 million people died. That is an average of 82 deaths a day.

The journey in the wilderness was a long march of grief and loss. Every day there seemed to be complaining and resentment because of the hardship of the journey and the uncertainty in their minds if they would ever reach the Promised Land.

In Numbers chapters 11-21 we read that something goes tragically wrong. It was a time of rebellion and willful disobedience against God. The rebellion started according to the scriptures with murmuring and complaining. Whenever you find yourself beginning to complain about your circumstances, consider this: You are on the threshold of rebellion, and rebellion always begins with complaining.

The people began complaining about their circumstances. God had given them manna and quail meat to eat and water to drink, but they complained because they did not like the taste of the meat and there was not enough water. God intended them to move into the land of Canaan, but they continually rebelled against God. They did not like God's way so they stood in His way and prevented Him from doing His will in their lives. It wasn't God's will for them to wander 40 years in a barren wilderness. The wandering was a consequence of their actions.

Whose fault was it they rebelled? It was not God's fault, because it was His plan for the people to possess a land of abundance and fulfillment. The people chose to turn their backs on God and so they continued to wander in a dry wilderness.

The people complained not only about their circumstances, but also about the blessings of God and His provisions for them. Then they complained about their leadership. They judged themselves by their own standards and rebelled against the properly, God ordained, constituted authorities in their midst.

Paul in the verse above reminds us we are to do all things without complaining so we may become blameless and harmless.

Christians today begin by complaining because their standards are different than God's. Then complaining turns into rebellion against God. Take a good look at all the times when you begin to complain. Are you complaining because of your standards? Most likely you are. Complainers cannot be what God wants His children to be. We are to be blameless and without fault so that we shine as bright lights in a crooked and sinful world.

TODAYS WORD FOR JULY 26

DOOR

Then Jesus said to them again, most assuredly, I say to you, I am the door of the sheep. I am the door; by Me if any man enter in, he shall be saved. John 10:7-8

Behold, I stand at the door and knock. If anyone hears My voice and opens the door, I will come into him and dine with him, and he with Me. Revelation 3:20

Possibly you have seen the picture of Jesus standing outside a door and knocking. This is the mental picture we get when we read Revelation 3:20. A door is a way in or out and is a barrier between those on the inside and those on the outside. The door must be opened in order to obtain access.

The verse above refers to Jesus standing at the door of our heart waiting for us to invite Him in and dine with Him. This refers to our accepting Jesus as our Savior.

Jesus is knocking at the door of our heart asking to come in. If we do open the door and accept Him and show our love to Him, He will come in and will dine (commune) with us. Jesus is standing ready for us to accept Him as we repent of our sins. He has paid the penalty for our sins and all we have to do is open the door of our heart and let Him come in. Then He opens the door to heaven for us.

In John 10:7, Jesus is called the door of the sheep. He is compared to the shepherd who kept his sheep in a pen to keep them safe at night. The shepherd then acted as the door to the pen, letting the sheep in so he could watch over them and protect them. It is only through Jesus that we can come to God. Once we have entered the door of salvation, Jesus becomes our shepherd and as our shepherd He is our protector.

In the two verses from John, above, John is proclaiming that belief in Jesus as the Messiah and Son of God is the only way to be saved from sin and hell. Knowing Jesus as the door to salvation is the only way to receive eternal life. Only Jesus Christ is the one true source for the knowledge of God and the one basis for spiritual security.

Jesus in these verses portrays Himself as the shepherd and the gate. The shepherd lets the sheep in and out of the sheepfold and as the gate He is the only way, the sole means to approach the Father, God, to partake of the salvation He offers.

One of the definitions of "door" (above) is: "any means to access." We urge you to open the door of your heart today, first to let Jesus into your heart and then open the door of your heart to let God and His Holy Spirit lead you through the day. God wants access to your heart. He is standing at the door of your heart and knocking. Do you hear Him?

TODAYS WORD FOR JULY 27

LEADERSHIP

Therefore we also, since we are surrounded by so great a cloud of witnesses, let us lay aside every weight, and the sin which so easily ensnares us, and let us run with endurance the race that is set before us. Hebrews 12:1

In Hebrews 12 the author likens living the Christian life to running a race. He is challenging us as believers to step out with confidence and run our Christian race with determination and endurance doing all we can to further the good news of the gospel. He says we have a great crowd of witnesses to lead us and encourage us. He lists the great heroes of faith from centuries past in the eleventh chapter of Hebrews.

He talks about the great faith of people like Abel, Enoch, Noah, Abraham, Sarah, Isaac, Jacob, Joseph, Moses, Rahab, Gideon, Samson, David and Samuel. They lived by faith and were led by their faith in God as a model for us.

People like these patriarchs of old, who followed God, serve to lead us today in our race of faith to keep us going in the right direction. God expects us to follow their example of faith. We will have to struggle against sin and endure hardship just as they did. All these leaders were commended for their faith. If we are faithful in our Christian race of life, we too will be commended by God for our faith.

The writer of Hebrews talks about running our race with endurance. Endurance is the steady determination to keep going, regardless of the temptations we run into that normally would slow us down or force us to give up. We need to remember the faith-filled life we are running is a demanding and grueling race.

God also expects us to honor our leaders. Our constant study of God's Word is a way we honor the patriarchs of the scripture as we develop our knowledge of the Bible and grow in our faith. Have you noticed the respect young men and women who are serving in the armed services have today when they are in the public? They have learned to respect those who lead them in defending our country. Those in leadership deserve our respect unless they are leading us to go against God's Word.

Leadership for running the race of life must begin in the home. It is only by faith parents can become successful leaders in their home. Parents are to be the encouragers of faith in their children's lives. This requires spending time daily with your children, not once a week, but daily.

We will tell you again, our family had dinner together every night. There was no television or radio on, no telephone calls or other distractions. It was a time to communicate. The two of us still do this every day even though our children are adults and living on their own.

Spiritual leadership is lacking today in every area of life. We lack leadership who honor God at the government level, our schools, our workplace, our families and even our churches. Without leadership who honor God our society and families will fail — and they are failing today.

TODAYS WORD FOR JULY 28

CHEERFULNESS

These things I have spoken to you, that in Me you may have peace. In the world you will have tribulation; but be of good cheer, I have overcome the world. John 16:33

How many people do you know who are always cheerful when you meet them? Frankly, the pressures of life today make it difficult for one to live a constantly cheerful life as our Lord wants us to live. We had a secretary for over 30 years who always was cheerful. Every day when you met her, she had a big smile and a cheerful comment. She loved the Lord and her face always radiated His love for her.

We all know we have good and bad days. On our bad days few of us feel naturally inclined to be cheerful. The scripture above tell us that cheerfulness comes from a merry heart. If our hearts are right with the Lord they can be merry.

Jesus warned us in John 16:33 that in this world we will have tribulation (trouble). Not every day will be a good day. But Jesus also tells us that we can be of good cheer because He has overcome the world and all the evil in it. We can have cheer because the victory has already been won. As believers we have peace in our hearts because our sins are forgiven and we have the gift of eternal life. Just thinking about all the Lord has done for us and remembering His promise to never leave us nor forsake us will bring cheer to our heart and life and our spirit.

All that we have belongs to the Lord, because He has given it to us. We are required to honor the Lord by giving back to Him a portion of what He has given to us. In II Corinthians 9:7 Paul reminds us God loves a cheerful giver.

Some can give more than others because they have been blessed with more to give. It isn't about how much we give, but about our attitude of giving. We should not give reluctantly or just because we feel we have to. We should give cheerfully. The Lord knows our heart and it is the cheerful attitude that is pleasing to God.

In Romans 12:8 Paul also reminds us we are all given different talents and abilities and we have a responsibility to use them for His glory and to grow the family of God, but we must do it cheerfully. It is by our cheerful attitudes others see in us that we are Christians and we have something they do not have.

We have been in many places around the world and have witnessed church conferences and church meetings. Probably our visits to Kenya have left the most lasting impressions of cheerfulness among believers on our hearts. These people who we worshipped with and ministered to were the poorest of the poor as to physical things, but they were the richest of the rich when it came to spiritual things. Their outward cheerfulness could only come from their love for God and the inward joy they had in their hearts.

Be cheerful to those you meet. Remember each person is facing frustrations and concerns, but a smile and a touch of cheerfulness from you will change their day. Proverbs 11:22 says a cheerful heart is good medicine. A cheerful word can be like a pain relieving medicine for someone having a tough time.

TODAYS WORD FOR JULY 29

JOY

These things that I have spoken to you, that My joy may remain in you, and that your joy may be full. John 15:11

Joy, as spoken of in the Bible, is not based on the happiness the world considers happiness. Joy will not come to a person because of wealth, possessions, fame or status. People work hard to obtain these things in order to find happiness, but as Solomon tells us in Ecclesiastes 1:2, it is all meaningless.

The best definition of JOY as used in the Bible is "exultant satisfaction." Only those who know the Lord understand the true meaning of JOY. Those who have accepted Christ as their Savior have peace in their heart and exultant satisfaction because they know their sins have been forgiven and that God loves them.

Jesus explains what He means when He says "MY JOY" in John 15:11 (above). In the previous two verses He says: "As the Father has loved me, so have I loved you. Now remain in my love. If you obey my commands, you will remain in My love, just as I have obeyed My Father's commands and remain in His Love." Jesus loved His Father and found joy in doing the will of His Father and obeying His Father's commands. When we do the will of our Heavenly Father and obey His commands, we will come to know that joy that Jesus has.

In Matthew 25:21 Jesus told the parable of the "Talents." He talked about the joy the master had in his heart when one of his servants responded. He said: "Well done good and faithful servant, you were faithful over a few things, I will make you ruler over many things. Enter into the Joy of the Lord." The servant's faithfulness and the success he obtained brought joy to his master and allowed the servant to share in the master's happiness. There is joy in doing well because it pleases God.

The apostle Paul lists the fruits of the Spirit that are evidenced in the lives of Christians through the work of the Holy Spirit in us. These are love, joy, peace, longsuffering, kindness, goodness, faithfulness, gentleness and self control. [Galatians 5:22-23]. Only those who have united themselves with Christ can understand the true meaning of joy. James reminds us in James 1:2 that when we face the trials in our day to day life we are to "count it all joy." He does not mean we are to be happy about our trials, but we are to face our trials with an attitude of joy because of what it can produce in our life for Christ's glory. When we have the "JOY OF THE LORD' in our life we will find it easier to face life.

Over the years we have had several close friends who were facing serious health problems. Each one had been through many tests, consultations, treatments and medicines and we often wondered how much they could humanly take. But the one thing that was true in each of their lives was they were living each day with a spirit of joy. They put everything into God's hands. They prayed for healing daily, as did scores of their friends. They were living their lives full of joy and hope.

TODAYS WORD FOR JULY 30

WRATH

Cease from anger, and forsake wrath. Psalm 37:8

He who believes in the Son has everlasting life; and he who does not believe the Son shall not see life, but the wrath of God abides on him. John 3:36

In Matthew 3:7 John the Baptist used the word "wrath" when he saw many of the Pharisees and Sadducees coming to see him as he was preaching and baptizing. He called them a "generation of vipers" and asked them "who warned them to flee from the wrath to come?"

What is the "wrath to come" John the Baptist was talking about? It is the wrath of God against sin. The wrath of God is seldom talked about. People like their concept of God to be a God of love, kindness, and peace. The question is often asked by non-believers how a God that is holy can get angry and still be holy. It is God's holiness that requires Him to be a God of wrath. God cannot tolerate sin and be holy. God hates sin and, therefore, must condemn it and judge it. It is because God is a God of love; He provided a way of escape from the wrath of His judgment. The escape is through His gift of salvation that is provided through the sacrifice of His Son who died on the cross for the sins of everyone. It is because He is a God of love and kindness that He is so patient with the ungodly and the wicked and gives them every opportunity to repent of their sins and accept Jesus as their Lord and Savior.

John 3:36 tells us about the reality of God's wrath. The writer, John, tells us all who do not believe on the Son of God will experience the wrath of God and will not spend eternity with God, but will spend eternity in hell.

The Bible also speaks to human wrath. Our wrath differs from God's wrath. Our wrath tends to be vindictive. God's wrath is untainted and tempered by mercy. Life is not fair and indeed it is not. Any theory that insists life is fair is really deceptive. David had many struggles in his young life running from trouble before he became king. He would be the first to tell you life was not fair. He had to live in caves and run from people who wanted to kill him. He had reason to be angry, yet he was able to advise us to cease from anger and forsake wrath (Psalm 37:8).

David in Psalm 37 prays he will not retaliate against those who have been unfair to him, but he will rest in the Lord and wait patiently for God to bring justice to the earth. In Psalm 37: 9 it reads those who wait upon the Lord will inherit the earth. .

In Ephesians 6:4 we have another reminder of the word wrath as in the scriptures. The reminder is as fathers and parents we are not to provoke our children to wrath. Very simply said, the lack of love, uncontrolled anger and constant harassment in the home will provoke children to wrath.

The key is what we feel in our heart. May we cease from anger in our lives, forsake wrath at all costs, and wait patiently on the Lord. Someone said: Revenge restrained is a victory gained. This is easy to say, but difficult to do.

TODAYS WORD FOR JULY 31

SIN

For the wages of sin is death, but the gift of God is eternal life in Christ Jesus our Lord. Romans 6:23

Many people today have a very nonchalant attitude about sin. In fact, very few non-believers have an understanding of what sin is. They have no concern or understanding they are a sinner. This is because of the philosophy to do what makes you happy and it is okay as long as it doesn't hurt someone else.

To these people there is no right or wrong. Therefore, in their minds there is no wrong so how can one be a sinner. Their rationale is that they are only doing what everyone else is doing. There are no eternal consequences to sin in their minds.

When we became parents it was quickly apparent our children did not have to be taught to do wrong. They had a natural inclination to use the same rationale the world uses today. They would say, "I was only doing what everyone else was doing."

What God calls sin is not understood by most people and whether they live in sin or not is irrelevant. They live for today and have no thought about the future. These people do not understand God sets the standards of right and wrong and not them. He has given His standards in the Ten Commandments (Exodus 20). To do wrong and break even just one of these commandments is sin against God. Everyone is a sinner and must pay a penalty for their sin. The scripture is clear but the problem is the people who are not concerned about sin do not believe the Bible is true.

When the first man and woman sinned against God in the Garden of Eden, their relationship and fellowship with God was broken. Thus began the suffering of man and woman and all mankind. From that point on, all of us will reap the wages of sin. We are all sinners with no exceptions. The only hope for us as sinners in order to escape the wages of sin, which is death and eternal separation from God, is for each of us to accept by faith the Lord Jesus Christ as our personal Savior.

"What is sin?" Sin is going our own way, doing our own will and ignoring what God has commanded us to do. There is a penalty each one of us must pay for our sins; however, God in His mercy has provided a way for our sins to be forgiven if we will only ask Him to forgive us for our sins. Then by accepting Jesus as our Savior, because He is the One who paid the penalty for our sins when He died on the cross, we will have our sins forgiven and will spend an eternity with Him in heaven. Sin is breaking God's law. In I John 3:4 we read whoever commits sin also commits lawlessness, and sin is lawlessness.

Sin causes human beings to fail in their most basic relationships. Sin is the so called monkey wrench that has been thrown into the human mechanics of our mind-set. Sin is the reason we behave in ways that are destructive to ourselves and others. Sin is the ultimate addiction one can face in life. We have to pay a penalty for our sin which is to spend an eternity in hell. However, God has provided His Son who died on the cross to pay our penalty for our sin.

TODAYS WORD FOR AUGUST 1

ANTICIPATION

Joshua told the people: Consecrate yourselves, for tomorrow the Lord will do amazing things among you. Joshua 3:4

When you think of times in your life when you anticipated something good or bad how did you react? Anticipation has an emotional effect on us. Excitement wells up within us when we are anticipating something good, such as the birth of a child, a trip, a reunion with someone close to us, etc. When we are anticipating something bad we are filled with dread and fear. We find after going through something we anticipated with dread, the anticipation was worse than the experience.

When our children were young, we often spent our vacation at the Pacific Ocean. Each of the children when experiencing the ocean surf for the first time were fearful of the breaking waves. They would stand at the water's edge and watch the waves. As they watched they noticed when the water receded sand was exposed. After a short time they would get daring and run out as the tide went out, chasing the water back to the ocean. They carefully would watch the waves in anticipation so they would have time to run ahead of the incoming wave back to the safety of the beach.

In Joshua chapter three, we find Israel standing on the edge of the Jordan River in anticipation of entering the Promised Land. For forty years God caused the Israelites to wander in the desert as punishment for their sins. Finally, a new generation was ready to enter the Promised Land; however, there was one major obstacle. Between the Israelites and the Promised Land was the Jordan River which was overflowing its banks due to the spring rains.

God always has a plan for carrying out His promises. God instructed Joshua what to do to solve their problem. The Priests who were carrying the Ark of the Covenant were to stand in the water at the edge of the Jordan River. As soon as the Priests' feet touched the water, the waters parted. Then the Priests, carrying the Ark of the Covenant, stood on dry land in the middle of the river until the entire nation of Israel had crossed over into the Promised Land. Have you ever wondered about the anticipation the Priests had waiting to see what God was going to do?

The anticipation of doing something new or dangerous is often accompanied by an element of fear. We can only imagine the fear the Priests must have felt as they stepped into the raging river. They stepped out in faith obeying God's command.

Think about all of the people and events we read about in the Bible. What was the anticipation of "things and events" like for them? What kind of anticipation did Noah go through building an ark in the desert and then waiting for it to rain? What about the anticipation David experienced when he was walking out to meet the giant Goliath with five stones and a sling shot?

What about the anticipation the disciples had as they watched Jesus die on the cross? It was not until after Jesus rose from the dead that they understood that Jesus would come again as a conquering King to reign over a new heaven and earth.

TODAYS WORD FOR AUGUST 2

DISCIPLINE

He who spares his rod hates his son, but he who loves him disciplines him promptly. Proverbs 13:24

Harsh discipline is for him who forsakes the way, and he who hates correction will die. Proverbs 15:10

In Hebrews chapter twelve there are some wonderful, expressive and powerful words concerning the discipline we need in our lives as believers. The Message translation of this passage from the Bible talks about the discipline needed for a long-distance race and relating it to the discipline we need in our daily lives.

The previous chapter gives us the experiences of all the godly men and women in the Old Testament and how they ran their race in life. They achieved victories in their lives in spite of difficulties and oppression. They all had one thing in common, faith. The examples of their great faith should challenge us to get on with it, start running our race and never quit.

To have victorious lives we need to keep our eyes on Jesus and never lose sight of where we are headed. Living the Christian life involves hard work and discipline.

In verses three and four we are reminded we are in an all out fight against sin and we may have to suffer hardships. But others have suffered far worse than we have and no one more than Jesus. He shed His blood.

Then in verse 5 the author of Hebrews reminds us not to feel sorry for ourselves when we get disciplined by God. He asks if we have forgotten how good parents treat their children and God regards us as His children. He writes: "My dear child, don't shrug off God's discipline, but do not be crushed by it either. It is the child He loves that he disciplines; the child He embraces, He also corrects."

These verses remind us that when God disciplines us He is educating us and treating us as dear children whom He loves. He is not punishing us through His discipline, but training us the same way good parents train children. We respect our parents when they train us so why not embrace God's training so we can truly live a life blessed by God. God is doing what is best for us, training us to live God's best.

In verse eleven the purpose of discipline is given to us. "No discipline seems pleasant at the time, but painful. Later on, however, it produces a harvest of righteousness and peace for those who have been trained by it."

The author of Hebrews continues to challenge us to not to sit on our hands, do not drag our feet, clear the path for the runners, help each other out and run for it. We are to work at getting along with each other and with God.

Discipline in our lives make us better people and better representatives of our Lord. Parents are reminded often in God's Word of the importance of disciplining because God considers us as His children and He disciplines us in the same manner.

TODAYS WORD FOR AUGUST 3

LIGHT

For you were once darkness, but now you are light in the Lord. Walk as children of light. Ephesians 5:8

There is no doubt we are living in a dark and sinful world. Darkness is a sign of evil and the world today for the most part is evil. Satan, the evil one, is running free in our world. Many people live today in situations where God is not acknowledged, where a Christian's faith is mocked and godless living is applauded.

As believers, Jesus told us in Matthew 5:14 "We are the light of the world." After we have accepted Jesus as our Savior, God expects us to represent Him in this world. A believer in Christ represents the opposite of evil and darkness and needs to shine as a light in a darkened world. When you as a believer live a life that honors God you are expected by your Lord to be a light for Jesus in this darkened world.

In most religions light is a symbol of God and godliness. The Bible is no exception. In 1 John 1:5 it reads that God is light. He is portrayed in James 1:17 to be the Father of lights and in Him is no darkness. He is said to be the light of the world in John 8:12 and in John 1:9, He gives (offers) light to everyone. In Psalms 119:105 it reads that His Word is a lamp to our feet and a light to our path.

We have been through two major earthquakes. The first one was in 1971 just before the birth of our sixth child. Earthquakes will knock the power out and at night it is really dark after an earthquake. There are many after- shocks following a major earthquake and some of these after- shocks would cause the lights to flicker or sometimes knock the power completely out. Being in total darkness was frightening to our young children. At the first hint of a tremor announcing a new aftershock they would come running and cling on to us for dear life. It was quite some time before they would go to bed unless the light was left on in their room.

Fear of the dark is very natural and common among children and adults. Since we live in an earthquake prone area we now keep flashlights and candles readily available. Darkness basically represents the evil side of life and light represents the good. This is not only true in the Bible, but in the world we live in today. The plot of many books and movies today, (such as Star Wars), are between good and bad, between light and darkness.

Darkness and light are completely opposite. They are opposing forces. Darkness blots out the light and depicts evil and light has the power to light up the dark and depicts honesty and love.

Each year, as our children were growing up we spent our vacation at the ocean. We always were awed by how clear and beautiful it was at night. Without the city lights; hundreds of stars could be seen which were never visible in the city. This is a vivid contrast; the light of the stars with the darkness of the sky is breath taking and always reminded us of the awesomeness of God. As the Psalmist said (Psalms 27:1) "The Lord is my light and my salvation, whom shall I fear?"

TODAYS WORD FOR AUGUST 4

SIGNS

And truly Jesus did many other signs in the presence of His disciples, which are not written in this book; but these are written that you may believe that Jesus is the Christ, the Son of God, and that believing you may have life in His name. John 20:30-31

Recently, we have received many emails asking us if there are signs or miracles in the scriptures that would help people know beyond a shadow of a doubt that Jesus is God. We have many wonderful new friends we have heard from in third world countries who are besieged with false teachings and they especially need this devotional to encourage them in their faith.

In the book of John, John records seven signs or miracles that prove the deity of Jesus Christ. The word "SIGNS" in the gospel of John is the key that unlocks the door to our understanding of the good news of the gospel. In this gospel of John there are signs in the form of miracles, powers, wonders, and words. John's purpose was twofold: First, we may believe Jesus is the Christ and the Son of God. Secondly, by believing we may have life in His name.

Following are the seven signs or miracles that John has given us to prove the deity of Jesus Christ:

- Jesus turned water into wine proving His power to create. John 2:1-11
- Jesus healed the Nobleman's son to prove His power to prolong life. John 4:46-54
- Jesus healed a sick man at the pool of Bethesda to prove His power to give life. John 5:1-18
- Jesus fed the five thousand with a lad's lunch to prove His power to supply the necessities of life. John 6:1-14
- Jesus walked on the water to prove His power to protect life. John 6:15-21
- Jesus gave sight to a blind beggar to prove His power to illuminate life. John 9:1-4
- Jesus raised Lazarus from the dead to prove His power to re-create life. John 11:38-44

In John 20:28 we read probably the most heartfelt confession of faith ever uttered or written. When Thomas saw Jesus after His death and Resurrection he said: "MY LORD AND MY GOD."

The words "MY LORD" indicate his full commitment to Jesus. The words "MY GOD" indicate his intellectual conviction that Jesus is God. Saving faith demands total commitment to Christ as Lord and Master and intellectual conviction that He is the God-Man.

TODAYS WORD FOR AUGUST 5

COMFORT

Praise be to the God and Father of our Lord Jesus Christ, the Father of compassion and the God of all comfort, who comforts us in all our troubles, so that we can comfort those who are in trouble, with the comfort we ourselves have received from God. II Corinthians 1:3-4

Therefore comfort each other and edify one another, just as you also are doing.
I Thessalonians 5:1

None of us go through life without being in need of comfort. We all experience sad and hurtful times and we are in need of comfort and reassurance. In those times in our life we need to have someone who is there for us, someone we can turn to and receive love and compassion and support.

We can give comforting words, but the only real comfort in our times of concern will come from our Lord. The verses we have written above give us the assurance that God our Father will comfort us in all of our troubles.

In the verses we have listed above, we look at the word comfort from two different perspectives. First, the comfort we receive as believers from Christ, and then the comfort God gives us so we can comfort each other.

God has set a high standard for all believers by saying He is the God of all comfort and the one and only source of comfort available to all believers. God then expects us to comfort those we meet and deal with daily. We have the responsibility of comforting others in their time of need, reminding them of the comfort God can give them when they turn their lives over to Him. We are also to comfort others by reminding them of God's saving grace and Jesus' second coming to this earth.

Children, when they are growing up rely heavily on the comfort they can receive from a parent, sibling or grand parent. We can remember when one of our children would get hurt, they fell down and skinned an elbow or a knee and came into the house crying like they had broken every bone in their body. Just sitting on mom's or dad's lap healed that hurt in about five minutes.

Our children found comfort in our caring and reassurance that we were there for them and that all was going well. Young people often look for comfort from their peers, but it is not always the right kind of comfort. As parents we must be aware of our children's hurts no matter what age they are and then be there for them to offer uplifting words of comfort and support.

Spouses must be a source of comfort to one another in their times of suffering and sorrow. Many spouses and children only have friends they can turn to for comfort rather than family. Unfortunately there are not many true friends.

TODAYS WORD FOR AUGUST 6

ROCK

Behold, I shall stand before you there on the rock of Horeb; and you shall strike the rock and water will come out of it, and the people may drink. And Moses did so in the sight of the elders of Israel. Exodus 17:6

The Lord is my rock and my fortress. Psalm 18:2

On the way to the Promised Land the children of Israel were upset there was no water to drink and the scripture says the people contended with Moses. They complained by asking Moses why he brought them out of Egypt if they were going to die of thirst? So Moses cried out to the Lord asking Him what he should do. In fact, he told God that the children of Israel were ready to stone him.

God again showed Moses that everything was in His hands and gave Moses his command. Moses responded by taking his rod, in front of witnesses, and struck a rock with his rod and water flowed from the rock. Moses' rod represented divine authority. The Israelites had forgotten who was in charge. God used the miraculous incident to not only remind the people Moses was His chosen leader, but it was God who had authority over them and He was ever present with them. Again God responded to the call of Moses and He responded so the Children of Israel knew it was God working through Moses.

In the New Testament, Matthew 16:18, Jesus tells Peter and the disciples He is building His Church. He said: You are Peter, and on this rock (Peter) I will build My church, and the gates of Hades shall not prevail against it. Jesus called Peter a rock to indicate He was giving Peter the responsibility of being the leader of the church after Jesus returned to heaven. To be the leader, Peter was going to need to be solid and strong like a rock.

The story is told of a young preacher, Augustus Toplady, walking through the English countryside when a sudden storm swept across the landscape where he was walking. This young preacher spotted a wide rock formation with an opening he could climb into for shelter against the storm. As he sat there waiting for the storm to end he contemplated the connection between his shelter and God's help in the storms of life he faced.

He had no paper to write on, but found a playing card on the floor of the cave like structure. He began to write the words to a song we still sing today.

Rock of ages, cleft for me, let me hide myself in thee: Let the water and the Blood, from Thy wounded side which flowed, be of sin the double cure, save from wrath and make me pure.

Think of your struggles. Do you need a rock to hide in? Do you need someone to shelter you from your problems of life? As the words from the song above say, You can find shelter and assurance from God.

TODAYS WORD FOR AUGUST 7

INFLUENCE

Do all things without complaining and disputing, that you may become blameless and pure children of God without fault in the midst of a crooked and perverse generation, among whom you shine as lights in the world. Philippians 2:14-15

We began training our children when they were very young alerting them concerning both good and bad influences they would run into in life. We often discussed the influence peers would have on their lives. We encouraged our children when they ran into negative influences to reverse the thinking and offer a positive substitute so that they would be a positive influence on their peers.

As they grew older we discussed influences that "role models" have on their lives. It was very important to us to let our children make choices. We would compliment them on good choices and caution them concerning questionable choices.

As the scripture says, we are living in a crooked and perverse generation. This is why our Christ-like influence on people is more vital than ever. In the verse above, Paul is telling the church at Philippi that they must shine as lights in the world. This is what we need to communicate to our children today. The stronger they are spiritually, the brighter their light will shine.

Children and adults have many influences on their lives today. Some of these are good and some bad. It is hard to overestimate the ungodly influence questionable literature has upon an individual. Several murderers have said in prison reading just one vicious romance book led them into crime.

Today it is the media that has the greatest impact upon our society. Also, just think about how the myriad of electronic devices available today, which have brought all sorts of evil influence right into the home.

Hour after hour and day after day we are bombarded with objectionable material in the press, on television and radio, and on the internet that can scarcely even be described. This kind of influence on our children and their parents undermines their moral values and sense of what is right and wrong. Is it any wonder our families are dysfunctional and our world is wracked by problems?

What kind of evil influences are impacting your family each day? Are you setting boundaries for your children and yourself? What kind of influences is your family facing at school, at the work place or with friends? Are you aware of whom your children spend time with each day and what kind of activities they are involved in? You need to eliminate the evil influences in your life and seek out positive influences. By doing this you will set a standard and example for your family. To begin on a positive note, read the Bible daily alone and with the family. Also, then pray daily alone and with the family. Watch carefully what your children are doing on the computer and their cell phones and IPods. Remember, a family that eats dinner together, talks, listens, reads the Bible and prays together will be putting positive values in their lives enabling them to overcome the evil influences they face.

TODAYS WORD FOR AUGUST 8

WEAKNESS

My grace is sufficient for you, for my power is made perfect in weakness. Therefore I will boast all the more gladly about my weaknesses, so that Christ's power may rest on me. That is why, for Christ's sake, I delight in weaknesses, in insults, in hardships, in persecutions, in difficulties. For when I am weak, then I am strong. II Corinthians 12:9-10

Have you at times felt weakness? We may feel weak physically to the extent we feel we cannot carry on. At other times we may feel weak spiritually knowing we desperately need a special touch from God. We can look at the lives of Samson, Joseph and Paul and see they had weaknesses they had to face too.

In Judges 16 we read about Samson, who was so strong he could kill a lion with his bare hands. He possessed physical strength that was unequalled by any human being. But all of his physical strength could not compensate for his inner weakness. Samson's problem was totally uncontrolled lust and because of this weakness he lost his sight, his strength, his honor and his life.

In Judges 14 we read about Joseph, who was in a great place of power. He faced similar temptations as Samson, but responded differently. He proved you can deal with your weaknesses so they will not destroy you. Joseph rejected the temptations he faced and relied on God's strength to overcome his weakness.

In the verses above from II Corinthians the apostle Paul had been struggling with some painful aspects of life, including some physical afflictions, and he kept praying daily for God to remove them from his life. In our weakness God's power is made perfect and God's grace is sufficient to meet our every need. This is the secret of true Christian strength. It is by God's grace and through His enabling power that we are able to face our weaknesses. It is not by any outward impressiveness, nor great prestige, pomp and favor nor degrees, honors and awards.

Spiritual power never lies in the place of human pride and might. Neither does it lie in a brilliant personality or in the ability to speak with eloquent oratory. Spiritual power is found in the heart of the humble human being who fully recognizes his or her dependence on the living Lord within himself.

May we remind you that "Out of weakness comes strength." Paul closes his writings to the church at Corinth by saying to them and to us today (13:5), examine yourselves to see whether you are allowing the strength of your faith to overcome your weaknesses. Test yourselves.

All of us have areas of weaknesses. God wants these character flaws to show us how totally dependent we are on Him. Weaknesses drive us into a deeper, more intimate relationship with Him. Given the slightest chance, sin will infiltrate your life and affect every aspect, including your faith, your integrity, your moral values, and your relationship with your family and friends. Nothing is off limits for sin.

TODAYS WORD FOR AUGUST 9

ARGUING

What causes fights and quarrels among you? Don't they come from your desires that battle within you? You want something but don't get it, you kill and covet, but you cannot have what you want. You quarrel and fight. James 4:1-2

But avoid foolish dispute, for they are unprofitable and useless. Titus 3:9

It seems people do love to argue. Take the time to carefully watch people around you and listen carefully to their conversations. Listen to children, youth and adults and count how many times you hear people arguing about issues both large and small. This, you will find out, is true among family members, neighbors and friends. It is human nature for one to argue. Some people like to argue just to argue.

James asks the question, "What causes fights and quarrels?" He gives us a straight-forward answer, "You want something but do not get it." These desires come from inside us because of our sinful and corrupt natures. And in this "ME" generation, arguing is a major cause of discord in the family, the community and in the world. Everyone is looking out for themselves. In the heat of the moment we forget Jesus' commandment "to love one another" John 15:17. Think about the truth in Paul's admonition in Titus 3:9: "foolish disputes are profitless and useless."

Even after we become Christians we have to contend with our sinful nature. Pride is a big factor in arguments. Both parties think they are right and they want it their way. Most arguments have bad endings. They lead to break up of marriages, loss of friend-ships and even in some cases physical harm.

Some argue to protect a past behavior. Children argue with parents and parents with children over choices made concerning their daily walk. The only way we can conquer our sinful desire to argue is to submit to God and ask Him to take away our pride and change our attitude.

When we know Jesus and put our trust in Him daily, we are expected to do all things without complaining or disputing. This means we must not put ourselves first in our personal relationships. By showing love and consideration to others we will avoid foolish disputes. When you look back on an argument, and if you are really honest with your-self, it probably was a foolish dispute. When arguments happen there is very rarely a winner. There is a saying "prayer changes things." More importantly, prayer changes us. Arguments are futile, but prayer is never futile.

We need to work daily on our relationships with others so an argument is not an option. We need to learn to respond to issues that normally would ignite an argument with kindness and in love. Seek to live a life that honors God and ask for His help in dealing with situations that lead to arguments. Work today on living a life that honors God despite issues that may arise that usually lead you to an argument.

TODAYS WORD FOR AUGUST 10

MEDITATION

Finally brethren, whatever things are true, whatever things are noble, whatever things are just, whatever things are pure, whatever things are lovely, whatever things are of good report, if there is any virtue and if there is anything praiseworthy, meditate on these things. Philippians 4:8

The book of the Law shall not depart from your mouth, but you shall meditate in it day and night so that you may be careful to do everything written in it. Then you will be prosperous and successful. Joshua 1:8

When you are out walking, riding the bus, driving the car or just sitting and relaxing, where does your mind wander to? Are you thinking about all your problems, family issues, all the work stacked up on your desk, or about someone or something that annoys you? Are you feeling envious or jealous of someone who has something you do not have? Are you thinking about the frustration of traffic and the aggressive drivers who are always cutting you off or are you just plain day dreaming?

These verses that we have listed above remind us to meditate on God's Word day and night. This means thinking about what you read in the Bible. You must first read God's Word before you can meditate on it. How else can God speak to you? Each day after you read the Bible take a few minutes to think about what you have read and apply it to your life. Ask yourself how the life you are living stacks up against God's principles you have read about. You cannot miss His principles because they are on every page of the Bible. .

After the death of Moses, Joshua became Israel's leader and had the responsibility to lead two million people to the Promised Land. God spoke to Joshua and reassured him just as He had been with Moses, He would be with Joshua. In Joshua 1:8 God gave a commandment to Joshua to be obedient to God's law and instructed Joshua to meditate on God's Word day and night.

When you read God's Word do you take time to really understand what you have read and reflect on what God is saying to you?

Paul, before he found Christ as his Savior, had allowed his hate for those who believed in Jesus to drive him to persecute them and to have them thrown into prison. Paul well understood how thoughts influence what we do and how they determine the kind of person we really are. If you want to change your life, Paul after he found Jesus, offers a solution as to how to change our thinking. In Philippians 4:8 (above) we are given his list of things that will lead us to a God honoring thought pattern which will lead to a positive change in how we live our lives. When we have God in our life and are meditating on His Word, God changes "things" because He changes us.

TODAYS WORD FOR AUGUST 11

DISTRACTION

Each one is tempted when he is drawn away (distracted) by his own desires and enticed.
James 1:14

Do you know that Satan's greatest goal for your life is not destruction, but distraction? Satan wants to daily distract you from doing what the Lord expects of you. When Satan cannot get you to succumb to temptation he works in more subtle ways to draw you away from the Lord. Corrie Ten Boom said, "When the devil cannot make us bad he makes us busy." That is so true.

Consider how busy your life is now. Typically in our homes today both spouses work and many have children to care for along with all the responsibilities of running a household. Then we have all the electronic diversions to keep us busy when we have a few extra minutes on our hands. We have TV's, computers, DVD's, texting, the internet and ipods. Satan can get us so involved in using these devices so we have no time to read God's Word or to communicate to Him through prayer.

Satan will use whatever he can to distract us from having a relationship with the Lord. Everything that consumes our time and keeps us busy is not bad in and of itself. What is bad, is letting distractions, like the things we have listed, keep us so busy we are not spending time with our Lord and Savior.

We raised six children and we were a very active family. We didn't have all the modern technology so the distractions were different, nevertheless there were many temptations to keep us busy. We had to set guidelines on the use of our time and we honored them. We must emphasize, we had to work at it constantly or our time would have been consumed by other things Satan could have used to distract us from spending time with the Lord. You will have to work at it also.

When Jesus was visiting Martha, He had to explain to her the importance of spending time with Him. Her sister Mary sat at the Lord's feet listening to what He was saying. However, Martha was distracted by all the preparations being made with the arrival of Jesus in their home. She came to Him and asked, "Lord, don't You care that my sister has left me to do the work by myself? Tell her to help me." "Martha, Martha," the Lord answered, "you are worried and upset about many things, but only one thing is needed. Mary has chosen what is better."

James tells us in James 1:13, "Let no man say when he is tempted, 'I am tempted by God'; for God cannot be tempted by evil, nor does He Himself tempt anyone." So when we are distracted and do not do what God would ordain for our life, who is to blame? We are distracted when we are drawn away from the Lord by our own desires. When we disobey God and make the wrong choice, do not try to shift the blame or justify your actions by saying that the devil made you do it. Instead take the full responsibility, confess your sin and pursue living a Christ exalting life.

TODAYS WORD FOR AUGUST 12

SIMPLICITY

For our boasting is this: the testimony of our conscience that we conducted ourselves in the world in simplicity and godly sincerity, not with fleshly wisdom but by the grace of God. II Corinthians 1:12

But I fear, as the serpent deceived Eve by his craftiness, that your minds may be corrupted from the simplicity that is in Christ. II Corinthians 11:3

We tend to make issues we face very complicated. In fact most people today live complicated lives and get overwhelmed when they need to face the daily issues of life. How do I pay all these bills? How do I handle my child? Why is my spouse upset with me? How do I get all this work done my boss has given me to do?

People complicate their lives by succumbing to worldly material pressures such as bigger houses, new cars, or the latest electronic devices. For those raising children there is the added pressures of parenting. There are many activities for children to participate in and parents are hard pressed to fit their children's schedules into their already busy schedules. Life is no longer simple. The hazard of today's complicated lifestyle is that it causes us to neglect our relationship with our Lord.

The apostle Paul lived a life that was uncomplicated by worldly distractions. He did not live by worldly wisdom, but by the grace of God, as written in the above verse. Paul was concerned about the Christians in Corinth because he had heard they were complicating the simplicity of the gospel message with false teaching.

Paul talks about the simplicity of our salvation (verses above). God did not make receiving Jesus into our hearts complicated. Paul preached the clear and simple plan of salvation given by Jesus in the third chapter of John (verses 2-19). In John 3, beginning in verse 2, we read about Nicodemus coming to Jesus and asking Him how to know God. Jesus responded very simply by saying, "Unless one is born again, he cannot see the kingdom of God."

Perhaps you are like Nicodemus and do not understand what "born again" means. Here is what it means to be born again according to the words of Jesus. One must first realize he was born a sinner and must pay the debt for his sins. Secondly, one must ask God for forgiveness and then ask Jesus to come into his or her heart, acknowledging that He paid the penalty, the debt, for your sins by dying on the cross. All those who believe in Jesus have eternal life.

This is the simplicity of the gospel. Jesus did the tough part. After you receive Jesus as your Savior you then must communicate with God daily by reading His Word and praying to Him. He is your new friend and as with all friends you should have a desire to communicate with Him. Then you give your issues to the Lord in prayer and seek His guidance in changing your standards in life so that you honor God in all you do. The writer of Hebrews warns us that there is no alternative. He wrote in Hebrews 2:3, "How shall we escape if we neglect so great a salvation."

TODAYS WORD FOR AUGUST 13

CONFRONTATION

You have heard that it was said, 'an eye for an eye, and a tooth for a tooth,' but I tell you not to resist an evil person. But whoever slaps you on your right cheek, turn the other to him also. Matthew 5:38-39

Far too often we are faced with situations that in our mind, invites confrontation. Before you confront someone for something said or done you need to carefully read what Jesus said about confrontation. It is our natural reaction to want to retaliate and confront the one that irritates us or speaks some untruth, but that is not what God wants from us as believers in Him.

We had a very good minister friend who had a large church in south Los Angeles some years ago. His name was Rev. E.V. Hill and he was known all across America. We can remember him telling us what he had said to his congregation the Sunday after there was a disturbance close to his church. He said, "Some people believe in an eye for an eye, but in this neighborhood it is two eyes for an eye." He went on to preach that you can never even the score you can only raise the stakes.

It happens every day. On a school playground a student gets pushed. In a home a sibling bumps, possibly on purpose, another sibling as they pass each other. A driver in a car forces you out of your lane. All of these situations and many more often grow quickly into a fight. It is a process of retaliation, confrontation and escalation that results from an attitude of revenge. Revenge is the desire to even the score.

Most children get into fights because they feel they must even the score for some issue they did not like. What parent hasn't heard these words: "He (or she) started it." When adults take actions of revenge they justify their response with the excuse of doing only what was done to them.

In Matthew 5 (above verse) Jesus tackles this key relational issue. He tells us to accept personal injury without retaliation. The person who slaps with his right hand, which most people do, has to strike with the back of his hand in order to slap the right cheek. In Jesus day hitting with the back of a hand was a way to insult or show disrespect rather than for the purpose of physically hurting or injuring. When you then turn the other cheek you send the message you are following Christ's example and returning good for evil. Before He was crucified Jesus was insulted, mocked, spit upon and beaten and yet He never retaliated.

By reacting in this manner the message you send is one of love and forgiveness. Someone once said that to return good for good is natural, but to return good for evil is supernatural. When we are confronted with evil and treated badly we will only escalate the situation if we try to get even. Instead, we must turn the matter over to God and allow Him to bring justice.

TODAYS WORD FOR AUGUST 14

JEALOUSY

For love is as strong as death, jealousy is as cruel as the grave. Song of Solomon 8:6

They have become filled with every kind of wickedness, evil, greed and depravity. They are full of envy (jealousy), murder, strife, deceit and malice. Romans 1:29

In the above verse from Romans, Paul is describing the sinful condition of fallen mankind. Right at the top of his list is envy or jealousy. Jealousy is often the root of deceit, malice, strife and even murder.

Jealousy led Cain to slay his brother Abel. Jealousy caused Joseph's older brothers to sell Joseph into slavery in Egypt. Jealousy caused Saul to try to kill David. Jealousy caused the Jewish chief priests to encourage the Romans to crucify Jesus.

We cannot be faithful to God and serve Him if we have jealousy in our heart. Jealousy is part of our sinful nature and if we continue to envy and be jealous we are then slaves to our sin. Romans 6:16 says: "You are slaves to whom you obey, whether you are slaves to sin which leads to death, or to obedience which leads to righteousness." Do not let jealousy lead you in the wrong direction.

Jealousy is a sin that cannot be hidden and cannot be tolerated. We have mentioned so many times in these daily devotionals that these "WORDS" we refer to daily are dramatically affected by choices we make in life. Some of us make choices based on how the world looks at things. Others make choices based on what the Bible teaches us. And some make choices based on advice, both good and bad, given to us by friends and family. You can be sure choices that come out of jealousy are always bad.

We have seen one family member jealous of another family member because they received something the other did not. We have also seen success bring on jealousy from others. Jealousy is a mood feeling one develops when one feels slighted and cannot accept that someone has more than they have. Jealousy leads to resentment and bitterness. A bitter person can never be happy and does not feel good about himself or herself.

In the Song of Solomon, it reads: Jealousy is as cruel as the grave. In other words, being jealous is cruel because it hurts us and makes us miserable.

The writer of Hebrews tell us to "be content with what you have because God has said, 'never will I leave you; never will I forsake you.'" Jealously leads to discontent. True contentment is found in knowing and trusting in the Lord.

TODAYS WORD FOR AUGUST 15

RESPONSIBILITY

Train up a child in the way he should go, and when he is old he will not depart from it. Proverbs 22:6

Bring them up (children) in the training and admonition of the Lord. Ephesians 6:4

A disciple is not above his teacher, but everyone who is perfectly trained will be like his teacher. Luke 6:40

Statistics tell us once a child becomes a teenager, age 13, over 80% of these teenagers never develop a personal relationship with God. We become very concerned when a child attains the age of accountability in God's sight and has never developed a relationship with God through His Son Jesus. When a parent is a believer in Jesus and does not train their child in the things of the Lord when they are young, they will have to face God and answer WHY? Every parent is accountable to God for their children.

The Bible gives us certain commandments that every mother and father can establish in their home today with their children. They first must make a commitment to God's commandment to know God, to love God, to obey God, and to train his or her child. Each parent must be disciplined enough not to quit.

We have listed three verses from the Bible (above). We suggest you read these three verses several times. They will give you three challenges that you and every parent have to act on if you want God's blessing on your home and on your family.

If you have never read the Bible with your children and have neglected to teach them to know and love God and Jesus then now is the time to begin.

You need to sit down with your child and explain what you are planning to do and why. Your child will most likely rebel, but as their parent you need to be firm and let them know because you love them you are going to begin this program in your home. Let them know their future for eternity is at stake.

Start reading the Bible daily with them and take time to pray with each child after you read the Bible and again before they go to bed. Explain that reading the Bible helps you get to know God and hear what He has to say to you. Then explain prayer is your way to communicate with God. Develop a habit, after you read the Bible and pray, to ask them if they have any questions and then listen not just with your ears, but with your heart. Children want parents to listen to their concerns and they want guidance and direction from their parents.

Children need to know there are two roads in life. There is a wide road that many will follow, but it leads to eternal damnation. They need to know you are leading them down a narrow road that leads to spending an eternity with God in heaven. It is the parent's responsibility to guide them on the right road, but the child's responsibility to obey their parents and God and choose the right road.

TODAYS WORD FOR AUGUST 16

USEFULNESS

And the angel of the Lord appeared unto him, and said, the Lord is with thee, thou mighty man of valor. Judges 6:12

The definition of valor as used here in this verse above is, boldness or determination in facing great danger in battle with courage and bravery. The Lord called Gideon a mighty man of valor and then told him to deliver Israel out of the Midian's hands. But Gideon replied to the Lord in verse 14 that his family was poor in Manasseh and he (Gideon) was the least in his father's house (verse 15). Gideon didn't feel like a mighty man of valor. All of his family, along with all the other Israelites, were being oppressed by the mighty Midianites who far outnumbered them. The Midianites destroyed their crops and their cattle and kept them living in fear and poverty.

Even after the Lord told Gideon He would help him defeat the Midians (verse 16), he was still afraid. Gideon then asked God for signs to confirm God's will and empowerment (Verses 17, 36-40).

Gideon was fearful because he felt inadequate and useless. He wanted to be useful to the Lord, but could not and would not believe God would give him the victory over the Midianites. Gideon looked at his own resources and felt his limitations would keep him from being useful to the Lord. It seemed impossible that even with God's help the Midianites could be defeated.

You may ask the question, "Why did the Lord address fearful Gideon as a 'mighty man of valor?'" The reason was God knew what kind of man Gideon would become when he put his trust and confidence in the Lord and allowed God to make him useful. Gideon finally put his full trust in God and was given the victory God had promised.

Just like Gideon, we doubt our abilities and potential. We look at projects from only our point of view and forget what God can do through us if we put our trust in Him to lead and guide us.

Many people are saying today they just do not have the talent or ability to be useful for the Lord. Conventional wisdom seems to question how much can be accomplished with little. We tend to believe a lot can be done if we have large financial resources, talented man-power, and innovative ideas. These things do not matter to God. What does matter to God is the attitude of our heart. Do we desire to serve the Lord and are we willing to let Him use us, no matter the cost?

Never doubt what God can do through you. When you put your trust in Him and obey Him, you can move mountains. Gideon's God is the same God we serve today. We can face any doubt or any fear and when we truly believe the Lord is with us we can be more useful to God.

TODAYS WORD FOR AUGUST 17

CONTENTMENT

Not that I speak in regard to need, for I have learned in whatever state I am, to be content.
Philippians 4:11

And my God shall supply all your need according to His riches in glory by Christ Jesus.
Philippians 4: 19

The more we talk to people we realize they are not content. When we think of contentment we go back many years and remember the contentment we saw on the face of all our children after feeding them and watching them fall asleep. Babies have that look of contentment because they have no concerns about life.

Concerns and pressures along with schedules and being lonely all cause people to have a feeling of discontent. The apostle Paul shared some thoughts that are most relevant to us today about contentment in his life.

Before his conversion, Paul was not in need for anything. He had it all, the best of education, prestige, and power and was living in plenty. Paul willingly gave it all up to follow the Lord and preach the gospel. As a result he often lived in need.

In the verse above from Philippians 4:11, Paul tells us he has learned to be content in any and every situation. Apparently, Paul was not naturally inclined to be content. Being in need was new to him. He continues in verse 12 to tell us he learned to be content "whether well fed or hungry, whether living in plenty or in want."

In verse 19 (above) Paul tells us what it was he learned. Paul said the secret of contentment is knowing, "God will supply all your need according to His riches in glory by Christ Jesus."

The message for us today is when we know Jesus as our Savior and put our total trust in Him and rely on His power and strength, then we will learn we can be content in all situations.

Our Lord is our strength, our energizer, the supplier of all our needs, and the one who enables us to keep going and going and going. In truth, we are no different from Paul. The same One who lived in Paul now lives through us. Christ is our life. He is our confidence and our energizer and we can be totally content in Him.

Many people feel empty inside. Often the desire for more possessions is a longing to fill that emptiness. That emptiness is a God-shaped void. It can only be filled by accepting Christ into our life and allowing God to fill that empty place in our life.

What gives you contentment in your life? Many people will say they have contentment if they have a home, a car, a job, and a few friends and can pay their bills. The apostle Paul tells us, as we have written above, that contentment is knowing God will supply all your needs. Our contentment comes from our relationship with Christ. Are you reading the Bible and praying daily. If not how can you have a relationship with God and how can you be content?

TODAYS WORD FOR AUGUST 18

INTERCESSION

This is the way you should bless the children of Israel. Say to them: The Lord bless you and keep you; The Lord make His face shine upon you, and be gracious to you; The Lord lift up His countenance upon you and give you peace. Numbers 6: 23-26

Is anyone among you sick? Let him call for the elders of the church, and let them pray over him, anointing him with oil in the name of the Lord. And the prayer of the faith will save the sick, and the Lord will raise him up. James 5: 14-15

When people hear we have six children they often ask, "How did you do it?" The answer is prayer. We prayed every day not only for them, but with them. God can do what we cannot do in the hearts of our children. We prayed daily and followed His leading and taught them His Words and let Him do the rest.

The scriptures give us several purposes of prayer (intercession) we should adhere to when we pray. We are to seek intercession for healing, to avert judgment, for deliverance, to give blessings, to obtain restoration and to encourage repentance.

Moses often had to intercede for his people on the long hard journey to their Promised Land. The people did not make it easy for Moses to lead them. They complained about food, they complained about the water, they complained about the leadership of Moses and they even complained about God.

In Numbers 21, God brought punishment in the form of fiery serpents. When the serpent bit someone the person died. "Therefore the people came to Moses and said, 'we have sinned, for we have spoken against God and against you. Pray that the Lord will take the snakes away from us'" So Moses prayed for them. God did spare the people from the serpents because Moses interceded for them.

The verses above from Numbers are the blessing we read when the Lord spoke to Moses. Moses and the priests were to bless the Children of Israel. God will not bless sinful men, but He blesses all those who have accepted Christ as their Savior.

In the verses above from James we are instructed to go to the pastors/elders in the church so they might be an intercessor for our specific needs. God then gives us a wonderful promise that our faith will save the sick and the Lord will raise us up.

When we offer intercession for others we must, according to the scriptures, plead on behalf of who we are praying for. Be specific as to the needs we are praying for, and then pray earnestly in faith believing we will have victory.

We have a responsibility to make intercession for our children. We must pray not only that the Lord will bring them to repentance and salvation, but that the Lord will protect them from evil and guide their steps and God would bless them.

The uniqueness of our relationship with Jesus is that as believers we have Jesus as our intercessor between us and God. This is why we pray in Jesus name when we pray. Do you have the confidence we have, that when you pray to God you have Jesus as your intercessor between you and God?

TODAYS WORD FOR AUGUST 19

REVENGE

Do not take revenge my friends, but leave room for God's wrath, for it is written: it is mine to avenge: I will repay, says the Lord. Romans 12:19

Be sure that no one pays back wrong for wrong. But always try to do what is good for each other. I Thessalonians 5:15

Do not repay anyone evil for evil. Romans 12:17

All parents discover early on children have a natural instinct to get revenge. When our children got into a disagreement it was often difficult to know which one was the bigger offender. One would say the other one hit him or her. The other would say their sibling had hit him or her first. It all was the other one's fault because of some unkind thing the sibling had done. Their justification for the fight or disagreement was they were just getting revenge.

The desire for revenge is not limited to children. Basic human nature drives most people to want to retaliate when someone does something wrong. This attitude of revenge is not acceptable to God. Every day we have situations that bring out our desire to show some revenge. A fellow worker blames you for an incident at work. A friend betrays you. A spouse causes hurt feelings to the other spouse. For all of these issues, and many more, your natural response is to retaliate even if it is just verbal.

When people try to even the score and get revenge it starts a vicious cycle. Every act done to retaliate and get revenge on someone who has wronged us, only results in another act of retaliation, and each act is more severe than the previous one.

People in deteriorating relationships have a strong tendency to bring up "ancient history." They feel they have to get payback or revenge. The result is that they can never truly forgive and resolve their anger. They end up suffering even more as the bitterness eats away at them like a cancer. Paul tells us in Romans to let the Lord be our avenger. He will punish with justness and fairness.

We have talked to people who have evidently been wronged years ago by a person and the relationship between the two people progressively gets worse every year. This is not acceptable in God's sight because He wants us to live a life honoring Him in all we do. When such an incident happens God expects you to respond with love and not repay evil for evil. (Romans 12:17).

As Paul advises us in I Thessalonians 5:15, "Always try to do what is good for each other." Paul also advises us it is not our role to retaliate, to punish or to seek revenge, but God's. When you respond with love and an understanding attitude it will make a lasting impression on the one who wronged you. It is a well known fact it takes two to fight and when your response is done in love and showing care it takes "all the air out of the balloon" of the one who wronged you. Next time you have a desire to retaliate, do something good, as the saying goes "bite your tongue."

TODAYS WORD FOR AUGUST 20

WEALTH

As for every man that God has given riches and wealth — this is the gift of God. Ecclesiastics 5:19

Honor the Lord with your possessions, and with the first fruits of all your increase. Proverbs 3:9

Wealth can be a wonderful asset or it can be a terrible liability depending on how one uses wealth. Let us share with you three principles concerning wealth:

* All wealth comes from God.
* God releases His wealth to His children.
* God releases His wealth to those who use it for His divine purposes.

We need to understand, as Christians, all wealth does come from God. He owns the cattle on a thousand hills; He created the world and all that is in it; He created us and we are blessed according to His will.

We have learned God really blesses those who practice what Proverbs 3:9 states: "Honor the Lord with your possessions." There are numerous other verses in the Bible that reminds us we are to honor the Lord with the first portion of our wealth. When one honors the Lord, no matter how wealthy he or she may be, God in turn multiplies what is given, in what He gives back to the giver. God will give you only what He can trust you with. Remember money or wealth is not evil. The scripture says it is the love of money or wealth that is evil.

The Lord also reminds us in Luke 12:48 "for everyone to whom much is given, from him much will be required." This includes not only our money, but our time and talents. For some people their wealth is in talents. If so, then God expects much to be done for Him in return for this wealth He has given to you.

In Ecclesiastics 5:10 we are told money never satisfies. If you take the time to read some of the biographies of some of the wealthiest people in the world, page after page will share experiences of unhappy lives. We read often in the newspaper of people committing suicide who seemed to have it all. They were rich and famous, but could not find true satisfaction in their fortune.

Money alone does not satisfy. In I Timothy 6:6-8 we are reminded that we bring nothing into this world and we take nothing out of this world when we die. That fact alone should cause each of us today to honor God with all of our possessions and use all of our wealth — money, talent and time — for His glory.

All of us need to reevaluate how we respond to what God has given to us. Are we seeking to please God with our wealth or are we hoarding our wealth and therefore limiting God in what He desires to do through us with our wealth?

TODAYS WORD FOR AUGUST 21

ARMOR

Put on the whole armor of God that you may be able to stand against the wiles of the devil.
Ephesians 6:11

Every believer can be assured we are in a spiritual war with Satan and all the demons of his army. The goal of Satan is to defeat Christ's church. In our own power we cannot withstand the attacks of Satan. There is no doubt we need armor to protect us. The scriptures give us a clear picture of the armor God has provided for us. We face a very real enemy in life who seeks to deceive and distract us from becoming who God wants us to be. So it is very important we remain alert, at all times, watching for the deception Satan will put in our way.

We need to prepare for spiritual warfare by taking time every day to communicate with God and by making sure we put on the various armor pieces God has provided for us. The apostle Paul has outlined for us what God has available for us in Ephesians 6:13-18.

It is important to note that Paul is taking us to the battle field just as the warriors existed. He is telling us to first take up the full armor and then put it on. The first three pieces of armor (girdle, breastplate and boots) were worn continually on the battle field. The last three (shield, helmet and sword) were kept ready for use when the actual fighting would begin.

We are to put on the "helmet of salvation" to protect our mind and imagination from Satan's weapons of doubt and discouragement he uses to destroy our assurance of salvation. We need to focus our thoughts on the love and power of our Lord that is ours because of our Lord's victory over sin and death on the cross.

We need to claim the righteousness of Christ by wearing the "breastplate' that will protect our heart and our emotions. The "belt of truth" should be wrapped around the core of our being to protect us from deception and so we will not be governed by feelings.

By putting on the "sandals of peace" God will guide our steps and see that our feet are planted firmly in the good news of God's redemption and His love and saving grace for all the world. These "sandals" will also empower us to stand firm against any and all attacks that will come our way by Satan.

We need to put on the "sword of the Spirit" which is the Word of God. There is no greater weapon to combat and defeat Satan. We must keep God's Word ready and available at all times by reading it and planting it in our hearts. This will allow us to always be ready to deflect and cut down Satan's lies against the truth of God and allow us to claim victory over all his evil ways. Since the fall of man, everyday has been evil, a condition that will persist until the Lord returns. Our goal should be to stand firm against the enemy without wavering or falling.

TODAYS WORD FOR AUGUST 22

ASCENSION

He who descended is also the One who ascended far above all the heavens, that He might fill all things. Ephesians 4:10

After the resurrection of Jesus He remained on earth for 40 days to give proof He had risen and that He was still alive. In Mark 16 we are told three women (Mary Magdalene, Mary the mother of James and Salome) came to the tomb. And in Matthew 28 we are told that two women (Mary Magdalene and the mother of James) came to the tomb. In John 20 we read about Mary Magdalene coming to the empty tomb and after talking to the two angels. Mary turned around and saw Jesus standing in front of her.

Over the forty days He appeared to the disciples many times and also appeared to many others. In I Corinthians 15 Paul tells us He was seen by over 500 people at one time, probably when He went back to Galilee. Yes, we can be assured we serve a risen Savior who is alive.

Forty days after the resurrection of Jesus we are told He ascended into heaven. The scripture above from Ephesians reminds us He who ascended into heaven is the same One who descended to this earth. This is a portrayal of Jesus being not only our deliverer, but now our Mediator. Jesus is in Heaven not only preparing a place for us as believers a place to spend eternity with Him (John 14:1-6), but He is our Mediator between God and us.

After the Lord ascended into heaven, having fulfilled all prophecies and all of His divinely-ordained redemptive tasks, He gained the right to rule the church and to give gifts. He was then filling the entire universe with His divine presence, power, sovereignty and blessing.

In Ephesians 4:11 we read when Jesus had ascended into heaven He gave not only spiritual gifts, but He equipped the apostles with the abilities to spread the good news of the gospel here on this earth. This is relevant for us today because He has given us all similar gifts. He has called some of us to be apostles, some prophets, some evangelists, some pastors and some teachers. These all are highly blessed gifts and each one carries a large responsibility in building up the body of Christ.

What a day it will be for us as believers when Jesus comes to take us to be with Him. But until He comes each one of us, as believers, carries a great responsibility to be a witness for our Lord. We will receive our rewards when we meet Him in heaven, so together let us do all we can to represent Jesus according to the spiritual blessings and gifts our Lord has given us. Sometime soon, we too will be resurrected and join our Lord and Savior in the air. Then we will begin our eternity with Him.

TODAYS WORD FOR AUGUST 23

LEGACY

The things that you have heard from me, commit these things to faithful men who will be able to teach others also. II Timothy 2:2

The wise shall inherit glory, but shame shall be the legacy of fools. Proverbs 3:35

I remember a famous musician saying the finest instruments today in the orchestra are those that were made years ago. If we remember right, he said that the wood used for instruments needed to be aged for 80 years in order to get all the moisture out of the wood. And then the instrument needed to be played for another 80 years before it reached its best sound. Just think, over 160 years just for the wood in a musical instrument to mature, so when it is played its tone is something special.

The point of this illustration is instrument makers craft instruments they will never play or hear. They make these so they can leave a legacy as to the greatness of their masterful craftsmanship. Such instruments become more valuable with time and become treasured possessions that are passed on from generation to generation.

Many of the things we do concern, "Next generation matters." In many cases teachers do not know how well they teach until a generation grows up and builds on what they learned from their teacher. A parent will not see the results of their training and tutoring their child or children until at least one generation passes.

The apostle Paul invested himself in people whose spiritual influence would continue long after he was gone. We read the words above, from II Timothy that show Paul wanted the message of his teachings to be his legacy. Paul told Timothy to teach what he has learned to men who would be faithful to passing Paul's teaching to generations to follow. Paul taught Timothy and other believers in the early church who then taught others to become faithful believers. Those believers then would teach others, thus fulfilling the commission given by Jesus to His disciples to go into all the nations and preach the gospel.

Are we living today for the short term or are we living a life dedicated to leave a legacy for our Lord? Are we giving ourselves to others or living exclusively for ourselves? Are those who we are training taking the time to train others? Living for Christ and making disciples are all about the next generation and the legacy we leave to them.

Are we influencing future generations by the way we are living for Christ today?

Do others see Christ in you during your good days and your bad days? Are you consistent in your walk and talk? All God expects from us is to perform our mission day by day asking Christ to lead us and bless us. Then, be encouraged by His presence in your life and be faithful to Him.

TODAYS WORD FOR AUGUST 24

DOUBT

O you of little faith, why did you doubt? Matthew 14:31

Be merciful to those who doubt. James 22:23

Why do we doubt? This is the question Jesus asked and a question each one of us must answer. Doubts come from the great deceiver, the "Father of lies," Satan himself. Satan uses false teachers to deceive believers in Jesus and this causes them to doubt. Doubt is Satan's tool. If our faith is little, it is easy for doubt to creep into our lives.

Jude, in his book, deals with the issue of doubt and weak faith believers have to deal with. Jude tells us (above) we should be "merciful to those who doubt." He wants us to be understanding and not judgmental toward those who struggle in their faith.

Believers are often critical of other believers. A person who has questions or doubts about his Christian faith should not be condemned or shunned as an enemy of the faith. Jude tells us rather than condemning such people we should show them compassion and endeavor to bolster up their faith so they can be strong and secure in their trust in the Lord.

Not only does Satan use others to deceive us and bring doubts about our faith, but he uses fear that comes when we face difficult circumstances and when life gets scary.

In the verse above from Matthew, we read when the disciples were in the middle of the Sea of Galilee being tossed by the waves they were troubled. They did not know it was Jesus walking on the sea. The disciples were troubled because they thought it was a ghost they were seeing and cried out with fear.

But Jesus spoke to them, "Be of good cheer, it is I; do not be afraid (or doubt)." Peter responded by asking if the person they saw was the Lord and if it was, to command him to come to Him on the water. Jesus said, "Come." Peter responded and began walking on the water toward the Lord. At that moment Peter was fearless. He was focused only on seeing Jesus.

The wind became boisterous and the waves became huge. Fear caused Peter's faith to grow weak and doubt began to take hold of him. The scripture tells us Peter took his eyes off Jesus and Peter began to sink and cried out, "Lord save me." Jesus held out His hand, and His words to Peter are so relative for us today, "O you of little faith, why do you doubt."

As believers when we have doubts because our faith is weak, the words of Jesus challenge us to reach out to Him and focus on Him, rather than on our circumstances. This is a challenge to all of us that should be a goal we work toward daily. Keep your eyes on Jesus and you will not be overcome with doubt.

TODAYS WORD FOR AUGUST 25

STEWARDS

As each one has received a gift, minister it to one another, as good stewards of the manifold grace of God. I Peter 4:10

Let a man so consider us, as servants of Christ and stewards of the mysteries of God. I Corinthians 4:1

As far back as we can remember, our parents trained both of us to be good stewards of our time, our talents and our material possessions. Both of us, because of this training, and probably because of our circumstances in life, have strived to be good stewards.

One thing we have learned and passed on to our children is the importance of being a good steward of the finances God has given us. We give our 10% tithe back to God plus offerings over and above. Your tithe already belongs to God. An offering is what is given over and above a tithe.

In Malachi 3:8-12 Malachi had to rebuke God's people because they were not honoring God and were not giving their tithes and offerings. He tells them they are robbing God when they withhold their tithes and offerings. He also tells them God will bless them if they bring their tithes and offerings to the Lord. Malachi challenges them to test God. We have tested God concerning the giving of our tithes over and over again. It is amazing to see how God blesses us when we give our tithes and offerings consistently.

The second area of stewardship is the talents God has given us. One of the saddest things in life is seeing a person just loaded with talent who sits back doing nothing. Then there are people loaded with talent and abilities and they use these for evil purposes. We have learned through the years God has given us different talents, and He has done this for a reason. We have learned to merge our talents together and Dottie does what she does best and Ken does what he does best. Then together, we have seen God do so much more through us than what either one of us could do individually.

The third area of stewardship is our time. God expects us to give of our time to others. Nothing is more important in our lives, except for our relationship with God, than to give time to our children and now our grandchildren. Time given is for bonding, listening, guiding, teaching and learning. God also expects us to give time regularly to our spouses, to our extended families, to our neighbors and to the world we live in.

Most people today spend their time on themselves. This is not what God wants from you. He wants you to invest it in your family, your church, your workplace, your neighborhood or through a mission project to a hurting world.

We have learned that we need to be faithful to God as to how we use the talents, time and material blessings that God has given to us.

TODAYS WORD FOR AUGUST 26

AUTHORITY

For there is no authority except from God and the authorities that exist are appointed by God. Romans 13:1

All authority has been given to me in heaven and in earth. Matthew 28:18

When the righteous are in authority the people rejoice; but when a wicked man rules, the people groan. Proverbs 29:2

As Christians, we need to look at the word authority from several perspectives. First the authority God has over us as Christians. Secondly, what God says about the authority we have in our individual roles we have been given or assumed in life.

The Bible declares God to be the supreme authority and the source of all authority. The scripture is clear there is absolutely no authority given to man other than by God.

When we are in a position of authority in this life, we must recognize all of our authority comes from God and we should exercise our power according to God's rules and remember God will judge us on our performance. Concerning the authority of our leaders in government and at our work place, unfortunately, we live in a corrupt and sinful world so we have corrupt leaders.

We must be wise in choosing those who are in authority over us. The words of Proverbs 29:2 are true. We will groan when we are under the authority of wicked rulers. We must choose rulers who are God-fearing and righteous. Believers must pray for those in authority to make righteous decisions. Nevertheless, we as Christians must accept the authority of those in positions of authority over us as long as it does not conflict with God's laws and moral standards. And remember, when we rebel against those in authority over us we are rebelling against God.

The scripture gives us in Ephesians Chapter 5 specific instructions on how family members in the home should relate to one another. As the head of the wife, husbands are to love their wives just as Christ loved the Church, and wives are to submit to their husbands. This does not mean the husband is the ruler nor is the wife inferior. It does mean the husband is the spiritual leader, always thinking of his wife's best interests and his wife should acknowledge and respect his leadership.

Unfortunately men no longer know how to lead their families properly under God's direction. They have abused their role. Wives want to be equal today and do not want to be subject in any way to their husband as is God's plan for marriage.

It is very important parents establish with their children that the parents are in charge. They must understand early in life it is God's plan for, "children to obey their parents." But most importantly, we need to recognize and respect God's authority in all that we do as individuals, a family, and in our work place.

TODAYS WORD FOR AUGUST 27

MARRIAGE

Marriage is honorable among all. Hebrews 13:4

He who finds a wife finds a good thing and obtains favor of the Lord. Proverbs 18:22

We knew when we were married years ago part of our marriage ceremony included taking a vow where we committed to be faithful and true to one another as long as we both lived. We both took that vow and have never regretted doing so. Honoring this vow is absolutely essential for those who are believers in Jesus. Marriage was ordained by God and is to be honored by all believers. Honor means highly esteemed, the most precious, warm, tender and the dearest of relationships.

The apostle Paul wrote in the book of Ephesians two important verses about marriage we have honored all of our married life:

In Ephesians 5:25 it reads, "Husbands, love your wives, even as Christ loved the church, and gave Himself for it."

In Ephesians 5:31-32 we are told by Paul, "For this cause shall man leave his father and mother, and shall be joined unto his wife, and they two shall be one flesh."

Marriage unites two people so they are no longer two entities, but one single entity. This is one of the biggest adjustments for newly married couples because they have been used to having their independence and doing what they wanted to do. After marriage it can no longer be, "I want" but "what do you want." It was an adjustment we had to make, but one that has great rewards. There is a joy in working together for common goals to benefit each other.

It was with these thoughts from scripture we began our married life together. And now, years later, with six wonderful children and their spouses and twenty grandchildren we continue to thank God daily for bringing us together and leading and blessing us as He has.

Often we are asked questions about the length of our marriage and the successes we have seen with our children and grandchildren. Our answer is always the same. It is because of the grace of God. We daily have put our trust in Him and our children in His hands. From the very beginning of our marriage we have read the Bible, prayed together, memorized God's Word and talked at every dinner time. We also read the Bible daily individually. We not only pray together each day but spend time individually praying. We tithe on all of our income that God blesses us with, and we do not sit back on our laurels, but daily press on to do more for Him. We feel this has brought the blessing of God on our marriage. Every day we wake up ready for God to do something special for us. The amazing thing is that He does and for this we praise Him daily. This is God's promise in 1 Samuel 2:30, "for them that honor Me, I will honor."

TODAYS WORD FOR AUGUST 28

EMOTIONS

The Lord is my shepherd; I shall not want. He makes me lie down in green pastures. Psalm 23:1-2

The book of Psalms is the book about human emotions. The Psalms are a collection of Hebrew poetry, songs, prayers and praises that express the deep emotions and feelings of the writers. Over the centuries these Psalms have been a source of comfort to Christians, in their times of distress and heartache. All the shades of emotion that surge in the human soul are reflected in the Psalms. The Psalms have words of encouragement for us that will lift our spirit and bring us hope during our times of deep human emotion.

These Psalms were the hymnbook of ancient Israel. Many were written to be sung in public. David is the author of approximately half of the Psalms. God gave this shepherd-king the inspired gift of capturing the rich emotions of his experiences. Other Psalms were written by Moses, King Solomon and King Hezekiah, to name a few.

We want to share with you some thoughts on Psalms you can read when you have certain emotions and you want to read scripture that relates to your needed emotion.

If you are happy and want a Psalm to express your joy, read Psalm 92. This Psalm expresses the jubilance of the psalmist as he recognizes how God is merciful, great in His works of creation, just in His dealings and faithful to His children.

If you are grateful and want to express your thankfulness to God, read Psalm 40 and Psalm 70. These Psalms begin with thanksgiving to God for all He has done and will do.

If your heart is full of praise and love for God, then read Psalm 84 and 116. The psalmist puts you in the role of a pilgrim walking in the presence of the Lord.

If you are troubled by fear and dread, read Psalm 56 or 23. The Lord is portrayed as a shepherd, our Shepherd, available in our time of need with grace and guidance for us.

If you are discouraged read Psalm 42. The psalmist seems to be facing a severe spiritual drought and looks to His Lord for refreshment.

If you are lonely read Psalm 62. David is facing deep concerns and turns his focus on God and then praises God's power and mercy.

If you are angry read Psalm 13. The psalmist points out that his pain comes because he has left out God. When he has to depend on his own resources he fails and the pain is overwhelming.

Controlling emotions for non-believers is most difficult because they have nothing or no one to rely upon. For a believer who faces emotions like depression, sadness, discouragement and loneliness they have their Savior who desires to comfort them and cheer them through His written Word.

TODAYS WORD FOR AUGUST 29

STRENGTH

And He said to me, My grace is sufficient for you, for My strength is made perfect in weakness. II Corinthians 12:9

For when we were still without strength, in due time Christ died for the ungodly. Romans 5:6

He is my strength in time of trouble. Psalm 37:39

Today's athletes spend hours every day working on increasing their strength so that they may excel in their sport. It is amazing how many hours they work at this and how committed they are for success.

Have you ever wondered what kind of world we would live in today if believers in Jesus spent the same amount of time daily as these athletes do, to increase their personal strength in the Lord and knowledge of God's Word?

We should learn something from this illustration and be challenged to spend more time working on increasing our spiritual strength by reading God's Word and communicating to Him in prayer.

When we think of strength as written about in the Bible, we think of Samson. He was a judge of Israel for about 20 years. He was known for his great strength, but later in his life his moral weakness became his downfall.

God promised Manoah, according to the account written about Samson in Judges 13-16, a son that would deliver Israel out of the hands of the Philistines. God instructed Samson's parents to raise him to be a Nazirite. A Nazirite was a person who was set apart from the things of the world for the service of God. A Nazarite was to never use a razor on his hair, but let it grow long. God then endowed Samson with great bodily strength.

God gave Samson the strength to be victorious when he was fighting against the Philistines, but foolishly Samson yielded to the temptation to use God's gift of physical strength for his own selfish purposes. Physically, Samson had great strength, but spiritually he was weak. Samson did not have the strength to resist the seduction of a Philistine woman named Delilah.

Samson fell in love with Delilah and revealed to her that he was never to cut his hair because of his Nazirite vow to God. Delilah betrayed him and told the Philistines. They captured Samson and cut his hair and he died a slave.

God is the source of our strength and He wants us to rely on His strength not on our own. Samson neglected to give God the glory for his strength and broke His commandment to serve the Lord. As believers we need to be committed to our Lord in a new and fresh way today and ask Him for new strength to serve Him.

Read carefully the verses we have written above and they will give you the assurance that GOD IS YOUR STRENGTH IN ALL YOU DO.

TODAYS WORD FOR AUGUST 30

STRESS

Come to me, all you who are weary and burdened and I will give you rest. Matthew 11:28

We live in a stressful world and it is fair to say we all have stress in our lives. Stress is a serious problem to many individuals and families today. Stress can come from so many sources such as our jobs, our family relationships, our health, our friends, our enemies, just to name a few.

The opposite of stress is peace and a sense of well being. How can we find peace when we seem to be overwhelmed with stress? God knows all about us, so He knows all about the stresses in our life and He wants us to turn to Him when the going gets tough.

In Matthew 11:28, Jesus invites us to come to Him saying, "Come to me, all you who are weary and burdened and I will give you rest." He is saying to us that He will give us rest from our stress if we will trust Him and not try to rely on our own strength and abilities.

The promise is given to us in Psalm 29:11, "The Lord gives strength to His people (those who have their faith in Him) and blesses them with His peace." There isn't a more powerful source of strength available to handle our stress than God almighty who is all powerful and the creator of all things.

Isaiah describes the peace that comes from God as perfect. Isaiah 26:3. "God will keep in perfect peace him whose mind is steadfast because he trusts in God."

Paul experienced stress in his life like very few others have. In Philippians 4:4-7 he tells us how he coped with stress and anguish in his life. He said to "Rejoice in the Lord always, I will say it again, REJOICE. Do not be anxious about anything, but in everything, by prayer and petition, with thanksgiving, present your requests to God. And the peace of God, which transcends all understanding, will guard your hearts and your minds in Christ Jesus."

In times of stress Paul recommends that we rejoice. No matter how much stress we are suffering, if we know the Lord we have reason to rejoice. Then he tells us to stop worrying and turn our worries into prayers and ask God to help us with the situations that are causing our stress.

There have been many times in our lives when we have faced stressful situations. When these situations come our way it is most difficult to, as the old saying goes, to let go and let God. When you face a stressful situation, first of all just sit back alone and set quiet your mind. When you relax, take your Bible and read a passage such as Psalm 23 or Psalm 100. Then stop and ask God to take over. You will be amazed how fast your attitude changes. Do not let stress linger in your life until you are in deep depression.

When we are really willing to turn our problems over to God, we will receive a peace that only God can give and that is beyond our own understanding.

TODAYS WORD FOR AUGUST 31

DOERS

Be doers of the Word and not hearers only. James1:22

All of us in our homes, in our churches, in our neighborhoods and at our workplaces have seen what we may call doers. When something needs to be done, they are the first to get into the project and work at it until the job is accomplished. In contrast, we have all seen the opposite happen. When something comes up that needs to be done, most people just sit where they are and will wait to see if someone else will do it.

In the verse above, James calls professing believers to be doers rather than simply to do. This emphasizes that the entire personality of a believer should be characterized as a doer. Professing Christians who are content with only hearing the Word have made a serious spiritual miscalculation.

We can remember in many of our ministry programs, people who always showed up and volunteered when we had a need. We can remember the need before Christmas to wrap several thousand Christmas gifts for inner city children. These children were the poorest of the poor and most would not even have one gift for Christmas. We wanted these children to have a gift. Year after year when we asked for help, many of the same people would return to help. They were the doers.

We have found out over the years the so called doers are the happiest people we know. This is because they have what we may call a servant's heart. They have followed the commandment of Jesus to serve others in their time of need. Many believers today seem to be too busy and involved to even consider what it means to have a servant's heart — to be a doer.

It was important for us to train our children to be doers if for no other reason it just made them better people. More importantly it taught them to respond when someone had a need. But the best reward was listening to a person who had reached out and became a doer, how it blessed their heart to help. This is what our Lord wants from us.

The world is a better place because of the doers of this world. Are you one of the doers of this world by always being ready to pitch in, to be involved, and even lead if necessary? Many of the doers of this world are also doers of the WORD. These are the followers of Jesus who have taken the challenge of James to heart: "Be doers of the Word, and not hearers only."

Are you doing all God wants you to do to further the good news of the gospel? What you do spiritually for the Lord will give you the crown God has for you in heaven. Start now by reading God's Word daily and then put into practice what you learned in your reading. You need to first — hear, and then — do.

TODAYS WORD FOR SEPTEMBER 1

TITHING

You shall tithe all the increase of your grain that the field produces year by year. Deuteronomy 14:22

Honor the Lord with your possessions and with the first fruits of all your increase; so your barns will be filled with plenty and your vats will over flow with new wine. Proverbs 3:9-10

Tithing is the setting aside of one tenth of all that God blesses us with to give back to Him. Tithing is of great significance in the lives of those who are believers. Tithing is an important part of serving and honoring the Lord. The purpose of tithing is to demonstrate that we put God first in our lives. We are to give God the first fruits (the first and best) of what we receive. (Proverbs 3:9-10)

Giving God the first part of our earnings shows what we value most. It is a temptation to take care of all other financial obligations first and give the Lord something only if there is money left over. If the Lord is not a priority, we cannot expect Him to bless us. Proverbs 9:10 tells us that those who honor the Lord with their tithe will have their "barns filled with plenty."

The Israelites were instructed by God, through Moses, to give the first and best portions of their harvest and the best of their flocks to the Lord. It was a reminder to them that everything they had belonged to God.

From the time we were children our parents taught us the importance of tithing. They instilled in us that we were to give the first tenth of all the money we received, before we spent it on anything else. I (Ken) can remember the cup that sat on the table for us to give the few pennies from our allowance each week. My (Dottie's) mother taught her three girls early on that if we received 10 pennies, we should give the Lord the shiniest one, signifying that we were giving our best to the Lord. It was a different day then, our allowance was in pennies.

This training helped us realize the importance of tithing. We believe that, because we were taught as children to tithe we have practiced tithing all of our lives. We also believe that faithful tithing may be the single most important reason that God has blessed us so abundantly.

If a tenth seems like a lot, remember two very important things. First, all we have belongs to God. Secondly, we cannot out give God. We have found that the more we give, the more God blesses us. We challenge you to tithe if you do not now. We could give you hundreds of examples of how God has blessed others just as he has blessed us. We learned to tithe even when it was difficult. We learned to give a tithe when we had to tighten an already tight budget. But every time we needed help or came to a crisis God provided far and beyond our need.

TODAYS WORD FOR SEPTEMBER 2

AWESOME

Let them praise your great and awesome name. Psalm 99:3

Come and see the works of God; He is awesome in His doings. Psalm 66:5

You shall not be terrified, for the Lord your God, the great and awesome God, is among you. Deuteronomy 7:21

We have teenage grandchildren and a word that we often hear in their conversations is "awesome." They talk about an awesome time, awesome events, awesome friends, awesome ideas and the list goes on and on.

In church we sing songs whose words refer to an awesome God whom we serve. This use of the word awesome is humbling to all believers as we consider the awesomeness of God. While our grandchildren often say "awesome" to describe everyday things, they understand that there is a difference because they know personally the awesomeness of their Lord.

Each one of us should stop for a moment every day and worship God who is awesome. He is all powerful; He is all knowing; He owns the cattle on a thousand hills (as the old hymn says); He is our creator and our Father. When we think about how awesome God truly is we cannot help but be filled with reverential adoration. We cannot begin to comprehend the awesome love God has for us. He loved us so much that He gave His only Son to die on the cross to pay the penalty for our sins.

When we accepted His Son into our hearts and asked Him to forgive us for our sins, He did, and at that point we began to serve our awesome God. It was then we began to understand how awesome our God really is.

We have traveled to many areas of our world and have viewed many sites that our friends and grandchildren would call awesome. When we saw these sites, we thought they were awesome. Places like the Great Wall of China and the Pyramids of Egypt are inspiring and leave a lasting impression that we will never forget.

But we have experienced other sites that have left an even greater and longer lasting impression on our hearts and minds. One such place was a garbage dump in the Philippians where 100,000 people, many of them were children, lived literally on top of the garbage. It was there that we met a young girl sitting in her lean-to shack with only a box inside serving as a table. There was one booklet on the box and it was a Sunday school booklet that we had sent to the Philippians months prior to our visit. In a dismal and seemingly God-forsaken place our awesome God had found a way to let a little girl know of His great love for her.

Let us never forget that we serve an awesome God. Remember today's words from the scriptures above (Psalms and Deuteronomy). We need not fear because our awesome God is with us. God's works are awesome so let us not neglect to "praise His great and awesome name."

TODAYS WORD FOR SEPTEMBER 3

EMPTINESS

He has filled the hungry with good things, and the rich He has sent away empty. Luke 1:53

Let no one deceive you with empty words, for because of these things the wrath of God comes upon the sons of disobedience. Ephesians 5:6

Surely God will not listen to empty talk, nor will the Almighty regard it. Job 35:13

We talk to so many people that have emptiness in their lives. They feel alone and many just feel rejected. The life style that many people live today initiates the emptiness that so many experience. When there is no hope in life the natural opposite is an emptiness that seemingly cannot be filled.

But the Bible has an answer for those who want to get rid of their emptiness. In the verse above from Luke, the writer describes the ones who feel emptiness in their lives as being hungry. And if you are one that is hungry, you are searching for righteousness. This verse assures us that if we come to God empty and searching for righteousness He will fill our lives with good things. He contrasts this with the rich who have everything and put their trust in "Things" instead of God.

The verse above from Ephesians reminds us that we face many temptations and evil pressures in this world. Paul refers to these as "empty words." False teachers use empty words to deceive us and pull us away from the cross which is the truth of our salvation. Throughout history and throughout the world there have been men, and sometimes women, who have claimed to know ways to truth, happiness, and even eternal life. These are all empty words that cannot fill empty, seeking hearts. It is the cross alone that stops the wrath of God against sin in the lives of those who believe in Jesus.

In the Old Testament we read about Job and all of the temptations and frustrations that God allowed him to go through to prove to Satan that he (Job) was a righteous man. In the verse above Job was accused of being empty and vain in his belief. This accusation was false, of course, but is an example for us today. Satan daily is going to tempt us, trying to make us think that our relationship with God is empty. When this happens how do you respond?

Emptiness is a tool that Satan uses. With the non-believer Satan uses empty words from false teachers to keep them distracted. The solution is for believers to live out our faith so non-believers have an opportunity to see and be filled by the truth of Christ. Satan uses feelings of emptiness to doubt God during difficult situations in our lives. Put your total faith in the Lord, your Father, and he will turn your emptiness into a life full of joy and hope.

TODAYS WORD FOR SEPTEMBER 4

MATURITY

Behold a sower went forth to sow, and when he sowed, some seeds fell by the wayside, and the fowls came and devoured them up; some fell upon stony places, where they had not much earth and forthwith they sprung up, because they had no deepness of earth; and when the sun was up, they were scorched; and because they had no root they withered away. Matthew 13:3-6

In the life of a tree, the key to survival is to have more roots than shoots. When we read about good and bad trees we notice if a tree puts on a lot of top growth and few roots it is usually unable to get the needed water and nourishment to sustain it and grow to maturity. A tree that puts down a great deal of roots and adds shoots more slowly has a chance to live longer and has more resistance to stress and strain.

The lives of people can be likened to that of a tree. Someone might seem to be on a fast track for success, but if they neglect to establish a healthy base they will most likely fail. People, like trees, that put up shoots faster than they put down roots are fragile and in danger of breaking, falling or dying.

In the parable told by Jesus in Mark 4, the seed that fell on rocky soil sprang up quickly but soon withered and died because it had no roots. Jesus said some people are like the seed sown on rocky soil because upon hearing God's Word they receive it quickly and joyfully, but they last only a short time because they do not develop any spiritual roots.

In this parable, Jesus taught us the importance of becoming mature in Christ. Maturity comes by hard work. Roots are not the least bit attractive, but they are the source for strength that makes the plant productive.

Trees need the nourishment that they receive through their roots in order to grow. Maturity in our spiritual life comes from reading and studying the Bible. In order for us to grow spiritually, believers need the nourishment that comes from the roots of their faith which has been given to us in God's Word. That is why it is not only important, but necessary to read God's Word daily. The more we study and learn the truths taught in God's Word the more mature we will become.

Maturity also comes through prayer. We need to communicate with our Lord and He will respond according to our needs. When God answers prayer in our lives our faith cannot help but be increased and deepened. Maturity also comes after we act by faith. We need to be a witness of our faith to those we see every day. The more we serve Him, the more spiritually mature we will become.

It should be the goal of every believer to become spiritually mature. Peter instructs us in II Peter 3:18, to "Grow in the grace and knowledge of our Lord and Savior Jesus Christ." If our roots grow deep in the knowledge of God we will have the spiritual strength and maturity to resist evil and survive the storms of adversity. The roots of stability come from being grounded in God's Word and in daily prayer.

TODAYS WORD FOR SEPTEMBER 5

STEADFASTNESS

Therefore, my beloved brethren, be steadfast, immovable, always abounding in the work of the Lord, knowing that your labor is not in vain in the Lord. I Corinthians 15:58

For though I am absent in the flesh, yet I am with you in spirit, rejoicing to see your good order and the steadfastness of your faith in Christ. Colossians 2:5

One of our many concerns when we were raising our children was that we would be consistent in encouraging them to be steadfast (firm) in their faith in God. We often reminded them that their steadfastness would be expressed in the way that they walked and talked.

Remaining steadfast in your faith is a difficult assignment in our world today. For young people there are many negative outside pressures and influences on them continually. If they are not resisted, it is difficult for young people to remain steadfast in their Christian standards. Young people often struggle to hold steadfast to Godly standards 0f speech, behavior, and in relationships.

While we often think of peer pressure as a problem for young people, it is also difficult for parents and adults without children. Negative behaviors that many people dismiss as normal because so many engage in them can tempt some to waver from their steadfastness in their beliefs. Adults struggle with remaining steadfast in their faith when it comes to Godly speech and relationships, but there are also standards for how we conduct business.

In the first verse above, the apostle Paul was talking to the believers of Jesus in the church at Corinth. His words to them should be taken seriously by us today. He challenged them to be steadfast, immovable, always abounding in the work of the Lord. If we live according to this challenge, we will be a shining light in a dark world to all who know us. Paul closes out this verse by reminding them, and us, that when we are steadfast in our faith, our labor will not be in vain.

Although we may not always see the results of our labor for the Lord, we should remain steadfast in our faith and not be discouraged. Anything done for the Lord is never useless. God will reward us, you can be sure, and the reward we receive in heaven will be greater than anything we could obtain on this earth.

In the second verse above Paul is speaking to the believers in the church at Colossi. He hears that they are walking with the Lord and daily working on establishing their faith. He is congratulating them for their steadfastness in remaining strong in their faith. Their unwavering faith caused the apostle Paul to rejoice.

Our desire as a believer should be to stay steadfast and strong in our faith so that we are a cause for our Lord to rejoice.

TODAYS WORD FOR SEPTEMBER 6

WITNESSING

You will receive power when the Holy Spirit comes on you and you will be my witnesses in Jerusalem, and in all Judea and Samaria, and to the ends of the world. Acts 1:8

When we think of the word witnessing, we may think of someone in a court of law telling his or her story about an issue that they either saw or experienced. The word witnessing, basically, to most people, refers to giving evidence about a situation. But to a person who knows Jesus, witnessing has a somewhat different meaning.

Witnessing, as we deal with the word today, is the words and actions that we share with others about our faith in Jesus. We are giving evidence as to how Jesus changed our lives. We are sharing with others the hope and peace we have in our hearts knowing Jesus as our Savior. In other words, we are testifying to what we have personally experienced as a result of accepting Christ as our Savior.

We have noticed different types of witnessing over the years. Some believers, with good intentions, button hole a person, force them literally into a corner, and tell them that they need to know Jesus. Others will say they do their witnessing through their actions and words. And then there are those whose style is somewhere between these two extremes.

There is a story about a woman who, every morning, pried open the jaws of her dog and forced liquid vitamins down his throat. She would always think that the dog did not know what was good for him and needed to be forced to take the vitamins. Then one day, the bottle of liquid vitamins fell and spilled all over the floor. At the same time, she lost her hold on the dog. The dog sniffed at the liquid on the floor and then began lapping it up. He actually loved the vitamins, but simply objected to being coerced.

There are some believers who force their testimony on a person and they feel coerced. They do not respond to the "in your face" type of confrontation. Many times the result is that the person will be driven away from God instead of wanting to know more about God. As believers we earnestly desire to share the good news of the Gospel by our witness (Acts 1:8 above), but our method just might end up repelling people instead of bringing them to Jesus.

We are not responsible for someone's acceptance or rejection of Christ. It is not our job to convict someone of sin. That is the responsibility of the Holy Spirit.

As you tell others about what Christ did for you, seek the Lord's guidance and rely on the power of the Holy Spirit. Learn to be sensitive, when to slow down, when to listen, when to answer questions. Let God's Holy Spirit and His Word do the convicting that will bring salvation to those to whom you witness.

TODAYS WORD FOR SEPTEMBER 7

CARES

Casting all your care upon Him, for He cares for you. I Peter 5:7

As believers we need to remember God cares for us in every circumstance. He cares about all of our anxiety. He cares when we are lonely, hungry and hurting. There is not a situation you may face that our God will not care for you.

Peter wrote these words in I Peter from the ancient city of Mesopotamia, also known as Babylon. Christians were living under dire circumstances. They were suffering from severe persecution because of their faith. They had been forced to flee for their lives, leaving everything behind: homes, jobs and possessions. They had only what they could carry by hand and fled to places they felt were safe.

They were, so to speak, an underground people, having to live, work, and worship in secret and to find housing and food wherever they could. They never knew when they would be discovered and have to flee again.

Imagine the agony, anxiety, pressure, tension and stress being experienced by these believers. It is in this setting that Peter wrote these words. He was assuring the believers, as well as us today, that there was great help available for them. God was available to help them.

If God could take care of these people in the terrible situation that they were facing, surely he will care for you in whatever situation you may be facing.

You need to note that the verse above as written by Peter is an exhortation, clearly stated but also a command. The word "care" in Greek is "merimna" and means anxiety. He is saying as a command: cast all your anxiety upon Him, for He cares for you. This verse is for us as well as for the Christians living in Babylon during Peter's time. God did not promise us that we would not suffer or go through difficulties. He promised to be there in the midst of our troubles.

When we cast all of our cares upon Him, His mighty hand will save and deliver us, look after and care for us, strengthen and secure us, provide and protect us, and give us assurance and confidence. What more do you need?

In I Peter 5:6, Peter tells the believers and us that before casting all of our cares upon our Lord we need to: "Humble yourselves under the mighty hand of God, that He may exalt you in due time." We are given a pre-requisite to accomplish before we cast our cares before the Lord. We are to humble ourselves.

There are three reasons for this. First, God is to be feared, for He resists and stands opposed to the proud. Pride keeps us from God. The proud cannot admit that they need God. Secondly, we need to humble ourselves under God because He is going to exalt the humble. The proud exalt themselves. Thirdly, we should humble ourselves because God cares for us.

By comparison to God's greatness and goodness we are nothing. God wants a relationship with each of us. He sacrificed His Son to have a relationship with us. It is indeed humbling when we consider how much He cares for us.

TODAYS WORD FOR SEPTEMBER 8

PREPARE

Do your best to present yourself to God as one approved, a workman who does not need to be ashamed. II Timothy 2:15

He will be an instrument for noble purposes, made holy useful to the Master and prepared to do any good work. II Timothy 2:21

We were proud of our children because it seemed to us that each child picked up and learned the trait of being prepared in most areas of their lives. They saw the importance of being prepared every day with their homework that they brought home from school. They were always prepared for their sporting events. Their competitive natures seemed to drive them to be prepared in most areas of their lives.

We also noticed that every week they would memorize our family scripture verse. They knew that at the end of the week we would have each one recite the verse and they all were prepared and recited it well.

The scriptures give us many examples of the preparation that God required of His children. We will discuss one of these examples today.

After God had miraculously parted the Jordan River so the Children of Israel could enter Canaan, they were anxious to conquer the surrounding nations so that they could occupy the land God had promised them. God however said, "Time out, not so fast!" God did not want them to rush into Canaan without being prepared.

The first thing God had them do in preparation was to set up the memorial of twelve stones. God had them do this to remind them that it was God who was leading them and they were serving a God of might and power.

The second thing God asked the Israelites to do was to circumcise every male. When God made His covenant (promise) with Abraham that He would make him the father of a great nation, God established that circumcision would be a symbol of cutting off the old life and beginning a new life with God, belonging to God.

The third thing God required them to do was to celebrate the Passover, a celebration of the night in Egypt that the angel of death passed over the Israelites homes sparing the lives of their first born. God wanted them to remember the mighty miracles He had done in bringing them out of Egypt.

There was special significance to these three steps of preparation that God asked the Children of Israel to do. He wanted to establish the importance of worshipping Him. They were to trust in God and in Him alone! They were to serve God and no other gods because they were His chosen people. They were set apart from the rest of the world and belonged to God.

Just as God wanted the Israelites to take time out and prepare for the challenges that were before them, God wants us to take time out each day to prepare for the challenges we will face. Taking time for God each day is just as important today as it was in the days of Joshua.

TODAYS WORD FOR SEPTEMBER 9

KNOWLEDGE

If you cry out for discernment, and lift up your voice for understanding, if you seek her as silver, and search for her as for hidden treasures; then you will understand the fear of the Lord, and the knowledge of God. Proverbs 2:3-5

Knowledge is not the same thing as wisdom. We have a lot of knowledge in this world, but real wisdom is scarce. Knowledge is knowing the truth, the facts and the principles. Wisdom is discernment and understanding in the use of our knowledge. Both wisdom and knowledge come only to those who seek it.

It is interesting to note that when God planted a garden in Eden he included a tree of the knowledge of good and evil (Geneses 2:9). From the beginning of time, God has been the source of knowledge. Before they ate of the tree of knowledge of good and evil, Adam and Eve knew only good. Satan told Eve that if she ate the fruit from the tree, her eyes would be opened and she would be like God, knowing good and evil. Adam and Eve had the knowledge of good and received the knowledge of evil by doing evil and suffered the disastrous consequences. The lesson for us is to make sure we pursue the right kind of knowledge.

Knowledge comes to us in various ways. We learn from schooling, reading books, and observing life experiences. Education equips us and helps us gain earthly knowledge. But it is more important for us to depend on the knowledge and wisdom that comes from God, through His Word, because it is truth and does not change.

We read in the Old Testament about Daniel. After Daniel was taken captive and sent to Babylonia, he was chosen by King Nebuchadnezzar to learn Babylonian culture. We read in Daniel 1:17 that God gave him knowledge and understanding in all kinds of literature and wisdom.

When the King had a dream that troubled him he called his magicians, sorcerers and astrologers and demanded that they tell him what he had dreamed and what it meant. When they told the king that no man could do what he ordered, the king had them executed. When Daniel heard about what the king was doing he went to the king and asked for some time so that he might be able to interpret the dream.

Daniel realized all of the education that he had been given was not sufficient to do what the king asked. Daniel asked God to reveal the meaning of the dream to him. Daniel knew that God was the true source of all knowledge. As a result of his faith, God revealed to Daniel Nebuchadnezzar's dream and the meaning of the dream.

We can learn from this illustration from the life of Daniel that all the knowledge we might get from schooling and books is not sufficient. The knowledge that comes from God and His Word is true knowledge and always sufficient to meet our every need. Knowledge without values is like a canoe without oars. In your pursuit of knowledge make sure you look to God for His direction and make sure you develop Biblical values in your understanding of knowledge.

TODAYS WORD FOR SEPTEMBER 10

BACKSLIDING

Your wickedness will punish you; your backsliding will rebuke you. Consider then and realize how evil and bitter it is for you when you forsake the Lord your God and have no awe of me, declares the Lord, the Lord almighty. Jeremiah 2:19

If we confess our sins, He is faithful and just to forgive us our sins and to cleanse us from all unrighteousness. I John 1:9

A backslider is a person who made a decision to follow Christ but then relapsed into bad habits that God considers sin. A backslider will fall victim to his or her sins and will eventually abandon his or her spiritual beliefs.

Backsliding brought about the downfall of Israel. God sent the prophet Jeremiah to confront the people of Judah with their sins and to warn them of the coming destruction of their nation if they did not repent. In Jeremiah 7:23-24, Jeremiah reminds them of God's command to them to, "Obey me, and I will be your God and you will be my people. Walk in all the ways I command you that it may go well with you." But they did not listen or pay attention. They went backward not forward.

When we do not listen to God or pay attention to what He tells us, we will become backsliders just like the Israelites. Instead of going forward with the Lord, we will go backward, following our evil desires. Jeremiah warned the people to repent and return to God or they would be punished. The Israelites did not repent and Jerusalem was destroyed.

When we look for a Biblical example of a backslider, we think of Jonah. God told Jonah to go to Nineveh to preach repentance to the Assyrians. Jonah fled because he did not want this assignment. He was fleeing on a ship when during a storm; he was thrown overboard by the crew and swallowed up by a big fish. We assume that this was a whale. Jonah was in the belly of the fish for three days and nights.

The MESSAGE translation of Jonah 2:1-9 gives a vivid and clear report of what Jonah then did while inside the fish. He cried out to God asking for forgiveness and God heard him. In his prayer to God from the belly of the whale he said, "I will sacrifice to You with a voice of thanksgiving; I will pay what I have vowed. Salvation is of the Lord."

The Lord then spoke to the fish and scripture says, the fish vomited up Jonah. Once again the Lord told Jonah that he must go to Nineveh and preach God's message. This time Jonah went to Nineveh and cried out to the people that in 40 days Nineveh would be overthrown unless the people repented. The people of Nineveh responded and believed in God and God did not destroy them.

God gave Jonah a second chance. He backslid and paid a severe penalty. When he was at his lowest point he prayed to God. God heard his prayer and responded. God will also give us a second chance if we cry out to Him.

TODAYS WORD FOR SEPTEMBER 11

GLORY

In those days there was no king in Israel; everyone did what was right in his own eyes.
Judges 17: 6

Apart from Israel, no other nation has had such a Christian beginning as the United States of America. Under the blessing of God, Israel began with a glorious heritage. Like Israel of old, God's blessing rested upon early America. Our pilgrim forefathers made it clear that they came to the shores of America to propagate the gospel. Yet like Israel, as told us in the verse from Judges above, America has not only forgotten her heritage, but we have forgotten God. America has lost her glory. .

In Judges 2:10 we read that a new generation arose in ancient Israel. This new generation forgot their relationship with God. Just like Israel of old, America is doing, "that which is right in its own eyes."

In Judges 9, Abimelech, an ungodly man, seized power in Israel through violence and deceit and led the nation straight into judgment. This came right after God honored Israel and its general, Gideon, by giving them a great victory over their enemy the Medianites. The scripture tells us that as soon as Gideon died, the Israelites forgot God. (Judges 8:33-35) Not only did they not give God the glory for all He had done, but they chased after other gods. They were ungrateful and their ingratitude led them into apostasy. For God's glory to shine again we must first become a thankful people.

Secondly, we learned that Israel's reward for its thanklessness was a godless leader who built his administration on a godless coalition by buying his support with silver. In America and other countries, in order for us to see the return of God's glory, we must have the courage to elect Godly leaders who have the courage to reverse the ungodliness in our countries.

We read in Judges 9:7-15 that the youngest son of Gideon stood up and told this parable of the trees. All the good trees and vines were "too busy" to take the reins of leadership, which is what we are seeing today in our homes, neighborhoods, churches and government. As a result, a useless thorn-covered bush gladly agreed to become king. The thorn bush represented Abimelech who became King when Israel no longer made godly leadership a priority. His ungodly leadership brought destruction to Israel. The apathy expressed here about Israel is true today across our world. We need committed believers to give Godly leadership so we will see the return of God's glory! Ungodly leadership leads to destruction all the time.

For glory to return to our countries we must have a mass return of our people to God. God works through His people. Who does He have to work through today? God would rather forgive than judge. We need to turn from our wicked ways and pray daily as we are told in II Chronicles 7:14. We need a mighty awakening in our land so we can all again witness the GLORY OF OUR LORD!

TODAYS WORD FOR SEPTEMBER 12

JUSTICE

For He is coming to judge the earth. With righteousness He shall judge the world, and the peoples with equity. Psalm 98:9

Therefore being justified by faith, we have peace with God through our Lord Jesus Christ. Romans 5:1

In Proverbs 1:3 we are told that we are to receive the instruction of wisdom, justice, judgment and equity from God. These standards are very consistent with the Ten Commandments that God gave Moses. In Psalm 82:3 we read that we are to defend the poor and needy and do justice to the offended.

Justice comes from God. God says that, "By me Kings reign and rulers declare justice." (Proverbs 8:15) Do our rulers, our leaders in government realize this today? We do not think they govern with this in mind.

The scriptures have much to say about God and justice. In Isaiah 61:8 it reads: "For I the Lord, love justice, I hate robbery and inequity." And in Isaiah 30:18 it reads: "Yet the Lord longs to be gracious to you; He rises to show you compassion. For the Lord is a God of justice."

In the New Testament Luke writes, "And will not God bring about justice for His chosen ones, who cry out to Him day and night? Will He keep putting them off? I tell you, He will see that they get justice and quickly," Luke 18:7-8. It does seem like there is so much injustice in this world. It seems, to many, that God is doing nothing about the injustice and certainly not as quick as many desire. These verses assure us that God is paying attention to those who cry out to Him. In His perfect timing He will see that those who love Him will get justice for the injustice done to them.

We must remind you that we are born into this world as sinners. Because of this we will each one be judged by God. We can be thankful that our Lord God is not only a just God but He is a merciful God. How grateful we should be that God, because of His mercy, does not give us what we justly deserve. It is because of God's mercy that He sent His Son into the world to pay our penalty for our sins.

There is no other way for us to escape eternal judgment other than through Jesus. The scripture makes it very clear in John 14:6 when Jesus said to Thomas, one of His disciples: "I am the way, the truth, and the life. No one comes to the Father except through Me."

There are no other options; either we except Jesus as our personal Savior or we reject Him. If we reject Him, then we face personal judgment and will spend eternity in Hell. Eternal judgment is terrible and most people do not take it seriously. Some say that God would never send someone to hell, and He does not. He gives us the option. It is our choice, not His.

TODAYS WORD FOR SEPTEMBER 13

COMPASSION

But He, being full of compassion, forgave their iniquity. Psalm 78:38

But when He saw the multitudes, He was moved to compassion for them. Matthew 9:36

We are living in a world where very few people have compassion for someone in need. It is a "ME" world where the person that one cares about is himself or herself. You constantly hear of someone leaving the scene of an accident or ignoring the call of a neighbor. Everyone is constantly in a rush and in crowded situations they bump people and never even smile or say I am sorry.

But for Christians it should be different because of the standard our Lord gave to us. When Jesus was going from city to city teaching in the synagogues, we are told that when He saw the multitudes, He was moved to compassion (Matthew 9:36).

True compassion moves us to action. In Mark 2:3 we read that, "Some men came, bringing Him a paralytic, carried by the four of them." These men saw their friend's helpless condition and their compassion moved them to take action. They carried him to Jesus. When Jesus saw the man, He saw more than his physical need. He saw his spiritual need for forgiveness of his sins. Jesus took care of the man's spiritual need first saying: "Son your sins are forgiven" (Mark 2:5). Then He healed the man and told him to get up and walk.

God's compassion for us surpasses all human understanding. He knew our need for salvation from the time of Adam and Eve in the Garden of Eden. It was because of His great compassion for us that He sent His only Son to die on the cross paying the penalty for our sins. Jesus took our sins upon Himself and then gave His life for us. There is no greater compassion than this.

Yes, true compassion leads to action. In Luke chapter 10 we read of the account known as the parable of the Good Samaritan. In verse 33 we read that when the Samaritan came across the man who had been beaten by the thieves and left to die, the Samaritan was moved to compassion and he took action. Unlike the two previous travelers who had come by the beaten man and continued on without helping, the Samaritan acted, came to his aid, and saved his life.

There are many people in situations in our world that would move anyone to compassion. We have talked to pastors in Kenya who have told us about the poverty of the people in their churches and tears filled their eyes. This shows real compassion.

These illustrations from life today and from the scripture need to be a reminder to us to live each day with a heart that is open to being compassionate. When you see someone in need, help them. When you see someone grieving, give them a word of encouragement. Work today on the concept of what my father (Ken) told me years ago: Live a life of JOY! JOY spelled out one letter at a time says JESUS, OTHERS and then YOU.

TODAYS WORD FOR SEPTEMBER 14

TONGUE

No man can tame the tongue. It is an unruly evil full of deadly poison. With it we bless our God and Father and with it we curse men. James 3:8-9

We both remember when we said something "bad" our parents would respond to us that if we repeated that word they would wash out our mouth with soap.

Now if you have ever had your mouth washed out with soap you will think twice about using your "tongue" that way again. The point that our parents made to us, and the point we made to our children in the same situation, is that we always need to be careful when choosing the words we use in our conversations. We need to think before we speak. We need to be sensitive to the feelings of those we talk to.

The tongue is a very small part of our body, but a most important one. Without it we could neither taste nor speak. While the tongue is small, it is mighty. James tells us that no man can tame the tongue and it is a restless evil, full of deadly poison.

The tongue has the power to do great damage. Once words come out of the mouth they cannot be taken back. In James 3:6 the damage the tongue can do is compared to a raging fire. Like a fire, you cannot control the damage words can do nor can you reverse the damage. In a matter of minutes a few words spoken in anger or with the intent to be hurtful can destroy the strongest of relationships.

In order to control our tongue we must think before we speak and consider whether our words have merit and are pleasing to God or whether the words are hurtful and destructive to the person we are speaking to.

Our society has changed so much, even over the last few years, that the words we hear in the work place, on the street, in movies, on television and even coming from the mouths of teenagers and children are appalling. Words that we hear today were never used in public even ten years ago.

We ask the question: "Why do we see this happening?" We have taken God out of our society. The media shows no restraint in the language used in movies and television. Unfortunately, the same is happening in every country of the world, no matter what the culture or beliefs are.

James tells us that what comes out of our mouth shows what motivates us and our words reveal what and who we are. Without God's help, it is impossible to control the tongue. If we claim to be Christians and have faith in Jesus we must submit our tongue to His control.

When we allow God to have control of our life and let the Holy Spirit fill our hearts with God's love then our tongue can be used for God's glory. Society's standards may have changed, but God's standards have not. What the Bible teaches about the tongue is still applicable today. We cannot control our tongue in our own strength. We must seek God's help and, through His Holy Spirit working in us, we will be able to keep our tongue from evil and our lips from speaking deceit.

TODAYS WORD FOR SEPTEMBER 15

HOLY SPIRIT

Do you not know that your body is a temple of the Holy Spirit, who is in you, whom you have received from God? I Corinthians 6:19

Most people have a pretty good understanding of God the Father and God the Son (Jesus Christ). But there are three persons in the God-head known as the Trinity. The third person is God the Holy Spirit.

When we accept the Lord as our Savior, God sends the Holy Spirit to dwell in us. The Holy Spirit is what sets believers apart from the rest of the world. There are two groups of people in the world. One group consists of those who are guided by their sinful nature. The other group consists of people who have chosen to die to their sinful nature and be guided by the Holy Spirit. When you accept Jesus as your Savior, your body becomes a temple of the Holy Spirit (I Corinthians 6:19 above).

Let us consider the power of the Holy Spirit and how He works in our lives.

THE HOLY SPIRIT CONVICTS: "When He comes He will convict the world of guilt in regard to sin and righteousness and judgment," according to John 16:8. It is the convicting power of the Holy Spirit that brings us to repent of our sins.

THE HOLY SPIRIT CONTROLS OUR MIND: "Those who live according to the sinful nature have their minds set on earthly desires, but those who live in accordance with the Spirit have their minds set on what the Spirit desires" (Romans 8:5). The mind controlled by the Spirit leads to life and peace. The Holy Spirit keeps our mind set on pleasing God and keeping His commandments.

THE HOLY SPIRIT GUIDES: "When He, the Spirit of truth, comes, He will guide you into all truth" (John 16:13). Jesus spoke these words to His disciples so we can be sure the Holy Spirit is working in us to enable us to determine truth from false doctrine and that He guides us in an understanding of all truth.

THE HOLY SPIRIT GIVES US ASSURANCE: "The Spirit Himself testifies with our spirit that we are God's children. Now if we are children then we are heirs of God and co-heirs with Christ" (Romans 8:16-17). The Holy Spirit gives us assurance that we have been redeemed and we have an inheritance of eternal life in heaven.

THE HOLY SPIRIT HELPS IN OUR WEAKNESS: "The Holy Spirit helps in our weakness" (Romans 8:26). God knows our weaknesses and that is why He sent the Holy Spirit, so that we do not have to rely on our own strength.

THE HOLY SPIRIT PRAYS FOR US: "We do not know what we ought to pray for but the Spirit Himself intercedes for us with groans that words cannot express" (Romans 8:26b). The Holy Spirit is wiser than we are and is interceding for us.

THE HOLY SPIRIT SANCTIFIES US: "God chose you to be saved through the work of the Spirit and through belief in the truth" (II Thessalonians 2:13). The Holy Spirit sanctifies us by working in us to make us desire to become more like Christ.

With all the Holy Spirit does for us, it is important that we as believers study and understand the Holy Spirits role in our lives.

TODAYS WORD FOR SEPTEMBER 16

ESTEEM

Let nothing be done through selfish ambition or conceit, but in lowliness of mind let each esteem others better than themselves." Philippians 2:3

Jesus is the Son of God and God could have sent Him to this earth in all His majesty as our glorious King. Instead he came into this world as a humble and suffering servant. Isaiah (53:2) describes Christ coming with no majesty and no beauty that would attract us to Him. The Jewish people, even though He was one of their own, did not esteem Him as their Messiah because He did not meet their expectations.

When we think of all that Jesus suffered for us and His great gift of forgiveness and eternal life, how can we not esteem Him as our Lord and Savior? Nevertheless, many do not acknowledge or esteem Jesus today. In fact, he is often despised and rejected. just as He was despised by those who knew Him when He walked on this earth.

Jesus is worthy of our esteem and all believers who accept Him as their Savior will one day sing with the angels in heaven: Worthy is the Lamb that was slain to receive power, and riches, and wisdom, and strength, and honor, and glory, and blessing (Revelation 5:12).

Paul wrote to the believers in the church at Philippi and instructed them to have the same attitude of humility as that of Jesus Christ. He encouraged them to be like-minded so that they would be one in spirit and purpose. In order to be unified, they would have to be humble and put aside their selfish ambitions and conceit.

Many people today think they are better than anyone else. They have such an elevated opinion of themselves that they think they know more about issues than anyone else. They seek to promote their own selfish ambitions with no regard for others. It is likely that we all have known such people and we have experienced the discord that is caused by that kind of person.

Esteem is a problem in our homes. Even spouses fight this problem. A spouse often thinks that he or she is king or queen of the house. This can only result in discord and unhappiness. The ego of one really affects the esteem of the other and destroys the family unit. The self-esteem of children suffers when they are constantly harassed and not praised in a humble way for their successes.

Many people (Christians included) evaluate themselves by the standards of the world. They are only concerned about how the world esteems them. What should concern us is not how the world esteems us, but how God esteems us. Are we true followers of Christ? If so we will show Christ-like humility and esteem others better than ourselves.

TODAYS WORD FOR SEPTEMBER 17

HONOR

Honor your father and mother, that your days may be long upon the land which the Lord your God is giving you. Exodus 20:12

Honor the Lord with your possessions, and with the first fruits of all your increase. Proverbs 3:9

Our life work has been dedicated to helping hurting and hungry children. We believe that one of the most important lessons you can teach children today is to honor their God, their parents and their friends. As the verse above states, children are to obey/honor their fathers and mothers. In our travels over recent years we have noticed that the farther one gets away from America, the more children honor their mothers and fathers. Here in America most children show very little respect for their parents but in most third world countries children honor their parents.

There are several thoughts that we need to understand concerning the word "HONOR." First and foremost we need to honor God for whom He is and for all that He has done for us. In John 5:23 we are told that all people should honor the Son (Jesus) just as they honor the Father (God). Anyone who does not honor the Son does not honor the Father who sent Him. The scripture also tells us (John 12:26) that anyone that serves Jesus will receive honor from the Father. Honoring God is not an option for Christians. When we honor God, He will honor and bless us in all areas of our lives.

We are also to honor our family with our words and actions. This includes children honoring their parents, spouses and honoring each other. Families need to show honor and respect to their extended families, neighbors and friends. Just today we were driving home from a visit to a store and a car came roaring up behind us and then swerved over one lane. As soon as he was half way past us, he cut back in front of us making us swerve and hit our brakes. This event reminded us that people today basically do not respect or honor any one else, let alone God. This typifies the culture that we live in today. There is no respect or honor for others.

When we think of the word honor, we also need to remember to honor the Lord with our possessions. This includes our wealth, our talents and our time. As Christians, sometimes we forget that God wants all that He has given to us to be available to Him to further His kingdom. It is not enough just to tithe of your wealth. If you have talents and time that God can use, He expects us to honor Him with these as well. Consider how you can honor God with what He has given you. Finally let God do His work through you. It might require sacrifice on your part, but if you honor God, He will bless you.

TODAYS WORD FOR SEPTEMBER 18

PRAISE

Let the Word of Christ dwell in you richly, singing with grace in your hearts to the Lord.
Colossians 3:16

Great is the Lord and most worthy of praise. Psalm 145:3

The apostle Paul tells us in this verse from Colossians to admonish one another in Psalms, hymns and spiritual songs, singing with grace in our hearts to the Lord.

These words remind us about when we visited Kenya for a two day conference with the Pastors, church leaders, choirs and people from some of the 75 churches we established there through our mission and the leadership of Rev. and Mrs. Rhoads.

Some of these people who were the poorest of the poor walked for days to attend this conference. But what we remember more than their poverty is the way they sang their praises to God. These people had very little of earth's treasures and they put us to shame in the way they praised God.

We have been too many places in our world, visiting programs we were assisting. So many times we would here an individual humming a song. This was their way to praise God. They sang and worshipped God even though they had so little.

We also remember our association with a ministry helping to establish churches for the deaf in the Philippians. You will never be the same when you sit in one of their churches and see these dear deaf people singing praises to God in sign language. They did not let their physical handicap keep them from praising God.

When we think of God's goodness to us and consider all He has done for us how can we not praise Him? No matter how you are feeling now; you can lift your spirits if you cultivate an attitude of praise. When we are praising God we won't be complaining about our problems. Think about what an impact and testimony it is to others when they see the joy we have in the Lord.

When our children were young we often sang children's songs of praise that they learned in Sunday school as we were driving in the car. Whether it is through song or conversation, let your joy for the Lord reverberate to others. You will be surprised by how many people you will encourage just by praising the Lord.

Remember, praise is a choice. Look at the many references in the Bible where individuals and groups chose to praise the Lord. The Israelites praised the Lord with song and dance after safely crossing the Red sea (Exodus 15:1-21). The apostle Paul praised God even when he was in jail (Philippians 1:13-18). And David wrote multiple Psalms of praise, many in the book of Psalms for us to read today.

We encourage you to begin every day by praising the Lord as you pray each morning. Throughout the day keep an attitude of praise and just watch what God will do for you.

TODAYS WORD FOR SEPTEMBER 19

COURAGE

*H*ave *I not commanded you? Be strong and of a good courage; do not be afraid, nor be dismayed, for the Lord your God is with you wherever you go." Joshua 1:9*

We have noticed that we hear of fewer illustrations of people showing courage. We know people, and have read about many others, that have been diagnosed with illnesses, sicknesses and/or diseases who have shown unbelievable courage in their fight for survival. We also must mention the men and women that serve in our armed forces because they really show courage. They are trained to be courageous and they respond so bravely to their call to duty.

But our concern is for the people we see in our neighborhoods, work places and in our churches. Courage as we saw it years ago has diminished. We have read about many people throughout history who have shown unbelievable courage in so many areas of life. This includes our founding fathers, government leaders, generals and many just average people from all walks of life that you might meet on the street.

God has given us many illustrations in His Word of people that showed courage. We also read how God stood with them from the beginning to the end of the task that they were trying to accomplish.

In Joshua 1:9, the final words to Joshua are given us in God's commission to him as he takes over the leadership of the Children of Israel. There is no doubt that Joshua was overwhelmed and even fearful of his new responsibility.

Three times God said to Joshua, "Be strong and courageous." But along with the command God gave Joshua the promise: "I will be with you; I will never leave you nor forsake you." (Joshua 1:6, 7, 9) This is the same command God gives us as we serve Him today. We are to be strong, have courage, and not be afraid because He has given us the same promise He gave Joshua. Jesus said, "I am with you always even unto the end of the world" (Matthew 28:20).

Joshua accepted the challenge that God gave him and rooted his courage on two promises. First, he knew that God would be beside him. God had made this promise to Joshua. Second Joshua knew that God would always go before him. God promised Joshua that He would take care of the enemies they must face going to the Promised Land. They would still have to battle, but God would give them victory. God has given us the same promises. He will go before us and take care of all the enemies we might face and He will be with us, through His Holy Spirit, every day.

The key for Joshua and the Children of Israel was that they were to have complete faith in God and obey His every command. Jesus has gone before us to heaven having won all Spiritual battles on this earth. He did this for us as believers.

Our redemption has been secured, our place in God's family established and our heavenly inheritance has been guaranteed. What kind of courage do you have? If you have fears or doubts, look to the life of Joshua and how he responded to God.

TODAYS WORD FOR SEPTEMBER 20

WORLDLINESS

And Jesus said unto them, you are from beneath; I am from above, you are of this world; I am not of this world. John 8:23

And do not be conformed to this world, but be transformed by the renewing of your mind that you may prove what is that good and acceptable and perfect will of God. Romans 12:2

In this modern day age of telecommunication we can hear and see what is happening in all parts of the world almost instantly right in the comfort of our own home. What we see on television and hear on radio is more the evils of the world than the good. It is very easy for a person to succumb to the evils of this world. It is a constant temptation made to look glamorous and enticing by the evil one. Satan is continually looking for weaknesses in our daily living and uses the enticement of worldliness to woo us away from our love for the Lord.

Worldliness captivates you by bright lights, great promises and the glitter of being popular. You can meet friends when you are involved in worldly activities but soon you will find out that those friendships are shallow and temporary.

In Luke 15:11-32 we read the well known account of the prodigal son. He asked his father for his inheritance and then left home. He journeyed to a far away country for a life of worldliness that he desired. The scripture says that quickly he wasted all his possessions with wild living, ending up with nothing, no food, no friends and nowhere to stay. The son had to hit the very bottom before he could see the futility and hopelessness of worldly living.

Jesus, in this parable, tells of the son's return home, repenting and being accepted by his father who welcomed him back with a great feast and celebration. What wonderful hope and assurance the parable holds for those who have reached the point of despair in living a life of worldliness. Our Heavenly Father is waiting with welcoming arms for all who repent of their worldliness and come to Him.

Consider these verses from the Bible concerning worldliness as we know it today and what God has for us in its place. In John 15:18-19 Jesus tells us, "If the world hates you, you know that it hated Me before it hated you. If you were of the world (worldliness), the world would love its own. Yet because you are not of the world (as a believer in Jesus), but I chose you out of the world, therefore the world hates you."

Worldliness is a real problem for new believers. They are easily tempted by Satan to want to hold on to some of their worldly sinful pursuits. John tells us in I John 2:15-16 that this is wrong. He says. "Do not love the world nor the things in the world. If anyone loves the world the love of the Father is not in him. For all that is in the world, the lust of the flesh and the lust of the eyes and the boastful pride of life is not from the Father, but is from the world." When a believer loves the Lord the evil ways of the world will no longer appeal to him. What a wonderful promise!

TODAYS WORD FOR SEPTEMBER 21

ENEMY

Love your enemies, do good, and lend, hoping for nothing in return. Luke 6:35

In Luke 6:27-36 Jesus gives us a long detailed expose on how believers are to deal with enemies. Jesus starts His comments by saying, "But I say to you who hear." He states it this way because He knows that many believers do not want to hear how He expects us to deal with our enemies. No one likes to hear anything that requires something difficult for us to do.

Jesus tells us to love our enemies and to do good to those who hate you. Jesus is initiating the most revolutionary lifestyle choice ever known in the history of mankind. No religion in the world can remotely compare with this. If you study other religions including Buddhism and Islam, they have absolutely no principles even close to this.

In verse 31, Jesus gives us what we know today as the golden rule. He says that we should treat others in the same way we want them to treat us. Jesus was restating what was recorded in Leviticus 19:18, "You shall not take vengeance, nor bear any grudge against the children of your people, but you shall love your neighbor as yourself."

The natural reaction today is to return good for good and evil for evil. Think of how you have reacted at times when someone does something that has hurt you. You immediately want to do something, maybe hurtful, to get back at that person.

It is natural to think that evil would not be returned for good, but it does happen, especially to anyone who is perceived to be an enemy. In Genesis 16:6 we read about Hagar and Sarah. Hager was a good and obedient servant to her mistress Sarah but they became enemies and Sarah treated Hager so harshly that Hager had to flee from Sarah.

David also did good serving King Saul, bringing victory to King Saul over the Philistines. It would be expected that Saul would feel grateful to David. Instead Saul felt jealous of David and considered him an enemy and plotted to kill him.

In Luke 6:32 Jesus says it is no credit to us if we love those who love us. Even sinners do that. Jesus wants us, as believers in Him (verse 33) to do the hard thing and love our enemies. Jesus goes on to say that when we give good we should give it without expecting anything in return. The Lord will repay us as is written in Proverbs 19:17, "He who has pity on the poor lends unto the Lord; and that which he has given will HE (God) repay him again."

God has been merciful to us. We are to be merciful to others. Everything we do needs to be based on what He has done for us.

TODAYS WORD FOR SEPTEMBER 22

HAPPINESS

And whoever trusts in the Lord, happy is he." Proverbs 16:20

Happy is the man who finds wisdom, and the man who gains understanding. Proverbs 3:13

But he who has mercy on the poor, happy is he. Proverbs 14:21

But happy is he who keeps the law. Proverbs 29:18

Recently we have commented to one another about how many people we see and talk to that are unhappy. Some people just look cranky and you wonder if every day is a bad day for them. We are living in a society where happiness does not abound. We think we understand why some people just do not know how to be happy. If they do not know Jesus as their Savior, they have no hope and no support, how can they be happy?

Everyone has things going on in their lives that are difficult and it is easy to let these things get you down. If you focus only on the down things of life it will make you cranky and unhappy. Happy people do not have it better than anyone else, but they focus on the good things in life. Everyone has bad days with bad things happening to them. However, everyone also has something to be thankful for so it depends on what you choose to focus on.

Look at the verses listed above from Proverbs. These verses are a short outline of what sets apart a happy person from an unhappy one. Happy is the man or woman who trusts in the Lord, keeps the law, (God's commandments) has mercy on the poor and who finds wisdom and gains understanding.

The starting point to finding happiness is to trust in the Lord. There is a void in everyone's life that only God can fill. People search in all the wrong places and try all the wrong things attempting to fill that void. Knowing your sins are forgiven and that you are saved from the penalty of your sins brings peace and contentment which in turn brings happiness to life.

Happiness comes to our lives when we are faithful in studying God's Word. This gives us wisdom, understanding and knowledge of how we are to live our lives in obedience to what God's Word teaches us.

Sometimes we get so busy that we just do not take the time to think about how much we have to be happy for. True happiness is not based on circumstances. True happiness is based on our relationship with God. When you go to a store, look at the faces of people. Do they radiate happiness? We urge you to look to the Lord and let Him fill you with a spirit of happiness every day.

TODAYS WORD FOR SEPTEMBER 23

BELONG

For whoever gives you a cup of water to drink in my name, because you belong to Christ, assuredly, I say to you, he will by no means lose his reward. Matthew 10:42

To the Lord our God belongs mercy and forgiveness. Daniel 9:9

As Christians we belong to the Lord. In Isaiah chapter 44 we read about God's blessing upon Israel and He clearly states that they belong to Him. In Romans 14:8 it reads, "We are the Lord's." Thus, we belong to Him. Galatians 3:29 reads, "And if you are Christ's then you are Abraham's seed and heirs according to the promise." So the scripture makes it very clear that if we know Christ as our Savior, we belong to Him.

The next question is, "What things belong to God?" In Job 12:13 we are told that all wisdom and power belong to God. And Job continues in Job 12:16 to say that all strength and victory belong to God. And in Job 25:2, all glory, dominion and awe belong to God. In Psalms we are told that "The kings of the earth belong to God." (Psalm 47:9) "The mountain peaks belong to God." (Psalm 95:4) "And the highest Heaven belongs to God." (Psalm 115:16)

Perhaps the most comprehensive statement of belonging is in Genesis 1:1 where it states that "In the beginning God created the heavens and the earth." Therefore all things belong to God. God blesses us by "loaning" to us what we have. When we recognize this fact, we realize our own insignificance. We do not understand so many of the things that happen in this world. Since the world belongs to God, who are we to question God's sovereignty, His wisdom or His justice? It blesses us to know that we belong to a God to whom all wisdom, all power, dominion, awe, strength and victory belong.

There was a young girl in Guatemala who asked us how she could be sure that she belonged to God. This girl came from a dysfunctional home and her family did not recognize that there was a God let alone mentioned God in their home. She attended the Christian school that our ministry sponsored. It was there that she heard about God and His love for her. She heard the plan of salvation and soon understood that she needed to accept Jesus as her Savior. She now belongs to God because she became a child of God.

Do you have questions about who God is? Do you understand that all we have belongs to God? And where do you stand in your relationship with God? Make sure you have answers for these important questions

TODAYS WORD FOR SEPTEMBER 24

HOPE

Be of good courage, and He shall strengthen your heart, all you who hope in the Lord.
Psalm 31:24

Psalm 31 is David's prayer to God. In it he speaks of his problems and his afflictions, his need for God's mercy, his complete trust in God, and praises God for His goodness. He closes in verse 24 by reminding us to be strong and take courage. These same words were spoken by Moses to Joshua in Joshua 1:7. Courage is used 20 different times in the Old Testament and always in anticipation of a battle.

David experienced many battles during his life. He was a giant killer, a victorious warrior, and a great King. In his personal life he did make serious mistakes, but he always sought God's forgiveness. It is neither his failures nor his greatness for which David is remembered. He is respected and remembered for his faithfulness to God. David put his complete trust and all of his hope in the Lord.

We as believers today can apply this Psalm to our lives. When we anticipate facing a battle in our lives, large or small, we need to read this verse and remember to be strong in the Lord and to be of good courage.

There is one key factor that cannot be ignored, which David points out in the last few words of this verse: "all you who hope in the Lord." Our hope must be in the Lord who is the one who gives us strength and courage. When our hope is in the Lord we can have confidence that God will be with us in any battle we face.

We all have seen or been in situations in life where things seem hopeless. David knew what it was to be in great despair because he had often felt he was in a hopeless situation. In life we are all in need of hope. Hope is what keeps us going.

The reason David encourages us to be of great courage is because in God he found hope. God will give us strength, just as he gave David, to get through our times of hopelessness. Only a person that believes in Jesus can have this hope. That is why we continually remind you that you need to know Jesus as your Savior.

When you commit to live your life honoring God, He will be faithful to you. He will always hear your cry for help in times of distress and hopelessness. For those that do not know Jesus, and do not have that hope, they are doomed to a life of discouragement and hopelessness because in troubled times they will have no one to turn to because their hope is in themselves and in their own strength .

Paul tells us in Titus 2:12-13 that we should live godly lives in this present age, looking for the blessed hope. The "Blessed Hope" Paul refers to is the second coming of Christ and believers return with Him to an eternity with God.

In Romans 5:5 we are reminded that our hope in God does not disappoint. The love of God has been poured into our hearts by the Holy Spirit to reassure us of our salvation. Keep your hope strong in the Lord and each day He will bless you and not disappoint you. He is our hope.

TODAYS WORD FOR SEPTEMBER 25

EVANGELISM

But you be watchful in all things, endure afflictions, do the work of an evangelist, fulfill your ministry. II Timothy 4:5

Jesus' last words of instruction to His disciples were to, "Go and make disciples of all nations, baptizing them in the name of the Father, and the Son and of the Holy Spirit and teaching them to obey everything I have commanded you." (Matthew 28: 19-20). This is known as the Great Commission. Soon after saying this, Jesus ascended to heaven because His work on earth was done. He gave His disciples the responsibility of carrying on His ministry and He commissioned them to be His evangelists. The disciples completed their work on earth and their commission of evangelism has been passed on to each one of us who are believers in Jesus.

In the above verse from II Timothy, Paul tells us to do the work of an evangelist, "fulfill your ministry." The word "ministry" here does not refer to any special group or class of people like pastors, teachers, or evangelists. The word "ministry" means "service" and all believers are called to be active in service of some kind. As it says in Ephesians 4:11-12, "And He Himself gave some to be apostles, some prophets, some evangelists, and some pastors and teachers, for the equipping of the saints for the work of ministry, for the edifying of the body of Christ."

Evangelism, New Testament style, is personal. Jesus set the example for us when He talked to individuals and ministered to people one on one. In Luke 19 we find Jesus ministering one on one to Zacchaeus. He had climbed up in a Sycamore tree to see Jesus over the crowd. Jesus saw him in the tree and said to him, "Zacchaeus, make haste and come down, for tonight I must stay at your house."(Luke 19:5) Zacchaeus welcomed Him gladly into his home and then into his life. Jesus said to him: "Today salvation has come to this house." (Luke 19:9) And Zacchaeus gave clear indications of his new found life in Christ. He welcomed Jesus joyfully; he determined to give half of his wealth to the poor and then promised to return four-fold all the taxes that he had collected dishonestly. Zacchaeus found Jesus and accepted Him as Savior in a one to one situation.

We think of evangelism as being the work of those who are good speakers. Jesus wants all of us who believe in Him to be His evangelists. The way we live our life speaks volumes to those watching us.

Jesus was the master soul winner. He witnessed to John and Andrew and they accepted Him as their Savior. He witnessed to Nicodemus and the Samaritan woman. Jesus gives us this call: Follow Me, and I will make you fishers of men.

There is no more important place to be an evangelist than in your own home. We taught our children about our commitment to Jesus by our deeds and then by our words. We consistently encouraged our children to share their faith by their actions and their words. There is nothing more rewarding for us as Christian parents than to see our children put into practice the Biblical principles we tried to instill in them.

TODAYS WORD FOR SEPTEMBER 26

RAPTURE

Therefore you also be ready, for the Son of Man is coming at an hour you do not expect.
Matthew 24:44

While it is heard frequently in Christian circles, the word "Rapture" is never actually used in the scriptures. Rapture, defined, means to be carried away. In scripture, rapture refers to events described by Paul in I Thessalonians 4:17. Paul is writing to the believers in Thessalonica about the second coming of Christ. He writes of Christ's return to earth and then describes believers, alive on earth, being "caught up together" with believers who have gone before "to meet the Lord" (NIV translation).

Recently we have read articles and seen television reports from people who claim to know the day the Lord will return to this earth and when the rapture will occur. However, the scripture (above) makes it very clear that the Lord is coming at an hour that no one will expect. There is no doubt on the clarity of this verse so do not be concerned with these stories as they come your way.

In Matthew chapter 24 we have a lengthy account of how Jesus responded to the disciples when they asked about the date of His return. He told them that only God the Father knows. In verse 36 He said, "But of that day and hour no one knows, not even the angels of heaven, but My Father only."

Then Jesus went on to tell them what they could do. He urged them to be prepared so that they would not be taken by surprise. In verse 44 He says, "Therefore you also need to be ready, for the Son of Man is coming at an hour you do not expect."

Therefore the most important question you will face in your lifetime is this: IF JESUS RETURNS TODAY, ARE YOU READY TO MEET HIM? There is nothing more important than for you, right now, to stop and make sure that you are ready if Jesus returns today. There is only one way to be ready. You must accept Jesus into your heart, ask for His forgiveness of your sins and then make that all important commitment to serve Him and Him alone.

Some people believe that they have done enough good things during their life, so they are ready for Christ's return. Others say they have been good parents or good workers at their jobs so God will accept them. But none of those things will get you into heaven with Jesus. Ephesians 2:8-9 is clear when it says we are saved by grace, through faith, not by any amount of work we could do.

We do not know when Jesus will return. No one does. The one thing we do know is that we need to be ready. If Christ comes today will you be ready? Are you prepared to meet Him? Have you accepted Jesus into your heart? Have you asked for forgiveness of your sins, and are you committed to serving Him and Him alone?

TODAYS WORD FOR SEPTEMBER 27

EXAMPLE

All these, obtained a good testimony through faith. Hebrews 11:39

I am ready to preach the gospel to you. Romans 1:15

Follow my example, as I follow the example of Christ. I Corinthians 11:1

The redeemed sinners listed in Hebrews 11 are all remembered for one common virtue — great faith. They all obtained a good testimony through their faith. Long after their deaths, the record of their lives of faith and obedience still inspires us today. They were, and are, examples to be followed.

John Wilkes Booth's place in history is that of a villain. He was an actor but became famous because he killed President Abraham Lincoln. After the south lost the Civil War, Booth wanted to be remembered as its avenger against the north. Instead he is remembered as an assassin who killed an unarmed Lincoln with a gunshot to the back of the head. His example in history is that of a murderous coward. In contrast Abraham Lincoln is remembered as an example of a president who preserved the Union, freed the slaves and exhibited malice toward none and charity for all.

Few of us will have a recorded place in history like that of Lincoln, Booth or those listed in Hebrews 11. Certainly we would want to be remembered as a good example like Lincoln and not as a bad example like Booth. But how much better to be remembered as a person of great faith like the people of God in Hebrews 11.

The apostle Paul is an example of a man of great faith and a committed desire to spread the good news of the gospel. Paul also showed, by his example, that he believed in the power of prayer. In Romans 1:9, he says he always remembered the people of the church in Rome in his prayers. He was eager and ready to preach the gospel to them. By example, Paul made it clear that he was not ashamed of the gospel he preached. He left for us a wonderful example of a life that honored God completely.

At the time Paul was teaching the Corinthians about Christ, the gospel had not been written. They only knew about Jesus Christ through Paul's preaching. Paul followed the example of Christ, therefore, he could say to them, "Follow my example"(I Corinthians 11:1 above). If we want to be a good example for our children and family to follow, we must make sure we are following the example that Christ has given us.

We will leave memories for our families and hopefully a positive example to those who knew us. We desire only to be remembered for living a God fearing life and a life of faith and obedience to Him. What kind of an example will you leave on this earth? A godly life speaks more eloquently than words.

TODAYS WORD FOR SEPTEMBER 28

CRITICISM

For the Lord will judge His people and have compassion on His servants. Deuteronomy 32:36

Judge not that you be not judged. Matthew 7:1

You judge according to the flesh, I judge no one. John 8:15

How many times recently can you remember being criticized? It was not easy to take, was it? But turn that thought around and think about how many times you have criticized someone. Criticism is easy to give but hard to take. Some criticism is justified and other criticism is not acceptable. Criticism is useful only if it is constructive and lovingly given.

In past years we have spent time with individuals who have been very critical of people, places and things. It seemed that no one could do anything right in their sight. In the world we live in there are many people that evidently need to be critical when evaluating others. These people are always negative in their thinking and do not seem to enjoy any of the blessings of life.

If you continually associate with someone who is critical, you will become just as critical yourself. Life is full of choices and we need to choose to associate with people who are kind, considerate and look at what is good in others rather than looking for something to criticize. People often criticize others because they are trying to boost their own egos.

The Bible gives us guidelines about criticism. When we criticize someone or something we are passing judgment on another person's actions. But we do not always know the circumstances or have all of the facts. In John 8:15 (above), Jesus was defending himself to the Pharisees. They were critical of His witness. Jesus was telling the masses that He was the Son of God. They did not believe that Jesus was who He said He was. Jesus responded to them by saying that they judged according to the flesh but He judged no one. This is a lesson for us today because when we judge or criticize someone or something, we are acting out of the flesh and not of God.

As parents, we taught our children to respect others no matter who they were, what they did or what disagreements they might have. We reminded them often that criticism hurts and hurting people is not of God. We also discussed the negatives that happen when you judge people. We tried to encourage our children to never judge a person and to always let God take care of the situation. Everyone must answer to God for their own actions. This is a difficult concept for one of any age to comprehend and practice. But we have learned, many times the hard way, to let go and let God take over.

TODAYS WORD FOR FRIDAY SEPTEMBER 29

GRACIOUS

For you have tasted that the Lord is gracious. 1 Peter 2:3 RSV Translation.

The words of a wise man's mouth are gracious, but the lips of a fool shall swallow him up. Ecclesiastes 10:12

Do you know many people today that are consistently gracious? To be gracious in the evil world that we live in is most difficult. People and situations can irritate and upset us to the point that we are not gracious. But God has given believers a standard that we should be living by each day.

In Exodus 34:6 God is speaking to Moses concerning the Children of Israel and how the Children of Israel were to honor and serve Him (God). God was making it clear to Moses that He expected the Children of Israel to worship and honor Him with obedience, love and graciousness. When Moses asked to see the Glory of God, the scripture says the Lord passed before him and proclaimed, "The Lord, the Lord God, merciful and gracious, longsuffering, and abounding in goodness and truth."

God made it clear to Moses that He expected the Children of Israel, just as He expects us today, to be gracious in all we do, because He is gracious.

In Luke 4 we read about Jesus' return to Nazareth, the place where He grew up as a carpenter's son. The town's people had all known Jesus as a boy but did not know Him as their Messiah. Jesus began to talk to them, telling them the scripture was being fulfilled with His return to Nazareth. He knew that He would be rejected by many in the place where He had grown up. According to verse 22 and after Jesus had spoken to them, all that bore witness to Him marveled at the gracious words which proceeded out of His mouth. And they said, Is this not Joseph's son?

Despite being rejected, misunderstood and persecuted, Jesus set a standard for us as believers to be gracious in any situation. As parents, we need to begin with ourselves and learn to be gracious to everyone, whether it is family or complete strangers. Probably the most difficult task that we have is teaching our children to be gracious. This will be difficult because they will have to deal with peers who are not gracious and to react and defend one's self with graciousness is most difficult.

One of our daughters came home from junior high school one day, very upset. Someone had taken her brand new jacket out of her locker during gym class. We tried to comfort her with the thought that perhaps the girl needed it more than she did. We reminded her that God expected us to be gracious in all situations and He would take care of the situation. In addition, we told her to think of the guilt the girl would feel whenever she would wear the blazer.

God has given us a standard to live by and we all need to learn how to be gracious to every person we face and to every situation that comes our way.

TODAYS WORD FOR SEPTEMBER 30

SYMPATHY

All of you, live in harmony with one another, be sympathetic, love as brothers, be compassionate and humble. I Peter 3:8

Bear one another's burdens, and so fulfill the law of Christ. Galatians 6:2

I have shown you in every way, by laboring like this, that you must support the weak. And remember the words of the Lord Jesus, that He said, "It is more blessed to give than to receive." Acts 20:35

Many people have trouble showing any kind of sympathy to others in their time of need. One of the reasons for this is because of the selfish "me only" era in which we live. When someone constantly thinks only of self, they really do not care about the feelings or situations of others. Thinking of self also indicates no communication with God, so there is no spiritual understanding of caring for others.

Do you have a sympathetic heart? How do you react when you see a hungry child, a lonely woman, a sick baby or a homeless family? Most people today, when they see these things, they walk right by showing no concern or interest.

Being in the ministry, we constantly run into situations where sympathy is needed. In today's environment people are losing jobs, losing their homes, facing economic concerns, need food, live in dysfunctional family situations and broken marriages. And then there are those who are physically injured, dealing with a dreadful disease or suffering physical pain.

It is also important to mention that there are many people today that are lonely. They have no one to talk to, no one to help them in a time of need, and no one to share their concerns. These people are looking for sympathy and they have difficulty finding anyone that cares.

In I Peter 3:8 (above), Peter gives us five qualities that should be evident in the life of every believer. These qualities are first, to live in harmony, second, to be sympathetic, third, to love each other as brothers, fourth, to be compassionate and fifth, to be humble. As believers we are to be sympathetic and compassionate. This means that when we see someone in need we must reach out to them in loving concern and do what we can to help and comfort them.

The scripture tells us that being sympathetic means we need to be willing to bear the burdens of others (Read the verse above from Galatians). Burdens are problems and issues that someone must bear. They can be physical or spiritual. The law of Christ, as discovered in the teachings of Jesus, instructs us to follow Him by showing love and sympathy to those who are burdened by heartache and trouble.

Read again the last part of Acts 20:35 where Jesus is quoted as saying that, "IT IS MORE BLESSED TO GIVE THAN TO RECEIVE." All of us need to learn to be sympathetic to the needs of the people we meet every day.

TODAY'S WORD FOR OCTOBER 1

BLAME

Just as He chose us in Him before the foundation of the world, that we should be holy and without blame before Him in Love. Ephesians 1:4

When we do something wrong we all are inclined to want to blame something or someone. When our children were young and we caught them doing something wrong they often blamed one of their brothers or sisters. How often we heard, it was his (or her) fault or he (or she) started it. It is very easy to pass blame to someone to cover a wrong behavior or a lie in order to avoid the consequences.

The "blame game" started long ago after God created Adam and Eve. God put Adam and Eve in the Garden of Eden (Genesis chapter 2-3) and told them not to do only one thing, "Do not eat of the fruit of the tree of knowledge of good and evil"(Verse 17). But they did, and by doing so they sinned against God and the BLAME GAME began. In Genesis 3:7-13, we read they first tried to avoid having to take responsibility for their actions and attempted to hide from God. When they were discovered, Adam first blamed Eve as to why he ate of the tree (verse 12) and even blamed God because God had given him Eve. Then Eve blamed the serpent (verse 13).

The result is sin came into the world because Adam and Eve were told one thing not to do and they did it. Because they did not want God to know what happened, they blamed someone else. To avoid taking responsibility for their own actions, people seem to constantly look for someone to blame.

In Mark 3:2 we read about Jesus and His disciples being in the temple with the Pharisees on the Sabbath. The Pharisees felt the popularity of Jesus was a threat to them and they wanted to find something they could blame Jesus for. They were watching Jesus carefully with the intent of criticizing Him for doing something on the Sabbath.

A man with a shriveled hand was in the temple. The scripture reads: "They watched Jesus closely whether He would heal a man on the Sabbath, so that they may (blame) him." Jesus was grieved by the hardness of the Pharisees hearts and looked at them with anger saying to the man who needed healing, "Stretch out your hands." The man obeyed and was healed. The Pharisees immediately left the temple to plot how they might kill Him by blaming Him for healing the man on the Sabbath thus breaking the Jewish law.

Every parent who has raised children has had to live with the BLAME GAME. The scripture gives us a guideline as to how we should handle blame as it happens with our children. In Proverbs 22:6 it reads: "Train up a child in the way he should go, and when he is old he will not depart from it." Children must be taught to accept responsibility for their actions and when they do wrong they should confess it and ask for forgiveness.

TODAY'S WORD FOR OCTOBER 2

OPPORTUNITY

Therefore, as we have opportunity, let us do good to all, especially to those who are the household of faith. Galatians 6:10

Be very careful how you live, not as unwise but as wise, making the most of every opportunity because the days are evil. Ephesians 5:15-16

The Apostle Paul in his writings (above) to the churches at Galatia and Ephesus emphasizes how the believers need to take advantage of the opportunity of time given to them by God. Paul points out that the believer's entire life provides the unique privilege by which he can serve others in Christ's name.

In Ephesians 5:15-16 (above), Paul tells us we are to make the most of our time in this evil world in fulfilling God's purposes, seizing every opportunity to tell others about Christ.

In Galatians 6:10 (above), Paul instructs us to do good to all wherever we have the opportunity. He puts emphasis on doing good not just to the non-believers, but also to our fellow believers. Believers are often critical of other believers. Jesus taught us we are to love one another.

The word opportunity suggests that it comes with a time limit. The term "windows of opportunity" is used to denote the period of time available to take action about something. Once the window is closed the opportunity is lost. In Isaiah 55:6-7 it says, "Seek the Lord while He may be found; call on Him while He is near."

The Lord can return at any moment and we as believers must be ready. For the unbeliever, the time of opportunity is critical to find Jesus. In Luke 13:25-28 tells us that the day will come if we missed our opportunity to find Jesus as our Savior, when He will say, "I tell you I do not know you or where you come from." When you find yourself standing at the door of heaven, will Jesus know you?

God does give second chances to listen and accept Him. Jonah refused to do what God asked him to do. God used the big fish to give Jonah a wakeup call and Jonah responded by doing what God wanted him to do. If God gives you a second chance, your wakeup call may not be as big as the whale, but will you respond?

Paul tells us about the many times God gave him opportunities to serve Him. Paul always took advantage of the opportunities God gave him and God blessed him because of his faithfulness to God. Even in times when Paul should have been concerned for his own welfare, his desire was to make it an opportunity to witness. In Acts 21 we find Paul being arrested and Paul asking the guards to allow him to speak to the crowd to give his testimony of how he had come to his faith in the Lord.

Paul always wanted to make the most of every opportunity that God gave him. He was concerned about the shortness of time and wanted to tell everyone he could about the love of Jesus. We must not ignore the opportunities that God gives.

TODAY'S WORD FOR OCTOBER 3

FRUITFUL

I am the vine, you are the branches. He who abides in Me, and I in him, bears much fruit; for without Me you can do nothing. John 15:5

We want to look at the word fruitful today as it refers to being spiritually fruitful. In the verse above (John 15:5), Jesus says He is the vine and we are the branches and if we abide in Him we will bear much fruit. When we read these words we think of bearing fruit by producing spiritual results relating to bringing others to know Christ. As believers that is what we are called to do.

The key words in this verse are "abides in Me." Abiding in Him gives evidence to our salvation and results in us bearing fruit. This fruit is not just soul winning, but abiding in Christ produces spiritual fruit that includes spiritual attitudes.

The apostle Paul tells us that "the fruit of the Spirit is love, joy, patience, kindness, goodness, fruitfulness, gentleness and self-control" (Galatians 5:22). Abiding in Christ also produces the fruit of righteousness when not only our attitudes change, but also our actions.

In Hebrews 12:11 we read, "No discipline seems pleasant at the time, but painful." Later on, however, it produces a harvest of righteousness and peace for those who have been trained by it.

When we think of being fruitful we think of a farmer. For a farmer to be successful he must have successful crops. To accomplish this he must have the right soil, rain, sunshine, seasons, cultivation, and then the blessing of God. Even a farmer who is not a believer in Jesus will tell you he needs the blessings of God on his crops if they are to be successful. He may refer to "Mother Nature" because he does not know God, but what he is really saying is he needs God to bless his crop.

When one becomes a believer in Jesus, he or she must first have a deep desire to abide in Christ and to live a life that honors Him so that one's life can be fruitful. Our desire should be "to walk in a manner worthy of the Lord, to please Him in all respects, bearing fruit in every good work and increasing in the knowledge of God." (Colossians 1:10)

As do the farmers, a believer must have the right soil; a personal relationship with Jesus. They must have the rain and sunshine; this is the daily communication with God through prayer and reading God's Word. Then there must be the sowing and the cultivation; the going out among the world and walking in your faith and talking about your faith in Christ. Finally, you need the blessing of God. It is God's blessing that brings a bountiful fruitful harvest.

This is a rough example, but it works. Do you want to be fruitful? Are you committed to serve God with all your heart, soul and mind? Have you experienced fruit in your Christian life? Read John 15:5 and you will see what the Lord says you need to do to bear fruit. Bearing fruit is not an option given to the believer. Our Lord expects us to bear fruit and He is standing near to make us fruitful.

TODAY'S WORD FOR OCTOBER 4

COMPANION

I am a companion of all who fear You, and of those who keep Your precepts. Psalm 119:63

And I urge you also, true companion, help these women who labored with me in the gospel." Philippians 4:3

For the most part we are living in a very lonely world. When we talk to people we find out that many do not have friends they can count on in their time of need. Most of you who read these daily devotionals have acquaintances, a few friends, but very few companions. Acquaintances are those we meet, but possibly do not know very well. Friends are those we know well and have a favorable relationship with. Companions are those we have a close relationship with and spend the most time with. Teenagers say today these are the ones we "hang" with. Companions have the same interests and values you have and this gives you a common bond. A true companion will stand by you and can be counted on for support in times of need.

No matter how self sufficient someone feels, we all have a need for a companion. This is why God instituted marriage because He said that man needed a companion. Marriages that put Christ first in their relationships are marriages that have spouses who share a common bond and a companionship based on God's love. When God is in the marriage the spouses will be true companions.

The writer of Psalms 119:63 said, "I am a companion of all who fear you and of those who keep your precepts (God's law)." The Psalmist desired to be obedient to God and faithful to keep God's commandments. He saw the importance of choosing the right companions who shared his same desires to love and obey the Lord. The danger for believers who choose close companions who are not believers is they will be drawn away from the Lord and be enticed to disobey God's commandments.

Children today look for companions. Parents have the responsibility to lead their children to choose the right companions. When our children went anywhere without one of us, we made sure we knew where they were going and with whom they were going. We always encouraged them to go with a trustworthy friend, a companion who would always be there for them. This also gave us assurance as parents, that our child would not be alone. The choices of companions can affect a child's lifestyle and standards for a lifetime.

Jesus wants to be our companion every day in all of our activities. He does not want us to be alone. With the Lord as our companion He gives us the confidence and boldness to live a life honoring the Lord. In Philippians 4:3 Paul uses the term "true companion." In another translation it reads "loyal yokefellow." These words describe the close relationship Paul had with the believers in the church at Philippi, and for that reason Paul could call on them.

TODAY'S WORD FOR OCTOBER 5

REBELLION

An evil man seeks only rebellion. Proverbs 17:11

These people have stubborn and rebellious hearts. Jeremiah 5:23

We are rebellious by nature going all the way back to Adam and Eve. Adam and Eve's downfall was rebellion against God.

Every parent knows about the terrible "two's." Two year olds do not like the word "NO." Just tell a two year old he cannot do something or he cannot have something and he will rebel, guaranteed. None of us like to be told we cannot have or cannot do something. We are all rebels by nature just like Adam and Eve. Adam and Eve found out quite quickly how God regards rebellion against Him. Today, we all must deal with God's penalty for Adam and Eve's rebellion.

The toughest job of Moses' job in leading the children of Israel was dealing with their rebellion against God. Moses knew the rebellious nature of the Israelites. Just before handing the leadership of the children of Israel over to Joshua he said he knew how stubborn and rebellious they were and he knew they would rebel even more when he was not with them.

In Deuteronomy chapter 32 we read the song of Moses which was his last message to the Israelites. He reminded them of God's blessings to them and warned them against rebelling against God. Then he commanded them to love and honor God and obey His commandments.

Rebellion is caused by pride. We think we know better than God and everyone else. It is especially arrogant to think we know better than God. Adam and Eve found that out very quickly.

We all know the story found in Luke 15:11-31 about the prodigal son. He was rebellious and took his share of his inheritance and left home. After he lost everything he had, he decided to start for home despite his rebellious nature. His father saw him coming and went out to meet him and gave him all he needed and more, including a great welcome home feast.

This is what God wants to do for us if we have been rebellious in our words or deeds. He is waiting with open arms to accept us back and all we have to do is come to Him.

Many parents today are concerned because of the rebellion they are witnessing in their children. If this is a problem you are facing, you need to show them at all times that you love them, but you will not tolerate their rebellion. Then give them a fair and just punishment. Be consistent in keeping the boundaries and standards you have set for them. No matter how rebellious they are, always love them, but be firm. The children of Israel were rebellious against God, but God never stopped loving them. But He did punish them and they had to suffer the consequences of their sins and rebellion against God.

TODAY'S WORD FOR OCTOBER 6

TIME

To everything there is a season, a time for every person under heaven: a time to be born, and a time to die. Ecclesiastes 3:1-2

The race is not to the swift, nor the battle to the strong, nor bread to the wise, nor riches to men of understanding, nor favor to men of skill; but TIME and CHANCE happen to them all. Ecclesiastes 9:11

Near the end of his life Solomon reflected back on his life and wrote down his analysis of his life in the book of Ecclesiastes. Solomon is known as the wisest man who ever lived. He not only had wisdom, but he had fame and fortune. He recognized there was one thing he had no more of than anyone else and that is time. In Ecclesiastes he wrote (above), Time and chance happen to them all.

God has given time to us on this earth so we can come to know Him and then to be a witness of Him to a world who needs to know Jesus. Time to God is different than time to us. In Psalm 90:4, the Psalmist says "For a thousand years in Your sight are like yesterday when it is past, and like a watch in the night." One day on God's calendar is like a thousand years on ours. God wants everyone to have time to repent and be saved. God's time table is not our time table.

After analyzing his life, Solomon came to his conclusion as to what is the most important priority of life not only for him, but for all of us as well. Solomon said, "Here is the conclusion of the matter: fear God and keep His commandments, for this is the whole duty of man." Ecclesiastes 12:13

The question for us as Christians is: "How do we spend our time when we know the Lord?" One of the great failings of Christians today is not having adequate time to give to God. In order for us to be in tune with God it demands time on our part. Specifically, it demands that we spend time daily reading God's Word, the Bible. This is how God communicates to us and how we learn how God wants us to live.

Secondly, God desires us to communicate with Him through prayer. Most Christians do not take the time to pray each day. Oh yes, some will say that they pray before each meal and before they go to bed each night. God wants more than that from us. He wants us to give Him time with our prayers so we can make known to Him our requests and our needs. And, more importantly, He wants us to thank Him and give Him our praise for all He has done for us.

Time is a valuable asset to each of us every day. How we spend our time depends on our priorities. Choosing how we use our time becomes a moral and spiritual issue. We always find time for the things that are important to us.

One of the reasons for the breakdown of the family unity is because parents and children do not spend time together. Time needs to be spent talking, praying and reading God's Word. Time also is needed for a family to play and relax together. We urge all parents to reevaluate today how you spend your time with your family.

TODAY'S WORD FOR OCTOBER 7

BLESS

Bless the Lord, O my soul; And all that is within me, bless His only name! Psalm 103:1

Bless those that curse you, and pray for those who spitefully use you. Luke 6:28

When we think of the word bless, we think of one of the most significant verses in the Old Testament. In Genesis Chapter 12, God made this promise to Abraham. "I will make you a great nation; I will bless you and make your name great; and you shall be a blessing." God fulfilled His promise to Abraham. Abraham fathered a great nation. God did make his name great.

And God goes on to promise: "I will bless those who bless you, and I will curse him who curses you." This nation today is Israel and God is promising us as individuals that He will bless each one of us who blesses Israel. In Acts 3:25 Peter preaches to the people, quoting Moses, "And in your seed all the families of the earth shall be blessed."

Have you thought about how all the world has been blessed through Abraham? First of all God chose him and his descendants to represent God to the world. God's Word, the Bible was given through Abraham to the children of Israel. And the greatest blessing the world has ever received is Jesus Christ who was given to us through the lineage of Abraham. The first chapter of Matthew lists the ancestors of Jesus. The list starts with Abraham.

In Psalm 115:13, the Psalmist says God will bless those who fear the Lord. Our daily strength comes from God and we can expect His blessing upon our lives when we fear the Lord. God does not give us a spirit of fear (II Timothy 1:7), but expects us to be obedient to His Word. When God promised to bless Abraham, He put a requirement on receiving the blessing. Abraham had to leave his homeland. He obeyed God and was blessed by God.

The instruction in Luke 6:28 is to bless those who treat you badly and this is very tough to do. Jesus wants us to follow His example and love our enemies. It takes a conscious effort on our part to want to bless those who spitefully use us and to pray for them. A kind word softens anger and prayer does change things. If we can bring ourselves to pray for an enemy our attitude toward them will change. Prayer works because it brings God into the situation and God can change the hardest of hearts.

In Mark 10:13-16 is the account when Jesus took the children into His arms, laid His hands on them and blessed them. The disciples had tried to keep the children away from Jesus and when Jesus saw it He invited the children to come to Him. When He blessed the children He demonstrated that His blessings are freely given and all are invited to come to Him. God "richly blesses all who call upon Him." (Romans 10:12)

TODAY'S WORD FOR OCTOBER 8

GRIEF

Who comforts us in all our tribulation (grief), that we may be able to comfort those who are in trouble, with the comfort with which we ourselves are comforted by God. II Corinthians 1:4

Sorrow is better than laughter, for by a sad countenance the heart is made better. Ecclesiastes 7:3

One of the most difficult experiences that one faces in life is the death of a family member, a friend or an acquaintance. We have experienced this several times in our immediate family losing dearly loved family members including our parents, a daughter-in-law and a nephew. The cause of the sorrow that comes with death is grief. The grief that one goes through for a person who has died knowing Jesus is entirely different than one experiences when the person did not know Jesus.

We have witnessed, first hand, both situations. When a Christian is grieving for a person who never knew Jesus, the grief includes personal feelings as to whether you did all you could to see that that person knew the Lord and therefore will spend an eternity separated from God. It is very hard, at times like this, to comfort the family of the deceased.

When a believer dies, we as believers have the blessed hope of spending an eternity in heaven with them. The depth of the grief is softened knowing the deceased knew Jesus as their Savior.

Job tells us in Job 42:5 that out of grief he saw Jesus as never before, "I have heard of You by the hearing of the ear, but now my eyes see You." Jesus, the perfect man, is described as "a man of sorrows," intimately acquainted with grief. (Isaiah 53:3)

In first reading the verse above from Ecclesiastes it is hard to understand how the writer could say, "Sorrow is better than laughter." There is a lot for us to learn that sometimes we only learn through grief. The writer of Ecclesiastes teaches us that sorrow does a work in one's heart that will make one a better person in the Lord.

We have traveled to many areas of our world and have seen suffering and grief that has moved us to tears although, we have learned through these many experiences that God used sorrow and grief to soften our hearts so we would be more sensitive to the needs of the suffering. It taught us to pray for those living in sorrow and made us aware of a hurting world that Jesus died for. God wants each of us to remember in times of grief and sorrow, He is in control and is our comforter. He wants us to be available to comfort others in their time of need as Paul wrote in the above verse from II Corinthians 1:4.

TODAY'S WORD FOR OCTOBER 9

PERSEVERANCE

Tribulation produces perseverance; and perseverance, character; and character, hope.
Romans 5:3-4

Have you ever watched a bird try to build a nest in a tree? We have watched as a bird would carry dry grass and twigs, one piece at a time into the spot in the tree they had chosen for their nest. It is painstaking work and takes perseverance, but the bird perseveres until the nest is built. Sometimes strong winds blow the nest away and soon the bird must begin the process all over again.

The perseverance of the birds in building their nests is inspiring. You can almost catch yourself cheering for the bird because it is a huge project for a small bird and yet they do not stop until the job is done. We just had a humming bird build a nest in a bush in front of our house. We have watched as the two little eggs have hatched and the mother bird faithfully perseveres in caring for her tiny babies.

Trying to live a Christ-honoring life in the world we live in today can leave us frustrated and discouraged. Many people today are facing insurmountable hardships including the loss of a job, the loss of a home and families who are in great turmoil.

Satan is alive and well in this sinful world. We can expect trouble and tribulation, especially as a believer. In times of difficulty it is easy to think God has forgotten us. This is not the case. God never forgets us. Often when times are good it is we who tend to forget God. It is when times are tough that we most need to depend on God to help us through our difficulties.

God will empower us to keep on going even when we cannot see the resolution of our problems. In many situations God is using a seemingly insurmountable challenge in our life to produce perseverance. And as the verse says, that we have written above, perseverance will produce in us character and through character, hope.

If anyone should be held as an example of what it means to persevere, in spite of hardships, it is the apostle Paul. Paul knew what it meant to suffer and be persecuted. In the first century, Christian persecution was the norm rather than the exception. In Paul's writings he gives words of instruction and encouragement concerning perseverance that he has learned from experience.

The Apostle Paul reminds us in Galatians 6:9 not to grow "weary while doing good." Paul then goes on to tell us not to give up. We are to persevere in everything we do and put all we are going through in His hands and He will get us through every situation.

When others around you suggest that you give up on a situation do not let them discourage you. Put everything in God's hands then hope will whisper to you, "Try one more time." Try it and we can assure you God will not fail you.

TODAY'S WORD FOR OCTOBER 10

BLOOD

The blood of Jesus Christ, His Son cleanses us from all sin. 1 John 1:7b

There is the old hymn that we sang often in church years ago. The words of the song began with, "What can wash away my sins, nothing but the blood of Jesus. What can make me whole again, nothing but the blood of Jesus?"

Just as the life we have in the flesh is in the blood we carry in our bodies, so the life of Christianity is in the atoning, life-giving blood of Jesus Christ. If the atoning blood of Jesus is rejected and the rejecter willfully rejects eternal life through the blood of Jesus, there no longer remains a sacrifice for his or her sins.

The words of this old hymn are the key to what has happened to someone who first recognizes that he or she is a sinner and then confesses their sin and asks Jesus to forgive them and come into their heart. The reason we have that privilege is because of the blood of Jesus.

God sent His Son to this earth to be born as a babe in a manger; to teach us His plan of salvation; to die on the cross, and rise again after three days. He is now in heaven preparing a place for us. It was His death on the cross and the shedding of His blood that paid the penalty for our sins once and for all.

Today, unfortunately, you do not hear many sermons in our churches about the shed blood of Jesus and why it is important for our salvation. Pastors seem to be fearful to preach this kind of sermon, but again as the old hymn stated: "Nothing but the blood of Jesus can wash away our sins.

The Hebrew word for blood "dam" is found 360 times in the Old Testament. Most of these references concern animal bloodshed in making a sacrifice for a person's sins. A few of these references concern the violent shedding of blood in war or a crime. In the Old Testament one needed to make a sacrifice of an animal for forgiveness of their sin. This was God's temporary provision since He had not yet sent His Son to die for our sins. The shedding of the blood of the lamb (animal) represented the giving of one life for another. Jesus gave His life for ours.

In Deuteronomy 12:23 it reads, "Only be sure that you do not eat the blood, for the blood is the life; you may not eat the life with the meat." This verse makes it clear that blood is a sacred fluid. It represents life itself.

As we stated above, when Christ came and died on the cross, He paid the penalty for our sins through the sacrifice of His blood. There is a crimson thread that begins in the Old Testament and runs through the New Testament. The New Testament focuses our attention on the "blood of Christ," in the context of Christ's crucifixion at Calvary. The sacrifices of ancient time foreshadowed Christ's self-sacrifice.

Now is the time for you to make that decision, if you have not already. "What can wash away my sins? Nothing but the blood of Jesus." There is no other way!

TODAY'S WORD FOR OCTOBER 11

TARGET

I press toward the goal for the prize of the upward call of God in Christ Jesus. Philippians 3:14

Our children were always very competitive not only among themselves, but also in sports and in their school classes. Now we see the same competitiveness among our grandchildren. As parents we encouraged our children to always do their best in every task they attempted whether it was work or play. A successful life by itself demands some sort of competitiveness. Being competitive drives a person to always have targets in life and to do all one can to meet those targets in a way to win.

In training our children we warned them they may not always win. Many times in our lives we may not win so when we lose we need to lose with graciousness and even humility. This is tough not only to teach, but to learn. No one ever wants to lose, but at times it will happen. Children today also need to be told that when one is "racing' toward a goal they have set, they need to "race" fairly and abide by the rules.

Part of winning is to know your target. In the 2004 Olympics the gold medal winner in rifle shooting was ready to win his second medal in another event. He had a commanding lead and everyone was certain he would win the second medal. In fact, it was his best event and he was highly favored. But something went wrong. He hit the middle of the target, but he had aimed at the wrong target. This is an excellent example for all of us to make sure that we are aiming for the right targets in life because it is so easy to get off course and aim for the wrong target.

In Paul's letter to the Philippians (above verse) he expresses the importance of focusing on the right target in our Christian life. Paul uses this word "goal" as the same word used as an athlete running a race. The same word is also used for the object to aim for in archery. In each of these definitions the prospect of winning depends on us being focused on the proper targets. For us as believers, we need to be focused on a lifetime pursuit of becoming more like our Savior, Jesus.

The prize the apostle Paul is referring to, also in the above verse, is the time God calls each believer up to heaven and into His presence. There will be the moment each believer will receive the prize which has been an unattainable goal or prize that could be won in earthly life.

To attain this prize, one of the desires God has is that we be Christ-like in all of our actions here on earth. This is a goal we all can try to obtain and it means daily work on our part.

Take a moment now and decide what your focus is on in your life. Are you preoccupied with getting ahead in life thus making life more comfortable for you? Are you focused on the target desiring to be more like Jesus? We encourage you today to make God's goals your goals and aim directly at that target. Keep your eyes on your target. If you take your eyes off your target you will be sure to miss it. Success in your Christian life depends on keeping your eyes on Jesus.

TODAY'S WORD FOR OCTOBER 12

PRIDE

For everything in the world, the craving of sinful man, the lust of his eyes, and the boasting (pride) of what he has and does, come not from the Father but from the world. I John 2:16

Pride goes before destruction and a haughty spirit before a fall. Proverbs 16:18

Take a moment and think about all the people you know. How many of them do you consider to be "proud?" When one is an unbeliever, he or she needs to have some way to feel successful, so most people tend to become very proud of what they do or who they are. As believers our pride should be in our faith in Jesus and not in the things of this world. This at times is very difficult because our nature is to become proud with success and accomplishment.

We have seen many proud people take terrible falls when their hope in life was built on success and accomplishments. When that success collapsed there was a steep fall into the reality that the things in this world are only temporary. Consciously and unconsciously pride creeps into our life and we must remember the fall can really hurt. We have often heard the saying, "Pride cometh before the fall."

Let us take a moment and look at what the scriptures say about pride. In the verse we have printed above from I John, we are reminded by the Apostle John that issues like lust of the flesh, lust of the eyes and pride are not of God. The book of Proverbs has a number of references reminding us that God is absolute in condemning pride. Proverbs chapter 6 verses 16-19 list seven things that the Lord hates. Pride is the number one item on that list. Pride is the devil's tool.

Proverbs 11:2 teaches "When pride comes, then comes disgrace but with humility comes wisdom." Also in Proverbs we find the results of pride contrasted with the results of humility. Pride brings downfall, destruction and disgrace and leads to quarrels. Humility leads to wisdom, honor and a willingness to take advice.

John wrote these words in I John (above) from Ephesus after he had been released from prison on the isle of Patmos. John's message was to distinguish between truth and the errors that were creeping into the churches of the day.

The danger of pride is that it comes between us and God. It is difficult for a prideful person to rely on God. When we are successful, it is human nature to want to take the credit and to become proud of what we have accomplished. We forget to remember to acknowledge that it is God who gives us strength and wisdom to do what we do. When pride takes over, we forget to give God the glory and we can no longer expect God to bless us.

As Christians we need to live with a humble spirit no matter how great or how little our accomplishments may be. As parents we need to teach humility and warn our children about pride. And as children we need to listen, watch and learn and then pattern our lives after the ones who show humility in all they do.

TODAY'S WORD FOR OCTOBER 13

CREATION

In the beginning God created the heavens and the earth. Genesis 1:1

Therefore, if anyone is in Christ, he is a new creation; old things have passed away; behold, all things have become new. II Corinthians 5:17

It is important that we consider several things when we read the first verse in the Bible. First, the Bible is not only the book from God; it is the book about God. Secondly, in the beginning refers to the beginning of creation. God created heaven and earth recently (not millions of years ago but thousands), and out of nothing. Remember that God was unformed, unmade, uncreated and had no beginning. He always was, always is, and always shall be. And finally God created the heavens and the earth, in other words the entire universe.

God is also our creator since the Word says he created man. Along with being our creator He is our sustainer, our judge and our hope in this world and for eternity. What an awesome series of events to understand. The six days of creation, as outlined in the book of Genesis, clearly tells us we are here and all we have is because of God and His love for us. God loves us so much that He not only created the world for us, but He created us in His image.

The apostle Paul talks about creation in II Corinthians 5:17. He is referring here to the creation of a new life when someone rejects the evils of this world and seeks Jesus and accepts Him as his or her Savior.

When a person accepts Jesus, this verse tells us he becomes a new creation of God saved by the blood of Jesus. He tells us old things are passed away. These are the things that ran our life before our salvation. He then tells us all things become new. As a new creation of our Lord the things that dominated our lives before we found Jesus are now history and no longer important. Now in serving Jesus everything has become new.

This verse that Paul speaks to the Corinthians begins with, "if anyone is in Christ." Paul is referring to the believer's security in Christ when he or she finds Christ as Savior. Paul also refers with his "in Christ" comment to the believer's acceptance of Christ for which God is well pleased.

In Psalm 139 David describes God as fashioning his tiny body together in the darkness of his mother's womb. God loved David before He ever created him and this is so with us. We came into this world with the inventive heart and hand of God.

Yes, God is our creator. He created the world we live in and He created our new life when we found Jesus as our Savior. The Psalmist prayed years later in a sinner's prayer, "Create in me a clean heart, O God, and renew a steadfast spirit within me." Psalm 51:10

TODAY'S WORD FOR OCTOBER 14

INDIFFERENCE

Those who have turned back from following the Lord, and have not sought the Lord, nor inquired of Him. Zephaniah 1:6

This verse in Zephaniah gives us an excellent definition of spiritual indifference. There are many people today who call themselves "Believers" and really have turned back from the Lord. They never seek the Lord through prayer or the reading of the Bible. And when you watch their daily living there is no indication of the person walking with God.

In Mark 14: 32-41 we read about Jesus going into the garden of Gethsemane to pray the night before He was betrayed and arrested. He told the disciples that were with Him to "sit here while I pray." Jesus was agonizing over the terrible suffering He would endure and needed to spend time alone with His Father in prayer.

When He returned to the place He left the disciples, they were sound asleep. The disciples in this situation showed indifference. Jesus asked the disciples "could you not watch for one hour?" You would think that would be a "wake up call" for the disciples, but it was not. Jesus went away again to pray and returned and found the disciples asleep. The scripture tells us that Jesus went a third time and came back and they were asleep again. Jesus responded after the third time "THIS IS ENOUGH." In Jesus' darkest hour, His disciples were not there for Him. They were indifferent to His needs.

Another example of indifference is the story of Jonah. When Jonah was running from God and in the storm at sea as recorded in Jonah 1:4-9, the crew was afraid and everyone was working hard to save the ship. But Jonah showed indifference and lack of concern, and went down to the lowest part of the ship and went to sleep.

Jonah was a prophet of God and should have been praying for God's protection. The crew had to wake him up and ask him to help by praying. To Jonah's credit he admitted he was the cause of the distress they were in because he had disobeyed God. He told them to throw him overboard to calm the storm. They did and God calmed the storm and saved Jonah by having him swallowed by a whale.

In many ways, today may be called the "Age of Indifference." Historian Arnold Toynbee has found that nineteen of twenty-one civilizations have died from within and not from outside conquest. Another historian, Dr. Lawrence Gould said he did not believe that our greatest threat is from bombs and missiles, but from our people not caring and showing indifference. Edmund Burke said in 1795: "Nothing is as fatal to religion as indifference." This is certainly accurate for today.

The problem with indifference or an "I just do not care" attitude is that it leads to inaction. Many people who call themselves Christians are indifferent Christians. Just as Jesus told the disciples and the ship crew told Jonah, we need to wake up from our indifference and take action to make a difference in this world.

TODAY'S WORD FOR OCTOBER 15

PROBLEM

My brethren, count it all joy when you fall into various trials (problems), knowing that testing of your faith produces patience. James 1:2-3

Be anxious for nothing, but in everything by prayer and supplication, with thanksgiving let your requests be made known to God; and the peace of God which surpasses all understanding, will guard your hearts and minds through Jesus Christ. Philippians 4:6-7

In life today everyone seems to be constantly talking about the problems they are facing. Many people just think the best way to solve a problem is to avoid it. Problems weigh on us even to the extent they can make us ill. Possibly the problems you face today include issues with the economy, your career or your family.

Do you have problems in your life? If you hear someone answer "NO" to that question, you can be certain they are in denial. Problems are part of living in a sinful world. Everyone has problems at one time or another. James doesn't say "IF" you fall into trials, he says "WHEN" you have trials. (Verse above)

First Peter is the letter Peter wrote to encourage believers who were going through trials. Peter calls problems trials in I Peter 1:6-7 where he says: "So be truly glad, there is a wonderful joy ahead, even though you have to endure many trials for a little while." Trials test how genuine and how strong our faith really is.

Peter goes on to say that trials test our faith like fire tests and purifies gold, though your faith is far more precious than mere gold. Just as gold is made more valuable when it is put through fire, we are made more valuable to God because we are strengthened by the problems and trials we go through. When your faith remains strong through trials, it will bring much praise and glory to Jesus Christ.

Also in I Peter 4:12, Peter says: "Dear friends, do not be surprised at the painful trial you are suffering, as though something strange were happening with you." People often ask: "Why is this happening to me?" when they have a problem. Peter warns us to expect problems or as he calls them trials. God allows us to have problems to test our faith. Problems come in many forms and each one brings pain, anguish, stress and worry. How we cope with problems depends on our attitude.

We need to do several things according to the verse the Apostle Paul wrote while he was in prison (Philippians 4:6-7 above). First we need to admit we have a problem. Then we need to turn that problem into a prayer. We need to face the problem straight on and do not let it linger.

When we turn it over to God in prayer, He will go through the problem with us and will use the problem to strengthen our faith and to give us peace that is beyond our understanding. Remember problems are not God's fault and there is no limit as to what God can do in solving your problem, if you turn it over to Him.

TODAY'S WORD FOR OCTOBER 16

OATHS

Keep the king's commandment for the sake of your oath to God. Ecclesiastes 8:2

You shall not swear falsely, but shall perform your oaths to the Lord. Matthew 5:33.

An oath is not to be made lightly. It is a solemn statement made with God as the witness. It is a sad commentary oaths are so often broken. It does not seem important to people that God is the witness when they make an oath.

We see this happening with marriage vows today, more than any other time in history. In America, the oath of marriage is broken more than 50% of the time. The marriage oath is two people making their vows to one another. This is a sacred promise to be honored for a lifetime. We read in Matthew 5:33 (above) God condemns taking oaths and then breaking them.

Even though oaths are meant to be kept, every day oaths are made with no expectation by one or both parties to keep the oath. People break their oaths because they have a change of heart or something better comes along. Most often "something better' never becomes a reality. There is an old adage: "The grass always looks greener on the other side of the fence."

Oaths are promises made and should be considered unchangeable. Probably one of the saddest oaths recorded in the scripture, was when Peter was asked if he knew Jesus when Jesus was arrested and taken to trial. In Matthew 26:72 it reads: "But again he denied with an oath, 'I do not know the man.'" And in the following verses, Peter denied he knew Jesus three times and then Peter remembered the words Jesus said to him (verse 75), "Before the rooster crows, (in other words before morning), you will deny Me three times." Earlier that night Peter had promised Jesus he would never disown Him even if he had to die for Him. Peter broke this oath and swore with another oath that he did not know Jesus. Not only did he break his first oath, but he lied in his second oath. Peter then went and wept bitterly because he was truly repentant for what he had done. We know Peter's repentance was genuine because he later did great things for the Lord.

In Matthew 23 when Jesus was talking to the Scribes and Pharisees, He said "Woe to you" several times because of their hypocrisy in their swearing of oaths along with other "things" they were doing that were against God's teachings. In Hebrews 7:21, the author quotes from Psalm 110:4: "The Lord has sworn and will not change His mind." Unlike us, when God makes an oath He keeps His word.

Oaths are to be made with a commitment to keep them. God is a witness to our oaths and God will honor those who keep their oaths.

TODAY'S WORD FOR OCTOBER 17

EXPERIENCE

Blessed be the God and Father of our Lord Jesus Christ, the Father of all mercies and God of all comfort, who comforts us in all tribulation that we may be able to comfort those who are in trouble, with the comfort with which we ourselves are comforted by God. II Corinthians 1:3-4

The above scripture reminds us why as Christians we go through trials and tribulations. One of the reasons God allows this, as it reads in the above scripture, is that we can comfort those going through their trial and tribulation because we have learned by experience — we have been there.

As we look back on our lives, we have had the privilege of going places, meeting people and seeing things that has given us a world of experience. We both also have had the joy of having Christian parents with experience, both spiritually and with life in general, to train us from our very young ages.

And then having God bless us with six children, their spouses and 20 grandchildren has given us wonderful experiences that God is now allowing us to share with friends like you.

Experience is invaluable and we as Christians need to realize the value of our experience in knowing Christ can help us share the good news of the gospel with others. Having made our decisions to accept Jesus before we were teenagers has allowed us to grow spiritually as children, teenagers, as a young married couple, and now as seniors so we can understand the mountains and valleys that one goes through in life. As they say, "We have been there and done that."

The actions and words of Paul the Apostle in Acts 14 reminds us that Paul was persecuted so he could be an encouragement to others who were or would be persecuted because of their faith.

The Apostle John wrote the book of I John to the believers, so they would be alerted to be able to distinguish between truth and error. In the first four verses he talks about the experiences the believers have seen, heard and touched concerning the Word of Life. John says to the believers that he reminds us about this so our joy may be full.

In life today, experience is very important. When someone has a job interview one of the first questions asked is about your experience. Asking about experience even relates to small children. We can remember choosing teams for our little league teams and we looked for children with some experience. We wanted to know if they had played the game before. When it comes to choosing a leader, a pastor or an executive, a key ingredient is their experience.

As Christians, those of us who have known Jesus for some time need to use the experience God has given us over the years to proclaim the good news of the gospel to those we touch daily.

TODAY'S WORD FOR OCTOBER 18

GOD

But without faith it is impossible to please Him, for he who comes to God must believe that He is, and that He is a rewarder of those that diligently seek Him. Hebrews 11:6

Do you know who God is? Do you think He is some supreme being up in the sky somewhere you can call upon when you have a serious need? What do you know about God? Do you know God wants you to know Him and He has made it possible for you to have a relationship with Him through His Son Jesus Christ?

According to the scriptures, God's Holy Word, the only way one can approach God is by faith. Anyone who comes to God must first believe that He is.

However, true faith is more than merely believing God exists. In Hebrews 11:5, Enoch is described as a man who pleased God. We are not told of any great thing Enoch did, but only that he "walked with God." To say Enoch walked with God indicates he made God the focus of his life and the major portion of his life!

In Hebrews 11:6, the writer tells us that without faith it is impossible to please God. He also explains what is necessary for us to believe to have that kind of faith. We must believe He is the one and only true God and He will reward all those who diligently seek Him in genuine faith. So genuine and great was Enoch's faith that God rewarded him by taking Enoch from this life to eternal life without facing death. God rewards all who diligently seek Him with the reward of eternal life.

Enoch is an example for those of us who seek to know and please God. To please God we must accept Him into our lives through His Son Jesus and then by faith walk with Him and live for Him. Without faith it is impossible to please God, and without faith it is impossible to know God.

God is a personal being. In Jeremiah 10:10 we read the Lord is the true God; He is the living God and the everlasting King. The personality of God is seen in certain characteristics ascribed to Him in the scriptures. God is not only all powerful and all knowing, but God is a caring God and He has feelings.

God is a God that grieves. In Genesis 6:6 we read, "He was grieved in His heart." God becomes angry. In I Kings 11:9 we read, "The Lord became angry with Solomon." God is a jealous God. In Exodus 20:5 we read, "For I, the Lord your God, am a jealous God."

Did you know that God laughs? In Psalm 2:4 the Psalmist writes, "He who sits in the heavens shall laugh." God also is a caring God. In I Peter 5:7 it is written, "Casting all your care upon Him, for He cares for you." God also hears us. In Psalm 94:9 the Psalmist writes, "He who planted the ear, shall He not hear?" And God sees. In Psalm 94:9 it reads, "He who formed the eye, shall He not see?"

God is eternal. The Psalmist tells us in Psalm 102: 24-27 that God's years are through all generations, God is the same throughout the years, and His years will have no end. God had no beginning, but "in the beginning God created the heavens and the earth." God has no ending. He is eternal and exists totally from Himself.

TODAY'S WORD FOR OCTOBER 19

PURPOSE

We were burdened beyond measure, above strength, so that we despaired even of life. II Corinthians 1:8

What shall I say, Father save Me from this hour? But for this purpose I came to this hour. John 12:27

Most people today live a life with no purpose really in mind. We are creatures of habit. We get up in the morning and go about a routine getting ourselves ready to go to school, to work or to do whatever we have planned for the day. Our days are routine and then we return home at night facing the same evening routine that we face daily.

Some people have a purpose in life. The problem with most people who have a purpose, that purpose has no hope or any kind of a future. The only people we know who really have a beneficial purpose in life are those who know Jesus as their Savior. Purpose comes from one's priorities. Those who believe in Jesus know that they have a purpose. Believers have the God given purpose to be Christ's witnesses that He died and rose again from the dead to save us and give us eternal life.

Shakespeare had a famous line: "To be or not to be, that is the question!" Hamlet, in the play, speaks these words. He had learned his uncle had killed his father and married his mother. The horror of this event was so disturbing to him that he contemplates suicide. The question for him was: "to be" (to go on living) or "not to be" (to take his own life). He had to make his decision based on what his purpose in life was.

In John 12:27 (above) Jesus reminded His disciples what His purpose was in coming to this earth. It was a moment He did not want to face, but He knew it was God's purpose for Him to go to the cross carrying all of our sins to die for us, paying the penalty for our sins.

The apostle Paul told the church at Corinth (above verse) his persecution was so intense that he "despaired even of life." But he knew this was God's purpose for his life. Because he kept his focus on God, he was able to endure joyfully instead of becoming overwhelmed. Paul learned not to trust in himself, but in God (verse 9). "Indeed in our hearts we felt the sentence of death. But this happened that we might not rely on ourselves but on God, who raises the dead."

Paul had such great faith that even in the direst of circumstances He knew that God was at work to accomplish His purpose.

God has a purpose for each of us and He wants us to fulfill that purpose. So many believers sit back and stay in the comfort zone of their daily routine and never step out in faith to fulfill God's purpose in their life. Trials in life may be part of God's plan to accomplish His purpose in our life. Trials make us think and thinking makes us wiser and wisdom helps us see our weaknesses and our need to rely on the Lord.

TODAY'S WORD FOR OCTOBER 20

SUBMISSION

Wives, submit to your husbands as is fitting in the Lord. Husbands, love your wives and do not be harsh to them. Colossians 3:18-19

You younger people, submit yourselves to your elders. Yes, all of you be submissive to one another. I Peter 5:5

One who rules his own house well, having his children in submission with all reverence. I Timothy 3:4

We are living in a day and age when one uses the word "submission" they will get in return a strange look or even a sneering remark. Many are saying that we are living in "the ME generation." This is when a person lives for "me" only and for no one else. To these people the word or thought of submission is not in their vocabulary. As you can see in the verses we have listed above, the Bible has a lot to say about God's requirement for us concerning being submissive.

We all have a mind of our own and a desire to do things our way and in our own timing. Our natural tendency is not to be submissive. This is nothing new. It goes back to the Garden of Eden. First Eve, then Adam, rebelled against submitting to God's command not to eat the forbidden fruit. That was when trouble began.

As new parents we were amazed at how soon our sweet little bundle of joy developed a mind of his or her own and had no desire to submit to our will. You just get to sleep and your child is wide awake demanding attention and just wants to play. You know whose will wins out. They only get more demanding as they grow up so it is soon quite evident they have a lot to learn about submission. Parents need to start training their children at a very early age the meaning of submission and what God requires of us as believers concerning being submissive.

Submission to God is necessary to prevent discord and chaos. The Bible teaches that we are to be submissive, first of all to God, and obey His commandments. The tragic actions of Adam and Eve and the consequences that resulted from them are evidence of the importance of being submissive to God. Jesus set the example for us by submitting to the will of the Father and was "obedient to death, even death on the cross." (Philippians 2:9). How can we do any less than to submit ourselves to God, the Father our Lord and Creator?

Peter tells us to submit to those who have a legitimate authority over us for the Lord's sake. It honors the Lord when we are law abiding and obedient to those in authority over us. The only exception is when obedience to an authority would cause us to be disobedient to God.

In today's society we have rebelled against being submissive to anyone except "me." It is time we begin to be submissive first to God, and then to our spouses, children, parents, family, leaders and the result will be that God will bless us.

TODAY'S WORD FOR OCTOBER 21

COMPLY

The seventh time around, when the priests sounded the trumpet blast, Joshua commanded the people to shout for the Lord has given you the city. Joshua 6:16

When the people gave a loud shout, the wall collapsed; so every man charged straight in, and they took the city. Joshua 6:20

Again today we look at an example God has given us in the scripture as to how He wants us to comply to His will. This example is from the adventures of the Children of Israel. They are now in the Promised Land.

Israel had set up camp at Gilgal which was about two miles to the north of the city of Jericho. Jericho was so well fortified that the Canaanites were sure that their city was invincible. It was situated on a hill and surrounded by a double ring of walls. The outer wall was six feet thick and the inner wall was twelve feet thick. Nevertheless God had determined that Jericho would fall.

God sent a messenger to Joshua to tell him God would deliver Jericho completely into Joshua's hands. God gave very specific instructions to Joshua to order the Israelites to comply with if they were to have the victory. Joshua and his army were to march once around the city for six straight days. They were to be led by seven priests blowing trumpets made of ram's horns who were then followed by the Ark of the Covenant. On the seventh day, they were to march around the city seven times and when Joshua gave the command all the people were to shout.

Joshua did everything just as God had instructed him and when all the people complied with the command to shout, the walls of the city collapsed and the Israelites were able to charge right into the city and take it.

The instructions given by God to Joshua were very unusual for a military conquest. When He directed that the Ark of the Covenant lead the soldiers, He wanted the Israelites to understand that He was in command and the outcome of the battle was dependent upon Him and not upon their military strength. With God's instruction the Israelites demonstrated their faith and trust in the Lord and their willingness to obey Him. In response to their obedience, God gave them victory.

Obedience to God and compliance to His laws always bring blessings. In Deuteronomy 28:2 it reads: "All these blessings will come upon you and accompany you if you obey the Lord your God." When you spend time reading the Bible and praying daily, God will make His direction clear to you. You will probably not hear His voice, but the still small voice within you will direct you.

In life today we need to, as individuals and as parents with our families, learn to set rules and boundaries for ourselves daily based on the scriptures and then to force ourselves to comply with them. When you set the boundaries up early in the lives of children they will normally learn much quicker the difference between right and wrong and will always know what it means to comply.

TODAY'S WORD FOR OCTOBER 22

GIVING

Jesus said, This poor widow has put in more than all those who have given to the treasury.
Mark 12:43

When you do a charitable deed, do not let your left hand know what your right hand is doing.
Matthew 6:3

These two verses above give us two important principles that apply to our spirit of giving to the Lord. The first principle is that it is not the size of the gift that matters.

In Mark 12:41-44, Mark relates the incident that took place when Jesus was with His disciples in the temple area where people brought their gifts of money. A poor widow put in two small coins. These were very little gifts in comparison to the large amounts given by others. Yet, Jesus said to His disciples the widow had put in more than all the others. The reason He said this was the others gave out of their surplus, but the widow gave sacrificially all that she owned.

Even if we have only a small amount to give, when it is given to the Lord He will bless it. We learned as children when we had little to give, we always gave ten percent of every dollar we received. This practice became part of our life style and we never stopped giving this way and God has blessed us abundantly.

The second principle that our Lord gave us as written in the above verse from Matthew is we need to give without fanfare. In other words, we do not need to announce what we give to anyone. Do not let your left hand know what your right hand gives. We are giving unto the Lord, not to gain favor from others on this earth.

Giving is much more than giving of our income. As believers we need to have a heart for giving. In James 1:22 James tells us to be doers of the Word and not hearers only. But he does not stop by telling us only to obey by being a doer of the Word He also gives us specific instructions as to how we can be a doer of the Word. He does this by giving us practical ways to be a doer. In James 1: 27 he says for us to "Visit orphans and widows in their trouble." In other words we are to give not only of our treasures, but of our time and talents. God expects us to have a heart of compassion and caring for the less fortunate among us.

We recently read about a young girl who kept coming home without her winter gloves. Her mother was driven crazy having to continually buy her new gloves. She finally told her daughter that she needed to be more responsible and bring home her gloves every night. The young girl responded by crying and through her tears told her mom that as long as she kept getting new gloves she could give them away to someone who did not have any and could not afford to get some.

The story continued when this young girl grew up, her hobbies included volunteering in the community and helping to mentor inner city children. As a child she developed the habit of giving and as she grew up it became part of her life style. We all need to ask God for a heart like this young girl.

TODAY'S WORD FOR OCTOBER 23

RECONCILIATION

First be reconciled to your brother, and then come and offer your gift. Matthew 5:24

In Judaism, the holiest day of the year is YOM KIPPUR, the Day of Atonement. On that day the people seek God's forgiveness for their sins both personally and nationally. The day before is called EREV YOM KIPPUR and is the last opportunity to seek forgiveness from other people before YOM KIPPUR begins. This is important because in the Jewish tradition you must seek forgiveness from other people before you can seek the forgiveness of God.

If we have wronged someone so there is a broken relationship, it can hinder our relationship with the Lord. If you wonder why this is so, it is because issues left unresolved fester and grow which often lead to bitterness and escalating acts of retaliation. This is sin in God's eyes. Sin separates us from God. Jesus pointed out in order to worship Him with all of our heart, and a pure heart, we first need to resolve matters with others. Jesus states this clearly in Matthew 5:24.

Our ability to truly worship God is hindered by our broken relationships with others. As believers we need to understand and practice reconciliation in our lives. Broken relationships are caused by wrong actions, bad attitudes and destructive words and these are all issues God expects us to make right before we should come to Him. If we do not, how can God bless us?

Jesus calls for reconciliation to be sought eagerly (Matthew 5:25), aggressively, quickly, and even if it involves self-sacrifice. He stated that it is better to be wronged than to allow a dispute between those who love the Lord to be a cause for dishonoring Christ.

It is tough, and for some tougher than for others, to get up the courage necessary to go to a person we have wronged and admit we were wrong and ask for forgiveness. Part of the process of reconciliation. As believers we have no choice, if we want to be obedient to God and used by God, but to act swiftly and completely.

Are you concerned enough that your worship with God will be pleasing and acceptable to Him, to take the necessary action to reconcile the issues in your life with those who have been affected by your actions? Remember what someone once said: An offense against your neighbor is a fence between you and God.

God, according to Paul who wrote in II Corinthians 5:18, has called us as believers to proclaim the gospel of reconciliation to others. Sinners alone cannot decide to participate in the realities that Paul is speaking of. We as believers must be there to proclaim the gospel to those who are looking for God.

TODAY'S WORD FOR OCTOBER 24

GENEROUS

Only they would that we should remember the poor. Galatians 2:10

And though I bestow all my goods to feed the poor, and though I give my body to be burned, and have not charity, it profited me nothing. I Corinthians 13:3

As believers how are we to be generous to others? God is a generous God who has given us everything we need and He expects us to be generous to others.

Giving to the poor and the needy was a mandate given by God to Moses which he in turn gave to the Israelites. At harvest time the Israelites were to leave the edges of their fields un-harvested to provide food for the needy.

In Galatians 2:10 we read when Paul was beginning his ministry as an apostle to the Gentiles, the apostles James, Peter and John instructed him to remember the poor. In Ephesians 4:28 Paul advises that we do something useful with our hands so we are able to have something to share with those in need.

In Proverbs 25:21 we are told to feed our enemies if they are hungry. We are not inclined to be generous to our enemies and to do so is most difficult. Jesus tells us to love our enemies and do good to them as we are told in Luke 6:35.

In Philippians chapter four, Paul thanks the church at Philippi for their generosity in sending him aid when he was in need. In verse 18 Paul says gifts to God's servants are "a fragrant offering, an acceptable sacrifice pleasing to God."

As believers we are not only expected, but commanded by our Lord to be generous to the poor and needy, to our enemies, and to God's servants.

Our parents trained us and constantly reminded us that God wanted us to be generous in helping the poor, the needy, our enemies and those who were God's servants. Our parents practiced what they preached to us. They were generous in their giving and this served as a great example to us. Just as God instructed Moses to teach the Israelites to be generous we must teach our children to be generous. Children are naturally inclined to be selfish. They must be taught to be generous.

The scripture gives us some guidelines on being generous. When we give we are to give in love. Love for the Lord and love for others should be what motivates our acts of generosity (I Corinthians 13:3). We are to give cheerfully because God loves a cheerful giver as recorded in II Corinthians 9:7. In Acts 11:29 we are first required to be generous to the poor and give according to our ability. If God has blessed us with time, talent or treasures we are to share with the needy, the poor, and our enemies and with those who serve Him in the ministry.

In Hebrews 13:16 we are told when we give with sacrifice, God is well pleased. In Acts 20:35, Paul tells us when we are generous to others we will be blessed by God. Proverbs 11:25 says being generous to others, enriches us and in I Timothy 6:17-19 we are told we will be rewarded.

TODAY'S WORD FOR OCTOBER 25

SUFFERING

For to you it has been granted on behalf of Christ, not only to believe in Him, but also to suffer for His sake. Philippians 1:29

Is anyone among you suffering? Let him pray. Is anyone cheerful? Let him sing Psalms. James 5:13

Many people in our world today are suffering because they are Christians and they are still standing firm in their faith. God is honoring these dear people and we pray for them daily. We see reports of churches being bombed, pastors being martyred, families being tortured, all because of their stand for their Lord.

We all can see families who are suffering for their faith in God right here in America. They are being ridiculed at their workplace because of their faith. Some are losing jobs because they live by Godly standards and will not compromise their Christian values in order to keep their job.

Children are being persecuted at their schools. It is heart breaking when a child going to school has to suffer because he or she has biblical standards and wants to live by them and is told they cannot. Praying and reading the Bible is forbidden today in primary schools. Teaching in our colleges and universities is anti-God.

There is tremendous suffering around our world and the scripture has a great deal to say to help us understand and to cope with suffering.

Jesus suffered so we can have eternal life. He suffered for us by dying on the cross to pay the penalty for our sins. Jesus, in His suffering, set an example for us to follow when we are faced with suffering for Him while we are on this earth preparing to spend an eternity with Him.

Having to suffer is not easy. The author of Hebrews understands this. He is writing to believers whom he knew had endured suffering and would most likely have to continue to endure suffering for their faith. He encourages these believers in Hebrews 10:32 to persevere by thinking about how their faith had enabled them to endure in times of suffering in the past. Again the author of Hebrews says in Hebrews 10:32 to those who had suffered for Jesus: "But recall the former days in which, after you were illuminated (accepted Jesus as Savior), you endured a great struggle with sufferings." For centuries, some have faced a great struggle as they suffered for the cause of Christ and Christians will continue to suffer until Christ returns. We must persevere for the cause of Christ in spite of suffering.

In the verse from Philippians above, Paul reminds us that in Christ we have a responsibility to suffer for Jesus. James tells us we should respond by praying when we are suffering. God will give us the strength, by praying, to get through every crisis. He will comfort and encourage our hearts. No matter what our suffering is, there is joy in the Lord that brings cheer to our lives. James tells us when we are cheerful, when we are suffering or not, we are to sing praises to God.

TODAY'S WORD FOR OCTOBER 26

FALSE TEACHERS

Beware of dogs, beware of evil workers. Philippians 3:2

Paul continues to warn the believers in the church at Philippi, just as he is warning us, to guard ourselves against false teachers by rejoicing in the Lord and by reading the scriptures daily and living by them. Paul was constantly facing false teachers who were savage in their attacks on him.

Paul tells us to be aware of false teachers who act like dogs. Both Jews and Gentiles of his day called each other dogs as a term of contempt. The word dog was the lowest title possible to convey contempt and ridicule. Dog refers to wild dogs that roamed the forests day and night. They were scavengers who could be vicious and dangerous.

Paul refers to false teachers just like wild dogs. They seek out all who will listen and consume them with their false teachings. When one responds to them defending their true belief in God they will snarl and become vicious and do all they can to destroy one's belief in the truth. In Matthew 7:15, Jesus tells us to beware of false teachers that come to us in sheep's clothing. These are whom Paul is talking about.

Secondly, Paul tells us to beware of false teachers who are evil workers. There were some people in the churches at that time who were teaching that the Gentiles had to be circumcised and keep the Jewish laws as part of salvation. These are people who hold to and teach high standards of righteousness, morality and religion. They are absolutely sure their righteousness and good deeds are what makes them acceptable to God. They think there is no way God would reject them.

Paul called them evil workers because they taught that it was by what we do through our own works that we come to God instead of by God's saving grace. Jesus died on the cross to offer His free gift of salvation. Any teaching that adds to God's plan of salvation by grace through faith is false teaching.

Paul also is referring to those who live and teach evil by the way they live and talk about morality, righteousness and religion. These types live immoral, indulgent and extravagant lives and do all they can to mix both a religious and indulgent lifestyle.

False teachers always oppose the Lord and His salvation by grace alone. By their actions they do not accept Jesus. They accept what they choose about His teaching, but deny or ignore salvation by His blood. Such false teachers are referred to by Paul as evil workers.

The Congress here in America has taken God out of the public schools. Children are not being taught about God, but they are being taught to be anti-God. Immorality, violence, sex, drugs, you name it, are all prevalent on school campuses today. Every parent must make it a priority to know what their children are being taught. You must teach your children to beware of false teachings and the evil doers on the school campuses. Parents must make it their business to know who their children are spending time with and what they are doing.

TODAY'S WORD FOR OCTOBER 27

THINK

For as a man thinks in his heart, so is he. Proverbs 23:7

We are often asked how to develop a Godly attitude in our daily living. Much of our actions and our desires are controlled by the way we think. Our thoughts motivate us to do the things we do. Many people we talk to have an inferior feeling due to fear that has come from sin in their life. They have a constant fear and want to overcome this fear.

Following are a few principles that if they become part of your daily thinking, they will motivate a change in your attitude from fear to faith. Allowing these principles to guide your daily thought process will soon help you to develop a positive Godly mental attitude.

Here are eight constructive suggestions you can think about daily and apply to your life as necessary:

Today I will think like a dynamic servant of God because as the scripture says (above), I am what I think.

I am not always what I think I am; I am what I think.

I am not what I eat; I am what I think.

Clothes do not make the man or woman; thinking makes the man or woman.

I will keep my thought processes active and open to the voice of God.

God did not call me to a life of failure, but to a life of success.

I cannot fail as long as I do His will. I will allow Him to work in and through me today, motivating my every thought.

Because my God is a great God, I will think with confidence on every issue that comes my way knowing that my thoughts never can be greater than my God's.

Make your commitment today to think like a dynamic servant of God. A dynamic servant of God thinks by faith and not with fear. You think by choice. You can think good or you can think evil. It is your choice, but remember you cannot have it both ways by thinking good and evil at the same time. We really have two ways to think, the righteous way or the unrighteous way.

In Isaiah 55:8-9 it reads: "For my thoughts are not your thoughts, nor are your ways My ways," says the Lord. "For as the heavens are higher than the earth, so are My ways higher than your ways, and My thoughts than your thoughts." When you really want to work at your thinking process remember to keep your thinking focused on the Word of God and open to the voice of God. Learn to listen for God's voice.

TODAY'S WORD FOR OCTOBER 28

FATHERS

Honor you father and mother, which is the first commandment with promise: that it may be well with you and you may live long on the earth. Ephesians 6:2

We exhorted, and comforted, and charged every one of you, as a father does his own children. I Thessalonians 2:11

Fathers are needed and wanted for much more than financial help today. A big concern is that over 50% of our homes do not have a father. The verse above from I Thessalonians is primarily directed to church leaders, but Paul talks about how their role is similar to a father's role in the family. He says, "You know how we exhorted and comforted, and charged every one of you, as a father does his own children."

It is not enough for fathers to think all they need to do is to bring home a pay check. Children and spouses need their love and encouragement. Nothing is more important to children than to have a father to listen and talk with them and to console and comfort them when they are hurting.

The word charged in this verse means to affirm. Fathers need to challenge their children by affirming the truth of God's Word as they live it out day by day. Good fathers reflect their heavenly Father. What we need today is for more fathers who know Jesus, to be spiritual leaders in their homes and to be there for their children to support, comfort and encourage them.

In Ephesians 6:2 Paul quotes the fifth commandment of the Ten Commandments which reads, "Honor your Father and your Mother." In Matthew 15:4 Jesus also quoted this commandment. This is not a commandment to be ignored, although it often is. What does God mean by "honor?" To honor our parents is more than just obeying our parents. It means to respect them, to love them, and to care for them.

Far too often we hear about children who are dishonoring their parents by talking back to them and showing continual disrespect for them. The nursing homes are filled with fathers and mothers who are never visited by their children. Fathers and mothers have the responsibility, first of all, to be the kind of parents children can respect, and then they must teach their children to honor and obey them.

But let us remind you that God never gave a condition as to when we should honor our father and mother. He stated it simply and clearly, "Honor your Father and Mother." If they abused you, you must still honor them. If they were unkind, you still must honor them. God never gave us any "ifs."

Yes, we know there are bad, even evil, parents in this world. A child may have to stand up against a parent who is leading him or her to do what is wrong. Even though a child's parents may not have earned the love or respect of their child, the mother and father are still the child's parents and the child should still honor them.

TODAY'S WORD FOR OCTOBER 29

REDEMPTION

For all have sinned and fall short of the glory of God, being justified freely by His grace through the redemption that is in Christ Jesus. Romans 3:23-24

Many people not only do not understand what redemption is, but do not know why they need redemption. So the question we want to answer is, "Why do we need redemption?"

The theme of the Bible is redemption. From Genesis to Revelation the Bible teaches the law of God has condemned us all, without exception, because as we read in Romans 3:23 (above) we have all sinned. By sinning we separate ourselves from God and miss the beauty of God's plan for our life. Because of our sinful nature we stand condemned and we need redemption. Because of the grace of God, He stands ready to rescue us from our sins and redeem us.

In the fourth chapter of Romans the apostle Paul speaks of three phases of redemption. They are justification, sanctification and glorification.

Paul illustrates the meaning of justification by saying that justification means that God gives us a right to stand before Him on the basis of the work of Christ, not because of anything we have done. Justification is God's act of declaring us not guilty. He wipes our record clean.

We can stand in God's presence because another One has died in our place to pay the penalty for our sins. Another One is available to meet our needs because we are incapable of pleasing God in our own strength or with our own shabby ideas of righteousness. Righteousness is not something we earn, but only comes to us when we accept the gift God gave us to pay our penalty for our sins.

Redemption also must include sanctification. Many believers stop with justification feeling all they need is an escape from going to hell. But Paul reminds us in Romans four, the necessity for all believers to be set apart for God and God's plan to deliver our soul, our mind, our emotions and our will from the control of our sinful nature. Being sanctified simply means that we as believers need to be dedicated to God or set apart for God.

And finally, when we are redeemed, it is God's plan for us to glorify Him through all of our words and actions. Nothing is more important for us today than to be certain we understand we all are born sinners and because we are sinners, we must pay the penalty for our sins. But God in His great mercy provided His Son to pay the penalty for our sins and for this we should glorify His name.

TODAY'S WORD FOR OCTOBER 30

PASSION

At one time we too were foolish, disobedient and deceived and enslaved by all kinds of passions and pleasures. We lived in malice and envy, being hated and hating one another. But when the kindness and love of God our Savior appeared He saved us, not because of righteous things we had done, but because of His mercy. Titus 3:3

Our children and grandchildren, for the most part, are sports enthusiasts. They not only play sports, but follow their favorite teams and players. Some get really involved at times and show "passion" for a certain player or team. Passion for our family in sports means at times great enthusiasm and even intense emotion.

In today's society the word "passion" usually refers to sensuality or sexuality. In Titus 3:3 (above) Paul tells us that passion for the sinful pleasures of this world enslave us. When we live for sensual gratification we become slaves to our sinful desires. Because of God's love and mercy He sent Jesus to free us from our slavery to sin. The meaning of passion is really an intense desire toward something or someone and can be applied to many areas of life. One place the word "passion" needs to appear is in the believer's life. We as believers should passionately seek to know the Lord Jesus Christ who saved us from our sins.

Even though our family has at times a passion for a sport or a team, it never overshadows our passion for our faith and our belief in Jesus. We are thrilled all of our children and grandchildren have put their faith in Jesus first.

When we claim to know someone, we often just mean that we have accumulated facts about the person or simply are aware of his or her existence. Unfortunately, too many Christians know Jesus in this superficial way. He is the world's Savior, the virgin-born Son of God who accepted death in our place and then rose again to sit at the Father's right hand according to the scriptures. Those are the facts, but just knowing these facts does not give a person the right to call themselves a Christian.

A believer in Jesus must not only know and accept these facts, but must with a passion accept Jesus into their heart to begin a daily relationship. One must become intimate with Jesus and this can only become a reality by daily opening the Word and making Jesus a reality in your life through the scriptures and then in prayer.

Studying God's Word is the essential first step to develop a passion for Christ. As we read the Bible we grow in understanding His ways and promises and see His great love for us. Our intimacy with Christ requires that we give Him our time to read His Word, talk to Him through prayer and listen for Him to speak.

Developing a passion for Jesus is not a one day affair, but a lifetime pursuit. This true passion will only become a reality in one's life when he or she will commit to lay aside everything that competes with one's devotion to their Lord and Savior. Fueling a passion for Christ brings the believer rewards as nothing else can.

As families today, we must develop a passion for our Lord and then we will have a deep passion for our spouse, children, parents and family.

TODAY'S WORD FOR OCTOBER 31

FOUNDATION

By the grace God has given me, I laid a foundation as an expert builder, and someone else is building on it. But each one should be careful how he builds. For no one can lay any foundation other than the one already laid which is Jesus Christ. 1 Corinthians 3: 10-11

The foundation of our faith as believers is Jesus Christ. We must continue to build our faith using high quality materials that meet God's standards. In the above verse from 1 Corinthians, Paul is writing to the church he founded in Corinth. Paul says he laid the foundation, but they, the people in the church, had not been building their faith properly. The new believers in the church were being undermined by the immorality that prevailed in Corinth.

Paul addresses them as babes in Christ because they are still worldly. Paul had carefully laid the right foundation, but the believers were not using the right building blocks of sound doctrine that Paul had taught them.

Many sincere professing Christians are spiritually starving, or spiritually ill, because they never have thought seriously about the quality of their Bible study.

If our physical diet is not in proper balance or if our digestive system is not functioning properly then our bodies will decline in health. Similarly, if we do not or cannot take full advantage of the spiritual food offered us in the Bible, we will become spiritually disabled.

Someone who is starving spiritually and not growing in their Christian way of life must regularly eat nourishing spiritual food which is the Word of God. All those who accept Jesus as their Savior have the one and only foundation for their faith. As Paul tells us in verse 11 above, there is no other foundation. As you study God's Word we recommend these important foundations for your spiritual growth.

First we must know what the Bible says about itself. Psalm 19:7 says that the law of the Lord is perfect. The Bible declares itself to be the Word of God.

Secondly, we must know what God intended the Bible to do for us. The Bible says in Genesis 1:1 — In the beginning God. The Bible is the only book from God, but also the only book about God and our guidebook for living.

Thirdly, the Bible stands above all human opinions. In John 10:4-5 we read about Jesus being our true Shepherd. Jesus tells about the shepherd who brings out his own sheep and goes before them and the sheep follow him because they know his voice. We must let the Word of God shape our opinions and then we will follow our Lord because we will know His voice.

We should know that the Bible deals in facts. In Colossians 2:8 we read to "beware lest anyone cheat you through philosophy and empty deceit, according to the tradition of men or according to the basic principles of the world and not according to the laws of Christ." We need to build our foundation in God's Word and to learn workable methods of Bible study and know how to use Bible commentaries.

TODAY'S WORD FOR NOVEMBER 1

CONTENT

Not that I speak in regard to need, for I have learned in whatever state I am, to be content. Philippians 4:11

Now godliness with contentment is great gain. For we brought nothing into this world, and it is certain we can carry nothing out. I Timothy 6:6-7

The apostle Paul wrote the two verses above, one to the church at Philippi and one to Timothy, to help them understand the true meaning of contentment and how to find it. Paul was well educated and held an esteemed position as a Pharisee, yet he willingly gave it all up to serve his Lord and Savior and preach the message of salvation to the multitudes. As a result he lived a hard life traveling from place to place, with no home and often without food, and suffering great persecution.

So why was he able to write that he could be content in all circumstances? It was because he had learned to rely on God for his contentment. As believers we need to rely on the Lord for contentment as Paul did. When God is blessing us with abundance we are to be content in Him. When we are in a state of crises we are to be content in Him. This is a difficult principle to learn but this is what God wants of us as believers and children of God. It is always easy to be content when all is going well but most difficult in a time of crisis.

We see people all around us today looking for contentment. Many find contentment in spending every moment of their free time sitting in a chair, eating food and watching the television or surfing the web on the computer. When the cable or the computer goes out they get frustrated and there goes there contentment.

There are others that are content only when they are working and making money. For others contentment is going places or doing "fun" things. These things are very temporal and do not bring contentment that satisfies for very long.

When we focus on what we don't have instead of all the good things we do have we will be discontent. Discontentment is Satan's way of drawing us away from the Lord. Eve had everything she needed in the Garden of Eden and she was content until she met Satan. Satan made her question her contentment by calling her attention to the one thing she didn't have. She yielded to Satan's temptation and ate the forbidden fruit. When we follow Satan and turn from the Lord we will know nothing but discontent.

As Paul said, "We brought nothing into this world and it is certain that we will carry nothing out." Whatever we have has been given to us from God. When we are thankful for what we have we will be content in whatever state we are in.

We have no control over crises that we may face like earthquakes, floods, hurricanes, civil wars or other disasters. God has a reason that He allows us to go through these situations. We may find ourselves in circumstances we are not content to be in, but God will protect us and bless us if we stay true to Him.

TODAY'S WORD FOR NOVEMBER 2

HOSPITALITY

Do not forget to entertain strangers, for by so doing some have unwittingly entertained angels. Hebrews 13:2

Share with God's people who are in need. Practice hospitality. Romans 12:13

When you read travel magazines and newspaper real estate adds you notice offers for travelers to rent a bedroom in a local family home. When you look up on the internet for such services you will notice one program founded by Casey Fenton has well over 250,000 homes available with bedrooms to rent. Many people across America open their home to offer hospitality to travelers.

This service sounds a little like biblical hospitality. In the verse above the writer of Hebrews instructed believers to practice hospitality and at the same time share their faith in Jesus Christ. This was defined by the early Christ followers as acts of generosity towards strangers.

When Paul talked about practicing hospitality he did not mean merely to entertain new friends but to pursue the love of strangers. In New Testament times, travel was dangerous and Inns were evil, scarce and expensive. So the early believers would open their homes to travelers, especially to fellow believers.

The writer of Hebrews when he wrote the verse we have put above, was encouraging believers to open their homes, despite possible persecution, because one never knows how far-reaching an act of kindness might be. The writer reminds the believers that their guests may be a spy or an evil person but God can protect them with angels. The important point is to share their beliefs with the travelers.

In the first century, hospitality often included housing a guest. This was hardest to do during days that Christians were being persecuted. Believers who offered this hospitality would not know if the guest was a spy or fellow believer. But the writer of Hebrews was suggesting that when they hosted a guest they well could be inviting a blessing into their home.

In today's world things are much different. We have hotels, motels and guest houses for people who travel. Also because of the great evil in the world offering a room in your house to someone you do not know could bring one who will bring disaster into your home. As God's people, we are called to be hospitable to others as part of our gratitude for the salvation we have received from God.

Times have changed from that first century but you can show hospitality today by helping a person in need, giving encouragement to the lonely, praying for the sick and much more. People who have a heart for God have a heart for people. As we have opportunity we as believers must make ourselves available to those who are in need of Christ-like love and kindness. The apostle Paul reminds us of the words spoken by Jesus, "It is more blessed to give than to receive." Acts 20:35

TODAY'S WORD FOR NOVEMBER 3

ALONE

I lie awake, and am like a sparrow alone on the housetop. Psalm 102:7

The Psalmist in the verse we have above is expressing that he is feeling like a solitary bird thinking that he has been abandoned by both God and man. These are the thoughts of an afflicted man that feels completely alone and feels that no one cares, not even God.

The writer of this Psalm is unknown but it is apparent that it was written when he was going through a troubled time in his life. Psalm 102 tells us that he was in great distress, so much so that he couldn't eat and he couldn't sleep. When we are in great distress we often feel deserted and that no one understands. This is how the Psalmist felt.

In verse 7 (above) he pictures himself as just a little sparrow all alone on a housetop. He feels so insignificant that he wasn't sure God even saw him or heard him. He cries out to God and asks God not to hide His face from him and to turn His ear to him. As he prays for God's help he feels reassured that God still sits on His throne and that He will respond to the prayer of the destitute.

Every day we receive emails from people that read our devotionals that share with us that they are distressed, frustrated and feeling helpless and alone, just as the Psalmist did. Being alone can be devastating for most people because they have literally no support in this life and have no one to turn to for support. They are truly lonely and alone. Loneliness usually leads to depression and the feeling that no one cares. We can, however, be assured that God cares and that He understands.

Just think how alone Jesus must have felt hanging alone on the cross. He cried out to God, "Why hast thou forsaken Me?" He endured separation from His Father in order to pay the penalty for our sins. Yes, because of God's great love for us, He sent Jesus all alone to the cross. Both Jesus and God, our Father, understand what it meant to be alone.

When you, as a believer in Jesus, begin to feel alone you have comfort that an unbeliever does not have. Knowing that you are a child of God, you have Jesus to turn to in prayer and you have the assurance that He is right by your side to comfort you and to encourage you. Those that do not know Jesus as their Savior are truly alone when they face struggles and loneliness.

Do you lie awake at night feeling like a sparrow all alone on the rooftop? Or do you lie down and sleep in peace because you have put your trust in the Lord? It is the Lord alone, nobody else or nothing else, who brings peace and allows us to dwell in safety.

TODAY'S WORD FOR NOVEMBER 4

GENTLE

See, your king comes to you gentle and riding on a donkey. Matthew 21:5

Take My yoke upon you and learn from Me, for I am gentle and lowly in heart, and you will find rest for your souls. Matthew 11:29

One of the characteristics of Jesus is that He is gentle. Matthew describes Jesus' triumphal entry into Jerusalem as the coming of a gentle king. Kings are usually tyrants and arrogant and war-like. Jesus is the opposite. He is gentle, humble and peaceful. Jesus is depicted as a shepherd and a shepherd gently leads his sheep and carries the lambs that need help. He never forcefully drives his sheep.

The prophet Isaiah tells of the coming of the Lord and in Isaiah 40:11 says "He will feed His flock like a Shepherd; He will gather His lambs with His arm, and carry them close to His heart, and gently lead those who have young." How comforting and encouraging to know that we have a gentle Savior who not only leads us in the right path but when the going gets hard He lifts us up and carries us close to His heart.

During Jesus' ministry on earth parents sought to bring their small children to Jesus for His blessing. The disciples tried to stop them, thinking that children were too insignificant to take up the time of Jesus and interrupt His ministry. Jesus rebuked the disciples and gently and tenderly called the children to come to Him, saying to His disciples, "Let the little children come to me, and do not hinder them, for the kingdom of God belongs to such as these." (Luke 18:15-16). Our gentle Savior invites all to come to Him.

The traits of power and strength are what people are most likely to respect and strive for. Gentleness is the trait that Jesus wants us to strive for. Jesus set the example for us. Jesus was gentle not only to those He had a close relationship with but to all. In Matthew 11:29 Jesus calls us to "learn from Me, for I am gentle and humble in heart."

Gentleness is demonstrated by showing consideration for others and by treating others with kindness. Paul tells us in Philippians 4:5 to "Let your gentleness be evident to all."

In II Timothy 2:24, Paul has this instruction for Christians: "A servant of the Lord must not quarrel but be gentle to all, able to teach and be patient." The scripture also reminds us that we need wisdom as given to us from God which is pure, peaceable and gentle. James 3:17.

In Proverbs 15:1 it tells us that a gentle or kind answer turns away wrath, but a harsh word stirs up anger. Our challenge to you today is to be gentle in your speech and treat people with consideration and kindness. It will make you a blessing to others and you will get a response from those who know you that will bless you.

TODAY'S WORD FOR NOVEMBER 5

STORMS

For you have been strength to the poor and a refuge from the storm. Isaiah 25:4

Life is much like sailing on a stormy sea. We feel we have no control and our very life is at the mercy of the waves. There is no choice but to ride out the storm.

We all will have to go through storms. Today, you may be in the midst of a storm in your life. Even though we as believers have our trust in the Lord, we all have many storms in our life. It might be a storm in your relationship with your spouse or a family member. It may be with a friend or a neighbor. Or it might be a financial crisis or even a health problem.

God does not cause these storms but He allows them for several reasons. Today let us take a few minutes and look at possible reasons and apply them to our lives.

God often allows storms to come into our lives to get our attention. We get so busy with the "THINGS" in our lives that we get caught up in just doing what we want to do and forget God. When we neglect to honor God as Lord of our life, we will rely on our own abilities and think we can handle every situation ourselves. When we get puffed up with pride God will allow a storm to happen in our lives to get our attention and help us refocus our relationship with Him.

God may use a storm in order to get sin out of our lives. God wants us to live a pure and clean life and since we are sinners we often fail to meet the standards that God wants from us. God will allow a storm to enter our lives to act as a warning. The longer you continue in that sin the stronger the storm will be.

God may allow a storm in our life because He wants us to surrender something. It is so easy in life to let a wrong relationship or obsession get between us and God. Success often separates us from God, and even "THINGS" can separate us from God. When He wants us to surrender something in our lives, He will make it clear to us and if we do not respond He will allow a storm to come to give us a wake-up call.

God is in control, not us, if we are willing to surrender all to God, He will not only go through the storm with us but He will bring us safely through it. When we successively weather a storm by taking refuge in the Lord and relying on the strength of His mighty hand, we will come out a stronger person with a deeper faith.

In Romans 12:1-2 Paul tells us that God can use a storm to conform us to His image. Paul goes on to tell us that God wants us to present our bodies as a living sacrifice which is Holy and acceptable to God and that we are not to be conformed to this world but He wants us transformed by the renewing of our mind so that we may prove what is that good and acceptable and perfect will of God for our lives.

God can use a storm to equip us to serve Him better. The storms we go through enables us to help others when they go through a storm. If we feel that we cannot accomplish what He wants us to do, we are reminded by a storm coming into our lives that He is ready to equip us to do the job He wants from us.

TODAY'S WORD FOR NOVEMBER 6

BLAMELESS

He whose walk is blameless and who does what is righteous. Psalm 15:2

One of the most difficult requirements Jesus asks of believers is to live a blameless life. Only our Lord is blameless because He is without any sin. The scripture is very clear that God expects us to work constantly on living a blameless life.

David exhorts us in the verse above to walk blameless and do what is righteous. To be blameless in our walk we must do what is right in God's sight and live moral lives that honor Him.

Believers in Jesus need to work daily on the goal of being blameless before our Lord. What do we need to do to be blameless in the evil world we live in today? In Psalm 15 David gives us nine standards for living a blameless life. He wrote, speak the truth, do not slander others, do not reproach (scold) our neighbor, reject evil people, do not cast a slur on others, honor those who fear God, keep your oaths, lend your money without usury and do not accept bribes.

Moses was talking to the children of Israel (Deuteronomy 18: 9-13) telling them when they entered the Promised Land they were not to live lives like their neighbors. The neighbors were pagans and the Israelites would face many temptations to join in their evil ways. The evil ways of the pagan Canaanites were based on the occult. Satan is the origin and the promoter of the occult. Moses told the children of Israel that they must not get involved with these evil practices because they were detestable to the Lord. God would hold them accountable for their actions. .

Today we as Christians also live in a wicked godless society. Occult practices are very prevalent in our world today. Parents must be alert to what is and who is influencing their children. The occult is intriguing but it is also very dangerous. Remember Satan is behind the occult. As parents we have the responsibility to teach our children to obey God's Word so they will understand how to live a blameless life and do what is right.

God did not want the children of Israel to follow the evil ways of their world and God does not want us to follow the evil ways of our world. God expects us to be blameless before the Lord. We all need to take a look back on our last 48 hours. Have we lived a life that could be considered blameless by God? Where have we missed it or broken down. Was it an action, a word or a deed?

The apostle Paul was praying for the people in the church at Thessalonica (I Thessalonians 3:13) when he prayed, "So that He (Jesus) may establish your hearts blameless in holiness before our God and Father at the coming of the Lord Jesus Christ with all His saints." Peter tells us in II Peter 2:14, referring to the coming again of Christ that we should be steadfast and strong in our commitment and beliefs. And we are to "look forward and be diligent to be found by Him in peace, without spot and blameless."

TODAY'S WORD FOR NOVEMBER 7

HELPER

Rejoice always, pray without ceasing, in everything give thanks, for this is the will of God in Christ Jesus for you. Do not quench the Spirit. I Thessalonians 5:16-19

And I will pray the Father, and He will give you another Helper, that He may abide with you forever. John 14:16

Have you ever wished you could have a 911 number that rang in heaven so you could call whenever you needed help with a situation or a crisis? We want to remind you that we all have, as believers, divine assistance that is even closer than a phone call. Our helper dwells within us and we know Him as the Holy Spirit. The problem is that many people today are unaware that He is available for us. Others fail to call on Him because they do not want to admit they need help. We miss so many opportunities to benefit from the greatest asset in our Christian life, the presence of the Holy Spirit.

Jesus knew when He left this earth, that His disciples would be totally inadequate to handle the task that Jesus was giving them. He knew they would need supernatural help and so would we. So He gave us the Holy Spirit who comes to our aid, empowers our service and transforms our lives from inside out. (John 14:16 above)

The Holy Spirit is a personal helper. He is a member of the Trinity and coequal with both the Father and Jesus Christ. He is a practical helper who involves Himself in every aspect of our lives. He convicts of sin and calls us to repentance (John 16:8). He guides us into all truth (John 16:9). The Holy Spirit helps us know the truth of the message of Jesus Christ and He helps us discern what is right and what is wrong. The Holy Spirit enables us to align our will with our Father's will so that we will receive God's best.

The Holy Spirit helps us with our prayer life if we involve Him. He burdens us to pray. The Spirit convicts by giving a strong sense that we need to pray. He does this because He may know we need strength because of a present difficulty or situation. The Holy Spirit also intercedes for us. Have you been in situations where sorrow or helplessness overwhelms you and you find it impossible to know what you ought to pray for. The Holy Spirit understands the depth of our thoughts, feelings and needs and He translates them into effective supplication according to God's will and intercedes for us before God's throne of grace. The Spirit helps in our weakness and even if we do not know how to pray the Spirit Himself intercedes for us with groans that words cannot express. Romans 8:26.

TODAY'S WORD FOR NOVEMBER 8

PEACE

Christ in you, the hope of glory. Colossians 1:27

Be anxious about nothing, but in everything, by prayer and thanksgiving, present your requests to God. And the peace of God, which transcends all understanding, will guard your hearts and your minds in Christ Jesus. Philippians 4:6-7

All of the restlessness of our times might be understood as an attempt by believers in Jesus to acquire the right things in the wrong way. There are essentially three things that believers desire, righteousness, peace and joy. Because our understanding is warped by sin, our search for these things gets skewed.

John F. Kennedy, former President of the United States said, "The absence of war is not the same thing as peace." Even when our society has enjoyed so called peace, there is often a sense of national tension, unease, and dissatisfaction. As a people, most of the time, we are not at peace with each other nor even with ourselves. This is because we seek peace in the wrong places and in the wrong ways.

For example, many people are dissatisfied with themselves because they feel they must have more than they have. It leads them to seek money, fame, or a higher standard of living as the key to having peace of mind, yet the more they get the more they want. One will never come to the place where he or she knows and has peace.

God gives believers a different peace, the peace that passes all understanding. This is what the apostle Paul wrote to us in the book of Philippians (above verse).

It is not what is out there in the world that gives us peace. It is Jesus Christ dwelling within us that brings peace as described by Paul in Colossians 1:27.

The song writer Edward Bickersteth wrote it beautifully in, "Peace, perfect peace." He wrote two lines in every verse. The first line ends with a question mark and the second line answers the question. Read carefully his words:

Peace, perfect peace, in this dark world of sin? The blood of Jesus whispers peace within.

Peace, perfect peace, by thronging duties pressed? To do the will of Jesus, this is rest.

Peace, perfect peace, with sorrows searching round? On Jesus' bosom naught but calm is found.

Peace, perfect peace, our future all unknown? Jesus we know and He is on the throne.

Peace, perfect peace, death shadowing us and ours? Jesus has vanquished death and all its powers.

Only the peace that Jesus gives will last for eternity.

TODAY'S WORD FOR NOVEMBER 9

GLADNESS

Serve the Lord with gladness. Psalm 100:2

You have put gladness in my heart. Psalm 4:7

Those who serve the Lord with a sad face, because for some reason they are unhappy about something, really are not serving Him at all. This type of person brings to the spiritual table a form of bowing down to God and seemingly worshipping Him, but their words and deeds do not show a love for their Lord in everyday living with true gladness and service.

Our God is a God of love and He wants no slaves to grace His throne. In God's sight a slave is one that has not given his or her heart to the Lord. Thus there is no true gladness showing from their heart each day. This type of person will continually show sadness on their face because they are carrying the heavy burden of their world on their back. God has His servants dressed in joy and gladness not with sadness. The angels serve Him with joy not with groans. A murmur or a sigh would be a mutiny in the ranks of the angels. The Lord looks at the heart and He can see that obedience that is forced and not voluntary is really disobedience.

Our service to God coupled with gladness and cheerfulness is true heart service and is what God wants from us. Cheerfulness and gladness is the support God gives us for our faith in the Lord. In the joy of the Lord we are strong. The joy of the Lord in our lives acts as a remover of difficulties. It is like what oil is to the wheels of a railroad car. Without oil the axle gets hot and accidents occur. We need the gladness and cheerfulness of the Lord in our lives. These act to oil our wheels. The man who is cheerful in his service to God shows the people of the world, non-believers, that it is a delight and joy to serve the Lord our God.

We encourage you first to take time to make sure you are doing all that God wants you to do by serving Him with gladness. Then take a few moments each day and look at the faces of those around you in the work place, your school, your neighborhood and even your church. You will see so many sad faces of concern. The least you can do is to pause a moment and ask God to give that person a heart of gladness. When you do this you will be surprised at the doors God will open for you to say a word of encouragement to someone.

You will soon find out as people talk to you the heavy burdens they are carrying. And most important your gladness will be increased and God will give you blessings beyond your most hoped for desire.

TODAY'S WORD FOR NOVEMBER 10

FAVORITISM

My brothers, as believers in our Lord Jesus Christ, don't show favoritism. James 2:1

Genesis 27 contains an ugly portrait of parental favoritism. This kind of favoritism is prevalent in families today. We read in this chapter that Isaac favored Esau and Rebecca, Isaac's wife, favored Jacob. Romans chapter 9 points out to us that even before Jacob and Esau were born God chose Jacob to carry on the covenant line of Abraham. God had also informed Isaac and Rebecca that "the older will serve the younger" (Genesis25:23).

Although Rebecca was well aware of God's promise, she would not refrain from allowing her feelings of favoritism toward Jacob to motivate her to take action. She schemed with Jacob to deceive Isaac, who was nearly blind, by disguising Jacob as Esau so that Isaac would give the blessing that was to be given to the first-born to Jacob instead of Esau. Rebecca's scheming to advance Jacob was both foolish and wrong. She was wrong to resort to deceit and make her son, Jacob part of it. She was foolish to think that God needed her help to accomplish His purpose and fulfill His promises. God does not need our help in carrying out His plans.

We ask you this question regarding this biblical account: Who was at fault, the parents or the children? Rebecca had no reason to lie and cheat to gain what she wanted. In choosing deceit, Rebecca so provoked Esau's hostility that Jacob, her favorite, was forced to flee and leave home. All that her conniving did was to divide the family and deprive her of her son for twenty years. The lesson we can learn from this is that "Ends never justify adopting sinful means."

To complete the story it is recorded in Genesis 27:33 that Isaac realized he had been tricked concerning his inheritance. He favored Esau, but he also knew that God had chosen Jacob. Nevertheless, Isaac tried to meddle with God's promise for Jacob. Isaac intended that Esau should have the blessing. When Isaac knew what had happened he began to shake violently, because he realized that he had tried to change God's plan but God had intervened to prevent it. So Isaac submitted to God's will and confirmed his blessing upon Jacob. Isaac could not change what had been done even though Esau asked for a blessing of his own. It is the parent's responsibility to counsel and guide their children in doing what is right.

As parents we need to treat all of our children equally and not show favoritism. Every child needs to be reassured that he or she is loved and valued for who he or she is. Children need to respond to parents the same way. Favoritism never works out for the good.

Have you ever considered how fortunate we are that God does not show favoritism? He sent His Son to die for all of us, no matter whom we are or how good or bad we are. He offers His gift of salvation to all who believe.

TODAY'S WORD FOR NOVEMBER 11

RESURRECTION

Jesus said to her, I am the resurrection and the life. He who believes in Me, though he may die, he shall live. And whoever lives and believes in Me shall never die. Do you believe this? John 11:25-26

These verses, we have written above, were words given by Jesus to Martha when Jesus went to Bethany four days after Lazarus died. He asked her if she believed and Martha responded saying that she did believe that Jesus was the Christ, the Son of God.

With this statement Jesus moved Martha from an abstract belief in the resurrection that will take place to a personalized trust in Him who alone can raise the dead. No resurrection or eternal life exists outside of the Son of God. Time is no barrier to the One who has the power of resurrection and life, for He can give life at anytime.

It was on a Friday over 2000 years ago that Jesus died on the cross to pay the penalty for our sins. He died for you and for us. He died so that we did not have to pay the penalty for our sins because we are all born as sinners and if we are to have eternal life in heaven with God we have to pay the penalty for the sins we have committed. All we have to do is repent of our sins, ask God for forgiveness, and then accept Jesus as our Savior and live for Him. We will then spend an eternity with Him in heaven.

In three days after His death on the cross we read of the Resurrection of Jesus. This resurrection of our Lord is what makes Christianity different from all other religions. The bodies of all the other religious leaders down through the centuries remain in their tombs. Jesus left an empty tomb. Jesus did what he said He would. He did rise from that grave and then about 40 days later, after He appeared to enough people to confirm His resurrection, He went back to Heaven and today is preparing a place for us to spend eternity with Him.

If for some reason you do not believe there was a resurrection you are saying Jesus is a liar and a hoax. If you believe Jesus did not rise from the dead you believe He has no power over death and thus no power to pay the penalty for your sins, which is death. Paul says in 1 Corinthians 15:14 that if Christ is not risen, then our preaching is useless and your faith is also useless. In verse 17, Paul goes on to say that if Christ is not risen that your faith is futile and you are still in your sins.

Those who are still in their sins cannot avoid God's judgment. We are asked in Hebrews 2:3, "How shall we escape if we ignore such a great a salvation?"

We urge you to make today the greatest day of your life. If you have not accepted the risen Jesus as your Savior, then do it now. If you have accepted Jesus as your savior make today and everyday a day of great celebration knowing that because of the resurrection of Jesus you will spend an eternity with Him in heaven.

TODAY'S WORD FOR NOVEMBER 12

EXPECTATION

My soul, wait silently for God alone, for my expectation is from Him. Psalms 62:5

We can remember so many times when we have experienced expectation in our lives. Our first such experience together was the year prior to our wedding. We were busy planning and working and lived 2000 miles apart but the expectation of our soon to be wedding grew day by day. Then the expectation of the birth of all six of our children was exciting. We experienced both quick births and long ordeals. In fact Dottie was in the hospital for 10 days, after our first child was born, and we both experienced the possible expectation of even death. But God answered our prayers as well as the prayers of many others and the expectation that we anticipated before our son's birth became a very positive reality.

There are exciting expectations and sad expectations in life. When you have people around you that you love like spouses, parents, children, grandparents and extended families then almost every day brings on new expectations, some happy and some sad. As the Psalmist says, in the above verse, the toughest part of expectation is the waiting.

Waiting on the Lord for His answer is very difficult at times. Together over the years we have asked God for direction and guidance and then we expected an immediate answer. But sometimes God made us wait and this was very difficult. Perhaps He needed to teach us patience or to better prepare our hearts for something. We have had to learn how important it is in God's sight for us to wait for His perfect timing. For us waiting has always allowed God to do something better through our lives.

It is the believer's privilege to say that my expectation is from Him (God). When we look to God for the supply of our wants, whether it is temporal or spiritual our expectation will not be in vain. We can look at our bank in heaven and receive our needs out of the riches of God's loving kindness. Our bank account with God can never be overdrawn.

Our Lord never fails to answer His promises and when we bring them to His throne through prayer, He never sends them back unanswered. Our problem is we forget to recognize when God answers He sometimes says "yes," sometimes "no," and sometimes, "wait." Therefore we need to learn to wait at His door and He will open the door according to His will.

Our greatest expectation in life is the expectation that one who believes in Jesus has in spending an eternity with our Lord. When that day comes, do you expect as you approach the heavenly gate to see the door open and hear the welcome invitation to come in to the kingdom prepared for you from the foundation of the world? Do you expect harps of gold and crowns of glory? Yes, one day we will see Him as He is. What is your expectation? We are waiting, excited and have great expectations of what God has for us in eternity.

TODAY'S WORD FOR NOVEMBER 13

BOASTFULNESS

In God we boast all day long, and praise Your name forever. Psalm 44:8

This is what the Lord says: Don't let the wise boast in their wisdom, or the powerful boast in their power, or the rich boast in their riches. For those who wish to boast should boast in this alone: that they truly know Me and understand that I am the Lord. Jeremiah 9:23

Most of us have met or know someone who is always boasting about something he or she has attained or accomplished. We have seen the rich flaunt their riches, the powerful brag about their power and the educated boast of their knowledge. Boasting may give a person a boost to their ego but boasting is not a positive trait. Boasting tends to drive a wedge in a relationship.

Occasionally we would hear one of our children boasting that they were better at something than another one of our children. This usually led to an argument about who really was best. We would often respond with something like, remember pride cometh before the fall.

I (Ken) remember some years ago a young man working in our warehouse at World Opportunities International. Constantly, day after day he was telling those he worked with and those from the inner city that came to our warehouse for food, story after story about some great accomplishment he had done the day before.

It did not take long for his peers and those that talked to him each day to find out that he was just a boaster and needed the attention. Most of the people we know who are boasters have very low self esteem and are very insecure.

The scripture tells us we should not boast about ourselves. There is only one way we should boast and that is to boast about our relationship with Jesus. People put a lot of value in riches, power, wisdom, knowledge, social status and appearance and they like to boast about them. These are all "things" that are temporary and can be taken away at any time. God does not value these "things" but what He does value is when we recognize that we know Him and love Him with all of our heart.

The opposite of a boasting person is a person who is humble. A humble person is not boastful about themselves but instead his boasting is in his relationship with Jesus. "Let him who boasts, boast in the Lord. For it is not the one that commends himself, who is approved, but the one whom the Lord commends." II Corinthians 10:17-18.

TODAY'S WORD FOR NOVEMBER 14

POSSESSIONS

For they did not gain possession of the land by their own sword, nor did their own arm save them; but it was Your right hand, Your arm, and the light of Your countenance, because You favored them. Psalm 44:3

But he was sad at this word, and went away sorrowful, and he had great possessions. Mark 10:22

We must realize in life that everything we have on this earth is because of God. He is the "owner" and all that we have is on loan to us. Possessions are "things" that God loans to us and He expects us to use these "things' to honor Him.

In Psalm 44:3 (above), the Psalmist recognizes the Children of Israel did not gain possession of the "Promised Land" by their own swords and arms or their own strength and might. They gained what God promised because God favored them and intervened to give them the victory in their conquest of the "Promised Land."

Most people we talk to do not understand this concept because they feel that their possessions are a result of their own abilities and hard work. Their possessions become a stumbling block in their relationship with the Lord. Possessions were in the way of the rich man that talked to Jesus, as recorded, in Mark 10:17-23. Jesus asked him to give his possessions to the poor so he could receive his treasure in heaven. He could not part with his possessions to gain the greatest possession of all.

In our travels we have visited many places where Kings and Queens, from thousands of years ago, had their most valuable possessions buried with them in their tombs. Today these possessions are still in their tombs, or museums nearby, for all to see. It is not in God's plan for one to take their possessions to eternity.

Many people work long hours today and spend money foolishly to acquire their goals so they can realize the "possessions" they have dreamed for. They do this at the expense of losing their spouses and family. How many people do you know who are captivated by a desire to have more and better possessions? Do you think they are really happy with what they have?

Our greatest possession in life today should be our personal relationship with God through His Son Jesus. Our second greatest possession should be our spouses and family. God will bless those that grasp this concept and honor Him in this way.

We remember a mother who lived in one of the poorest areas in the heart of Los Angeles. She had two children. One was mentally disabled and the other was in good health. She loved children and took six other children off the street and raised them in her very small home. Cathy had very few earthly possessions and had to make contact with our mission to receive food and other supplies weekly to feed these children. Cathy had her priorities right. She invested her time and energy to raising her "children" to love the Lord. She had very few earthly possessions because they were not important for her. She will receive her reward in heaven.

TODAY'S WORD FOR NOVEMBER 15

JUDGING

Judge not, that you be not judged. Matthew 7:1

Our law does not judge a man unless it first hears from him and knows what he is doing. **John 7:51**

What better way is there to tell people to mind their own business than by quoting what Jesus said, "Judge not, that you be not judged." Judging others happens especially among believers and non-believers. But if you read this seventh chapter of Matthew (verses 1-5) you will see what Jesus meant.

In these verses Jesus pulls no punches concerning the criticizer, the one who judges. In verse one Jesus says, do not judge and do not criticize. In verse two He says the criticizer will be judged. In verse three He mentions that the one who judges fails to examine himself.

In verse four Jesus says that the criticizer is deceived about himself when he judges others. In verse five Jesus calls the criticizer a hypocrite and in verse six He says the criticizer is undeserving of the gospel.

Take a moment and review all of the sins listed here by Jesus, committed by the criticizer. Christ says the criticizer will stand in the day of judgment guilty of inconsistency, self-righteousness, spiritual blindness, self deception, uncharitableness, lack of love, hypocrisy and abuse of the gospel.

The word judge means to criticize, condemn or censor. It is fault-finding and most often picky. But when someone thinks judging is necessary they often miss the point the scripture shares with us. When a person slips it is a time for compassion not censoring. It is time to reach out with a helping hand and not a time to use your hand and push one away. It is a time to speak kindly and encourage, not negatively or destructive.

Most people judge others because it boosts one's self image. It is simply enjoyed by the criticizer and makes one feel better than the other person. It allows one to justify their decisions at the expense of someone else's decisions. And unfortunately it is an outlet for one to hurt or show revenge to the one who possibly failed.

We should not judge, first, because the scripture tells us not to judge. Secondly, we do not know all the circumstances and facts. All people fall short and when we fall short we want someone to comfort us, to show compassion and to lend a helping hand.

God is our final judge and believers will be judged by the quality of fruit they produce. This fruit cannot be judged by earthly values but by heavenly values. Galatians 5:22 lists the fruits of the Spirit which are love, joy, peace, longsuffering, kindness, goodness and faithfulness.

TODAY'S WORD FOR NOVEMBER 16

CHASTISEMENT

My son, despise not the chastening of the Lord, neither be weary of His correction: for whom the Lord loves He corrects. Proverbs 3:11-12

As a man chastens his son, so the Lord thy God chastens thee. Deuteronomy 8:5

The word chastisement as used in the scriptures may be understood as correction. In the verses above from Proverbs, the author reminds us as children of God not to despise or get weary of the correction (chastisement) that God gives us.

In the verse from Deuteronomy we are reminded that God corrects us as do fathers who love their children. As children we did not like it when our parents corrected us even though they told us they corrected us because they loved us. We did not enjoy disciplining our children but we knew we must do so because we loved them and were concerned about them. This is a concept that most people do not understand today, both from the position of giving and receiving the correction.

Chastisement was designed by God to correct us, to prevent us from sinning and to bless us. In Jeremiah 24: 5-6 we are given the story of two baskets of figs, one of good figs and one of bad figs. God allowed king Nebuchadnezzar to defeat Jehoikim, the king of Judah because of Judah's sin and disobedience. The baskets of figs represented the exiles that were taken from Judah to Babylon. This was God's chastisement on His people. The good figs represented the good exiles whose hearts were responsive to God. God blessed them and eventually brought them back to Judah. The bad figs represented the bad exiles that continued in their sins and eventually were destroyed. When God disciplines us it is never without a reason and it is always for a purpose. The lesson for us is to keep our hearts responsive to God's fatherly correction, and He will bless us as He did the good exiles.

In II Corinthians 12:7-9 we are told that Paul was tormented by Satan with what Paul called a "thorn in the flesh." Three times Paul prayed that the Lord would remove it, but when the Lord did not remove it Paul realized his "thorn in the flesh" kept him humble and showed him he must depend on the Lord and not on his own abilities. God has designed correction to prevent us from sinning. And finally he corrects us so that we can be blessed. In Psalm 94:12, the psalmist says, "Blessed is the man whom You instruct (correct) and teach out of Your law."

Both the Old Testament and the New Testament give us guides as to how we should respond to correction given us by our Lord. In II Chronicles 6:24-31 we see that God desires that we repent in response.

In II Corinthians 12:7-10 we see that we are to show submission to God our Father. It is only as we are willing to submit to God that we can experience His power and blessing in our lives.

We encourage you to be open to the chastisement that the Lord has for you so you can repent and change the behavior that hinders your relationship with God.

TODAY'S WORD FOR NOVEMBER 17

PERFECT

There was a man in the land of Uz, whose name was Job; and that man was blameless and upright, and one who feared God and shunned evil. Job 1:1

Keep back Your servant also from presumptuous sins; let them not have dominion over me. Then I shall be blameless (perfect) and I shall be innocent of great transgression. Psalm 19: 13

We are all born in sin and therefore we are imperfect. Our daily experiences teach us that we are imperfect. Every tear that comes from your eye, every negative word from your mouth, and every bad step taken by your feet reminds you of the imperfection in your life.

A person who has any drive seems to be doing all he can do to obtain perfection, but most people do not want to do any more than just get by. The world has developed an entitlement mentality wanting the government to take care of them.

In the verse above from Job we looked at the Hebrew word for "perfect" as used in this verse. It is TAMAN and has several meanings. First it means consumed. Job was in deep sorrow and exhausted after losing all of his family and his possessions but he remained consumed (perfect) in his trust in God.

Job is a wonderful example for us. Often in times of great loss or suffering, doubts about God creep in and our perfect trust in the Lord grows weak. Just when we need the Lord the most, we turn away from the Lord. Job's faith in God never wavered. When our faith grows weak the first thing we should do is get back to reading God's Word and praying. When we seek the Lord we will find Him.

TAMAN also means upright. The psalmist writes in Psalm 19:7: "The law of the Lord is perfect restoring the soul." God's law is perfect because it keeps us away from sin and upright (perfect). TAMAN also means to be complete, without blemish and blameless. This was Job's status when we read about him in Job 1.

Our Lord and Savior is perfect and as believers He has set the standards in life that we need to strive for in our lives. In Psalm 18:30 we read that as for God, His way is perfect; the word of the Lord is proven; He is a shield to all who trust Him. What a wonderful promise of assurance this is for us as believers. We are not perfect nor has anyone in our world been perfect after Adam and Eve sinned in the Garden of Eden. It is only by the blood of Jesus that we can be made perfect. When we get to heaven we will be made perfect.

In Matthew 19:16-22 Jesus counsels the rich young ruler. In verse 21 Jesus tells him, "If you want to be perfect, go, and sell what you have and give to the poor and you will have treasure in heaven; and then come and follow Me."

Our Lord wants us as believers to give of our time, talent and treasure to Him and follow Him. When we do we will store up our treasure in heaven that will endure forever.

TODAY'S WORD FOR NOVEMBER 18

HURT

Look! He answered, I see four men loose, walking in the midst of the fire; and they are not hurt, and the form of the fourth is like the Son of God. Daniel 3:25

We all have hurts in our lives. Some hurts are physical caused by sickness or injury. Other hurts are emotional caused by how we are treated by others. How we respond to these hurts can affect our daily life. Fortunately most physical hurts heal with time. Emotional hurts are difficult to heal and can affect us for a lifetime. As believers it is important how we respond to hurts when they come our way because the way we respond can affect our spiritual life. Hurts and the threat of hurts can cause us to doubt and lose our faith when we most need it.

The scriptures give us numerous examples of those who went through times of great hurt yet remained faithful to God. In the verse above we are reminded about Shadrach, Meshach and Abed-Nego and how they responded when they faced physical harm. They believed in God and stayed true to their faith refusing to obey the command of King Nebuchadnezzar to bow down to the King's statue in worship.

They faced a most painful death, but God protected them and they were not hurt. Three people were thrown into the fire but when the King looked he saw four men. God sent someone from heaven to protect them. It is possible that it was Jesus Christ. One thing the King was certain of was that the fourth person was a heavenly being. God intervened because they stood true to their faith so they were not hurt.

Later in Daniel 6:16 we read about Daniel being thrown into the lion's den. King Darius made it a law that no one could pray to any god but him. The punishment for breaking the law was to be cast into a den of lions for thirty days. Daniel continued to pray to his God, the true and living God, just as he always had done in spite of facing a painful death of being eaten by lions.

When the King ordered Daniel taken out of the lion's den, no injury or hurt was found on him. God protected him. Daniel told the King, "My God sent His angel, and he shut the mouths of the lions. They have not hurt me." Daniel 6:22

In Acts 18:9-10, we read about the Apostle Paul who was in Corinth preaching to the Jews telling them Jesus was the Christ. The Jews opposed Paul and became so abusive that Paul decided to quit preaching to them. The scripture tells us that the Lord spoke to Paul in the night and told him to preach without fear and no one would hurt him. Paul realized that he must remain faithful to what God called him to do in spite of the threat of hurt, so he continued preaching.

These are great examples for us, teaching us to rely on God's protection. We urge you that when a hurt comes your way, lay that hurt in the hands of Jesus and never waver in your faith but continue to serve and honor Him.

Many people that we know today are hurting physically and spiritually. We continue to see such a difference between one that knows the Lord as to how they deal with a hurt opposed to one who does not know the Lord.

TODAY'S WORD FOR NOVEMBER 19

COLLAPSE

When you pass through the waters, I will be with you; and through the rivers, they shall not overflow you. Isaiah 43:2

Have you ever been in so much despair that you felt as if you were sinking in deep water? The difficulties in life can be oppressive and many people today feel they are sinking fast. God does not promise we will escape the turbulent seas of life, but He does promise, "I will never leave you nor forsake you." Hebrews 13:5. This promise is one each one of us should continually remember because it is true that Jesus does care for us. He cares so much for us that He gave His life for us.

In the verse above, Isaiah reminds us we can trust our faithful God to always be there in all of our struggles including when we feel we are collapsing under the pressures of life and there is no hope.

We are living in an age where the lives of people all around us seem to be collapsing. The everyday situations include such things as questionable life-styles, economic frustrations and dysfunctional families. We see nations collapsing economically and we see families collapsing with over 50% of all marriages failing. We see children, victims of both broken homes and homes with no standards or boundaries set for them, collapsing because they fall victims to drugs, sex and the evil ways of the world.

People are losing jobs, losing their homes, lacking the money to buy food and most of these people have nowhere to turn. If you are facing what you feel is a "collapse" in your life, there is a verse found in I Corinthians 10:13 that we both memorized when we were children and it has been one of our favorite verses. This verse has always helped us when we felt our world collapsing and we have faced situations when we felt that was happening. The fear of collapsing is the result of temptation trying to overcome you. Here is the verse:

"No temptation has overtaken you except such as is common to man; but God is faithful, who will not allow you to be tempted beyond what you are able, but with the temptation will also make the way of escape, that you may be able to bear it."

When difficulties seem to be sweeping over you like a flooding river remember the words said by Isaiah, "God will be with you." When our world seems to be collapsing all around us, as believers we can be sure that God will be with us. He will protect us against a loss of our faith and will see that we will survive to see the wonders of His faithfulness. But we must keep our eyes on Him and put our complete trust in Him.

Before your burden overcomes you and you feel a collapse coming, trust God to put His arms underneath you.

TODAY'S WORD FOR NOVEMBER 20

GRUMBLING

Do all things without complaining and disputing. Philippians2:14

These are grumblers, complainers, walking according to their own lusts; and they mouth great swelling words, flattering people to get advantage. Jude 16

Children often grumble. We experienced it often when we gave our children a job to do that they were not happy about. They would often reply with words like, "but why me?" As they reluctantly went on their way to do as they were told (we did not give them an option) they would grumble under their breath saying that they didn't understand why they had to do everything and none of their siblings had to do it. Of course, none of the siblings would agree as they had their equal share of jobs to do. It is hard not to observe that grumbling is contagious. When one person starts grumbling or complaining it can stir up a whole group.

I (Ken) can remember in high school a teacher telling our class that he would not tolerate griping in his class room because grumbling and complaining cause's dissension and can undermine the spiritual and emotional health of an entire group. Grumbling of course is not limited to children. We all grumble at times and grumbling is nothing new. Moses heard grumbling and griping among God's people just three days after he led them from slavery into freedom. The people complained against Moses saying, "What shall we drink." Exodus 15:24. As a result of their grumbling they forgot the joy of their new God given freedom from slavery and they lost their trust in God to provide for them.

Centuries later, Samuel felt the weight of grumbling people as he sought to represent God to his generation. The elders came to Samuel (I Samuel 8:4-9) telling him he was old and his sons did not walk in His ways honoring God so they wanted a King appointed so they could be like all the other nations. Their grumbling led them to reject God's plan for them. God gave them their way and the result was the eventual destruction of Israel.

In the verse from Jude (above) written by Jude the brother of James, who were both the brothers of Jesus, Jude describes the apostate members of the body of believers in the early church. He tells us that they were grumblers and complainers and had the ability to express themselves in "great swelling words' to impress and deceive people. In verse 9, Jude says, "These are the men who divide you." Paul admonished us to; "Do all things without complaining and disputing" because grumbling was divisive and harmful. In addition to being grumblers they followed their own evil ways.

We need to avoid a grumbling and complaining spirit because we belong to God and we are serving Christ. We are to rejoice and thank God for all that He has done for us. When you feel like grumbling or griping start counting your blessings and see what God has done for you and what He can do through you.

TODAY'S WORD FOR NOVEMBER 21

AMBITION

Let nothing be done through selfish ambition or conceit. Philippians 2:3

And you shall love the Lord your God with all your heart, with all your soul, with all your mind, and with all your strength. Mark 12:30

We have been involved in Christian ministries now for over 60 years. During that time we had responsibilities of working with all kinds of people. The one thing we have noticed is that all things being equal, such as talent, ability, and experience, the person that had ambition excelled far and above those that he or she worked with. But we also learned that a person with ambition needed to be guided to make certain that ambition was not motivated by selfish desires to elevate themselves above others or have a conceited attitude of superiority.

Probably one of the worst things that one could have on his or her performance review is lack of ambition. When it comes to work, those who lack ambition seldom rise to the top of their profession or ministry. Without a strong desire to achieve something, nothing is accomplished.

But ambition also has a dark side. Often one with ambition is dedicated to elevate themselves to a higher level and not to what the Lord has called them to do. This was the case of many of the kings of Israel, including the first one.

Saul started out with humility and with great ambition but soon Saul grew impatient waiting for God's leading and he decided to take matters into his own hands (I Samuel 13:8-10). He forgot that he had a special assignment from God to lead His chosen people in a way that would show other nations the way to God.

Not only did Saul disobey God by not allowing God to lead him, but he failed to give God the credit for his victories in battle. After the victory over the Amalekites, Saul set up a monument to honor himself (I Samuel 15:12). We are told in I Samuel 15:30 that when God rejected Saul as king, Saul's only concern was for his own honor.

We are living in a world where people only think of themselves. Often ambition compels people to do whatever it takes to put themselves in a position of power over others. God calls His people to a different way of living. We are to do nothing out of selfish ambition (verse above).

In addition in Hebrews 12:1 the writer tells us to lay aside the weight of sin that ensnares us. Sin is what causes us to seek our own selfish ambitions instead of seeking the will of God and then to give ourselves the credit and honor for our successes. This is not acceptable in His sight. God should receive the honor for the successes He has given us.

If you want to be someone who truly wants to rise above others that you work with and meet daily, then make your ambition to humbly love and serve God with all your heart, mind, soul and strength. God honors those who honor Him.

TODAY'S WORD FOR NOVEMBER 22

WALK

Enoch walked with God, and then he was no more, because God took him away. Genesis 5:24

How will you live your life today? What will your walk be like? When we refer to your walk we refer to your words and deeds and if they will honor God.

We read in the Bible about one man, named Enoch, who was very unique. It is said about him that "he walked with God." The references to Enoch in the Bible are very brief. There are only nine verses but these verses give us a very strong message and an excellent guideline as to how we should walk with God.

The Bible says that for 300 years Enoch put God first in his life. The Lord was pre-eminent in everything he did, in his thinking, in his ways, and in his walk. God was first in who he loved, who he served and who he worshipped. He was one of only two men who the scriptures say "walked with God." The other man was Noah.

In nine verses referring to Enoch, we are given four examples in Genesis, Hebrews, Micah, and Amos how we are to walk with God that is relevant for us today.

First, we are told that Enoch walked with God consistently and without failing for 365 years and then God took him to heaven without experiencing physical death (Genesis 5:21-22).

Secondly, we are told that Enoch walked by faith and that without faith it is impossible to please God (Hebrews 11:5-6). When we walk by faith we must believe that God is and that He is a rewarder of those who diligently seek Him. God rewarded Enoch for his walk by not allowing him to experience death. All those who walk faithfully with God will be rewarded in heaven.

Thirdly, Micah writes about walking humbly with God and we are to do the same (Micah 6:8). Walk humbly before our God should be our daily goal.

Finally, Amos writes we are to walk in agreement with God. Amos writes asking the question, "Can two walk together, unless they are in agreement?"(Amos 3:3)

So what we have been reminded of in these verses is that as believers we are required to walk with God without failing, by faith, humbly and in agreement. Enoch has given us this standard to live by walking with God daily.

In our homes today there is very little discussion as to how we should walk with God. Young people, for the most part, have never been taught how to walk with God. Parents have failed and our churches have failed. And of course our schools, businesses, and political leaders will never teach this to our young people.

In order to walk with God one must begin each day by reading the Bible so God can talk with us. We must spend time praying. This is our communication with Him. By praying and reading the Bible daily God can teach us how to walk with Him and He will give us the faith we need to walk with Him. We all need to stop just living our daily lives on our own and begin walking with God every step that we take.

TODAY'S WORD FOR NOVEMBER 23

THANKS

Oh, give thanks unto the Lord, for He is good; for His mercies endure forever. I Chronicles 16:34

Oh, that men would give thanks to the Lord for His goodness, and for His wonderful works to the children of men! For He satisfies the longing soul, and fills the hungry soul with goodness. Psalm 107: 8-9

When the American colonies were first settled one man suggested as a group they were dwelling too much on their problems. It was time to focus on their blessings. Thus we had the first thanksgiving celebration in America.

As Christians every day should be a day of thanksgiving. Just take a moment and list in your mind all the things that God has given you to be thankful for. Our health, our family, our salvation, our job, our home, our neighbors, our church, our Bible, our automobile and the list goes on and on. Many people in our world, in fact over 85%, do not have anywhere near the many things we as Americans have to be thankful for. How much more should we be thankful to God?

In Psalm 103:2 it reads: "Praise the Lord, Oh my soul, and forget not all His benefits." It is easy to forget all the benefits God has given us. How often do we really thank God for all He gives us?

As far back as we can remember we spent time every day praying and thanking God through prayer for His blessings. As a child we prayed before every meal, we prayed every morning and we prayed every evening before we went to bed. Christian parents have the responsibility of teaching their children the benefits they received from the Lord and to be faithful in thanking Him for them. In Psalm 103: 3-5 David reminds us of the benefits we receive. Be sure to read these to your children. We are thankful for the marvelous heritage we received from our Christian parents of being thankful which we in turn passed on to our children.

If you do not have that heritage now is the time for you to take time every day to thank God for His blessings and establish that heritage with your children. Our God is a loving God and yearns for your gratitude. And He will respond by multiplying His blessings upon your life if you just take the time to thank Him.

Have you thanked God recently for sending His Son to pay the penalty for your sins? Have you thanked God for the assurance that you have that He is in heaven preparing a place for you for eternity? The apostle Paul calls God's gift of salvation and grace that he gave us by giving His only begotten Son to die on the cross as "God's indescribable gift." We should be so thankful for this gift that Paul says is above all else.

If you pause to think, you will be aware of how many benefits you have from God that should give you cause to thank God.

TODAY'S WORD FOR NOVEMBER 24

CALAMITY

For the day of their calamity is at hand, and the things to come hasten upon them.
Deuteronomy 32:35

Therefore his calamity shall come suddenly; suddenly he shall become broken without remedy. Proverbs 6:15

At some time or the other we all face a calamity in life. Calamities are most often accidents, but we do bring calamities on ourselves. In Proverbs 1:26-27 it reads: "I will laugh at your disaster (calamity); I will mock when calamity overtakes you." This sounds like a heartless reaction but we have no one to blame but ourselves. Those who foolishly laugh and mock God will one day find that God has the last laugh. Solomon tells us in verses 24-25 that the reason why calamities overtake us is because we have rejected God, His wisdom and advice. And Solomon goes on to say: "Then they will call on me and I will not answer; they will seek me diligently, but they will not find me."

God is not the author or the cause of calamities but He will let us experience calamities because of our pride and arrogant ways when we turn our eyes away from God. When we put our trust in God and listen to Him, He will lead us away from calamity. He wants to protect us from calamities because of His love for us Proverbs 1:33 says: "Whoever listens to me will live in safety and be at ease, without fear of harm."

In real life we have calamities. These are normal events that just happen because of circumstances. After all, we are all human. One of our children over the years became lovingly known as "Calamity Jane" to our family. For some unknown reason she had nine accidents and nine broken bones. Yes, she was very athletic but so were all of our children. She was just in the wrong place at the wrong time and became the victim of calamities. Calamities like these come and go and do not affect a relationship one has with God unless one starts to blame God.

The calamities we are concerned about today deal with the calamities that result from not having a relationship with God. In the Old Testament there were so many illustrations given to us that involved men and women who God was ready to use but because of their actions they became calamities in God's sight. When this happens, God can not use a person that turns away from God and accepts living without God in a sinful society. And God will only wait so long for one to get on track with Him.

TODAY'S WORD FOR NOVEMBER 25

UNSHAKEABLE

Who shall separate us from the love of God? Shall tribulation, or distress, or persecution, or famine, or nakedness, or peril, or sword? In all these things we are more than conquerors through Him who loved us. Romans 8:35, 37

Our world is literally changing daily. In this changing world many people seek security in wealth, relationships, and power. But what people are finding out is that putting their security in these things is not guaranteed from one day to another. No wonder there is so much despair and fear in our world today.

For believers reality is not based in what we see or feel. Our foundation for life is not found in this world of uncertainty. We build our trust and hope in the Lord and believe the truth that is in His Word.

The verses we have written above tells us that even in chaotic times like today our certainty is found in our relationship with God. We are His children and He cares for us and tells us, NOTHING CAN TEAR US AWAY FROM THE LOVE OF OUR LORD JESUS CHRIST.

No matter what circumstances we might be in, and no matter what happens to us, God's love for us is unshakeable. We can never lose God's love. Bad things happen to all of us. Many have been abandoned by those who should love them. Children are abandoned by parents and spouses abandon one another.

In tough times, especially, we may feel God has abandoned us, but we can be assured that God will never abandon us nor stop loving us. God proved His love for us when He gave His life for us on the cross. We must not allow our circumstances to shake our faith in our Lord and Savior.

As believers we are in a very unique position today. In the midst of turmoil and trials we have the assurance our lives are in the grip of almighty God. We can rely not only on His love and presence in our lives but also on His uninterrupted attention, faithfulness and perfect care.

Is your faith in the Lord today unshakeable? When difficulty arises in your life and circumstances seem overwhelming, can you respond with confidence and strength because of your relationship with Jesus? The psalmist said in Psalm 91:2, "My refuge and my fortress, my God, in whom I trust."

TODAY'S WORD FOR NOVEMBER 26

BLESSING

Let us not grow weary while doing good, for in due season we shall reap if we do not lose heart. Galatians 6:9

Shall we indeed accept good from God, and shall we not accept adversity? Job 2:10

When we mention the word blessing to many people they think of the prayer that they say before a meal or the prayer that a minister gives at the end of a service. These are called blessings but we want to look at the word from the perspective of the blessings that God has for us as believers in Him.

We are convinced that God gives us the greatest blessings in our lives when we invest our time, talent or treasures in other people or projects that benefit people. Let us share with you just one example. One of the ministries that we have worked with for years is a ministry called CERT. They recruit doctors, dentists, nurses and other professionals to give a week or two of their time and talent to go on a mission trip to a remote area of our world where the people have no access to medical or dental help.

The President of CERT promises the volunteers hardship and discomfort. He warns them that they will not receive financial help but they have to pay their own expenses. But he does promise them that they will receive one of the greatest blessings they have ever experienced. A doctor who accepted that challenge (and over 100 do every year) came back from the trip he went on and said, "I never knew that life in a remote third world country could be so bad but the blessings that I received from this trip has driven me to look for ways every day for me to share my talents, treasures and time into the life of someone that needs help."

Take the Apostle Paul's encouragement that he wrote in the verse above from Galatians — to do good to all and do not grow weary. In the verse above from Job we are asked the question about receiving good (blessings) from God. Sometimes we feel a little guilty when God blesses us so abundantly when others have so little. As Job asked his wife (above verse) if they should accept good (blessings) from God and not accept adversity?

When things are going well in our life most believers are happy to acknowledge God as the source of their blessings. However, when trouble comes their faith wavers and they blame God. Satan uses difficult times in life to cause us to doubt God. Job and his wife suffered great disappointments but Jobs faith never wavered. The principle here is for us to be grateful for the blessings that God gives us and to be strong in our faith in both the good times and the bad times in our life.

The Apostle Paul tells us how he learned to rejoice in plenty and in want (Philippians 4:10-13). God has an interest in teaching us to be content both in blessings and in losses. The message for us today is to know that we are at our best when we serve others and we are to accept what God gives us in all circumstances.

TODAY'S WORD FOR NOVEMBER 27

GREED

Now it came to pass when Samuel was old that he made his sons judges over Israel. But his sons did not walk in his ways; they turned aside after dishonest gain, took bribes and perverted justice. I Samuel 8:1, 3

They have a heart trained in covetous practices, and are accursed children. They have forsaken the right way and gone astray. II Peter 2:14

It is interesting to watch children when a plate of cookies is being served. They will look the plate over carefully and select the largest cookie. If they think no one is looking they will take two or possibly a handful. We can say that that is just what kids do, but unfortunately it is not just children that are greedy.

All around us we see greed today. Many family members are driven by greed. They always want more "things" and are never happy with what they have.

We see the same greed in politicians, our government leaders and in the work place among owners, supervisors and workers. We sometimes listen to people in church that are professing believers and comments of greed come from their mouths. Greed prevails not just in our "worldly society" but also in our churches.

The two verses that we have written above give us two illustrations about how greed affected people in Biblical times. The first verse deals with Samuel and his two sons. The second verse deals with false prophets in the early church.

Samuel was about 60 years old when he appointed his sons as Judges. There is no hint of any kind in the scriptures that Samuel asked the Lord for guidance. As we read in the verse above from I Samuel, his sons allowed greed to corrupt them. We learn that Samuel, although he was a godly man, was human just like us and he put his sons in positions where they were to have spiritual authority.

As so often happens, when people have power they use their position of authority for personal gain. Greed is the motivating factor in most cases. Greed caused Samuel's sons to "accept bribes and pervert justice" to satisfy their excessive desire for riches. Thus Israel no longer had the spiritual leadership that Samuel had given Israel in the past. As a result of the greed of Samuel's sons, the elders of Israel rebelled against the evil sons and demanded that Samuel give them a king.

Most false teaching is based in greed and appeals to our sinful nature's desire for the riches and pleasures of this world. In II Peter (above) Peter was warning the believers about false teachers. These false teachers were not only greedy but they were trained in greed. They took their eyes off the message of the Cross and preached a modern word of faith that contradicted all that Jesus taught.

Those that followed these false teachers, Peter said, would be unable to cease from sin. These false teachers were very deceptive and spoke appealing and seductive thoughts. Peter warns us to stay true to the message of the cross and not to let greed entice us to follow the teaching of false teachers.

TODAY'S WORD FOR NOVEMBER 28

COUNSEL

So Moses heeded the voice (counsel) of his father-in-law and did all that he had said. Exodus 18:24

Because of the busy lives that many of us have, it is not hard to recognize ourselves in an over-extended situation, such as Moses was in, as recorded in Exodus 18. As God's chosen leader of the Israelites, Moses had a huge responsibility. He had to teach God's laws and show how to live lives that were pleasing to God. Moses was also the sole judge for all of the children of Israel and he was surrounded, "from morning until evening" verse 13, by people who needed his help and counsel.

We have talked to many people over the years, particularly parents that identify with Moses. They are overburdened and stressed out because they have too much on their plate. It seems that we need to learn two life skills for survival in today's world. We need to have an eagerness to listen to wise counsel as Moses did to his father-in-law in the verse we wrote above and willing to accept it. Secondly, we need to develop a willingness to accept the help of quality people as Moses did. In verse 25 we read that Moses chose able men to assist him and made them heads over people.

Many are not willing to listen to others and they do not want to accept help. This is mostly because of pride. But sometimes it is only because life is moving so swiftly for us and making so many demands on us that we barely have time to react, let alone to contemplate or go to someone for advice.

Many people would rather do it themselves to make sure it is done right. Others say that it is easier to do it themselves rather than take the time to train someone else. But the scripture is very clear when it tells us to surround ourselves with counselors who will offer their wisdom and experience even when we are too busy to ask for it.

Moses recognized that wise counsel includes God. His father-in-law Jethro, told Moses that if he followed his advice he must do it only if God commanded him to do it (Exodus 18:23). Jethro also advised Moses that those men that Moses chose to help him must be men who feared God and are trustworthy.

We can all learn from Moses and his father-in-law. Do not put yourself in the position of being overwhelmed. Instead, seek godly counsel and then follow through on what you are told. God will go before you and lead you through every step. Also remember that he who will not be counseled will not be helped.

TODAY'S WORD FOR NOVEMBER 29

PURGE

As for our transgressions, thou shall purge them away. Psalm 65:3

Purge out the old leaven, that you may be a new lump, since you truly are unleavened. For indeed Christ, our Passover was sacrificed for us. I Corinthians 5:7

Many Chinese families several days before their New Year give their home a thorough cleaning. They practice this tradition because they believe the cleaning sweeps away the bad luck of the preceding year and make their homes ready for good luck.

In the verse above from I Corinthians the Apostle Paul was writing to the church at Corinth asking them to give their lives a thorough cleansing, not for good luck but to please God. He told them to purge out the old leaven. Paul in this verse used the Jewish feasts of Passover and Unleavened Bread (Exodus 12) as a backdrop for this statement. Leaven (yeast) was a symbol of sin and corruption and was to be removed from the Jewish homes to celebrate these festivals.

When Paul says to be a new lump he is saying for us to start acting like what we are, a new creation in Jesus. As a new creation we have a new standing with God and we can have victory over all sin because of the cross and our relationship with Christ.

Jesus is our Passover Lamb who cleanses us from sin and corruption which separates us from God. The Corinthian church had acknowledged that Jesus was their Passover Lamb, but they had not gotten rid of their old sinful ways. Paul wrote them and admonished them that they must purge out (get rid of) the old leaven (sin).

The Corinthians were to scour their hearts and remove all evil and sexual immorality, malice, and wickedness from their lives. Out of gratitude to Jesus for His sacrifice, let us purge out the sin in our lives and celebrate the holiness that only God can bring to us.

The NIV translation of Psalms 65:3 reads, "When we were overwhelmed by sins, You forgave our transgressions." David, the writer of this Psalm acknowledged he was a sinner and knew where to go when sin overwhelmed him. He knew that no matter how great our sin, there is no sin God will not forgive and enable us to purge from our life.

By faith, David looks forward for the purging of his sin at Calvary. Our faith now looks back to Calvary where we were purged of our sin and iniquities.

TODAY'S WORD FOR NOVEMBER 30

FRIENDSHIP

A friend loves at all times. Proverbs 17:17

A man of many companions may come to ruin, but there is a friend who sticks closer than a brother. Proverbs 18:24

He who walks with the wise grows wise, but a companion of fools suffers harm. Psalm 13:20

In the book of Proverbs Solomon gives us words of advice how to live a godly life. Solomon gives us words of wisdom on three aspects of friendship: the foundation of a true friendship in Proverbs 17:17; the necessity of choosing friends wisely in Proverbs 18:24; and the influence friends have on a person's life in Proverbs 13:20.

In Proverbs 17:17 he notes the foundation of a friendship is love. A true friend is a constant source of love. To love at all times requires loyalty. Friends may not always agree but loyal friends will continue to love each other. Loyal friends will be there for each other in the good times and in the bad times.

Many people base their friendship on what they can get out of it. These kinds of friends do not last and either you will leave them or they will leave you as soon as one sees they cannot benefit in some way with the friendship. Genuine friendship means being available to help in times of trouble and distress.

In Proverbs 18:24, the writer Solomon is telling us the person who makes friends too easily and indiscriminately does so to his own destruction. On the other hand a friend chosen wisely is more loyal than a brother. The word "friend' here is a strong word meaning one who loves. Friendship was used in II Chronicles 20:7 to describe Abraham's close relationship with God.

The type of friends we choose as close friends speaks volumes about us. Friends that we spend a lot of time with have a significant effect and influence on our life. Proverbs 13:20 admonishes us that, "He who walks with the wise grows wise, but a companion of fools suffer harm." We must choose our friends wisely.

It is of most importance that parents get to know who their children's friends are and to make sure that they are the right kind of friends. Friendships are important to everyone, but especially to teenagers. Christian parents have a responsibility to get their children involved in church and with groups that uphold Biblical values so that their children can choose wholesome friendships.

Abraham Lincoln said that the better part of one's life consists of building and keeping friendships. Mark Twain once said that friendship is only purchased with friendship. True friendship begins with the certainty that you must have in your heart that you are a friend of God. Do you communicate with Him daily? He alone can help us to be a friend that loves at all times.

TODAY'S WORD FOR DECEMBER 1

CREDIBILITY

Beloved, I beg of you as sojourners and pilgrims abstain from fleshly lusts which war against the soul, having your conduct honorable among the Gentiles, that when they speak against you as evildoers, they may, by your good works which they observe, glorify God. I Peter 2:11-12

As parents raising our children we constantly stressed the importance of always being credible. Unfortunately, most people in today's culture do not consider the importance of being credible with their friends and acquaintances. When one loses his or her credibility it is almost impossible to get it back. We taught our children the necessity of being honest, truthful and trustworthy because those were the character traits that would give them credibility. You do not win in life if you lie or mislead people. The truth will always come back to hurt the one who misleads another.

Credibility is not something that you buy, it is something you work for and earn. We may be able to "borrow" credibility for a while by associating ourselves with credible people, but sooner or later we will need to establish our own credibility.

As Christians it is essential our lives are lived in a way that honors God. We are known as Christians and are held to a higher standard by the world. We are Christ's witnesses in this world and therefore our actions reflect on Christ's purifying power to enable us to be trustworthy and honest. If we fail in some way then our credibility failure affects God's reputation. We must earn credibility as Christians by living each day in an honorable way. When we take care of our character, by building it on God's laws, our reputation and credibility will be honorable.

In verse 21 of I Peter 2, we are reminded that Christ suffered for us and left us an example. It then says we are to "follow" His steps. In the Greek, the word "follow" means to take the same road. We need to walk the same road Jesus walked and in turn we will be more Christ-like and have real credibility.

In the verse we have written at the top, Peter is telling us we are living in a hostile world. We are like pilgrims waiting to go to our home which will be in heaven. We are foreigners in a secular society because our citizenship is in heaven. Jesus set an example for us by living in this world a perfect life in a hostile environment.

As believers we have learned how to live a pure and honorable life. Therefore, we must outwardly live among non-Christians in a way which reflects the inward discipline we have learned by studying God's Word. Each one of us needs to work daily on our credibility. The way we walk and the way we talk must exemplify our Lord.

TODAY'S WORD FOR DECEMBER 2

REST

Come to Me, all you who labor and are heavy laden, and I will give you rest. Matthew 11:28

And He said to them, Come aside by yourselves to a deserted place and rest a while. Mark 6:31

Rest is needed and important. God demonstrated that to us at the time He created the world as it is written, "On the seventh day God ended His work which He had made; and He rested on the seventh day." If God needs to rest then we surely need to as well. God also ordained for us in the writing of the Ten Commandments that the seventh day be a day of rest and a day of worship. We need to have time to refresh ourselves not only physically, but spiritually.

Jesus also needed rest when He ministered here on earth. Jesus and His disciples were followed everywhere by large crowds. It was often difficult for them to find a time and place to rest. In Mark 6:31, Jesus saw it was time for rest so He called His disciples to come to Him to find a quiet place so they could rest awhile.

As we walk our Christian walk there are many times we need to stop a moment and take a rest. Jesus has given us a place to rest. In the verse above from Matthew He says to come to Him and He will give you rest.

We think of the song, "Near to the heart of God." The verse reads, "There is a place of quiet rest, near to the heart of God. A place where sin cannot molest, near to the heart of God."

We are told that Cleland McAfee wrote this song in 1901 after the death of his two nieces from diphtheria. The words offered hope to a family who was hurting and needed rest that could only come from God.

Single moms probably need times of rest more than any other group of people today. They carry the heavy burden of working to support their children financially and also need to carry the burden of caring for them physically and emotionally. They are on duty 24-7 so there is little time for physical rest. If you are a single mom, let us remind you that Jesus knows you are heavy laden and He calls you to come to Him for physical rest and spiritual refreshment. Just a few moments of quiet time, alone with God, reading His Word and praying will refresh your soul.

Paul tells us in Romans 8:31-39 nothing is able to separate us from the enduring love of the Lord. Yes, the heart of God is the place for us to rest from the pressures of life. Leave it all to Him for He cares for you, as it is written in I Peter 5:7.

The Psalmist tells us that rest is longed after. In the verse above from Mark, taking time for rest is encouraged by Christ. In the verse above from Matthew we find the real source of rest is from our Lord.

TODAY'S WORD FOR DECEMBER 3

HERITAGE

Behold, children are a heritage from the Lord. Psalm 127:3

Many years ago today we were having dinner in our house with fellow missionaries in Seoul Korea. The doorbell rang and a telegram was delivered. I (Ken) opened the envelope with the telegram and read it quietly and then announced to everyone that my father had a heart attack and was not doing well. He was in the hospital in Los Angeles close to the airport, the telegram read, because he was getting on an airplane when the heart attack occurred.

It was no more than 15 minutes later and the telephone rang. It was Bob Pierce calling and he said quietly and caringly words such as, "Ken your father is in heaven." At the young age of 46 God decided to take him home. Everyone who knew my father would say he left a wonderful heritage for us.

We are reminded the Hebrew word for heritage is NACHAL. This Hebrew word has several interesting definitions. One is to receive as a possession or to acquire as used in Proverbs 3:35: "The wise should inherit glory." NACHAL is also used in Psalm 119:111, "Your testimonies I have taken as a heritage forever."

In the verse we have chosen to write above we are reminded that children are a heritage (NACHAL) from God. When Ken's father died, we were in Korea working on establishing orphanages to house abandoned GI babies and orphans, who were living on the streets. Ken's father had challenged us both to spend some time on the mission field working to help children because they were, and still are, a wonderful heritage from God.

Today we look back on our heritage. We both had loving and caring parents who trained us in the Word of God leading us to know Jesus as our personal Savior. Both of our parents involved us in church, Sunday school and missions so that our hearts would be sensitive to those in need. We look back on the heritage our parents left us and we thank God for this wonderful blessing.

Now for these years since the death of my (Ken) father, we have raised our six children hopefully giving them a portion of the rich heritage we were given. Now our six children are raising our twenty grandchildren with the same spiritual emphasis on godly family living as we trained them and our parents trained us.

God told Moses in Exodus 6:8, "I will bring you into the land which I swore to give to Abraham, Isaac and Jacob; and I will give it to you as a heritage." The Psalmist said in Psalm 61:5, "You have given me the heritage of those who fear Your name." Today we as a family benefit from the heritage our parents left for us. It is our prayer that we will leave for our grandchildren and their children a rich heritage that God can use to bring them into a productive relationship with Him. What kind of heritage are you leaving for those who love you?

TODAY'S WORD FOR DECEMBER 4

BLESSED

Blessed be the God and Father of our Lord Jesus Christ, who has blessed us with every spiritual blessing in the heavenly places in Christ. Ephesians 1:3

Most everyone who has read the Bible realizes Old Testament people lived under the age of law based on the Ten Commandments. However, after Christ's earthly ministry, He gave us the "BLESSED HOPE" of His return for those of us who have put our trust in Him.

This "BLESSED HOPE" is the most important aspect of our knowing Jesus as our Savior. Every believer who has accepted Jesus as Savior is looking for that Blessed hope of His coming again to take us with Him. This "BLESSED HOPE" is prophesied many times. In fact for every prophecy recorded in the Bible concerning the first coming of Jesus, there are eight prophecies on His second coming — which is our" BLESSED HOPE." In fact, to make sure we understood Jesus was coming again, the second time; there are 2,163 references in the scriptures. Let us all as believers look forward to that day.

In Matthew chapter five we read the words of Jesus as He preached the Sermon on the Mount about the Beatitudes. Jesus told the multitudes who were listening, the words that have been mentioned often down through the centuries. Jesus said, blessed are the poor in spirit, blessed are those who mourn, blessed are the meek, blessed are the hungry, blessed are the merciful, blessed are the pure in heart, blessed are the peacemakers, and blessed are the persecuted.

Through this Sermon on the Mount, Jesus was clarifying whom He blessed. He set a standard in this sermon that He honored thereafter and expects believers today to do the same. Today Jesus blesses us when we honor Him.

When the building of the Temple was complete and the Ark of the Covenant was put in place, Solomon (I Kings 8:56-61) first prayed and praised God for His blessing on the building of the Temple. And then the scripture says that Solomon rose from his knees, as he was kneeling in front of the Ark praying to God, and spread his hands to the heavens and blessed all the assembly of Israel with a loud voice saying: "Blessed be the Lord."

Solomon recognized Israel had been blessed by God and he praised God for those blessings.

Daily God blesses us as it is written in James 1:17, "Every good gift and every perfect gift is from above, and comes down from the Father of lights, with whom there is no variation or shadow of turning." Just as Solomon gave his praise to God, we should give praise to God for all the ways he has blessed us.

TODAY'S WORD FOR DECEMBER 5

UNIQUENESS

And they were astonished at His teachings, for He taught them as one having authority, and not as the scribes. Mark 1:22

In life there are many unique people, places and things. All of us have seen people who have unique ability. There are places on this earth that are unique because of the topography, wildlife and climate. We all have seen unique things, but we want to talk about the most unique person who ever lived.

Jesus came to this earth as a man who possessed moral integrity and divine righteousness that marked Him different from all men. He was unique and set apart from all others.

HE WAS UNIQUE IN HIS PERSON. In Hebrews 1:1-13 His uniqueness is proclaimed as the Son of God, the Christ and the God-Man. He spoke in times past to the fathers of the prophets (verse 1), was appointed heir of all things (verse 2), He made the worlds (verse 2), He is the out-flowing of the glory of God and expresses the perfect character of God (verse 3). He purged our sins (verse 3), and sat down at the right side of God (verse 3).

HE WAS UNIQUE IN HIS BIRTH. In Luke 1:26-35, He was born of a virgin, was the incarnate God (born in flesh), and was born in the city of Bethlehem. His birth announced by Angels. He was born in a stable, cared for in a feeding trough, but worshipped by Kings. Hosts of angels sang praises.

HE WAS UNIQUE IN HIS MINISTRY. In Mark 1:21-28 it reads that He preached with absolute authority, was the greatest teacher who ever lived, performed the mightiest of miracles. He was absolutely Holy and sinless in His person, actions and standards, a friend of sinners offering them salvation.

HE WAS UNIQUE IN HIS DEATH. In John 19:16-30 we are told that He died for people's sins. He prophesied He would be put to death. He died as the Passover Lamb as prophesied. He died voluntarily doing His Father's will.

HE WAS UNIQUE IN HIS RESSURECTION. In John 20: 1-31 we read He arose according to the Old Testament prophecies. He prophesied His own resurrection. He rose from the dead from a sealed and guarded tomb.

HE WAS UNIQUE IN HIS ASCENSION. In Acts 1:1-9 we are told how He was taken into heaven. He went to be with the Father. Jesus made a promise at His ascension that the disciples would receive power to witness for Him after the Holy Spirit came. Jesus made a command at His ascension to go into all the world and be witnesses of Him. He went to heaven to take the right seat next to God and to make continual intercession for the believers to God.

HE WILL BE UNIQUE IN HIS SECOND COMING. In Matthew 16:27 we are told Jesus will return to this earth in power and majesty. He will raise the dead in Christ and come as a thief in the night. He will begin the promised millennium Kingdom on this earth and rescue the tribulation saints.

TODAY'S WORD FOR DECEMBER 6

HEROES

These all died in faith. Hebrew 11:13

For living to me means simply "Christ" and if I die I should merely gain more of Him. Philippians 1:20 (J B PHILLIPS TRANSLATION)

All of us during our lifetime have had heroes in our lives. When we were younger we had many more heroes than now. Part of that was due to our age and lack of maturity. Over the years we have seen some of our heroes fail in some way and burst our so called bubble, because we thought they were the greatest. It is a great disappointment when someone turns out *not* to be what we thought they were.

In Hebrews chapter 11, we read about heroes of faith from the Old Testament. They include Abel, Enoch, Noah, Abraham, Isaac, Jacob, and Sarah. When you look to the Bible for your heroes in life you will find role models that you can confidently build your life upon.

The key to those who are listed above in Hebrews II, is that they all lived by faith. If we pick these as our heroes and our role models we need to do all we can to live as they did. In their faith they found their comfort, their daily guide, their motive for living and their support.

They believed the promises that came from God and lived their lives relying on those promises. They were assured that their sins were blotted out through the mercy of God. These heroes were confident of their acceptance by God. They enjoyed living in His love and resting in His faithfulness.

They agreed that they were foreigners and nomads here on earth just as we are as believers today. They were looking forward to a country of their own, a better place than where they were or had been. They all were looking for their heavenly home and knew that one day they would arrive there and live an eternity with their maker. Is this the kind of hero you have chosen in your life?

In the verse we have written above from Hebrews 13 we read they all died in faith. Dying in faith looks to the future. They died as men and women of faith. They knew that faith is the confidence that what we hope for will actually happen; it gives us assurance for what we cannot see. They died knowing the Messiah would surely come and one day they would rise from their graves to behold Him in the air.

Faith was the orbit that these heroes moved in while they were here on this earth. If you are looking for heroes in your life, look no further than these heroes we read about in Hebrews. And you can be a hero just like them if you will look to Jesus, the author and finisher of your faith. Thank God today for giving you similar faith like He gave those great Bible heroes of faith who are now in glory.

TODAY'S WORD FOR DECEMBER 7

DECEPTION

They refused to pay attention; stubbornly they turned their backs and stopped up their ears. Zechariah 7:11

They made their hearts as hard as flint and would not listen to the law or to the words that the Lord Almighty had sent by His Spirit through the earlier prophets. So the Lord God Almighty was very angry. Zechariah 7:12

Think back on the many times you have felt you have been deceived. Deception is rampant in the world today. We are all guilty of deception at one time or another. We not only deceive others, but we deceive ourselves into thinking we are better than we are. This is because we measure ourselves by our standards, not God's standards.

In the 7th and 8th chapters of Zechariah the prophet is communicating God's plea to the people to be honest and open before Him. God reminds them of their failures and reminds them while He is unfailing in mercy and grace, He is also unchanging in His standards. He always supplies to them what is necessary, but never lowers His standards.

The people reacted in three ways. First, they refused to pay attention and turned their backs on God. They basically ignored God by pretending not to hear.

Secondly, they made their hearts hard and would not listen to God. They deliberately disobeyed God. Thirdly, they began to play the hypocrite role. At the beginning of this chapter, verse 3, the people asked if they should mourn and fast during the fifth month as they had done for years. God answered them by asking why they would celebrate — because you mean to worship me or just for a religious show.

They fasted, but did not fast with a proper attitude of repentance and worship. They deceived themselves that they were pleasing God. Many of us do the same today. We use these same evasions to avoid God's will in our lives.

Think about this: We go to church, but we do not hear. We deliberately disobey and we become hypocritical. This is because we do not have a sincere desire to know the Lord and worship Him. He wants us to repent of our sins and do what is pleasing to Him. This passage in Zechariah portrays the human heart in the very act of deception.

God's Word tells us the results of our repeated turning a deaf ear to God's voice. We become blind to the truth. We lose our ability to see and hear what God is saying to us. This is what happens when God tries to move in our life and we do not listen. You lose the ability to see and hear God.

TODAY'S WORD FOR DECEMBER 8

WALLS

And I went out by night through the Valley Gate to the Serpent Well and the Refuse Gate, and viewed the walls of Jerusalem which were broken down and its gates which were burned by fire. Nehemiah 2:13

Down through the ages walls were built to protect the people and things inside the walls. But walls are more than just a barrier of stone and mortar. The walls of the city of Jericho symbolized the pride and arrogance of that godless city. God chose to pull them down with nothing, but the faith of the Children of Israel and their leader.

The Berlin wall not only symbolized the division between east and west, but also the misery and despair of the people living under communism. The 1500 mile long wall of China symbolized the vast power of the China Dynasty and was built to defend China from the warring tribes of the north.

The walls of the city of Babylon, according to Daniel, were not as long as the Great Wall of China, but were much higher and more massive.

The wall Nehemiah went to look at by night was the wall around Jerusalem God had called him to rebuild. And it had even a deeper spiritual meaning than any of the other walls ever built. The walls of Jerusalem were symbolic of God's protection and power. The rebuilding of these walls around Jerusalem, symbolizes an act that must be taken by everyone who is spiritually broken down. They must rebuild the walls of their lives.

There were 5 steps Nehemiah took in the process of rebuilding the walls of Jerusalem. We need to adhere to these steps as we rebuild the walls of our lives.

First, Nehemiah had a CONCERN about the ruins. We will never rebuild the walls of our lives unless we have a concern and mourn the ruins of our lives.

Secondly, Nehemiah wept and prayed for days over his concern for the way the nation of Israel had forsaken God. He prayed and CONFESSED the sins of his people and asked God for forgiveness.

Thirdly, Nehemiah was COMMITTED. He didn't just pray. He got to work and took immediate steps to fulfill his commitment. Rebuilding the wall would have not been possible without God's enabling power.

Fourthly, Nehemiah needed COURAGE to rebuild these walls. Nehemiah was mocked and threatened, but he did not give up because he knew God was directing him. Whenever one says that they will arise and rebuild, Satan always responds by saying he will arise and destroy.

Finally, Nehemiah approached the rebuilding of the walls of Jerusalem with CONFIDENCE. He did not just rush out and start laying bricks or recruiting people to help. He went out at night and secretly surveyed the damage to the wall to determine exactly what needed to be done. When he was ridiculed Nehemiah confidently replied, "The God of heaven will give us success." Nehemiah 2:20.

We can learn by these 5 steps as we work to rebuild the walls around our lives.

TODAY'S WORD FOR DECEMBER 9

GROW

Grow in the grace and knowledge of our Lord and Savior Jesus Christ. II Peter 3:18

New believers come from all sorts of backgrounds. Some may have gone to church before they found Christ, but never accepted Jesus as their Savior. Others may have come from a very worldly and sinful background and never darkened the door of a church or ever even opened a Bible to read it. Spiritually they are as newborn babies. Just as a baby needs to be fed to thrive and grow, a new believer needs to be fed from God's Word in order to grow and mature in their new found faith.

In Ezekiel 47, Ezekiel shares with us a vision of a river flowing out from the temple. The temple symbolizes God and the river reflects the Gospel of Jesus Christ. In this vision, stages of spiritual growth are depicting those who have accepted Christ.

When we first find Jesus it is likened to walking ankle deep in the water, as portrayed by Ezekiel, and we experience only a shallow sense of God's grace and power in our life. If a person does not begin to learn more about Christ the Scriptures calls one a babe in Christ. Such a person has not learned how to live a Spirit-lead life which is a life of obedience, trust, surrender and peace.

A lot of people who say they are Christians want to wade ankle deep into the grace of God. They are not motivated to want to take the next step by wading into knee deep water which is hungering and thirsting for God. At this stage a Christian is not satisfied by being merely born again, but hungers for a deeper knowledge and closer relationship with their Savior and Lord.

In Ezekiel 47:4 the prophet talks about walking into the water up to the waist. The Holy Spirit is now captivating the believer in Jesus to be possessed by His Lord.

You can see we live today among so many Christians who are still just babes in their faith and need to be motivated to wade up to their waist in God's Word in order to be possessed by God. This motivation is not coming from our families or churches. The result is we live in a world where Christians are living according to the will of the flesh rather than living according to the will of the Spirit.

The motivation comes from the Holy Spirit, but we must be willing to listen to Him and allow Him to lead us into the deep water of His Word. It is only by reading God's Word we can grow into the mature Christian our Lord wants us to be.

The apostle Paul tells us in I Corinthians about how the people in the church at Corinth were divided into factions and cliques. They were continually at each other's throats, dragging one another into courts of law, gossiping against each other and undermining each other. Does it sound a little like what you may be facing among those you know and perhaps even among your friends and family?

The source of these divisions is pride, the fleshly desire for preeminence, and to be idolized and praised. Paul reminds us as long as the desire to live for worldly pleasures is alive and well in our lives, we will remain spiritual infants.

TODAY'S WORD FOR DECEMBER 10

DELIVERANCE

And the Lord will deliver me from every evil work and preserve me for His heavenly Kingdom.
II Timothy 4:18

When Adam and Eve were driven from paradise for their sin they condemned all mankind to live in a world subject to the evil devices of the evil one (Satan). Because of God's love for us, He had a plan of deliverance through Jesus' death on the cross to redeem us from death into eternal life. As believers we are saved from the penalty for our sins, but we must live in a world subject to the evil Satan brings into it.

We can't listen to the news without being made aware of all the evil that exists in our world. When Jesus gave us His example of how we should pray, He taught us to ask for deliverance from evil (The Lord's Prayer, Matthew 6:9-13). There should be no doubt this is what we need to pray. We need deliverance from the evil that surrounds us.

Even God's most faithful servants will not be shielded from dealing with the evil in this world. Paul went through many trials and persecutions and in II Timothy 3:11 he said the Lord delivered him from all of them. It is from experience Paul is able to confidently say in the verse above that the Lord will deliver us from all evil and bring us safely to His heavenly kingdom.

Paul also tells us God delivers us from death in II Corinthians 1:10, and in Colossians 1:13 He delivers us from the power of darkness. In I Thessalonians 1:10 Paul tells us to look forward to the return of Christ and the deliverance He will bring from the wrath of God to come. What a wonderful assurance we have, as believers, of the deliverances from evil we have through Jesus Christ each day.

There are so many examples in the scriptures we have concerning the way God delivered those who honored His name and believed in Him. We will give you a short list to encourage you. You may want to look up each passage we leave with each example. Here are just nine examples:

· Noah: Genesis 8:1-22. (Deliverance from the flood)
· Lot: Genesis 19:29-30. (Deliverance from the destruction of Sodom)
· Jacob: Genesis 33:1-16. (Deliverance from the fierce anger of Esau)
· The Children of Israel: Exodus 12: 29-51. (Deliverance from slavery in Egypt)
· David: 1 Samuel 23:1-29. (Deliverance from King Saul who wanted to kill him)
· Jews: Esther 9:1-19. (Deliverance from execution)
· Daniel: Daniel 6:13-27. (Deliverance from the lion's den)
· Jesus: Matthew 2:13-23. (Deliverance from being killed by King Herod)
· Paul: II Corinthians 1:8-10. (Deliverance from life threatening affliction)

There is no evil of any kind our Lord cannot overcome. We are living in a sinful and cruel world, but as believers we have so much to thank our Lord for daily, including the deliverance He gives to us from our trials and temptations. Take the time to thank Him for the way he delivers you from evil and the trials you face.

TODAY'S WORD FOR DECEMBER 11

INQUIRED

And David inquired of the Lord, and He answered. II Samuel 5:23

When David made this inquiry of the Lord for advice, he had already achieved great victories. He killed the giant, Goliath, with a sling shot and a stone. He defeated the Amalekites and the great hosts of Philistines. The people were singing praises to David for his great victories. But David continually gave God the credit saying this all happened because God led David and went ahead of him to protect him. David knew these were all the Lord's victories.

The Philistines now came the second time and David would not go out to fight without inquiring to the Lord first (verse above). Once David had been so victorious in his battles one would think he would just go out and fight feeling confident he would be victorious once again. But David would not venture out based on past victories, but wanted to ask the Lord first for the same assurance the Lord had given him before.

He asked very simply, "Shall I go up against them again?" He then waited until God gave him an answer. He did not move ahead of God. David did as the Lord commanded him (verse 25). We need to learn from this. David asked, listened, and obeyed. As we walk down our path of life, we need to allow God to be our compass.

Most of us today act on our own, feeling confident that we can win at a situation we may be facing. But that is not what God wants from us. The big problem that most believers face is waiting on the Lord for an answer. David did not move ahead of God and He expects us to be patient and not move ahead of Him.

God promises us He will instruct us and teach us in the ways we should go. The words of a Puritan some years ago were, "As sure as ever a Christian carves for himself, he will cut his own fingers." Another Puritan said, "He that goes before the cloud of God's providence goes on a fool's errand." When we trust in ourselves alone we are sure to fail.

As believers in God we need to learn to inquire of Him in all we do. It is so easy for us to rely on our own strength feeling we are invincible. The times of failure will come your way often unless you make it a practice to begin each day inquiring of God. Our confidence must be in the Lord, not in ourselves. Every believer needs to ask God daily to give them wisdom, to give them direction and to open and close doors according to His will for their lives. Ask God daily what you should do, how you should do it and then march out every day to face your battles as David did. Walk with confidence that God is with you and leading you.

We learn from David to acknowledge that God is the one who gives us victory. David said in Psalm 60:12, "With God we will gain victory." When you have victory remember it is God who made you victorious and give God the glory.

TODAY'S WORD FOR DECEMBER 12

WINGS

Oh, that I had wings like a dove! I would fly away and be at rest. Psalm 55:6

David wrote freely about his circumstances in his life. He had violence, oppression and strife around him on all sides. Much of this was stirred up by disloyalties from old friends and even family. On many occasions fear and terror, pain and trembling, anxiety and restlessness overwhelmed him. No wonder he wrote in the verse above that he wanted wings so he could fly away. He was facing in his life an escapist feeling.

When many of us face strife, pain or anxiety we want to go somewhere to get away to just rest, think, read the Bible and pray. So we can understand how David felt when he wrote this verse (above). You can hear him sigh and say, oh, if I only had wings like a dove, I would get out of here and fly away and be at rest for a few days.

But escape for David was not an option. He could not evade his concerns. He could only give his circumstances to God. In verses 16-17 he writes, "As for me, I will call upon God, and the Lord shall save me. Evening and morning and noon I will pray, and cry aloud, and He shall hear my voice."

David was confident when he called upon the Lord, the Lord would hear him and would protect him. Isaiah 40:31 tells us that those who wait for the Lord (after calling on Him), will gain new strength. They will mount up with wings like eagles, they will run and not be weary, they will walk and not faint. There is a general principle here in this verse for believers. We are to be patient in our praying, learn to wait on God, and then we will be blessed by God with strength, that only He can give us, in our trials.

Isaiah also was reminding us that the Lord expected His people to be patient and await His coming in glory at the end to fulfill the promises of national deliverance, when Israel would become stronger than ever.

Whatever our circumstances, a difficult marriage, a problem child, a loss of a job, the loss of a loved one, neighbors who are hurtful, or deep loneliness, we can give them to God.

God has lifted the burden of our sins so will He not lift the weight of our sorrows? We have trusted Him with our eternal souls, can we not trust Him with our current circumstances? In Psalms 55:22 it reads, "Cast your burden upon the Lord, and He shall sustain you." Because God cares for us, we can leave our cares with Him. In Psalms 91:4 the psalmist tells us He will cover you with His pinions (like the protection of a parent bird), and under His wings you may seek refuge. What a glorious promise for us as believers.

TODAY'S WORD FOR DECEMBER 13

GUARD

False Christ's and false prophets will appear and perform signs and miracles to deceive the elect, if that were possible. So be on your guard; I have told you everything ahead of time. Mark 13:23

Finally, my brethren, rejoice in the Lord. It is no trouble for me to write the same things to you again and it is a safeguard for you. Philippians 3:1

Our parents regularly reminded us to be alert and guard ourselves from things in life that could be harmful to us. We did the same to our children. Spiritually, children and adults need to guard themselves against false teachings concerning the scriptures and the evil temptations they face in life.

This third chapter of Philippians is noted as one of the great chapters in the Bible. In it Paul gives his personal testimony and speaks of the principles that governed his life. His desire was always to grow in the Lord and to become more Christ-like. That should be our goal as well. In this chapter Paul emphasizes a believer must guard his faith against false teaching and gives us practical advice to safeguard our faith.

During trials in life we can be vulnerable to Satan's attempts to destroy our faith. However, we can guard our faith during the trials of life by rejoicing in the Lord. When we focus on rejoicing in the Lord the trial becomes insignificant. As we walk our daily walk we face physical and spiritual challenges and we must face them straight on. It is important not to allow these trials to take our eyes off Jesus, because Satan will use them to destroy our faith.

Satan loves to have his evil-minded followers belittle our Lord and our faith in Him, by making us feel that the Lord has forgotten us because He allows us, as believers, to suffer trials.

Peter also warns us in I Peter 5:8 to be on guard and watch for the devil and false teachers because they are our enemies and are on the prowl to destroy us. Satan seizes every opportunity to overwhelm us with enticing temptations, so we can never let our guard down allowing Satan any kind of an open door into our lives. Therefore, always be on guard and watch out!

The greatest thing that "rejoicing in the Lord" does for the believer is that it places and keeps a person in the presence of Christ. Nothing can separate us from the love of Christ (Romans 8:35-39). We will face trials in this sinful world, but there is no trial so big that it can separate us from our Lord.

Paul faced so many trials in his life including being stoned, beaten, was homeless without food and water, and imprisoned, but always continued to rejoice in the Lord.

Rejoicing in the Lord according to the apostle Paul is the sure way to guard your faith in the midst of the trials of life you will face. In Philippians 4:4 he said it twice, "Rejoice always in the Lord."

TODAY'S WORD FOR DECEMBER 14

DISASTER

For My thoughts are not your thoughts, nor are your ways My ways, says the Lord. For as the heavens are higher than the earth, so are My ways higher than your ways, and My thoughts than your thoughts. Isaiah 55:8-9

When a disaster strikes, many people respond with what they feel are legitimate questions. They include: Why does the Lord let such things happen? Couldn't God have stopped this? Doesn't God care? The magnitude of disasters like earthquakes, tornadoes, tsunamis and floods cause death and destruction and our thoughts change from day to day activities to concerns about surviving and wanting explanations for the suffering that results.

Non-believers in our Lord have a most difficult time answering these questions because they have no relationship with God, thus they feel hopeless and alone. They have no frame of reference for understanding God.

Believers in the Lord have the Bible to guide them as they wrestle through the issues they face. Coming to the proper conclusions on issues will depend on one's knowledge of the Bible and the depth of one's relationship with God.

We must not allow disasters to cause us to doubt God. When a disaster happens we want to ask, "How could God allow this to happen?" Isaiah reminds us that we cannot know the mind of God. God does not think as we think and His way is not our way. Isaiah assures us, however, that God's thoughts are higher than our thoughts and His ways are better than our ways.

Many believers have a tendency to design a box in their mind that the Lord will fit into. But if He does not fit into that box we get upset, confused and even angry at God.

We may not know why disasters occur, but we have several Biblical truths that we know with absolute certainty that will allow us to trust God in even the greatest times of our suffering.

We know God is in control. "The Lord has established His throne in heaven, and His kingdom rules over all." Psalm 103:19. Nothing in heaven or earth is outside of His control, rule or authority. We can always trust in His goodness and mercy.

The Lord loves people and wants them to be saved. "For God so loved the world that He gave His only Son, that whoever believes in Him shall never perish but have eternal life." John 3:16. God cares for us, even when we cannot feel it or even when we will not accept it.

God ordains or permits events for His good purpose. All though we cannot comprehend what God is doing, in every incident, every disaster is a wakeup call for humanity. God is alerting us to repent. Catastrophes open our ears to hear from God.

TODAY'S WORD FOR DECEMBER 15

PROVIDENCE

The Lord is righteous in all His ways, gracious in all His works. Psalm 145:17

Just think how difficult it would be, if you are a believer in Jesus, to face the situations you face daily in your life without the assurance that God is not only looking out for you, but that all things are under His control.

With all the uncertainties in our world today, we as believers can be certain of one thing which is we have divine guidance watching over us every moment of every day. Providence is God in control. When people can't find a reason to explain why something happened they often say, "It was just one of those things." Others say, "It was just meant to be." Those of us, who believe in the Lord, our God, know that what happens in this world is by Providence. Providence is the sustaining power of God at work in our world and His ever present hand guiding our destiny.

The scripture clearly tells us that if we cast all of our cares upon Him, our Lord, He will take care of us. Divine guidance in a clear term means God taking care of those who are known as His believers.

In Psalm 103:19 we are told by the Psalmist the providence of God is universal. "The Lord has established His throne in heaven, and His kingdom rules over all." The Lord's rule is righteous (Psalm 9:4) and He rules forever (Psalm 9:7).

In Daniel 4:35 we read it is impossible to fight against the providence of God. Nebuchadnezzar is quoted praising God by saying, "No one can restrain His (God's) hand or say to Him, 'What have you done?'"

God's providence is manifested in how He preserves the world. In Nehemiah 9:6 it reads that You alone are the Lord; You have made heaven and earth and everything on it — and You preserve them all.

We need the providence of God (His care) upon our lives in so many areas. We need His divine guidance and protection when we travel by car, train, bus, bicycle or airplane. We need the providence of God on our lives when we are at church, at school, at meetings, at events and even in a crowd in a store. There is no place that God's providence cannot reach us.

We cannot forget so many people living in our world who are suffering daily with a sickness, a disease, civil unrest as well as those who are being personally attacked because of their faith in the Lord. God is aware of each one. In all these things God will guide and sustain us as believers when we put all of our trust in Him.

In Proverbs 3:6 we are reminded to, "In all your ways acknowledge Him and He will direct your paths". If we acknowledge God as Lord of our life, God's hand will be on us in all that we do and will always be there to guide us and to care for us.

TODAY'S WORD FOR DECEMBER 16

EMPATHY

All things work together for good to those who love God, to those who are the called according to His purpose. For those God foreknew he also predestined to be conformed to the likeness of His Son. Romans 8: 28-29

I will never forget when our oldest daughter dislocated her little finger playing in her high school basketball game. They stopped the game and we saw her finger totally bent the wrong way. To say the least it looked grotesque. We took her to the doctor and he carefully twisted and turned the finger until it went back in place.

As parents we felt "the hurt" probably as much and maybe even more than our daughter. It is difficult for parents to see their children suffer. As parents we want to make the pain go away and we would rather go through the painful experience ourselves rather than have our children go through it. Parents have deep empathy for their children when they suffer whether it is the physical pain of sickness or injury or whether it is emotional and mental pain resulting from the pressures of life or from harmful relationships.

It is empathy for the physical pain and suffering of others that people become doctors. If we trust earthly doctors to care for our children, how much more should we be willing to trust God, our great a physician to heal our broken body and to reset our broken lives "to be conformed to the image of His Son" (Romans 8:29). God's empathy for our suffering is so much greater than any doctor.

One of God's purposes of pain is to mold us into the image of Jesus in our hearts. The next time you feel pain remember what God wants to do for you through the pain. God wants us to be able to weep with those who weep and may need to stain our cheeks with a few of our own tears so that we will empathize with others in their time of need just as Jesus did.

In the verse above the writer uses the word, "foreknew." This speaks of a predetermined choice that God has made to set His love on us, showing empathy, and establishing an intimate relationship with us as a believer. God predestinates, marls out, appoints or has determined beforehand to have a likeness to His Son. What a wonderful promise for us as believers.

God may need, at times, to strip away our security, when we are happy sitting in our comfort zone, to conform us to the God-sufficiency that Jesus displayed while on this earth.

Next time you feel pain or discouragement or you are broken hearted, do not panic. The Lord our God, heals the broken hearted and bandages their wounds. Psalm 147:3. Just stop and praise God knowing that He is at work in your life.

TODAY'S WORD FOR DECEMBER 17

ENLARGE

Enlarge the place of your tent, and let them stretch out the curtains of your dwellings; do not spare; lengthen your cords and strengthen your stakes. Isaiah 54:2.

The prophet Isaiah in this passage (above) is talking about God's everlasting love for Israel and His covenant promise to Abraham to make of him a great nation. As a growing nation Israel is to make their tent larger. This verse refers not only to Israel, but applies prophetically to the future Kingdom of Jesus Christ and the need for the church (all believers) to enlarge its tent by spreading the good news of the gospel.

The verse goes on to tell us to "Lengthen your cords" so the church can increase its influence in the community throughout the world. Jesus commanded that we, "Go into all the world, and preach the gospel to every creature." (Mark 16:15)

The illustration of a tent is understood by all. When you put up a small tent you tighten the cords and it will house a few people. But when the need arises to hold more people we must enlarge the tent. We do this by lengthening the cords and strengthening the stakes that hold the cords in the ground.

In the Hebrew dictionary the word for "enlarge" is RACHAB. It means to become wide like chambers, like the chambers of a heart. It also has the meaning of increasing the size such as a city's borders or a church.

To enlarge our tent we must enlarge our heart by filling it with more of God's love and enlarge our capacity to love others. It is only as each one of us has more love for the Lord that the church "tent" will be enlarged.

We, as believers in Jesus today, need to enlarge our tents. Our tents include our ministry, our vision and our testimony to others. We need to spread out and think big. When a tent is enlarged the cords must be lengthened and stronger stakes are needed to keep it from collapsing. We need to lengthen our cords by looking for new and fresh ways to serve our Lord. We need to strengthen our stakes by reading God's Word and praying daily for something special that God has for us.

In this chapter of Isaiah the prophet is speaking of the day when Israel accepts Christ as their Messiah and Savior. "With great compassion I will gather you." Isaiah 54:7. At that time they will need enlarged spaces where they can sing and be blessed with a rich reward of everlasting joy and peace.

The Message translation of this verse makes it very clear: Clear lots of ground for your tents; Make your tents large; spread out; think big; use plenty of rope; drive the tent pegs deep; you are going to need lots of elbow room for your growing family. Just as Israel needs to enlarge their tents, we as believers need to enlarge our tents so we too can honor and bless our Savior.

TODAY'S WORD FOR DECEMBER 18

IGNORE

He does not ignore the cry of the afflicted. Psalm 9:12

How shall we escape if we ignore such a great salvation? Hebrews 2:3

It is easy to ignore things in life that we do not want to deal with. It was annoying to have our children ignore what we would say to them. We are all guilty of ignoring someone or something at one time or another. As the saying goes, "It goes in one ear and out the other." We ignore people even though we do not like to be ignored.

Some people just plain shut the outside world out of their mind when they are involved in certain projects. They are often accused of ignoring a word or conversation being carried on with them. In many of these situations they do not hear what is being said because their entire concentration is on what they are doing.

But there are many who are in the same situation and they hear, but do not want to admit that they are listening. They do this on purpose and then use as an excuse, an outward lie, that they did not hear what was said.

How fortunate we are that we have a loving God who does not ignore us even though day by day we continually ignore Him. You ignore God when you do not read the Bible, His Word, daily. God speaks to you through your reading what He is saying in His Word. You also ignore God when you do not take time everyday to pray to God. How else can you communicate to God?

In Luke 19:10 we read, "for the Son of Man came to seek and to save those who are lost." God seeks each and every one of us, but unfortunately the majority of people in our world, both in past centuries as well as today have chosen to ignore Him.

We often said our children had selective hearing. They heard what they wanted to hear. If they were engrossed in what they were doing they would act like they were listening and even answer, "Uh-huh", when they were asked if they heard what we said. It would be apparent they had not really heard a word and were tuning us out, because they did not respond to do what they were asked to do.

In Matthew 13:13 Jesus warned the crowd that some of them, "though hearing, they did not hear." Many respond to God's offer to us of His gift of salvation in this same way today. They do not hear because they choose not to hear.

We often hope by ignoring something that it will just go away. Some things in life, no matter how much we ignore them, will not go away.

The writer of Hebrews asks this vital question: "How shall we escape if we ignore such a great salvation?" Everyone must ask themselves this question because no one will escape God's punishment for their sins if they ignore the wonderful gift of salvation that God has provided for us through Jesus Christ. All of us who are willing to come to God can be sure that He will hear our cry of repentance. "He does not ignore the cry of the afflicted." No sin is so great that Jesus will not forgive.

TODAY'S WORD FOR DECEMBER 19

PROSPERITY

Beloved, I pray that you may prosper in all things and be in health, just as your soul prospers. III John 2

After Jesus ascended back to His Father in heaven, He left His disciples the task of tending His sheep (the followers of Jesus). The disciples were faithful to encourage the believers and to uphold them in prayer. John III is the apostle John's personal letter of encouragement to Gaius, a fellow believer and faithful worker in the early church for the Lord. John wrote Gaius to commend him for his faithfulness and to let him know he was praying for him. John noted that Gaius' spiritual state was so excellent; he was praying that his physical health would match his spiritual vigor.

It was a common practice for one to be asked when being met how his health was. Our physical condition is not something that is always apparent. Our spiritual condition, however, should be very apparent. Our Christian walk and the way we conduct ourselves should give evidence to our spiritual condition. John wrote Gaius that others had testified to him that Gaius was "walking in truth." By the way Gaius lived his life it was apparent to others he had his priorities right.

The world has its priorities wrong. The priority of the world is making money and gaining power. If that is accomplished one is considered prosperous. On the road to obtaining this prosperity people destroy their physical health with stress, lack of sleep, sexual immorality, alcohol and drugs. People seem to be willing to pay this price for what they consider prosperity.

People who are so called prosperous in the world are fearful that if they come to the Lord they will have to give up their prosperity. They do not understand God wants to bless and prosper those who love Him and honor Him in their lives.

Jeremiah writes in Jeremiah 29:27 a promise that was given to the nation of Israel. "I know the plans I have for you, plans to prosper you and not to harm you, plans to give you a hope and a future." Throughout the Old Testament God promised prosperity to the people of Israel as long as they honored Him. When they failed God they not only lost their prosperity, but eventually the whole nation was lost and scattered.

God's first desire for us is that our souls will prosper. Our prosperity in life is dependent on what God blesses us with and as we learn in the Old Testament we will prosper in life depending on how our soul prospers. It must be our priority to walk in truth so that God can prosper us.

Our family is not what the world would call wealthy, but we feel we have been very prosperous. God has blessed us far beyond what we deserve, but not in riches or wealth. Our prosperity has been in good health, God given enabling strength, sound minds, loving, God fearing children and unusual ministry opportunities that could have only come from God.

TODAY'S WORD FOR DECEMBER 20

GUIDE

Trust in the Lord with all your heart, and lean not on your own understanding; in all your ways acknowledge Him and He shall direct your paths. Proverbs 3:5-6

Life is like an untraveled trail with complex twists and turns. Have you ever gone hiking on a trail in the mountains? There are always signs that clearly mark the trails and signs that remind you to stay on the trail. If you make the mistake of leaving the right trail you become lost and may never reach your destination.

There are many examples in life where one needs a guide. How many times have you been driving on a road and run into a construction crew making the road impassable? Many times you will see guides at the beginning of the construction zone to help you through. We have guides when we travel in unknown territory. We need guides in many situations. We have guides that direct us in hospitals. Without signs it would be hard to find what we want in large malls and stores.

In our daily life we run into appealing activities that if we take our eyes off of our guide, Jesus, we can easily be detoured to the quicksand of sin. We may at times have to journey over some hard terrain or deep valleys. The only way to be sure we are walking right is to follow a guide who knows the way perfectly.

In John 16:13 John, the writer, points out to us as believers that the Holy Spirit will give us supernatural revelation of all truth by which God has revealed Himself to us through Christ. It reads: "But when He, the Spirit of truth, comes, He will guide you into all truth, for He will not speak on His own initiative, but whatever He hears, He will speak; and He will disclose to you what is to come." He is our guide today and will always be our guide.

We remember seeing years ago a large picture on an office wall. An artist painted a picture of the Lord Jesus standing behind a young man whose eyes were focused in the direction the Master was pointing. Jesus' hand was on the man's shoulder, and you could only imagine He is saying, "This is the way we are going. I will get you to your destination."

If you are honest with yourself you will admit you are ill-equipped to go through life alone. God created us knowing we would need His guidance. In our own knowledge and reasoning power we are simply not able to figure out how to consistently make wise decisions. Some people feel they are wise enough to make their decisions on their own, but sooner or later they fail.

The assuring hand of our Lord on our shoulder will always lead us down the right path to good choices if we put our total trust in Him as our guide. We urge you to choose to follow the lead of Jesus by reading His Word and then by applying biblical principles to your walk in life. Also learn to pray through both large and small decisions you need to make and seek the path that He wants to guide you through.

TODAY'S WORD FOR DECEMBER 21

PRODIGAL

And he arose and came to his father. When he was yet a great way off, his father saw him, and had compassion, and ran, and fell on his neck, and kissed him. Luke 15:20

Luke 15 contains information many say is one of the most important chapters in the Bible. It includes three of the most famous parables told by Jesus. Jesus was teaching His disciples and a crowd came around Him. The scripture says the crowd included Pharisees and scribes, tax collectors and sinners.

The parable of the Lost Son, better known as the Prodigal Son, has many messages. There are five stages in the life of the prodigal son we can learn from.

As the story begins we first see a wayward son. The scripture indicates that he was selfish, hard hearted, independent, stubborn and worldly. He was the son of his father by birth, but did not belong to his father in heart, mind and spirit as God wants us to belong to Him. The son demanded from his father his inheritance by saying; give me the portion of goods that belongs to me. Even though he had not earned his portion or even deserved it, he demanded it, and was only thinking about himself. He did not take into consideration how it would hurt his father's estate because that mattered very little to the son. The father gave his son his freedom and his possessions and the son was free to do what he wanted with his life and goods.

Secondly, we read the son wasted his life in riotous living. He rebelled, revolted and journeyed into a far away country (verse 13). Finally he met the day when all began to go wrong. He had been living a worldly life, living for the pleasure of this world only. When his money was gone he was left with the fruits of his life of sin: poverty, bondage, enslavement, suffering, no friends, dissatisfaction, emptiness, destitution and hunger. He was alone, broken, humiliated, and facing starvation.

In the third stage the young prodigal sees himself as he really is. He snapped out of his insanity and remembered how good life was in the home of his father. He thought of his father and the enormous provision he had given him. His life had been reduced to feeding swine. He knew that he needed to humble himself and repent and confess his sin and unworthiness to his father.

So he responded to the conviction in his heart and took action. He got up and returned to his father. At the final stage we see a restored son, forgiven by a loving father. When the father saw his prodigal son returning, he ran out to meet him and greet him with a loving embrace. The father not only accepted the son's repentance and forgave him, but he restored him to his place in the family.

What a story (parable) for us to learn from. We are the prodigal son. We have left God to live a life of sin. Our Father is waiting for us to repent and return to the loving embrace of His arms. He wants to restore us to our position in His family as one of His children. God wants us to always trust Him, but if we fall away, He is big enough to accept us if we will return to Him. In verse 31 the father said to the son, "You are always with me, and all that I have is yours." He is an awesome God.

TODAY'S WORD FOR DECEMBER 22

IDOLATRY

You turned to God from idols to serve the living and true God. I Thessalonians 1:9b

It is important for us when we talk about the word idols we understand what it means. Most people think of idols as a statue or figurine representing a god or the worshipping of an unknown god, but it goes much farther than that. The "things and people" in your life can become idols when they are more important than your relationship with the living God. The great concern that we have is that the majority of the people in this world have idols that come before God.

If you were to ask people if they believed in God, the majority would probably answer "Yes." If you were to ask what they considered most important in their life, their answer would not be God but most likely money, fame, power or pleasure.

Many people create their own god. A report in the magazine NEWSWEEK said that a youth pastor asked teenagers "who they think God is?" One said that "He was like a grandfather. He is there but I never see Him". Another said, "He is an evil being who wants to punish me all the time." The report went on to say that most people form their own gods in life. What consumes one's time becomes one's god.

Creating one's own deity today is common place, but the god's we create have no lasting value. It is extremely dangerous because it robs a person of knowing who their heavenly Father really is. God is a Spirit, infinite, eternal, holy, just and unchangeable and He is waiting for us to establish a relationship with Him and make Him the one and only God in our life.

Idol worship has been prevalent through the centuries and throughout the world. During Moses' time there was a Pharaoh (AKHENATEN) who pointed to the rising and setting sun as the great deity who gave life to earth. The religious symbol for him was a single disc of light with sunrays coming from the sun. This was his god and Moses warned the Israelites to only worship the one and only God and not the god of Pharaoh.

When Paul came to Athens he saw all their objects of worship. The Athenians built beautiful temples to their gods. The remains of those temples can still be seen today. Paul was grieved by the idolatry in that city. He used the people's imperfect understanding of God to point them to the God of scripture.

In Acts 17:24 Paul wrote, "God, who made the world and everything in it, since He is Lord of heaven and earth, does not dwell in temples made with hands." He wanted them to see the one true God is greater than all their worthless idols.

The people around us may worship a god that they have invented for their life. It is our first responsibility to make sure we have a daily relationship with the one and only true God and His Son Jesus. Then we should reach out to those who have their own idols to worship and through our words and deeds show them there is only one God, the living and eternal God who is the God of all creation and the God of salvation.

TODAY'S WORD FOR DECEMBER 23

RUIN

You are of your father the devil, and the desires of your father you want to do. He was a murderer from the beginning, and does not stand in the truth, because there is no truth in him. When he speaks a lie, he speaks from his own resources, for he is a liar and the father of it. John 8:44

Jesus pulls no punches in this verse we have written above as He speaks of the devil as it relates to the ruin of man. Jesus is talking to the Jews telling them that they exhibited the patterns of Satan in their hostility towards Him. Their failure to believe in Him as their Messiah was the exact opposite of their claims. Therefore, Jesus said, they belonged to Satan.

Man today would have to be spiritually blind, deaf and mute not to know the whole world lies under the sway of the wicked one. The verse in 1 John 5:19 reads, "We know that we are of God, and the whole world lies under the control of the wicked one."

In this verse from 1 John God reveals two classes of people. First there are those who are no longer spiritually blind, deaf or mute to God's message. They are saved by the grace of God and know it.

Secondly there is a whole world of unsaved souls that lie in the hands of the evil one, Satan. Satan is the father of the wicked and the one who has ruined mankind. Every nation, every tribe, every family, the rich and the poor, the educated and the uneducated, all participate in the ruin of man because we all have a common origin in Adam. We all share a common heritage, a common legacy and that is the ruin of man.

The Bible clearly tells us because of the sin of Adam and Eve, "The wages of that sin is death, but the gift of God is eternal life" (Romans 6:23). This verse describes two absolutes for us. Spiritual death is the paycheck for every man's slavery to sin. Death is universal because the ruin is universal.

The second absolute is that eternal life is a free gift God gives undeserving sinners who believe in His Son. Thanks be to God for this free gift He gave to us if we ask.

Yes, because of the sin of Adam and Eve, mankind was ruined, but in Jesus we have complete redemption. Peter reassures us of this in 1 Peter 1:18-19 where it reads, "Knowing that you were not redeemed with corruptible things, like silver or gold, from your aimless conduct received by tradition from your fathers, but with the precious blood of Christ, as a lamb without blemish and without spot."

As one who believes in Jesus you can rest assured that your ruined life is no longer ruined? Now, you need to do all you can to become more Christ-like every day and love and serve God as you never have before.

TODAY'S WORD FOR DECEMBER 24

CHRISTMAS EVE

Glory to God in the highest, and on earth peace to men on whom His favor rests. Luke 2:14

We encourage you today to start preparing for tomorrow. It is our prayer for you that CHRISTMAS DAY will be one of the most Christ honoring and special days of your life.

It has been a family tradition for our family to get together on Christmas Eve. As part of our celebration we have a Christmas Eve play featuring our grandchildren. We portray the Christmas story with Mary and Joseph sitting by the manger with the animals, Kings, shepherds and wise men all standing by the manger scene.

Tonight, take a moment with your family, and read the Christmas story found in Luke 2:1-14. To make it easy for you here are the verses.

"In those days Caesar Augustus issued a decree that a census should be taken of the entire Roman world. This was the first census that took place while Quirinius was governor of Syria. And everyone went to his own town to register.

So Joseph also went up from the town of Nazareth in Galilee to Judea, to Bethlehem the town of David, because he belonged to the house and line of David. He went there to register with Mary, who was pledged to be married to him and was expecting a child.

While they were there, the time came for the baby to be born, and she gave birth to her first-born, a son. She wrapped Him in cloths and placed Him in a manger, because there was no room for them in the inn.

And there were shepherds living out in the fields nearby, keeping watch over their flocks by night. An angel of the Lord appeared to them, and the glory of the Lord shone around them, and they were terrified. But the angel said to them, 'Do not be afraid. I bring you good news of great joy that will be for all the people. Today in the town of David a Savior has been born to you; he is Christ the Lord. This will be a sign to you: You will find a baby wrapped in cloths and lying in a manger.'

Suddenly a great company of the heavenly host appeared with the angel, praising God and saying, GLORY TO GOD IN THE HIGHEST, AND ON EARTH PEACE TO MEN ON WHOM HIS FAVOR RESTS."

The story goes on with the shepherds going to find Mary, Joseph and the baby. (Luke 2: 15-20) After you have read this account to your family this Christmas then take time to pray together, thanking God for sending His Son to pay the penalty for your sins.

Make tonight and tomorrow a real celebration as you celebrate the birth of Jesus.

Have a Blessed Christmas and remember that JESUS IS THE REASON FOR THE SEASON!

TODAY'S WORD FOR DECEMBER 25

CHRISTMAS

For unto you is born this day in the city of David a Savior, which is Christ the Lord. Luke 2:11

There were some unusual events that happened in the world when Jesus was born. These events had a dramatic effect on history.

Jacob gave us a prophecy of the birth of Jesus. In Genesis 49:10 Jacob said, "The scepter shall not depart from Judah, nor a lawgiver from between his feet, until Shiloh (the Messiah) come; and unto Him shall the gathering of the people be."

When Jesus was born this prophecy was being fulfilled. The scepter of rule had departed from Judea and they were now under the rule of Rome with Caesar Augustus reigning as emperor. Cyrenius was governor of Syria and Judea was part of the province of Syria. Herod was now King of Judea. So you see that a foreign, alien power, now ruled over Judea.

With the birth of Jesus, the prophecy of The Messiah coming was fulfilled in Jesus Christ. Jesus Christ was the Messiah (Shiloh) and His coming into the world not only fulfilled prophecy, but was surrounded by the most unusual events.

One of these unusual events was the unexpected taxation. It had been prophesied Messiah was to be born in Bethlehem and this scripture had to be fulfilled. Joseph and Mary lived in Galilee and as the scripture says, "Mary was now great with child." The taxation happened just at the right time and in the right way. Every one needed to return to the city of his family ancestry to register and pay his taxes. God was controlling these events so that all things worked so He might fulfill His promise to send the Savior into the world.

Joseph and Mary were both descendants of David so the taxation forced Joseph to take Mary and to go to Bethlehem. The city of Bethlehem was prophesied to be the city of the Messiah's birth. The taxation led to the fulfillment of Scripture. Without the taxation decree Joseph and Mary would certainly have not had any reason to make such a long difficult journey of more than 70 miles from Nazareth to Bethlehem, especially with a baby on the verge of being born.

The Scribes understood where Jesus the Messiah was to be born (Matthew 2:5-6). The common people understood where Jesus was to be born (John 7:42).

Jesus had to be born in Bethlehem because it was prophesied the Messiah was to be the Son of David. David had been born in Bethlehem therefore it was necessary for Jesus the Son of David to be born there. The "Son of David" was the most common Messianic title used to refer to Jesus in His day. And finally the scripture prophesied the Messiah would be born in Bethlehem. (Micah 5:2)

How can we not only be amazed, but also have our hearts blessed when we consider how God miraculously worked out His plan of Salvation for us? Caesar Augustus could never have imagined he would play a role in fulfilling prophecy concerning Christ our Messiah.

TODAY'S WORD FOR DECEMBER 26

LONGING

I am hard pressed between the two, having a desire to depart and be with Christ, which is far better. Philippians 1:23

Paul is sharing with the Church at Philippi in this verse his struggle in his mind as to where he would rather be at that moment. He is relating that equal pressure is being exerted from both sides. Here he is speaking of his personal desires and not necessarily that which the Lord would desire. He makes it clear that his personal will is to be swallowed up in the sweet and perfect will of God.

At the time he wrote Philippians Paul was in prison. It was not where he longed to be. Paul is longing to be with Christ, but he knows that his mission on earth is not complete. The centerpiece of this entire dialog from Paul is Christ. In verse 21 Paul says simply and concisely, "For to me to live is Christ." As long as the Lord had a purpose for him to live, even if it was in prison, he would accept that.

There are many examples in life today where children and adults face longings in their lives. How many children have you heard about who went on their first overnight camping experience and in the middle of the night they had a longing for mother and father at home?

There were times in our lives before we were married living 2000 miles apart that we faced a longing to see one another. We needed to look beyond that longing anxiously waiting the day we knew we would see one another again. We long to be with those whom we love.

Many times we have talked to or heard about friends who were fighting sickness, economic struggles or strained relationships and they had a longing to call it quits and go to heaven and leave their troubles behind.

It is easy for us as believers to think longingly about being with Jesus, just as Paul did. As God's children we know this world will never truly be home to us. Paul loved serving Christ as we should, but a part of him longed to be with the Savior as we do. It is comforting to know that being with Jesus in our eternal home will be far better than being here on earth.

We, as believers, can be confident when we face those moments of longing to be free of life's struggles we have strength that comes from our Lord. He will give us all we need to step up and live above our worldly longings. As Paul said, for him to live was Christ and was all he needed and longed for. This is what the Lord wants to be our reason for living. When we put our trust in Jesus, He will take our worldly longings away. What do you long for? Do you long to be with Jesus who loves you so much that He was willing to die for you?

TODAY'S WORD FOR DECEMBER 27

JUDGMENT

Jonah rose up to flee to Tarshis from the presence of the Lord. So he went down to Joppa, found a ship, paid the fare and went to Tarshis. Jonah 1:3

The Lord is good. A stronghold in the day of trouble; and He knows those who trust in Him. Nahum 1:7

The book of Jonah has the makings of a great movie plot. A runaway prophet; a terrible storm; the prophet swallowed by a great fish, God spares the prophet's life and then the repentance of a pagan city. This is the account we receive from the book of Jonah and the result was repentance.

But in the book of Nahum the story has a different ending. Nahum ministered in Nineveh about 100 years after Jonah was there. The Ninevites had no interest in the message Nahum was preaching and no interest in repentance. They rejected repentance and thus chose, by not responding, judgment. They seemed to be willing to welcome judgment into their lives. Finally, Nahum condemns Nineveh and on behalf of God pronounces judgment on the people.

God is patient. He withheld His judgment for several decades. God never judges in haste. He patiently waits for repentance, but those who defy God will receive His judgment. God fulfilled Nahum's prophecy of judgment through the nation of Babylon who destroyed Nineveh and toppled the Assyrian empire.

In Nahum 1:3, Nahum preaches to the Ninevites, "The Lord is slow to anger." In verse 7 (above) he tells the people the Lord is good. The Ninevites did not listen and the result is the Ninevites rejected repentance and accepted judgment.

We learn by these two accounts, Jonah and Nahum, that every generation has their individualistic responses to God and His message. In Jonah's time the people repented and God blessed them. In Nahum's time they did not repent and thus received God's judgment. We have the same choice in our lives, repentance or judgment.

When we are told, "The Lord delights in those who place their trust in Him." We are being reminded this concerns the delight the Lord takes in those who place their trust in Him and His Word, and not on the frail arm of man.

Here in America we are fast becoming like Nineveh. It was not so many years ago that this country respected God. People were allowed to pray in public, and our leaders honored the Christian-Judean principles that this country was founded on. This is not so true today. Will we repent as a nation or receive God's judgment?

The most important point we can make today is the individual decision we make about repentance and the judgment that must be considered. Remember God honors those who repent of their sins and honor Him.

TODAY'S WORD FOR DECEMBER 28

ACCEPTED

To the praise of the glory of His grace, by which He made us accepted in the beloved.
Ephesians 1:6

While we were raising our children we saw firsthand the pressures that were on our children to be accepted by their peers. It seems the world thrives on being accepted. And when you stop and think, the way a non-believer thinks, ask yourself the question, "What do they have to rely on to obtain acceptance?" Usually it means following the crowd, doing what they do and saying what they want to hear.

Everywhere the Apostle Paul went among believers, he was accepted. But that was not true from the world of non-believers he ministered to daily. He was persecuted verbally and physically for his preaching about Christ and Him being crucified. In his "world" centuries ago Paul was not accepted among non-believers, because not only did he not do what they did, but he strongly spoke against the sinful things that they did and he did not say what they wanted to hear.

Today, we see crowds of protestors on the street to take a stand against what is not acceptable to them. The world of non-believers is quick to react against something or some person they do not accept, especially if it goes against what they seem to believe or against what they live by in their "ME" philosophy. We all have our own ideas and we find it hard to accept what does not conform to them.

We also see the problem of acceptance at times in the church. If someone different attends a service, maybe his dress, his actions or his beliefs are different, and they often are looked upon negatively and not accepted. The same happens for children in school. If a child is different than his or her peers by the way he or she dresses, acts or thinks, he or she is not accepted by "the group." Think what this does to the self-esteem of the one not accepted.

The scripture is clear. We are all sinners and are unacceptable to God. Ephesians 1:6 tells us that God has provided a way for us to be acceptable. By His grace God gave us His Son Jesus to provide that way. "He made us accepted in His beloved."

We may look different, think different or talk different, but God loves us all and all that accept His Son are made acceptable to God. Romans 5:8 says, "God showed His great love for us by sending Christ to die for us while we were yet sinners."

If God could love us when we were still unacceptable, and what is even more incredible, love us so much that He was willing to give His only Son to die to pay the penalty for our sins, how much more should we be willing to accept others?

Children can be very cruel to other children who are different in some way. They can be unmerciful in mocking and teasing those who do not fit in. As parents we must teach our children to accept and love all children and adults as people but they should reject the possible sinful life they are living. To do this we must look at ourselves first and evaluate how we accept others. Our children will learn from our actions more than our words.

TODAY'S WORD FOR DECEMBER 29

CHRISTIAN

And the disciples were first called Christians in Antioch. Acts 11:26

Then Agrippa said to Paul, You almost persuade me to become a Christian. Acts 26:28

If anyone suffers as a Christian, let him not be ashamed. I Peter 4:16

The word "CHRISTIAN" is found only three times in the Bible. We have listed all three scripture references above. The name "CHRISTIAN' began to spread as the gospel was preached away from Antioch to the whole world.

A Christian is a believer in Christ and one who really believes that Jesus is who He says He is, THE ONLY BEGOTTON SON OF GOD. A Christian must believe in his heart that Jesus died on the cross to pay the penalty for his sins and that He rose again from the dead and is alive today in heaven preparing for all those who believe in Him a place to live for eternity.

A Christian is not living by a ritual or a series of "do's and don'ts." Being a Christian is when one believes and receives Jesus as their Savior and then begins a relationship with Jesus. A Christian has accepted God's gift of salvation through Jesus. By accepting this gift, God thus cancels one's wages for sin which is death.

We are warned by Jesus not everyone who calls himself Christian is a true Christian. Jesus said in Matthew 7:21 "Not everyone who says to Me, 'Lord, Lord,' shall enter the kingdom of God, but only he that does the will of My father in heaven."

Many people go to church regularly and know all the right words to talk a good talk about God. But what Jesus is saying, is that it is not about our talk, but about our walk that sets us apart from those who just say they are Christians. This is what some may call a "fake Christian." It is easier to say the right things than it is to walk the right walk. Christians are to be "doers of the Word and not hearers only." James 1:22.

Becoming a Christian is a miraculous transformation. We cannot do it for ourselves. The following references describe the miracle changes that occur when one is a true Christian believer.

A Christian has been born into the family of God by a spiritual birth. We were born once into this world as a baby. John 3: 1-8

A Christian is a new creation in Christ. 2 Corinthians 5:17

A Christian is made the righteousness of God in Christ. 2 Corinthians 5:21

A Christian is declared just because of his or her faith in God. Romans 5:1

A Christian has accepted God's gift of eternal life in Jesus Christ, and God has cancelled the penalty of his or her sin, which is death. Romans 6:23

TODAY'S WORD FOR DECEMBER 30

CROWN

There is laid up for me a crown of righteousness. II Timothy 4:8

He will receive the crown of life which the Lord has promised to those who love Him. James 1:12

James tells us that all who love the Lord will receive the crown of life. The crown was the wreath put on the victors head after Greek athletic events. Here the crown denotes the crown of life the believer's ultimate reward, eternal life, which God has promised.

Timothy tells us we have a crown of righteousness waiting for us. The crown of righteousness represents the eternal righteousness we receive through Jesus Christ when we get to heaven. What a glorious day that will be!

How many times have you either wondered or silently said to yourself "I fear I shall never enter heaven?" Are you one who doubts? Fear not because every person in our world who put his or her trust in the Lord shall enter heaven and has no reason to fear.

Recently we read about the remarks made by a man who was dying. He said he had no fear about going to heaven and, in addition, he had sent before him all the things of importance. God, he said, had forgiven his sins and he had accepted Jesus as his Savior so he was on his way to heaven. He also said God had His finger on the latch of his heart's door and he was ready for Him to enter and take him home.

Then someone said to this elderly man, "Aren't you concerned about losing your inheritance, all that you have worked for on this earth for years?" NO, NO, NO, NO he responded. He went on to respond further by saying he sent his inheritance ahead of him and there is one crown in heaven God has made for him and it will only fit his head and even the apostle Paul cannot wear it because it fits only me.

This little story, which is a true story, serves as a reminder to us as children of God, we cannot lose our inheritance and crown God has for us in heaven. If you have repented of your sins, believe in the Lord Jesus, and have asked Him into your heart, there is not only a place reserved for you in heaven, but a crown and some say even a special harp just for you.

In Revelation 3:11 we read, "I am coming quickly; hold fast what you have, that no one may take your crown." Christ is coming quickly, a hopeful event, to take His church out of its hour of trial. We need to hold fast to our faith, waiting for that day of His return.

TODAY'S WORD FOR DECEMBER 31

RENEW

Let the people renew their strength. Isaiah 41:1

And renew a steadfast spirit within me. Psalm 51:10

But those who hope in the Lord will renew their strength. Isaiah 40:31

All things on earth need to be renewed. This is the last day of an old year and tomorrow is the first day of a new year. It is time for us to renew the good things and get rid of the bad ones in our lives.

We all know that God created all things, but no created thing continues by itself. But God provided ways for the things that He created to be renewed. For example consider trees. They must have the water of the rain that falls and must be fed with the nourishment from the soil that God provides for them.

Years ago we were in the country of Lebanon. We had read so many times in the Bible and in other books about the Cedars of Lebanon. We went to the part of Lebanon where many of these beautiful Cedars of Lebanon trees grow. God planted (created) these trees, but they only live because God provided for them an environment that met their daily needs for renewal and growth they could draw from the earth.

Our lives as believers are so similar to these trees. We can only be sustained by receiving a daily renewal from God. For example, just as it is necessary for us to replace the waste and liquid from our bodies with frequent food and water daily, we must replace the waste we lose from our soul by feeding daily on reading the Bible.

Just think how depressed we would be if we missed many meals. Even so we will get more depressed spiritually when we miss reading and studying God's Word. Without constant spiritual renewal in our lives we will not be ready for the constant evil assaults on our lives or the strife we have from within. If we do not renew our strength in the Lord daily, we will grow weaker spiritually and evil will gain a stronghold in our life and soon it will have mastery over all we do and say. We need to not only read the Bible daily, but we need to pray daily asking God to renew the spirit within us as the psalmist said in Psalm 51:10. "Create in me a clean heart, O God, and renew a steadfast spirit within me."

The apostle Paul wrote in II Corinthians 4:16 "even though our outward man is perishing, yet our inward man is being renewed every day." Yes, every day we get bolder and the aches and pains get stronger, but when we are in a right relationship with God, He will renew us inwardly with spiritual strength through His Holy Spirit who works within us.

We urge you to practice the words of Isaiah (40:31) in your daily life. "They that wait upon the Lord shall renew their strength." It is our choice!

CPSIA information can be obtained at www.ICGtesting.com
Printed in the USA
BVOW030537040313

314572BV00002B/4/P

9 781625 093523